Haitian Connections in the Atlantic World

Haitian Connections in the Atlantic World

RECOGNITION AFTER REVOLUTION

Julia Gaffield

The University of North Carolina Press Chapel Hill

© 2015 The University of North Carolina Press
All rights reserved
Designed by Alyssa D'Avanzo
Set in Quadraat by codeMantra, Inc.

The paper in this book meets the guidelines for permanence and durability of the Committee on Production Guidelines for Book Longevity of the Council on Library Resources.

The University of North Carolina Press has been a member of the Green Press Initiative since 2003.

Cover illustration: Mural of Jean-Jacques Dessalines in Port-au-Prince, Haiti, and original printed copy of the Haitian Declaration of Independence, issued by the Government of Haiti (photographs by the author)

Library of Congress Cataloging-in-Publication Data

Gaffield, Julia, author.
Haitian connections in the Atlantic World: recognition after revolution / Julia Gaffield.
   pages cm
Includes bibliographical references and index.
ISBN 978-1-4696-2562-1 (pbk : alk. paper)
ISBN 978-1-4696-2563-8 (ebook)
1. Haiti—Foreign relations—1804–1844.
2. Haiti—History—1804–1844. I. Title.
F1922.G34 2015
972.94'04—dc23
2015018761

To my mum and dad, Pam and Chad Gaffield,
whom I love and appreciate so very much

Contents

Acknowledgments xi

Introduction 1

CHAPTER ONE
I Put Fear in the Hearts of Those Who Engage in This Trade:
French Efforts to Isolate Haiti in the Atlantic World 17

CHAPTER TWO
I, Leader of a Country, Treat for My Citizens:
Haiti and Jamaica after the French Defeat 61

CHAPTER THREE
Legislators of the Antilles:
British Regulation of Trade with Haiti 93

CHAPTER FOUR
Aiming a Blow at Their Very Vitals:
U.S. Interdiction of Trade with Haiti 124

CHAPTER FIVE
The "States of Hayti" and the British Empire 153

Conclusion 182

Notes 197

Bibliography 237

Index 245

Figures

1. "Currents of Air" 26
2. Map of the Caribbean 42
3. Draft map from the 1801 accord between Saint Domingue and Jamaica 75

Acknowledgments

In 1816, King Henry I of Haiti wrote to British abolitionist Thomas Clarkson to express his gratitude. "I do not know of any better way of thanking you," he wrote, "for your wise and good advice than to beg you to continue it."* Many times I have thought about these words in reflecting on my good fortune for having such a wonderful mentor, colleague, and friend. I am forever indebted to Laurent Dubois to whom I offer a million sincere thanks for providing invaluable guidance on academia and life. I am truly lucky.

Early on, I benefited from the kindness, intellectual rigor, and encouragement of a number of scholars. Melanie Newton first introduced me to Caribbean history and invited me to participate in the scholarly community in Toronto. Ken Mills showed me how to look at primary sources and demonstrated the importance of asking thoughtful questions. Michael Wayne introduced me to the art of storytelling in history, and his kind advice, tough teaching, and encouragement over the years have been invaluable. I would also like to thank Michele Johnson, David Trotman, Adrian Shubert, and Marcel Martel, who supported my research as I began exploring Haiti's connections with the broader Atlantic World.

I am lucky to have benefited from the thoughtful comments of a number of scholars who read earlier drafts. Elizabeth Fenn was always available with honest, kind, and tough critiques. Deborah Jenson pushed me to think more creatively and inspired me with her passion and drive. Barry Gaspar continually renewed my love for history. Vince Brown has shown me how to think about history beyond the texts that dominate our field and encouraged me to explore new ways of researching and teaching. I owe great thanks to my writing group and my accountability club, Fahad Bishara, Doug Leonard, Willeke Sandler, Jacob Remes, and Jillian Powers.

I have been welcomed into a collegial, intense, and inspiring group of scholars, and I am grateful for the joy that they bring to academia.

*Henry Christophe to Thomas Clarkson, 18 November 1816, in Griggs and Prator, *Henry Christophe and Thomas Clarkson*, 101.

I offer my sincere thanks to David Armitage, Lauren Benton, Madison Bell, Jean Casimir, Matt Childs, Marlene Daut, Ada Ferrer, Doris Garraway, John Garrigus, David Geggus, Malick Ghachem, Jean-Pierre Le Glaunec, Eliga Gould, Allan Greer, Philip Kaisary, Jane Kamensky, Paul Lachance, Sue Lanser, Christina Mobley, Graham Nessler, Andrew O'Shaughnessy, Nathan Perl-Rosenthal, Grégory Pierrot, Jeremy Popkin, Richard Rabinowitz, James Robertson, Rebecca Scott, Matthew J. Smith, Philip Stern, Anoush Terjanian, Chantalle Verna, Laura Wagner, Ashli White, Peter Wood, Charlton (Chaz) Yingling, Paul Youngquist, and Erin Zavitz. I am lucky to have joined a friendly community at Georgia State University, and I thank Michelle Brattain, Jared Poley, and Denise Davidson for their support.

Archivists and librarians are key to good research projects, and I had the good fortune of collaborating with many. In particular, Patrick Tardieu at the Bibliothèque Haitienne des Pères du Saint-Esprit in Haiti has been extremely generous and inspiring in his enthusiasm for collaboration in archival research. Poul Erik Mouritzen at the Danish National Archives saved me from tears and kindly allowed me access to their stacks after an untimely truck accident in their West India collection. I would also like to thank Chris Barnes at The National Archives of the United Kingdom for keeping me company over lunch and helping me track down and follow up on sources. Finally, I had one of the greatest archival experiences at the National Library of Jamaica, and I would like to thank the staff in the manuscript division for their help.

I owe great thanks to David Jarmul, Camille Jackson, and the rest of the crew at the Office of News and Communications at Duke University for taking an interest in my research and for helping the public learn a bit more about Haiti. I have thoroughly enjoyed engaging with a community beyond the university, and I am grateful to the journalists that made this possible, in particular those at the *New York Times*, the *Times of London*, and the *Globe and Mail*. This experience helped me see the value of connecting academic research to a broader public and to current events. I saw this approach at work at the New-York Historical Society, and I thank the members of the staff for their scholarly and community engagement.

This project would not have been possible without generous funding from a number of institutions. The Social Sciences and Humanities Research Council of Canada; the Canada-US Fulbright Program; the Center for Latin American and Caribbean Studies and the Franklin Humanities Institute at Duke University; the Harvard Atlantic World

Research Seminar; the Andrew W. Mellon Sawyer Seminar at Brandeis University (2013–14); the Department of History, the College of Arts and Sciences, and the Center for Latin American and Latino Studies at Georgia State University; the Latin American and Caribbean Section of the Southern Historical Association; the Robert H. Smith International Center for Jefferson Studies; the University of Warwick; and the John Carter Brown Library provided the funds for my research trips in seven different countries and the time and backing that I needed to complete this project. I thank all of these institutions for their help and support. Many thanks to the members of the staff at *William and Mary Quarterly* and at the *Journal of Social History*, who graciously allowed me to draw upon material in my articles for Chapters 2 and 5. Thank you to the David Rumsey Historical Map Collection for allowing me to use one of their maps in this book and for providing an invaluable research and teaching resource.

I am appreciative of the keen editorial insights of Elaine Maisner at the University of North Carolina Press and of the hard work and responsiveness of Alison Shay. The book benefited greatly from the thoughtful comments and suggestions of the anonymous readers, and I thank them immensely for their time and generosity.

My friends have helped this project in more ways than I can express. I am lucky to know Kristin Cullen, Mitch Fraas, Erin Parish, Liz Shesko, Orion Teal, and Kaila Wingrove. My life is better because they are in it. They have supported me throughout this journey, and I appreciate their friendship and love more than I can say.

Mark Kohler has been my best friend, someone to lean on, and the person with whom I have shared the most laughs. The birth of our son, Stevenson Thomas, during the final round of editing put everything in perspective, and he has brought so much joy and happiness to my life. My family members have supported me through the best and worst of times. I owe all the thanks in the world to Scott Gaffield, Jillian Gaffield, Johanna Spaans, Aaron Spaans, Pam Gaffield, and Chad Gaffield. I am who I am because of the tough love, the quick banter, and the unwavering confidence that I learned from my family.

Haitian Connections in the Atlantic World

INTRODUCTION

On 1 January 1804, General-in-Chief Jean-Jacques Dessalines, leader of the Armée Indigène (Indigenous Army) in the French colony of Saint Domingue, announced the founding of Haiti by proclaiming the world's second successful Declaration of Independence.[1] The Acte de l'Indépendance (Act of Independence) was the culmination of the thirteen-year Haitian Revolution and brought to an end the two-year war for independence. But this ending was also the beginning of a whole new array of challenges for Haiti. As the country's first leader, Dessalines now faced the monumental work of establishing Haitian sovereignty and making the new nation a part of the community of empires and nations in the Atlantic World. It was a hostile world, one in which slaveholding powers dominated the seas and the political landscape, and, unlike in the American and French Revolutions, the successful slave revolution in Haiti overturned the racial hierarchy of the colonial slave system. The basis of the economic system of the Atlantic was under attack.

The first leaders of this radical project of abolitionism and nationhood—particularly Jean-Jacques Dessalines, Alexandre Pétion, and Henry Christophe—employed innovative means to negotiate new economic and political relationships with the surrounding empires and nations. Their strategies reflect an international context in which ongoing warfare among European empires informed the actions of these governments and created openings for the new nation of Haiti. The early rulers recognized such opportunities amid the serious challenges, and they exploited them by pursing the ambitions laid out in the Declaration of Independence and other proclamations that circulated widely in the Atlantic World.[2] In response, the international community's reactions to events in Haiti were both diverse and constantly changing. The distinct and competing interests of empires and nations, as well as the layers of governance within the dominant empires, created a shifting geopolitical landscape upon which Haitian leaders were able to build a viable economic, ideological, and legal foundation. Understanding how they did so helps to explain how Haiti succeeded in remaining independent in the precarious years after 1804.

The reinterpretation of Haiti's initial success in establishing independence during a crucial period of international uncertainty rejects the long-held scholarly consensus that Atlantic World states and empires collectively isolated Haiti after the Declaration of Independence. Because foreign governments withheld official diplomatic recognition, scholars assume that this prevented either diplomatic or economic contact with Haiti during the period of non-recognition. Scholars have explained the supposed initial isolation and slow subsequent acceptance of a sovereign and independent Haiti by focusing on the Haitian Revolution's potent challenge to colonialism and slavery. They highlight the fear and racism of the international community, which attempted to contain the implications of the world's only successful slave revolution.[3] Haiti's public denunciation of colonialism and slavery made it a target not only for the defeated French government but also for other groups, since slave-owning powers were desperate to prevent the spread of the revolution. Haitian freedom and independence, this perspective assumes, were so anomalous in the Caribbean in the early nineteenth century that the country posed a threat that could only be met with full refusal.[4]

The claim that the rest of the Atlantic Word immediately isolated Haiti has persisted because of an emphasis on the heightened importance of racial fears and the future of slavery elsewhere in the Caribbean and beyond. In the established studies of the postindependence years, Haiti's identity as a "black republic" often overshadows all of its other characteristics—agricultural gold mine, pawn in the Napoleonic Wars, victor of a war for independence—that foreign officials and individuals also used in their equations when they considered how to react to the Haitian Declaration of Independence. The evolution of racism over the course of the nineteenth and twentieth centuries and, in particular, the specific racism directed toward Haiti in recent history has shaped the way that scholars characterize the initial decades after 1804. Haitian history, from this perspective, becomes a linear path from an unsuccessful experiment in independence to "the poorest country in the western hemisphere."

This approach to nineteenth-century Haitian history—a perspective that historian Thorald Burnham refers to as the "isolation thesis"—does not capture the many and varied ways that foreigners interacted with Haiti during and after the period of diplomatic non-recognition.[5] In fact, a great deal of evidence that will be presented in the following chapters makes clear that Haitian independence unfolded with multiple connections across the Atlantic World. Specifically, local, regional, and metropolitan reactions to and interactions with Haiti call into question the established emphasis on race in the early nineteenth century. Race and slavery were certainly important factors in foreign reactions to news of Haiti's independence, as fear of the spread of revolution and the impact that it might have on other Caribbean slave societies terrorized (or inspired) the international community.[6] But these were not the only factors, and indeed they do not adequately explain the years after 1804. Historian Patrick Bellegarde-Smith has come to this conclusion with respect to the intellectual and political networks connecting Haiti and the Atlantic World during and after the Haitian Revolution. His study emphasizes the inadequacy of the current historiography: "Although race prejudice has played a dominant role in Haitian diplomatic relations with Western Europe and North America and although color has increasingly become a code word in Haiti, masking a virulent class struggle with cultural overtones, race and color cannot satisfactorily explain Haitian (and for that matter, West Indian) historical development."[7] The significance of Haitian independence, especially during the first decade, did indeed go far beyond the usual tropes of antiracism and antislavery. In order to fully understand this chapter in the Age of Revolution and the early nineteenth century, we must recognize the extent to which Haiti succeeded in establishing diplomatic, economic, and legal connections in the Atlantic World after 1804.

The Declaration of Independence raised unprecedented and profound questions about revolutionary legitimacy and national sovereignty, and these concerns were intertwined with changing political, military, and economic interests. In order to address these central questions, this book systematically examines the first years of independence by focusing on Haiti's connections with France, Britain, Denmark, the Batavian Republic (Netherlands), and the United States. The chronic warfare of the period shaped the reactions of foreign government leaders to news of Haiti's Declaration of Independence, and Haiti's relationships with Atlantic nations, empires, and colonies highlight the complex and layered set of priorities for both the Haitian government and the established powers of the Atlantic. France and Spain were waging war against Britain, and, as "belligerent" nations, all three were subject to particular rules under the customary practices of the law of nations. This distinction gave the British more freedom to officially interact with Haitian leaders, despite

France's continued claims over the island. In contrast, the United States, the Danish Empire, and the Batavian Republic operated under the rules governing the actions of "neutral" nations, and the customary practices of the law of nations forced them to tread a careful line when challenging French authority in Haiti. This context helps to explain why foreign observers did not simply see Haitian independence through a lens of racism and colonialism but also considered a larger and more complicated and nuanced Atlantic World that was connected by warfare, economics, and political change.

The archival evidence reveals a story of strategic contact between foreign governments and private businesses and the new Caribbean nation. One major reason why scholars have been quick to conclude that foreign diplomatic non-recognition resulted in Haiti's complete isolation after the Declaration of Independence is the paucity of sources in Haitian archives. Factors such as natural disaster, underfunded institutions, political turmoil, and theft have worked against the proper curation of official archives within the country. Fortunately, a number of repositories in Haiti have maintained important parts of the archival record, although their collections relate mostly to the latter half of the nineteenth century and the twentieth century.[8] In contrast, archives in France are rich with respect to both the colonial and early independence period, and I began my research in Paris at the Archives Nationales where I studied key documents relating to the French evacuation and French plans to reconquer the colony. But it soon became evident to me that the French archival holdings were only one part of a much larger evidentiary record about Haiti in the early nineteenth century. Indeed, in undertaking research for this study, I discovered how one document connected to another and then another in an extensive network of archival sources produced both by Haitians and by many others in disparate locations in Europe and the Americas. In other words, the historical evidence relating to contact and communication about and with Haitians after 1804 is scattered (but not randomly) throughout the Atlantic World. The multiple repositories of this evidence emphasize the importance of recent studies in Atlantic World history that reveal the interconnectedness of diverse people and places east and west, north and south, during the early modern era. An increasing number of studies are revealing how the movement of people, goods, and ideas created a significantly integrated Atlantic community that cannot be adequately understood in terms of divided nationalities or even empires.

To study the historical evidence of the connections between Haiti and the rest of the Atlantic World, my research took me from Haiti and France to Jamaica, England, the United States, the Netherlands, and Denmark. Through their dealings with Haiti and their internal debates about the question of trade with the new nation, each of these states and their former colonies produced a rich archive of correspondence, as well as a diversity of other primary sources, which, taken together, not only enhance our understanding of why France was unable to enforce its rejection of Haiti's independence but also reveal an intense interest in engagement with Haiti throughout the Atlantic World after the Haitian Declaration of Independence. Specifically, parliamentary and congressional debates as well as diplomatic correspondence shed light on official state policies and how local and metropolitan representatives viewed the benefits and drawbacks of a relationship with Haiti. Furthermore, they expose the conflicts, disagreements, and resolutions that eventually led to official diplomatic, economic, and legal policies. Merchant correspondence, often catalogued with court and state documents, reveals the extent to which the economic interests of individuals and companies influenced and shaped diplomatic and legal decisions. Merchants directly and indirectly informed (often intentionally) how local and metropolitan officials reacted to news of events in Saint Domingue/Haiti. As trustworthy sources of information for officials and as powerful influences on state governance, their letters describe the day-to-day connections between Haitians and the international Atlantic community as well as the processes by which officials settled on policies and procedures. For their part, court records reveal the interpretations and implementation of state policy both in the courtroom and on the high seas. The testimonies of merchants and captains as well as the rulings of judges indicate how state policy affected the actual connections between foreign individuals and Haitians after 1804, including how individuals were able to manipulate the vagaries of these policies in order to pursue their own interests and ambitions.

Of special importance is the record of the communications between local agents in the Caribbean and their home governments as well as with Jean-Jacques Dessalines, Alexandre Pétion, Henry Christophe, and other Haitian officials. These sources reveal the strategic political, economic, and military importance of Haiti during the early nineteenth century. At times, the leaders of foreign governments grappled directly with the question of Haitian sovereignty, but the task of confronting this question largely fell to the local representatives, who were placed in the position of dealing with the consequences of laws and developing policy. These representatives sometimes operated with very little direction from the metropole, while in other cases they collaborated closely with their home governments. This interwoven international context emphasizes the importance of focusing on Haiti in the broader context of the Atlantic World, especially in analyzing the years following the Declaration of Independence.

In examining for the first time in an integrated way the rich archival sources related to Haiti held in diverse locations, it becomes clear that the obstacles that Haiti faced after the Declaration of Independence were not unique. Only decades earlier, the United States had experienced similar problems of unequal power relationships with foreign governments. The American Revolution began an international discussion about the integration of new states into the community of nations in the Atlantic World, and the discussion would continue as Haiti and then almost all of Spain's American colonies declared their independence in the early nineteenth century. In the final decades of the eighteenth century, the new United States of America was sometimes able to form relationships with its Atlantic neighbors as equals but was often forced into a hierarchical relationship.[9] Inclusion "among the powers of the earth" was something that the new republic had to work for, and the process was not immediate.[10] Indeed, participation in the Atlantic community rested on a concept that historian Eliga Gould describes as "treaty-worthiness." Gould reveals that this was a hierarchical concept, but that after the American Revolution Americans sought to achieve treaty-worthiness equal to the powers of the Atlantic. This status would have integrated the new nation into the system of rights and duties that governed foreign relations in the late eighteenth- and early nineteenth-century Atlantic World. Treaty-worthiness was an extremely valuable and fickle possession, and the international community could revoke these privileges as easily as it could give them.[11] The United States only formally joined the community of nations in the Atlantic World after it entered into a Treaty of Alliance in 1778 with France, but the new country's struggle for full equality on the international stage continued into the early nineteenth century.[12] The American precedent made clear that new states would have to earn this status, and Haitian leaders similarly advocated for their own inclusion in the community of nations and empires in the Atlantic World.

The American Declaration of Independence sparked a broader debate about the rights of new states, and this debate would deepen in the early nineteenth century as Saint Domingue and then Haiti gained more and more autonomy.[13] Much of the discussion surrounding Haiti's right to declare independence paralleled the discussion that had occurred decades earlier with respect to the United States, and many observers and government leaders even made direct connections between the two. According to Haitian historian Dantès Bellegarde, the Declaration of Independence "marked both the birth of the second independent nation in America (after the United States) and the entrance of a Negro people into the society of civilized nations. It was also an eloquent affirmation of human liberty and of the equality of race."[14] While these statements may have been the intended results of the proclamation, outside nations had to ratify Haitian independence and the new country's participation in the "society of civilized nations" or "treaty-worthy nations." The Haitian government hoped to be treated as the leadership of an independent and sovereign territory, but foreign governments had to decide whether they would recognize this claim to national independence.

Foreign recognition of Haitian independence, however, was complicated, in part due to the confusing terms under which the French army left the island. Foreign governments found it difficult to decide whether they should follow the de jure sovereignty of the island—still claimed by France—or the de facto sovereignty—clearly secured by Dessalines and his army. Marcus Rainsford, the early nineteenth-century British chronicler of the Haitian Revolution, emphasized that the Haitian army had indeed secured de facto independence, and he supported British recognition of the new nation. "Their reduction to their former situation is impossible," he argued in 1805, "and though Europe waste her armies, and exhaust her navies in the endeavor, the blacks of St. Domingo will be unsubdued."[15] In his opinion, 1804 marked the end of French colonialism on Hispaniola.

French claims to title of the island after the Haitian Declaration of Independence nevertheless left foreign governments in a bind. There was no legal document conceding France's defeat and the granting to Haiti of its independence and sovereignty, as had been the case with the Treaty of Paris in 1783, through which the British Empire had acknowledged the independence of the United States of America. On the other hand, Dessalines proclaimed and published the Haitian Declaration of Independence in the midst of a long and violent war between France and Great Britain.

Haiti's independence, therefore, provided an opportunity for the British to land a blow to France's war efforts. The centrality of war, in the end, trumped any kind of allegiance among European empires. Even Spain, France's ally in 1804, was reluctant to invest resources in helping France reclaim their colony; some individuals in Cuba, however, capitalized on the situation by allowing French privateers to process and condemn ships caught trading with Haiti in their admiralty courts—in doing so, they received part of the profits.[16]

Warfare also proved to be more important than the fears of white planters and government officials in the British Caribbean that the revolution might spread to the other Caribbean colonies. Military strategy, in fact, encouraged the British to provide aid to Dessalines's forces at the end of the 1803 and to withhold aid from the French forces. Support to Dessalines's army against the French, however, did not necessarily mean that they would also accept Haiti as a sovereign nation and as an equal. The Haitian Declaration of Independence, therefore, posed a series of new questions to which military victory by itself did not necessarily demand answers. Haitian leaders, however, took the initiative and demanded recognition of their sovereignty and equality by explicitly affirming their break from France in a public statement, as the United States had done just under three decades earlier.

In doing so, Haitian leaders sought to integrate their new country into the system of laws—explicit and implicit, documented in treaties, theorized by philosophers, and established over time through custom—that governed the relationships between Atlantic nations. The debates about whether to include Haiti in this system of international diplomacy focused on evolving theories of the law of nations and centered primarily on the work of political and legal theorist Emer de Vattel and his guidelines for the incorporation of new polities into existing codes of international conduct.[17] Vattel emphasized that states possessed natural rights to independence and equality, but, as historian David Armitage shows, "the means by which new states might acquire that right, if they had not previously possessed it, became a central topic of international legal argument only in the late eighteenth century, partly in response to the issues of recognition raised by the [U.S.] Declaration of Independence itself."[18] In the discussions among foreign officials regarding Haitian independence and sovereignty, it is clear that the two concepts were closely related and that the relationship between the two concepts was a product of the American Revolution and the U.S. Declaration of Independence close to three decades earlier. Armitage argues that the Americans, by successfully creating an independent state, applied "Vattel's conception of independence [as] the touchstone of external sovereignty."[19]

In declaring independence from France, Dessalines and his generals did not explicitly address the issue of national sovereignty; the word "sovereignty" (*souverainté*) does not appear in the text of the Declaration. Instead of "sovereignty," the Haitian Declaration of Independence referenced the "liberty" (*liberté*) that they sought to secure from the "dominion" of France. This liberty could only be achieved by national independence. In the Declaration, Dessalines described Haiti as "a nation proud of having recovered its liberty" and referred to himself as "the protector of the liberty which the nation enjoys." While these references to liberty may have referred to freedom from individual enslavement—which had been abolished in the colony in 1793—it is more likely that these references to liberty referred to the metaphorical or political slavery of colonialism. American revolutionaries had deployed the language of slavery in their battle against the "tyranny" of the British Empire, and Dessalines similarly sought to affirm and secure Haiti's "liberty" from France's dominion.[20] The emphasis on liberty stresses the central goal of the Declaration of Independence—or, as Armitage shows, any declaration of independence—the achievement of the country's "international legal sovereignty."[21] By "living free and independent," Haitians could secure their "place on the list of free nations" or, as the United States' Declaration argued, "among the powers of the earth." The Haitian Declaration of Independence, therefore, united independence and sovereignty (or liberty).

Just as the context and content of the Haitian Declaration of Independence drew on the experiences of the United States just three decades earlier, international actors also returned to the incorporation of the United States into the community of recognized nations when they considered how to apply the various theories, customs, and laws relating to independence and sovereignty to the case of Haiti. But, while this experience characteristically framed their discussion in important ways, Haiti was also viewed as exceptional. The fact that the majority of the population in Haiti was not white and that most Haitian citizens had formerly been enslaved meant that the debate about Haiti's participation in the international community of recognized nations had a racial dimension that was unique, not only in comparison to the United States but also in comparison to later independence movements throughout Latin America. Could

Haiti be considered within the customary practices of the law of nations? Or would the situation require a new set of guidelines that accounted for the socio-racial hierarchy enforced by the powers of the Atlantic World? The overt challenge that Haiti represented to the economic investments of European empires in the Americas and to slave owners in the United States meant that foreign observers saw the Haitian Declaration of Independence as qualitatively different from its precursor in the United States. At the time, understandably, no political theorist had written guidelines that could account for the particular nature of the Haitian Revolution and the Haitian Declaration of Independence. Foreign officials, therefore, combined the customary practices of the law of nations with racial and colonial ideologies and theories in order to justify the policies that they ultimately adopted—or tried to adopt—in engaging Haiti for their own political, military, and economic interests.

Previous studies have suggested that Haiti remained economically and strategically important for other powers after the Declaration of Independence, including evidence of merchant travel to Haiti after 1803. But scholars have been dismissive about this evidence, emphasizing that such contact occurred outside the laws of the merchants' nations. While this was sometimes the case, much of the foreign trade with Haiti was legal throughout the period of diplomatic non-recognition. Furthermore, the merchant interest influenced political decisions in important ways, and this trade is therefore central to discussions about the diplomatic place of Haiti in the Atlantic. Merchants sometimes served as unofficial agents in Haiti since official non-recognition prevented traditional methods of communication between foreign and Haitian officials. More generally, merchants intersected with lawyers, judges, newspaper editors, governors, and other interested parties. The persistent willingness of merchants to trade with Haiti, even under risky circumstances, forced such other parties to make difficult decisions about Haiti's place in the world. In other words, diplomatic non-recognition after the Haitian Declaration of Independence did not prevent economic recognition, and, moreover, the line between the two layers of recognition was blurry. Legal trade with Haiti helped sustain the island's political break from France, and international trade with Haiti directly violated France's claims over the island.

Considered as a whole, the documentary reconstruction of Haiti's relationship with the larger Atlantic World during the first years after the Haitian Declaration of Independence reveals that foreign governments did not form an alliance in an effort to isolate Haiti. In the years following

1 January 1804, the international community reacted with a diversity of opinion rather than with a homogeneous quarantine. Neighboring nations, on the one hand, refused to recognize Haiti's independence, but on the other, they were keen to capitalize on the new trade opportunities and to incorporate Haiti into their military strategies. The movement of manufactured goods and agricultural products facilitated the movement of ideas and created what historian Julius Scott has famously called the "Common Wind," connecting Haiti to other Caribbean islands and nations in the Atlantic in a way that the emphasis on diplomatic isolation ignores.[22] The familiar scholarly focus on Haitian isolation masks the many and diverse ways that Haitians and their leaders interacted with Atlantic World empires, nations, and colonies outside the constraints of official diplomatic non-recognition and how these other forms of recognition impacted Haiti's diplomatic status. Haiti's various relationships with foreign officials and individuals sparked profound discussions about the country's status and how this new entity might enter into existing international codes of diplomatic and economic conduct.

State leaders in Haiti certainly presented their cause as a universal one, with implications for all oppressed people in the Americas. Yet they understood well that they were pursuing their radical experiment in state formation and freedom in a constrained space, one surrounded by empires based on the wealth produced by slave economies. Even as neighboring states and empires broadly sought to contain the influence that Haiti might have on their own slave and colonial systems, they also had countervailing interests in continuing connections with the country. Economic, military, and political interests often trumped concerns about the spread of revolutionary ideas. The result was that, as I show in this book, the relationships between Haiti and other powers in the early nineteenth century were layered and sometimes contradictory. Haiti's successful preservation of its independence was deeply connected to the broader Atlantic World.

In proclamations, speeches, and correspondence, Dessalines and other revolutionary leaders announced to the world the principles upon which they would build the Haitian state. Their rhetoric highlights a perceived community of humanity that they pitted against the French. "Toward these men who do us justice," Dessalines, Henry Christophe, and Augustin Clervaux proclaimed in November 1803, "we will act as brothers." The three revolutionary heroes also called on the "God of Freemen" for protection. They condemned slavery and declared that the "tribunal of Providence . . . has not created men to see them groaning under a harsh and shameful servitude."[23] An article in the *Times* (London) echoed this sense of a common humanity that had been tainted by the institution of slavery. "Is it ordained that a degraded race of men," the article questioned, "shall be the only race who resent the cruel wrongs done to themselves and to humanity?"[24] Though the British report maintained a racist tone, the parallels between such arguments and the proclamations issued by the Haitian state suggest that the leaders of the new Caribbean nation were part of a larger discussion about humanity and the legitimacy or rightfulness of slavery.

The rhetoric of independent Haiti, however, was much more forceful. "Thus perish all tyrants over innocence," Dessalines proclaimed in the solemn sermon of the Declaration of Independence, "all oppressors of mankind!"[25] This anger and outrage was directed at the French, and, as the Haitian state sought new political friendships in the Atlantic, it overlooked the British, American, Dutch, and Danish slave systems in order to form new economic partnerships. Political necessity narrowed the application of universal principles to Haitian territory, and Haitian leaders did not condemn slavery as a labor institution throughout the Atlantic. Instead, they courted the goodwill and friendship of other foreign governments and merchants, focusing most of their attention on the United States and the British Empire.

After the French evacuation, Dessalines understood that Haitian independence would come under attack. "It is not enough to have forced out of your Country the Barbarians who have ensanguined it for the Space of two Centuries," he argued in the Acte de l'Indépendance; "it is not sufficient to have put an End to factions reviving from the Phantom of Liberty, which France exposed to our Eyes." Dessalines announced that there was still work to be done to secure Haitian sovereignty. "We must convince the inhuman Government which has hitherto kept us in the most humiliating State," he continued, "that all hopes of ever enslaving us are at an end, and we must live Independent or die."[26] He called on the people to stand guard to protect these sacred achievements.

In this context, the following chapters build not only on specific work on Haiti in the larger Atlantic context but also on research that is uncovering the multifaceted character of official authority and influence across all the vast imperial territories in the early modern era. In particular, historian Lauren Benton's global study of sovereignty reveals the many and diverse power structures within empires that produced a system of "layered sovereignty."[27] Benton's research highlights the need to "imagin[e] sovereignty as a divisible quality whose component parts could be apportioned in various combinations."[28] More recently, Benton has studied the implication of "layered sovereignty" for independence movements in Latin America. "Precisely because empires were structured as systems of layered sovereignty," she argues, "it was possible to imagine a range of different types of new polities operating with some state-like capacities."[29] These important insights encourage a closer examination of how different actors both in the Caribbean and elsewhere helped determine the meaning of Haiti's Declaration of Independence.

While Benton's research focuses on these different layers within empires, the case of Haiti shows that these layers were also significant in an international context. Official non-recognition did not result in diplomatic isolation, and indeed foreign governments extended partial or temporary recognition of Haiti's independence from France. Furthermore, the layers are visible not just in diplomacy but also in economic connections. Foreign governments were willing to extend economic recognition to Haiti even while they withheld official diplomatic recognition. This economic recognition meant that Haitians were not isolated in the Atlantic World after the Declaration of Independence, despite their exclusion from the international diplomatic community. Just as sovereignty was divisible, so was foreign recognition. After 1804, therefore, we see multiple layers of recognition in Haiti's connections with foreign governments and individuals. Moreover, the close analysis of Haiti's interactions with the rest of the Atlantic World points to the value of looking beyond official policies as articulated in the metropolitan centers to understand the meaning of the Declaration of Independence. The years after 1804 reveal that Atlantic empires could imagine in the case of Haiti "a varied set of potential outcomes."[30]

The following chapters trace both the reactions of foreign governments—in the Caribbean, the United States, and Europe—to news of the Haitian Declaration of Independence and the ways that Haitian leaders attempted to shape their own trajectory during this crucial period. I focus on the decade after 1804, a period during which foreign officials and many others debated intensely how to react to Haitian independence while also taking specific actions. During this time, policies changed as governments responded to local and international needs and concerns. After these years, governments settled on their respective policies, which lasted until they extended official diplomatic recognition in later decades (France in 1825; the British Empire, the Netherlands, and Denmark in 1826; Spain in 1855; and the United States in 1862).

Since the most important challenge that Haiti faced was the continued opposition of France, the first question I address in my analysis is why France was unable to convince foreign powers to isolate Haiti. While active representatives of the French government energetically tried to convince the governments in Curaçao, St. Thomas, and the United States to withhold recognition of Haiti's independence, they were not able to assure the complete failure of Haiti's independence project since merchants from each of these places continued to travel to Haiti—both legally and illegally. France's frustration in trying to ensure Haiti's isolation focuses our attention on how Haiti was able to take advantage of the centrality of economic interest in the Atlantic World. While Haiti had to deal with France and its efforts to establish solidarity with other powers, it worked intently to carve out a new economic space for itself in the Caribbean.

It was able to do this in part because France's enemies—primarily the British—were willing to explore the possibility of an alliance with the new Haitian government. Representatives from Jamaica negotiated with Jean-Jacques Dessalines with the hope that they could establish a friendly economic relationship. The proposals by the Jamaican governor, however, would have trapped Haiti in a hierarchical relationship that would have undermined the country's sovereignty. Dessalines, therefore, rejected the proposed treaties.

Following the failure of the negotiations between Jean-Jacques Dessalines and the governor of Jamaica, the British government did not issue an official statement regarding its relationship with Haiti. Given that Britain was indecisive and inconsistent in coming to grips with Haiti, what happened when ships were caught trading with Haiti? How did the courts deal with them? Despite the continued silence regarding Haiti's diplomatic status, the British explicitly allowed and regulated trade with Haiti beginning in late 1806 and therefore extended economic recognition of Haiti's independence. The British Admiralty Courts, however, expanded these terms and extended some degree of diplomatic recognition to Haiti between 1806 and 1826.

The U.S. government similarly resisted making an official statement regarding Haiti's diplomatic status, and it took a full two years after the Haitian Declaration of Independence for the U.S. Congress to prohibit trade with Haiti. This prohibition, however, was only in place for a total of four years (1806–10). Between 1804 and 1806 and 1810 and 1862, therefore, the United States withheld diplomatic recognition but allowed American merchants to travel to Haiti to capitalize on the economic opportunities available because of the country's proclaimed break with France. The brief economic prohibition, however, had implications for Haiti's perceived diplomatic status, despite the fact that the U.S. government did not explicitly address the issue.

By 1806, the British Empire was the only Atlantic empire that had not prohibited trade with Haiti and instead supported and regulated the trade. This connection inspired Dessalines's two successors, Alexandre Pétion and Henry Christophe, to attempt to reopen the failed negotiations between the Jamaican governor and Dessalines. The new Jamaican governor, however, refused to communicate with either Haitian president, and so Pétion and Christophe turned to London for diplomatic and economic support. Their new treaty proposals conceded to many of the demands that Jean-Jacques Dessalines had found unacceptable in 1804. The situation in 1807, however, was drastically different, since all of the other important empires and nations in the Atlantic had prohibited trade with Haiti. The British government refused to respond to these proposals and thus concluded the official conversation with the Haitian government. Trade and unofficial and local communication, however, continued.

After 1 January 1804, did the nations of the Atlantic consider Haiti independent and sovereign? Rather than emphasizing the French-led insistence on isolation and the length of time it took before foreign governments officially recognized Haiti as an independent state, the historical evidence reveals a multilayered strategy on the part of governments other than France and its ally Spain as they grappled with the unprecedented and profound questions posed by events in Haiti. Governments and individuals in the United States, Britain, Denmark, and the Batavian Republic (Netherlands) all debated the best course of action in response to France's defeat in the Haitian Revolution and the Haitian Declaration of Independence. During this time, Haiti succeeded in launching its independence and in creating a new fragile space in the turbulent Atlantic World.

1

I PUT FEAR IN THE HEARTS OF THOSE WHO ENGAGE IN THIS TRADE

French Efforts to Isolate Haiti in the Atlantic World

On 19 November 1803, Dessalines signed a proclamation with the adjutant commander of the French forces in Saint Domingue coordinating the evacuation of the French army from Cap Français, the last French stronghold in Saint Domingue. This proclamation gave the French army ten days to leave Cap Français, and it listed eight articles, including a guarantee for the safety of the white inhabitants who chose to remain on the island, as well as the means for others to leave the island with the French army.[1] In one sense, this proclamation officially began the postcolonial process that led to the emergence of a new country in the Atlantic World. In hindsight, we know that when Napoléon Bonaparte's troops set sail from Cap Français in November 1803 and when Dessalines declared independence a month later, it signaled the end of French rule in what had been the French Empire's most profitable colony. While many French citizens and officials dreamed of reconquest, neither Bonaparte nor his successors ever launched a military campaign designed to defeat Haitian independence. At the time, however, French government and army officials and refugee Dominguan planters variously ignored, denied, and challenged the fact of Haitian independence. They largely saw the situation as temporary and continued to claim that Haiti was simply a "belligerent" colony.[2] The details of the proclamation make clear that France viewed this retreat as a temporary setback. It did not announce a French surrender; it simply stated that the French forts and war matériel would be given to Dessalines and that the French troops would leave the city. This omission allowed the French to continue to claim to be the legal authorities and to embark on a campaign to isolate Haiti in order to cut off international trade, weaken the rebel forces, and thereby facilitate reconquest. For this reason, the point of departure for understanding how Haiti was able to establish new connections within the Atlantic World is to examine why France was not able to fulfill this imperial ambition.

At the outset, the Haitian leaders had to contend with the continued threat from a small contingent of French soldiers on the eastern side of the island in the city of Santo Domingo, led by the French general Jean-Louis Ferrand. In late 1803, after he refused the opportunity to escape the island on a British ship, Ferrand assumed command from the less senior François de Kerversau.[3] As would be expected, the French government viewed Haiti's Declaration of Independence on 1 January 1804 as an illegitimate document, and officials worked to convince other powers—both enemies and allies—that the territory officially remained a French colony and would soon be functionally reunited with the French Empire. Ferrand worked intently to reestablish French authority and to undo the abolition of slavery. "At its core," historian Graham Nessler argues, "the underlying logic behind the policies of the Ferrand regime was the desire to crush the new Haitian state and reestablish a rejuvenated French plantation colony on its ruins."[4] Despite the relatively small size of his military force, Ferrand was able to instigate a great deal of trouble for the new Haitian state, especially by helping French privateers police the waters around the island in order to prevent other foreign nations from trading with the claimed colony.[5] In addition to challenging slave emancipation and unleashing French privateers along the Haitian coasts, Ferrand launched a war of proclamations in order to undermine Haiti's independence. "He [Ferrand] established the foundational textual basis," French studies scholar Deborah Jenson has shown, "for a cascading series of political and legal conclusions that the free citizens of the new black republic were simply revolted colonized subjects of France."[6]

In order to help prevent the supposedly illicit trade between foreign merchants and the ports of Saint Domingue, French privateers patrolled the waters around Hispaniola and other islands in order to capture merchants whom they suspected were trading with the "brigands." In this effort, they received help from Spanish corsairs and courts in keeping with the Spanish-French alliance in the war. When Jean-Jacques Dessalines declared Haitian independence on the first day of 1804, France and Spain were waging a brutal war against the British. Therefore, when France outlawed trade with Haiti, they had the support of Spanish privateers from Cuba in their efforts to suppress international trade.[7]

French privateers captured over 100 American ships accused of trading with Haiti in the two years after the Haitian Declaration of Independence.[8]

According to a British emissary writing in early 1804, the American trade with Haiti had been "completely interrupted by privateers from Cuba."[9] Because of Ferrand's precarious position in Santo Domingo and because of the geographic location of his base relative to the Haitian waters and to the British islands, French privateers used Spanish ports to process and condemn their prizes.[10] "Often the property was condemned *de facto* and without trial," historian Ada Ferrer reveals, "the vessels and their (human and other) cargo sold, and duties that should have been paid to the King and state instead were divided among local Cuban officials complicit in the enterprise."[11] Spanish support for their French allies and opportunism on the part of individual actors in Cuba led the Haitian state to declare war on the Spanish Empire and to retaliate in the waters west of the island of Hispaniola. Haitian ships captured Spanish vessels and brought them to Haitian ports for processing and condemnation.[12] While allied with France, however, Cuban authorities were reluctant to react to Haitian independence with explicit policy either in support of or in opposition to Haiti's new proclaimed status. Thus, while they continued to refer to the island as a "foreign colony," "Cuban authorities pretended that Haiti was a nonentity, and pretending, they hoped, would make it true."[13]

Ferrand's challenges meant that the war between the Haitian and French armies was, as the French believed, clearly not over. Frustrated by the harassment from Ferrand and keen to assume control over the entire island of Hispaniola, in 1805 Dessalines and 20,000 soldiers marched from the western side of the island to launch an attack on Santo Domingo. Despite Dessalines's advantage in terms of manpower, his campaign was met with defeat because of the arrival of a French naval force.[14] In fact, Ferrand and his band of troops were able to hold out at Santo Domingo until 1809, when they were defeated by a joint Haitian, Spanish, and British effort. Afterward, the eastern side of Hispaniola again became a Spanish colony, despite continued claims by the Haitian government.

Meanwhile, the schemes to reinvade Haiti began soon after the retreat of the French army at the end of 1803.[15] Between 1804 and 1815, French action vis-à-vis Haiti was characterized by efforts to collect information about the former colony in order to "simply turn the clock back to 1789." If such action were successful, "slavery would be re-imposed and the plantation system re-established in an effort to return the colony to its former glory."[16] Even a decade after Haitian independence, French citizens continued to submit reconquest schemes with the hope of reclaiming the lost colony.[17] The French government hoped to regain control over Saint Domingue/Haiti for a variety of reasons: they worried about the spread of the rebellion to their remaining Caribbean colonies, Martinique, Guadeloupe, and Guiana; they wanted to prevent the British from achieving a monopoly on the colonial markets; and they sought the revitalization of French commerce in the Atlantic.[18]

In the immediate years after 1804, the key problem for the French was that other imperial governments and their local representatives—as well as Caribbean and Atlantic merchant communities—had their own well-established connections with Saint Domingue/Haiti. Both before and during the revolution, Saint Domingue's economy was organized around foreign trade, specifically the exchange of plantation crops for provisions, manufactured goods, and war supplies. The Haitian Revolution disrupted colonial trade regulations and opened Saint Domingue to a range of international trade. Merchants flocked to the island to take advantage of the opportunities presented by the multifaceted war. The free ports of Curaçao and St. Thomas provided immense opportunities for merchants of diverse nations and empires since goods could cross between imperial boundaries and circumvent the restrictive laws of mercantilism.[19]

At the time, the French ambition to ensure the isolation of Haiti must have been a quite attractive alternative to military reinvasion as a strategy to reject the Declaration of Independence and reassert imperial control. In the midst of the Napoleonic Wars and on the heels of a disastrous attempt by the Leclerc Expedition to regain control over the colony, the French military could not spare the forces that would be necessary for such a feat. French officials could not count on renewed military support and therefore had to find an alternative method for suppressing the Haitian Declaration of Independence. The conviction that trade was vital for Haiti's prospects as an independent country was also shared by Haiti's new leaders, who focused on continued Atlantic commerce as the key to their survival. They welcomed foreign merchants and assured government officials that trade with Haiti was a safe and profitable undertaking.

Foreign onlookers, however, feared that the influence of the revolution in Saint Domingue might spread beyond the boundaries of the island or that Haitian leaders might initiate foreign military campaigns in order to overturn the slavery-dependent economic systems of the Atlantic World. France was indeed justified in expecting the support of foreign governments; the Napoleonic Wars worked against the prospect of France getting everyone's support for any particular project, but, in this case, the hope of coordinated actions seemed reasonable since the economic underpinnings of European empire in the Caribbean were at stake. It is understandable, therefore, that scholars have assumed that French officials succeeded in their attempts to isolate Haiti after the Haitian Declaration of Independence. But to what extent does the archival record support this theory? Were the French agents in the Caribbean able to orchestrate and enforce trade policies in the region that would thwart Haiti's economic ambitions? Did the rest of the Atlantic World support, in practice as well as in theory, the isolation of Haiti?

In order to address these key questions, we must focus on the efforts of French agents at two central trading hubs in the Caribbean—Curaçao and St. Thomas—to convince the governors of those islands to outlaw trade between Dutch and Danish merchants and the "rebels" in Saint Domingue/Haiti. Fortunately, the extant historical evidence includes substantial correspondence between the local agents and the French general Jean-Louis Ferrand in Santo Domingo, to whom they reported.[20] This evidence is worth examining in detail in order to understand the difference between aspirations in France and everyday life in the Caribbean after 1804. In particular, the experiences of three agents in Curaçao and St. Thomas who attempted to carry out the critical mission of stopping trade with Haiti reveal why implementation proved so difficult. In Dutch Curaçao, J. Thilorier served as French agent during late 1803 and early 1804 before Jean-Pierre Gouges replaced him and served until 1807. In Danish St. Thomas, Arnaud André Roberjot Lartigue served as the French agent beginning in 1805 and ending in 1807.[21] The British Empire occupied both islands beginning in 1807. During their time as agents, all three men wrote frequently to Ferrand in order to ask for advice, assistance, and aid while also informing the general of the actions undertaken, decisions made, and publications issued in the foreign colonies. One of the governors of Curaçao, Pierre-Jean Changuion, also wrote regularly to Ferrand, not only to update him regarding the prohibition of trade but also to complain about French encroachments on Dutch sovereignty. Taken together, a detailed analysis of the flows of correspondence within the Caribbean sheds new light on the meaning and significance of Haiti's Declaration of Independence. Moreover, this evidence helps explain why France did in fact lose its colony, why the ambition to isolate Haiti failed, and why Haiti achieved considerable sovereignty despite all odds in the early nineteenth-century Atlantic World.

Challenging and Strengthening Haitian Connections within the Atlantic Economy

Until the end of the eighteenth century, Saint Domingue was immensely profitable, a draw for merchants in the Greater Caribbean and across the Atlantic World. Although Toussaint Louverture was able to stabilize the economy during the latter half of the 1790s and revive the plantation export system, trade never returned to the prerevolutionary levels, primarily as a result of the steep decline in sugar production.[22] Louverture and postindependence leaders, including Jean-Jacques Dessalines and Henry Christophe, tried to reconstruct the sugar economy, but they did so only with partial success. A British agent reported in 1804 that the only crops being produced in Haiti were coffee and cotton and that he doubted that the sugar plantations could be restored.[23] Two years later, a British merchant reported that sugar production had been completely wiped out. "The Cultivation of the Sugar Cane (which used to be its *first* staple)," Robert Sutherland wrote, "from the destruction of the works the want of capital as well as Artificers to replace them, has of late years been almost totally abandoned but this Branch may again revive in Some *degree* and other articles of produce experience a gradual increase."[24] There were, however, other export crops—including cotton, mahogany, and, most important, coffee. Already a significant export crop during the eighteenth century, coffee became the country's major agricultural export in the early nineteenth century. It could be cultivated on small farms, in combination with other crops, and therefore fit well with the broader aspirations of the Haitian population after independence. This transition was successful because Haitian coffee was a sought-after commodity in the Atlantic market.[25]

Thanks to coffee and other agricultural exports, trade with Haiti continued to attract merchants from around the Atlantic. Furthermore, Haiti was a profitable market for manufactured goods and war matérials. "There was a great Appearance of Business in most of the ports of St. Domingo," the Governor of Jamaica reported at the end of 1804, "profuse importations of goods of all descriptions, and an abundant supply of produce (sugar excepted)."[26] In this context, Dutch and Danish merchants had good reason to see trade opportunities in Haiti.

The French therefore had their work cut out for them as they tried to convince merchants to forgo trade with Haiti. Leading the charge to isolate Haiti was General Jean-Louis Ferrand, who, from his base in Santo Domingo, ordered French agents in other parts of the Caribbean to convince foreign governors to prohibit trade. He received support from France's remaining colonies in the Caribbean, mainly Guadeloupe and Martinique, but there may also have been some competition between the islands. Soon after Haitian independence, on 5 June 1804, the captain-general of Guadeloupe published a proclamation prohibiting trade with the "brigands."[27] "The Corsairs of Guadeloupe," Article One of this proclamation stated, "will stop all Ships destined for the ports of St. Domingue that are occupied by the brigands, as well as those which are leaving them." Article Two then condemned those engaging in the trade as more than criminals: "The ships whose destination is proved to be for the Ports, or coming from the Ports occupied by the revolted [révoltés], will be considered enemies of France. They will in consequence be considered good prize and condemned as the Rules dictate." In effect, the French government declared war on all those who collaborated economically with Haitians. As they had done during the 1790s in their war with the English, the French insisted that any merchants who traded with Haiti were trading with the enemy; such merchants lost their neutrality and became legitimate targets for navy vessels and privateers.[28]

Less than a year after the proclamation from Guadeloupe, Ferrand published another proclamation from Santo Domingo and sent it to government representatives around the Caribbean. This proclamation of February 1805 stated that "all individuals, whoever they may be, who are found on allied or neutral ships, destined for the ports of Saint-Domingue, that are occupied by the revolted, will be punished with death." Ferrand did not distinguish among types of cargo. All trade was deemed illegal. The result was that trading with Haitians was worse than simply trading with the enemy.[29]

Merchant Islands

As small islands in the Caribbean, Curaçao and St. Thomas based their economies on trade activity rather than plantation agriculture. Their status as merchant hubs meant that before the Haitian Revolution, both islands had solid commercial relationships with Saint

Domingue. Curaçao was already known by the mid-seventeenth century as a major regional trade center, with merchants of all nations coming to the island to exchange their goods—particularly because of the island's role as a hub for the slave trade.[30] "In 1675," notes historian Linda Rupert, "at a time when most European powers imposed severe trade restrictions and colonies were only allowed to trade with their Motherland, Curaçao was opened to ships of all nationalities, an exceptionally bold move for the times."[31] The population of Curaçao, despite the fact that the island's economy was not based on plantation agriculture, included an enslaved majority. Of the 20,000 people in Curaçao at the end of the eighteenth century, about 13,000 were enslaved. The white and free colored population equally made up the remaining 7,000.[32] The enslaved population in Curaçao was employed in diverse jobs, most in the shipping industry, either as sailors or in the ports. Others, however, worked on smaller plantations that were geared toward local consumption.

Rupert's detailed study of the commercial activities of Curaçao reveals a pivotal shift in the island's trade relationships in the late eighteenth century. British dominance in the Caribbean and on the high seas signaled the demise of Dutch commercial supremacy.[33] Furthermore, French armies occupied the Netherlands between 1795 and 1813 and created a "satellite state" called the Batavian Republic.[34] The struggles between the French agents and the governors of Curaçao, therefore, took place in a context of economic decline and animosity toward the French Empire.

The relationship between the Batavian Republic and France was contentious and changing between 1803 and 1806, and the tension is clear in the correspondence between the French agents and the governors of the island. Batavia was a French satellite state, but the Dutch ruling class maintained constant resistance to French domination. The Dutch, therefore, were not quite neutral in the Franco-British war, but they were also not clear allies. Despite the combative nature of the relationship between the Dutch and the French, observers from both empires described Curaçao as either an ally of France or a neutral nation at this time period. A more commonly used term, however, to describe the relationship was "friendly," although, as is clear in the correspondence between the French and Dutch representatives in the Caribbean, the relationship was not always congenial and supportive. Friendship, however, suggests some obligation on the part of the Batavian Republic toward France but nothing as strong as an alliance. This distinct status blurred the assumptions about the colony's commitments to France. And, despite France's official power over Batavia, scholars emphasize the resistance to this occupation in Curaçao. "In practice," Rupert argues, "Curaçao did not feel like a French possession to its inhabitants, even though the French had stationed a government agent on the island."[35] Even this government agent's power was not guaranteed, because the governor in 1804 received notice from his superiors in Europe that he could no longer recognize the post.

French and Spanish privateers patrolled the waters around Haiti, ready to enforce the proclamation issued by Ferrand, but the merchant community in Curaçao still appeared willing to undertake the risky economic ventures. Indeed, foreign observers reported that merchants from Curaçao continued their relationships with Haiti. "The Dutch from Curacoa [sic]," the governor of Jamaica reported in 1804, "are now beginning to carry on a trade with the South side of Saint Domingo particularly Aux Cayes and Jacmel."[36] International jockeying over power during this period of international warfare may have induced the Dutch merchants to ignore the directions from the French in the city of Santo Domingo as well as the proclamations issued by their own governor. Indeed, Rupert quotes an insightful witness to these types of actions: "'In fact, the best commercial periods for Curaçao were those in which war in neighboring countries brought a wind of prosperity to our coast,' noted one contemporary observer. The difference between legitimate and illegitimate commerce was neither understood nor heeded."[37]

At this time, the island was experiencing significant change at a local level, most notably the transfer of authority from the West India Company to the Dutch government. West India Company rule ended in 1791, at which point a Dutch-appointed governor administered the island with the help of the Colonial Council, which was primarily composed of wealthy merchants.[38] Indeed, the island's history as an economic hub continued to influence the government and political culture since the island's economic leaders also held political representation.[39] Economic considerations, therefore, were central to government decisions.

St. Thomas occupied an economic role in the Caribbean similar to Curaçao. Until 1755, the island had been the property of the Danish West India Company. After this rule, ownership transferred to the Danish crown, and, beginning in 1764, it was opened to international trade under the designation of a "free port."[40] This status stipulated that "anyone was permitted to set up an enterprise in St. Thomas and engage in

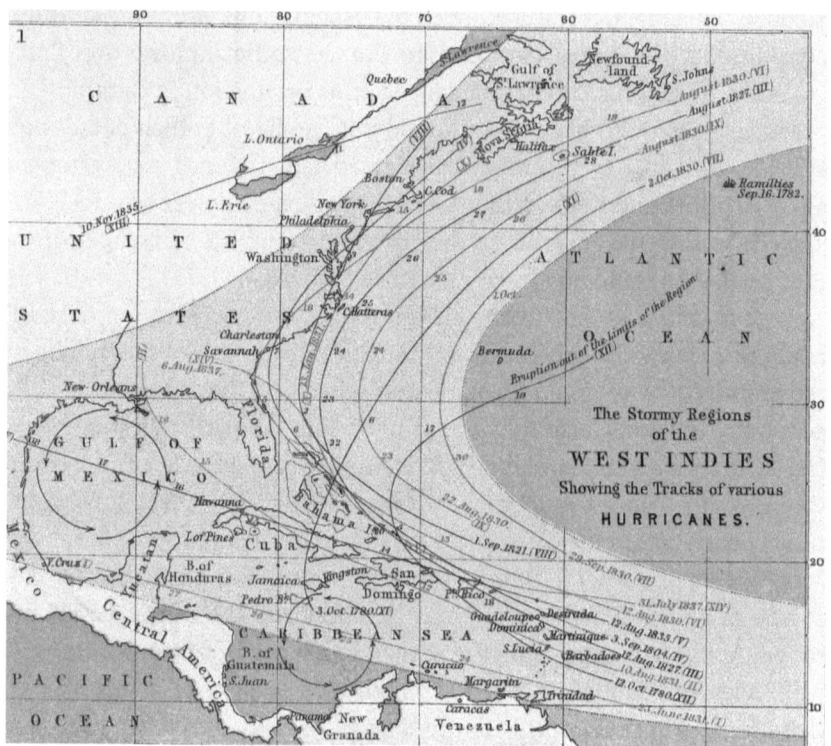

FIGURE ONE A portion of Alexander Keith Johnston's map "Currents of Air," published by William Blackwood and Sons, Edinburgh, 1854. (Courtesy of the David Rumsey Historical Map Collection.) The wind currents drawn on this map show the easy accessibility from Curaçao to the south of Haiti and from St. Thomas (just east of Puerto Rico) to the north of Haiti.

trade in either European or American goods."[41] The Danish in St. Thomas were able to capitalize on the free port status during the European wars of the late eighteenth and early nineteenth centuries because of their neutral status. The island was small, "and though St. Thomas had but little of these productions of her own to export [West Indian products], great quantities came pouring in for sale, and were transmitted to Europe and America in neutral vessels, in order to avoid the cruisers of the nations that were at war with each other." At the time of Haitian independence, St. Thomas was home to only about 3,000 enslaved individuals, most of whom were employed in the port cities.[42]

The island served as a distribution center of sorts for European goods. "Large importations of merchandise arrived from Europe," John P. Knox, a nineteenth-century historian, noted, "and of flour and other provisions from the United States, which were immediately sold and dispersed among the British, Spanish, and French colonies."[43] Another nineteenth-century author argued that since St. Thomas was a "rendezvous where vessels of all nations could meet on neutral ground, where their business could be transacted, where prizes could be sold, a little piracy planned, supplies of all sorts procured, or a cargo of slaves landed, it is not at all surprising that it flourished and did well."[44] After the Haitian Declaration of Independence, the Danish continued to trade with the island. The trade was so widespread that the governor of Jamaica noted that "the [trade to the] northern and western ports of the island, and that of the south is in the hands of Danes from St. Thomas,' or at least vessels bearing their flag, from Jamaica and other West India Islands."[45]

French Pressure at Curaçao

In 1803, General Donatien Rochambeau, leader of the French army in Saint Domingue, sent J. Thilorier to Curaçao to serve as a French agent on the island. Rochambeau's situation in Saint Domingue was increasingly desperate; by the end of November, his troops would evacuate the island. He sent Thilorier to Curaçao to prevent Dutch merchants from supporting the rebel armies in Saint Domingue and to help procure military supplies for the dwindling French army. Thilorier arrived in Curaçao on 10 November and immediately began gathering information regarding the alleged relationships between the "*mulâtres* or blacks of this colony [Curaçao] and the brigands of Saint Domingue."[46] These relationships, he reported, had been formed during economic engagements in which merchants from Curaçao sailed to Saint Domingue and returned with a fresh cargo. He learned from a Guadeloupe-based French agent at Curaçao that ships from Curaçao officially cleared out for Cuba but then traveled instead to Jacmel and other areas in the south of Saint Domingue. These voyages, he argued, supplied the "brigands" with "powder and other war munitions."[47]

By the last few months of 1803, the French troops in Saint Domingue were starving and losing hold on their precarious post in the colonial capital, Cap Français. Thilorier was therefore outraged that the rebels were receiving aid and military supplies from a colony that was France's alleged friend. Thilorier reported in his first letter to Rochambeau that the agent from Guadeloupe had not been able to prevent the trade for "lack of proof or direct knowledge of the guilty individuals."[48] The other French agent probably lacked the necessary evidence because the vessels avoided documenting their trips to Saint Domingue by clearing out for other islands. Despite this fact, the French agents were absolutely convinced that the trade was widespread. Thilorier was hopeful that he could do a better job than the agent from Guadeloupe in preventing this "illicit" trade. He reported to Rochambeau that the Curaçaoan government had reassured the French agents that they would take all necessary measures to stop this trade.

In addition to gathering information with a view toward stopping trade between the merchants at Curaçao and the rebel army in Saint Domingue, Thilorier tried to help Rochambeau's troops in Saint Domingue. One of his tasks was to acquire badly needed supplies for the French army.[49] The deteriorating French army had been cut off from external supplies by a British blockade of Saint Domingue, and Thilorier tried to find friendly suppliers who would be willing to challenge the British ships in the waters surrounding the western side of Hispaniola. In addition, in order to contribute to the privateering strategy, Thilorier requested that Rochambeau send him commissions for the French privateers operating out of Curaçao, licensing them to capture ships engaged in illegal trade.[50]

Given Curaçao's "friendly" relationship with the French, the British had occupied Curaçao between 1800 and 1803, and during Thilorier's early months in Curaçao, the island remained under siege by British ships. Despite the occupation and the continued threat of military invasion, Thilorier complained that he perceived a significant amount of pro-British sentiment on the island, and he argued that another British occupation might have been welcome. He may have been correct. "Faced with occupation by one or the other European power," Linda Rupert reveals, "Curaçao's Colonial Council judged it better 'to place the territory under the protection of his Britannic Majesty than to allow it to fall into the hands of the ferocious gang of robbers laying siege to us.'"[51] The period between British occupations, 1803–06, saw increased economic difficulties and a scarcity of commercial activity, and, therefore, officials on the island had to find a way to stop the economic downfall.[52]

At the same time that Thilorier complained about the residents of Curaçao favoring British interests, he also noted that the French in Santo Domingo should not hope to receive any aid from the island; and the two observations may have been connected. When Ferrand asked Thilorier to help him secure badly needed provisions and supplies from

Curaçao, Thilorier responded that he "should not anticipate anything from Curaçao without money or merchandise."[53] Apparently a number of previous transactions had spoiled the French reputation in Curaçao, and, as Thilorier argued, "there is a general air of distrust, and it exists entirely among those in government who will not be useful to us."[54] Despite these obstacles, Thilorier's correspondence suggests that he was able to secure a supplier for a large order of leather shoes for the French army.

The Unofficial Agents in Curaçao

J. Thilorier and Jean-Pierre Gouges pressured the governors of Curaçao in ways that reflected the changing international alliances as well as certain assumptions about how the Dutch should act to support France's efforts. These perspectives, however, did not take into account Dutch self-interest and their wariness about trusting French economic relationships. The conflict between French and Dutch authority in Curaçao intensified in December 1803, just over a month after Thilorier's arrival. The governor of Curaçao received notice from the Batavian government in Europe that the government of Curaçao was no longer allowed to recognize foreign agents on the island; the records do not suggest why the metropolitan government made this decision. The governor told Thilorier that he would allow him to stay on the island but that he could not occupy an official position and that he would have his powers limited to those matters concerning French corsairs and prize vessels.[55] The governor did not follow up on this concession, and Thilorier argued that he was "paralyzed" as a government agent.[56]

Thilorier's inability to influence the activities of Curaçaoan merchants was particularly frustrating for him because he perceived a general culture of lawlessness on the island. In a letter written to General Rochambeau in December 1803 (not knowing that Rochambeau's troops would have set sail from Cap Français by that time), he described his views on Curaçao. "Curaçao can be considered," he argued, "a haven for scoundrels of all colors, and of all nations." "They are good friends of our rebels," he continued, "for whom they are very useful by the different envoys sent to them daily."[57] The connection on the western side of Hispaniola between the merchant communities in Curaçao and Saint Domingue dated from the French colonial period.[58] The friendship that Thilorier described had been ongoing for over a century and did not stop during the Haitian

Revolution. The new conflict between France and Haiti, from Thilorier's perspective, should have cut off these trade networks. This argument, however, did not immediately convince the governor of Curaçao. "The government here supervises, and supervises only for the form," Thilorier claimed in the same letter; "he does not seem to want to meddle in the quarrel of their neighbors."[59] This may have been because the "quarrel of their neighbors" was the ideal context in which to capitalize on trade. Thilorier was doubly upset at this fact since the governor had, with "zeal," promised to prohibit this trade. According to Thilorier, this trade was inherently illegal; however, according to the governor of Curaçao, the conflict was a local affair and should not have affected the trade of neutral nations.

Thilorier soon received word of the French evacuation of Saint Domingue, but he continued his correspondence with General Jean-Louis Ferrand, who stationed himself in the city of Santo Domingo on the eastern side of Hispaniola. Ferrand claimed to be the legal authority for the entire island and denied that the rebels had formed a legitimate government. After the Haitian Declaration of Independence, Thilorier maintained the same goal of cutting off the supply source for Haiti, but he became increasingly annoyed at the rate at which the merchants from Curaçao were allegedly traveling to Haiti to supply Dessalines's army. "Our rebels will continue to receive resources," he reported to Ferrand, "especially under the two Commissioners that make up the government of Curaçao, who have no other view than money, and no other guides than baseness and ignorance."[60] Thilorier perceived that economic activity motivated the Curaçaoan government, and this focus took precedence over the friendly relationship between the French and the Dutch and any other moral objections that the government might have had in establishing trade relationships with former slaves.

Since the government representatives of Curaçao were unwilling to prohibit and police the trade with Haiti at the beginning of 1804, Thilorier undertook measures that placed this responsibility in the hands of the French. He once again asked for commissions for French privateers, who were apparently begging for permission to arm their ships in order to patrol the waters between Haiti and Curaçao with the hope of capturing the merchants who were engaged in this trade. Ferrand sent Thilorier four of these commissions, which he quickly distributed to privateers in Curaçao.[61] Despite Thilorier's energetic attempts to secure the appropriate documentation for the departure of the French privateers at

Curaçao, the Dutch governor prohibited him from engaging in the regulation of the ships that they captured. Once, when a French privateer brought a captured ship into the harbor, Thilorier described to Ferrand how two members of the Colonial Council boarded the ship to oversee the unloading of the ship and the sale of the prize, an act that he claimed should have been his job. The money amassed from these transactions was deposited into the Curaçaoan treasury instead of being passed to the (unrecognized) French agent. Thilorier would only receive the money if the Dutch government concluded that the capture was legitimate.[62] Prize cases in the Atlantic were typically brought before the captors' own judges, but in this case the privateer carried the captured ship to Curaçao, perhaps because they expected that the French agent would oversee the case. Thilorier expected to have authority over French captures on foreign territory, but the Curaçaoan governor would not let him have this power.

In the first months of 1804, Thilorier became understandably disillusioned with his job as the French agent at Curaçao. The government at Curaçao did not recognize his position, and he was so limited in his power that he complained to Ferrand that the only task that occupied his time was the payment of debts that he had accrued in order to live on the island. Accordingly, he notified Ferrand that he felt that his services were no longer required—especially in the context of British interest in controlling the island as evident in the continued British blockade of certain ports. Thilorier felt that he could not accomplish anything, and he assumed that the British would control the island in a short time anyway. But this assumption proved incorrect in 1804, because it was not until 1807 that the British took control of the island. As a result of these feelings of futility, Thilorier notified Ferrand that he would return to France in June 1804.[63]

Despite being a former colonist of Saint Domingue, Thilorier gave up his dream of regaining the colonial possession. "Saint Domingue lost," he explained to Ferrand; "I have no other resources in the colonies and so I will benefit from the remaining possibility to return to the heart of my family in Europe."[64] While many former plantation owners from Saint Domingue continued to hope that the colony would once again return to its prerevolutionary structures and production levels, at least some of them conceded defeat and searched for new opportunities in Europe or elsewhere. Before departing, Thilorier appointed an interim contact person for Ferrand in Curaçao, Jean-Pierre Gouges, a French merchant based out of Curaçao. At the request of Thilorier, Gouges agreed to tend to any business, including commissions for corsairs, supplies for Ferrand (the leather shoes for the troops), and any business relating to prize ships.[65] The Curaçaoan government, however, still did not recognize him in any official capacity.

Instead of following Thilorier's directions, Gouges took on the role of activist for French interests, especially the goal of shutting down any supply source for the rebels in Haiti. In a letter to Ferrand in September 1804, Gouges, in his role as the new (unrecognized) French agent at Curaçao, referred to a proclamation issued by Ferrand on 27 July 1804, which stated that "the tribunal of St Domingue [at Santo Domingo] is the only one competent to judge the prize Ships illegally on the Coast of St Domingue."[66] Ferrand might have issued this proclamation to prevent foreign courts from having control over the regulation of trade to Haiti. Thilorier's experience in early 1804 reveals that some French privateers brought their prizes into foreign ports, against the general custom of prize courts in the Atlantic, but Ferrand's publication made it clear that it was in the interests of the French to judge their own prize cases. This was perhaps because other foreign governments had not yet prohibited this trade and therefore had to rely on their own legislation and their own systems for enforcing it. In response to this proclamation, Gouges asked Ferrand what he should do in the case of a prize brought in by a Guadeloupean or Martiniquan privateer. Would the tribunal at Santo Domingo overrule even French authority in the Caribbean? This question may have arisen out of a context of inter-island competition within the French Empire. Ferrand badly needed extra revenue, and the governors of Guadeloupe and Martinique might not have shared the profits of a capture. Indeed, privateers from Guadeloupe and Martinique also sought to capture ships trading with Haiti and provided competition for Ferrand's interests.[67] Even within the French Empire, Ferrand could not secure complete support.

Badgering the Governor

Shortly after Jean-Pierre Gouges replaced J. Thilorier as the (unrecognized) French agent, a new provisional governor, Pierre-Jean Changuion, arrived in the colony. Changuion corresponded regularly with Gouges in Curaçao and General Ferrand in Santo Domingo. His initial communications convey friendship and solidarity between the French and Batavian governments, particularly in the context of the British blockade and potential siege at Curaçao. Changuion emphasized that the island was in desperate need of military and provisional supplies because of the continued British blockade of certain ports, and he told Ferrand that he had heard a rumor that Ferrand had these in excess. He noted that it was in the best interests of both the French and the Batavian governments to keep Curaçao under Dutch rule, and he asked Ferrand to send support.[68] Seven months later, Changuion was still asking for provisions and noted that a citizen of the island was sailing to Santo Domingo to get a cargo of flour.[69] Given the desperate situation in which Ferrand found himself for his entire occupation of Santo Domingo, it is unlikely that he had any excess supplies.[70] Perhaps Ferrand had started these rumors in order to lend legitimacy to his proclamations and to his plan to reconquer the western side of the island. This rumor could have been a scare tactic in order to convince the Haitian government that a French invasion was still possible and likely.

Gouges believed that these expressions of allegiance to France were honest, and he assumed that the new governor would do more to prohibit the trade between the merchants of Curaçao and those in Haiti. "The Government here has recently changed and there arrived here a new Dutch Governor named Mr. P. J. Changuion," Gouges reported to Ferrand on 7 September 1804; "this change might enable you to put a stop to the almost open trade (only hidden by a Spanish or Danish flag) that is done here with the rebels."[71] While the previous governor of Curaçao had not explicitly outlawed trade with Haiti, it appears that ships continued to sail under foreign flags and therefore suggests some degree of perceived French authority in Haiti—although it is not clear why a Spanish flag would have benefited the merchants, since trade between the Spanish islands and Haiti was illegal. Perhaps the Spanish flag might have protected the ships if French privateers intercepted them on the high seas. Thilorier noted that merchants prior to the Haitian Declaration of Independence cleared out for other foreign ports to cover up the fact that they were sailing to Haiti, and Gouges's reports reveal a second tactic that merchants used to circumvent a possible implicit prohibition on trade with Haiti. The implicit prohibition, however, appeared to Thilorier and Gouges to have had no effect in actually preventing the trade.

Three months later, Gouges was still hopeful that Governor Changuion would help the French prohibit international trade with Haiti, but he also noted that the trade between Curaçao and various southern ports in Haiti continued unabated. "I see with horror," he wrote to Ferrand, "that this commerce happens without even any concealment except to say that they arrive from Cuba and they [even] bring a quantity of letters from des Cayes or Jacmel."[72] The merchants appear to have become increasingly brash in their ongoing trade with Haiti.

Despite the friendly relationship between the Batavian Republic and the French Empire, the government of Curaçao did not immediately or explicitly outlaw trade with Haiti after the Haitian Declaration of Independence. The conflicts between the local representatives in the Caribbean, despite the inter-imperial alliance, suggest that colonial interests sometimes trumped the broader frameworks of foreign relations. Eventually, however, the French officials in the Caribbean succeeded in convincing the governor of Curaçao to outlaw trade with Haiti. After a year of constant letters and conversations with the governors of Curaçao, the French finally had the support of their "friends." "I detest the relationships with the negro rebels with all my heart," Governor Changuion declared on 11 December 1804 in response to a letter from Gouges, "knowing well to what horrors they have often given way."[73] Finally, on 18 December 1804, Governor Changuion notified the residents of Curaçao that any "Dutch (or Batavian) ships entering this Port [the Port of Amsterdam and Willemstad in Curaçao] and being convinced that they came from any Port or Place in the island of Saint Domingue that are actually in the possession of the Negro Rebels, or who have done Commerce with the Revolted, their Ships and Cargos will be Confiscated."[74] Close to a year after the Haitian Declaration of Independence, the Curaçaoan government finally issued a statement that explicitly condemned the ongoing trade between Dutch and Haitian merchants.

The week after Changuion published this proclamation, Gouges remained critical of the governor's efforts. Frustrated by the ongoing commerce between the merchants of Curaçao and those in Haiti, Gouges decided that he had to pressure Governor Changuion to do more than simply issue a proclamation. "The arrival in this port of a Schooner loaded with coffee coming from des Cayes, inspired me to go see Mr. de *Changuion*," he reported to Ferrand. "I notified him," he explained, "of the illicit trade that occurs from this place with the rebels [and] I instructed him of all the maneuvers that they [the sailors] use in order to prove that the Ships come from Cuba."[75] Changuion, however, deflected the accusation that the Curaçaoan merchants were not obeying the new law, and he reminded Gouges that he had no authority on the island.[76]

Since the governor of Curaçao would not recognize him as an official governmental delegate, Gouges was not able to regulate and condemn ships that were thought to have been trading with Haiti. Despite the fact that Gouges challenged the effectiveness of Changuion's proclamation, he remained confident that the governor would prohibit the trade. "I believe that Mr. de *Changuion* has very good intentions," Gouges reported to Ferrand, "and that he will prevent the continuation of this trade." Gouges still regretted that he could not actively participate in the processing of captured ships and in the condemnation of ships found guilty of trading with Haiti. He argued that Changuion's efforts would not play out "with the same energy as he would have done if I had been recognized as a Delegate, in this position I could have given him proof."[77] Gouges assumed that he had insider knowledge on how the trade occurred, perhaps because of his experience as a merchant before he assumed the role of (unrecognized) French agent.

Ten days after his proclamation prohibiting trade, Changuion published another proclamation noting that Ferrand was pressuring the governor to stop this trade and highlighting the dangers, both for the ship captains and for the colonies in general, if this trade continued. General Ferrand, Changuion announced to the citizens of Curaçao, "complained, that the inhabitants of Curaçao who have the most interest in opposing the success of the brigandage on the island of Saint Domingue, instead fuel this brigandage, and provide supplies to the revolted . . . and that he will hang all those who are found to have relationships with the rebels of Saint Domingue, and who are stopped by the privateers that the General has stationed along the coasts of the revolted."[78] Ferrand's approach emphasized two key reasons why he thought that the merchants of Curaçao should stop supporting the rebels. First, that they should be more conscious of the implications that this economic relationship might have for their own island since it might facilitate collaboration between the rebels in Haiti and the enslaved laborers in Curaçao. In his proclamation, Changuion suggested that he also perceived that this trade could more broadly affect Curaçao, and he stated that each merchant was accountable for the effects of their actions: "We render each person responsible for all the calamities and all the suffering that by their own fault could result, spread and extend to this island (Curaçao) because of this dangerous Commerce."[79] Second, Ferrand reminded the merchants that he would have them killed if a French privateer caught them trading with Haiti.

By the end of December 1804, Gouges appeared convinced that this illegal trade would stop. The additional materials published by Changuion that emphasized the consequences of this trade appear to have reassured him, and they may also have influenced the actions of Curaçaoan merchants, at least temporarily. "I report with pleasure that I don't believe that there will be another Expedition from this Place to the Rebels," Gouges reported to Ferrand. "Mr de Changuion is not known and he is feared," he reassured Ferrand, adding "afterward I put fear in the hearts of those who engage in this Trade by saying that they will be hunted even during peace, our Emperor will not leave unpunished the villain who has traded with rebels."[80] If the merchants of Curaçao continued to trade with Haiti, the French would use any means necessary to stop them.

Just over a month later, Ferrand again pressured Changuion to up the ante with respect to the illicit trade between the merchants at Curaçao and the rebels in Haiti. When he received notice of Changuion's 18 December proclamation prohibiting trade with Haiti, Ferrand wrote to Changuion to ask that he expand the regulations outlined in the document. Changuion's proclamation punished merchants trading with Haiti by ordering that their ships and cargo be confiscated; however, the punishment in Ferrand's court was much graver. "I take faith to invite you, in the name of French Government, to give orders to ensure that all Communication ceases, between Curaçao and the coasts of St Domingue that are occupied by the revolted. I have the honor to send you herewith, six copies of a Decree, that I published on the 16th of this month."[81] Ferrand also sent this proclamation to the Danish government in St. Thomas and announced to both nations that "all individuals, whoever they may be, who are found on allied or neutral ships, destined for the ports of Saint-Domingue, that are occupied by the revolted, will be punished with death."[82] A week later, Changuion made sure to publicize the *Arrêté* with the "sound of the drum" and again warned his citizens of the dangers involved in this trade.[83] Gouges reported that the merchants were shaken by this news.[84]

The proclamations prohibiting trade with Haiti by Changuion and Ferrand appear, however, to have had a limited effect in the long run. At the end of 1805, Changuion again wrote to Ferrand to express his own horror at the ongoing trade between Curaçaoan merchants and the rebels in Haiti. Evidently, neither Changuion's nor Ferrand's proclamations and pleas with these merchants could counterbalance the financial opportunities available through this trade.

Jurisdictional Power

The (unofficial) French agents expressed extreme frustration in their efforts to ensure that merchants from Curaçao did not sail to Haiti, at least partly because their ability to control the actions of citizens in foreign colonies had clear limits. In Curaçao, Governor Changuion had warned his citizens that they might suffer death if a French privateer captured them while they were trading with Haiti, but he was not willing to allow French officials jurisdiction over his island. These limits are exemplified in a conflict over the processing and decision of a captured ship brought to Curaçao by a French privateer for sentencing. "I am irritated to have to inform you," Changuion wrote angrily to Ferrand at the beginning of 1806, "that I recently had a small altercation with *Mr. Gouges*, whom you recommended to *me* in your last letter, on the subject of a prize brought into this port."[85] The French privateer L'Eulalie brought a neutral ship into the port of Fort Amsterdam and accused the captain of trading with Haiti. Just under two years earlier, Thilorier had been frustrated that he was not allowed to process a captured ship, and perhaps this prior experience encouraged Gouges to take the initiative before the Curaçaoan officials had the opportunity. Changuion reported that the Dutch tax lawyer went on board the ship, as per protocol on that island, to take inventory, collect the papers, and seal the ship before sentencing, but when he arrived he found Gouges already in the process of sealing the ship.[86] Gouges had scrambled to circumvent Dutch protocol so that he could assume control of the sentencing. Changuion argued that Gouges did not have the authority to undertake such tasks because he was not an official delegate. He reminded Gouges that the Batavian government had prohibited him from recognizing foreign agents and that he had notified Ferrand of this fact.

Despite the fact that Changuion had expressed his personal opposition to the ongoing trade between Curaçaoan merchants and Haitians, Gouges perceived that he was being pressured by local residents to resist French pressure to prevent the trade. "The people interested in the Continuation of this Trade viewed with pleasure the fact that the Governor did not want to recognize me as a Delegate of the French Government (after the orders of his Government), they find it extraordinary that he listens to me when I lodge complaints on this subject, one of the leaders of this place, even went so far as to say that if he had been in the place of the Governor, he would have made me leave the Colony."[87] Gouges continued to complain about his constrained position in Curaçao and marveled at the audacity of the Batavian government to prohibit the recognition of a French agent, even though the Batavian "Government in Europe [was] under the Dependence of the French Government."[88] Gouges interpreted the friendly relationship between the two empires to be hierarchical, a perspective with which the governor of Curaçao would not have agreed.

Changuion insisted that the Curaçaoan government would be the one to rule on prize cases in the colony. He explained the procedure to Gouges: first, the tax lawyer would be responsible for sealing the ship and establishing a guard in order to prevent fraud; second, the tax lawyer would question the crews of the prize ship and that of the captor on the circumstances of the capture; third, the government's secretary would take the ship's papers for inventory.[89] Gouges clearly did not follow these guidelines when the Lille was brought into port as a prize. Instead, he sealed the vessel and obtained possession of the ship's papers, arguing that he had the right to supervise prize cases involving French privateers. When Changuion rejected this claim, Gouges used the ship's papers as leverage to try to secure official recognition as a French agent at Curaçao. He sneakily requested that Changuion ask for the ship's papers in a letter addressed to him as the French agent at Curaçao. Such a letter would provide evidence that Gouges was in fact a recognized agent. Changuion, seeing through the devious plan, refused.[90]

Changuion concluded his letter to Ferrand about Gouges's unacceptable behavior by saying that his main goal as governor of Curaçao was to "*obey and to be exactly faithful to his Instructions and to the Orders of the Batavian Government.*"[91] Between the time that Changuion first wrote to Ferrand in mid-1804 and this letter in January 1806, a noticeable change occurred in his tone. In early 1804, he highlighted the friendship and alliance between the Batavian Republic and the French Empire and emphasized the need for collaboration and support against the rebels in Haiti and against the British. Two years later, however, Changuion confronted Gouges and insisted that his only allegiance was to his home government and not to the parallel efforts of the French and Dutch. One factor that may have contributed to this change in attitude was that the island was experiencing some respite from British attacks and blockades. In addition, the French were now flagrantly challenging the authority of Dutch representatives. The bigger empire was walking all over the smaller empire and casting aside the customs and rules outlined by the Batavian Republic and the law of nations.

The conflict between Dutch authority and French authority climaxed during the sentencing of the ship captured by the French privateer in the port of Fort Amsterdam at the beginning of 1806. According to Changuion, Gouges should have deferred to Curaçaoan policy and authority when the *Lille* was brought to port. "*Good principle* requires that we conform with the *Laws of the Country* in which we find ourselves," he argued in a letter to Gouges. "I am convinced," he continued, "that the French Government would never allow the *Batavians* to exercise jurisdiction, to give the freedom to initiate acts of authority within its territory *without* [permission], because that would be Against the Rules of Sane Reasoning."[92] The tax lawyer responsible for sealing the prize ship even spoke condescendingly to Gouges. According to the unrecognized French agent, "The tax lawyer told me in an ironic and insulting tone that he did not recognize any French agent in Curaçao, and that he had to enforce the Batavian flag."[93]

From Gouges's perspective, the Dutch were setting him up for failure. In addition to feeling shunned and constrained by the governor, he perceived a general anti-French air on the island. For example, when the captured ship *Lille* came into port, Gouges reported that "everyone on shore shouted against the French, that they were pirates and that they should be hanged."[94] This claim suggests that the Dutch citizens in Curaçao thought that the French were acting outside the law and that their assumed control over international maritime trade with Haiti amounted to piracy.

Gouges did not want to argue about spheres of legal authority, but rather about the need to do the right thing (from his point of view). And this meant squashing the success of the rebels in Haiti. Gouges turned the practical legal battle into a discussion of moral responsibility. He regretted that the French were forced to "pronounce against the ships, and the particulars of the friendly and ally powers." He further claimed "that the appeal of gain brings madness to the point of sustaining the monstrous rebellion, by supplying them with the means and provisions, and also war munitions that keep them in a state of being able to oppose resistance to the force, that His Majesty will direct against them."[95] From Gouges's perspective, the Curaçaoan government should have put international legal norms aside for the sake of preserving the Caribbean colonial and slave systems.

The captain of the *L'Eulalie*, Roullit, also argued his case to Changuion by claiming, "It appears as though you favor the Ships coming from the rebels, over the Ships of the French nation."[96] Roullit felt that Changuion evaded the question of the legality of the capture by focusing on the larger legal issue of jurisdiction: "He told me that I wanted to give laws in his country."[97]

The laws that were relevant to this particular prize, Changuion argued, had to do with the geography of Dutch jurisdictional authority in the waters around the island. According to a law passed in 1798 by the Batavian Republic, no foreign privateer could capture a neutral ship sailing within the limits of the territory, that being "within the shot of a cannon from this port [Piscadera]." The Colonial Council concluded that the L'Eulalie was definitely within the territorial waters of the island of Curaçao at the time of the capture. The governor and the members of the council of justice of Curaçao, therefore, found Roullit guilty of capturing a neutral ship within Curaçaoan territory.[98] In concluding that the ship was not a legal prize, the council justified its decision on the basis of territorial jurisdiction. "The resolution that was concluded was principally founded on the Publication [from 1798] of the Batavian Government," Changuion told Ferrand, "on the subject of prizes made inside the territory that leave no doubt about the accuracy in the present Case."[99] The sentence handed down to Roullit included a 3,000 Dutch florin fine in addition to any costs accrued by Roullit. The prize would also be freed.

Changuion then returned to the illegality of French privateers capturing vessels within the territorial waters of Curaçao. He reiterated that the illegality of the capture rested on the fact that the French corsair had made the capture within the boundaries of Curaçao. Whether Captain Roullit of the L'Eulalie could provide sufficient proof of the neutral vessel's voyage to Haiti was a moot point because of the location of the capture. "The territory was notoriously violated and the prize was made *without our consent . . . and under our Cannon.*"[100] The central issue was "*the violation of our Territory.*"[101] Because of this focus, and since the ship was outside French jurisdiction, Changuion noted, "the council had no intention to want to assume the judgment on whether the ship *was condemnable or non-condemnable under the laws of France.*"[102]

But the debate did not end there. Changuion was quite willing to consider Gouges's argument after coming to the conclusion that it was irrelevant. Changuion did attempt to address the question of whether the Lille had come from Haiti. In this scenario, Changuion also concluded that the Lille could not be considered good prize because he did not have sufficient evidence to prove that the ship sailed from Haiti. This argument, however, simply fueled Gouges's outrage because he interpreted this conclusion as evidence of the unwillingness of the governor to fully investigate the ship's voyage.

Gouges explained two simple strategies that Changuion might have followed if he had actually wanted to find out the truth. First, Gouges argued that it was simply a matter of comparing the produce on board the ship with the crops cultivated in the alleged port of departure. This, he argued, made it obvious that the ship had arrived from Haiti because the goods on board the *Lille*, including coffee, dyes, and beans, were not products of Santa Marta on the Spanish mainland—the declared port of departure—and were in fact available in Haiti.[103] He offered additional advice in case this method was not conclusive. All Changuion had to do, Gouges argued, was to ask the captains of ships laden with coffee for their papers. The governor could then verify these papers by sending a notice to the purported points of departure. To prove that these ships had in fact come from Haiti rather than Cuba or Puerto Rico, "all we have to do is send an express to Cuba and to Puerto Rico, to ask whether in such a time they sent a ship laden with coffee, and we will soon have proof of the contrary."[104] He assumed that the reports from the ports noted in the ship's papers would not corroborate the story communicated by the ship's captain.

Despite Gouges's suggestions to Changuion about how he might discredit the ship's papers, Changuion concluded that "until now there does not exist an ounce of proof."[105] Changuion informed Ferrand that the council had in fact suspended judgment on the issue of jurisdiction in order to gather information on the legality of the capture. They had interviewed members of the ship's crew two days after the ship's requisition, but, Changuion reported, "the result was that all of the individuals of the crew and two passengers declared under the solemn faith in the Oath that the ship came from *Baracoa* on the Spanish Coast and that they did not touch at or see Saint Domingue."[106]

A report by the Council of Civil and Criminal Justice of Curaçao concluded that the *Lille*'s voyage, as articulated by the captain and crew, was legitimate. The ship had left St. Thomas, in October 1805, destined for the Bay of Baracoa on the coast of Santa Marta on the Spanish mainland. The ship, the crew reported, had not even seen Haiti. The *Lille* stayed in the Bay of Baracoa for three months to collect coffee and wood; according to these testimonies, Santa Marta did indeed produce coffee, contrary to Gouges's claim. The ship sailed on a return voyage to St. Thomas, during

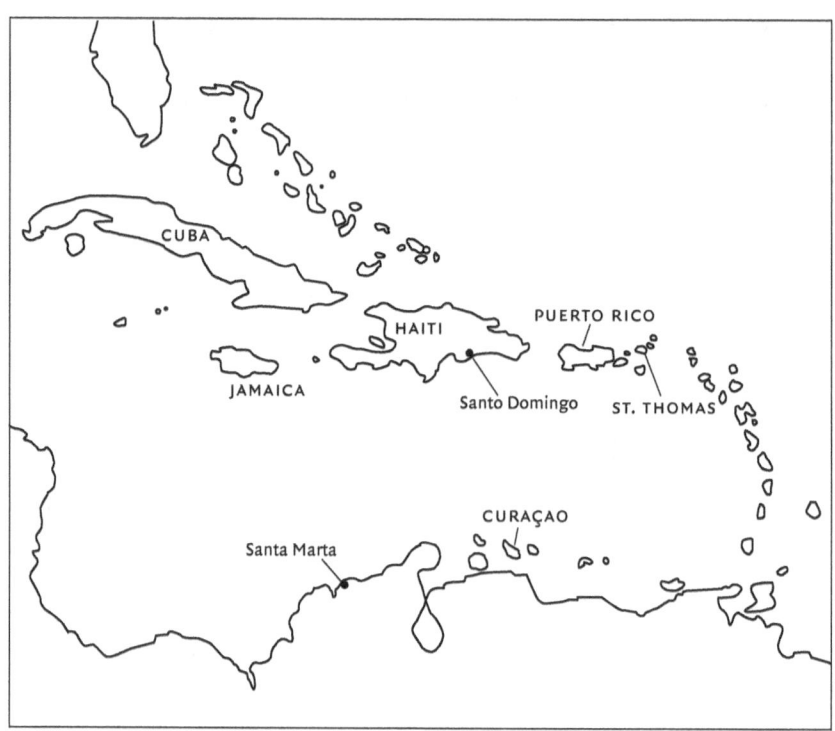

FIGURE TWO Map of the Caribbean

which the ship sprang a large leak and was forced to change course to Curaçao for repairs.[107]

The Colonial Council at Curaçao found this narrative to be true for two reasons: first, all of the testimonies given by the people on board the *Lille* were consistent; and second, their testimonies did not raise any suspicion of trade with the rebels in Haiti. It is worth noting that the captain of the Danish ship, Jan Valentin Curiel, was Dutch, and Roullit classified him as "*mulâtre et créole de curaçao*" (a creole person of mixed-race from Curaçao). Perhaps he had connections within the Dutch merchant community at Curaçao, even though he was sailing a Danish ship.

Gouges appealed the Council's decision and tried one last time on 14 February 1806 to convince Changuion that the *Lille* should be condemned as good prize. "Because of the certainty that I have that the Schooner conducted into this port (by the French Privateer *L'Eulalie*) comes from trading with the revolted of Saint Domingue, in defiance of the laws established by the French government on this subject, I would not be fulfilling my job . . . if I did not denounce to Your Excellency the said

Schooner for having traded and engaged in illegal commerce as per our laws with the revolted in the Colony of Saint Domingue."[108] Roullit also tried to convince Changuion to reverse the fine in an appeal. He asked for more time to collect proof, but his request was denied and the Council upheld the ruling.[109]

According to Gouges's reports, Ferrand wrote to Changuion to express his concern with this ruling, as well as the ongoing trade that he was convinced was happening between Curaçao and Haiti. According to Changuion's response, Ferrand accused several rich citizens who were members of the Council of being invested in the decisions of prize cases and who were "*personally interested in the Commerce with the Revolted!*"[110] While not entirely unbelievable, Changuion vehemently denied this claim. "That is a strong accusation, *monsieur capitaine general!*" Changuion responded, and he challenged Ferrand to provide evidence for it. "I invite you with *every assistance* possible to *nominally denounce* to me these particular rich people, these members of the council, and to bring to me unequivocal proof of their infernal conduct."[111] Changuion again professed his loyalty to the French Empire and Ferrand's cause and denounced any merchants willing to support the rebels in Haiti. "The Political Consideration in the interest of the Colonies undoubtedly requires," Changuion argued, "that all the Powers with Colonies reunite in a common accord, to exterminate forever down to the smallest trace that Detestable Rebellion!!"[112] This common accord, however, did not allow for French encroachments on Batavian jurisdiction. Following this profession of loyalty, Changuion provided Ferrand with a detailed report showing that the *L'Eulalie* had captured the *Lille* within Curaçaoan waters.

To circumvent this issue, Ferrand asked Changuion to send Jan Valentin Curiel, the captain of the captured ship, to Santo Domingo so that he could be tried in a French court—where his ship, presumably, would have been condemned as good prize and Curiel would have been hanged. To this, Changuion noted that he had informed Curiel of this request but that he could not force him to surrender himself at Santo Domingo since he was a Danish citizen. Earlier, Rouillit had described Curiel as a Dutch citizen, and so either Rouillit or Changuion was mistaken or Curiel professed a more fluid definition of his own nationality. Changuion additionally emphasized to Curiel that, "in the opinion of the Government and Council of Curaçao, the French Government is the *only competent judge* on the subject of the *Condemnability* of the ship that was captured."[113] This comment—that received no further explanation—apparently referred to the fact that Changuion and the Colonial Council would have judged the legality of the prize based on proclamations that had resulted from French requests to prohibit trade to Haiti. Furthermore, the *Arrêtés* that Ferrand himself had published and sent around the Caribbean might have been taken into account. Was Changuion saying that the French government could be the only nation to recognize the independence of Haiti? Or just that it was best for the French courts to try prizes captured by French privateers? Changuion reiterated the justifications for the decision that the Council had made: the distance from the shore, the depositions, and the ship's papers. He confirmed that, from his perspective, he had made the right decision.

Perhaps Changuion felt the need to make amends with Ferrand and Gouges after this conflictual prize case, because, soon after this incident, after two years of back and forth with Gouges, Changuion appeared to be willing to accommodate to Gouges's wishes and allow him some form of authority with respect to decisions regarding prizes. "I am ready to *concede* to your proposal respecting Mr. Gouges," he wrote to Ferrand, "to *receive* him as your *personal* delegate and *special* representative, and to admit him in this quality as an interested party in the decisions of prize cases."[114] Changuion agreed that there would be limits to his powers; he would still not be an official government delegate. This half-hearted concession has noticeable similarities to the constraints placed on Thilorier in 1803 and 1804. Changuion, while giving the appearance that he was willing to compromise, still refused to recognize Gouges as an official French agent.

This case highlights the deep tensions between empires that Haiti's Declaration of Independence brought to the surface of the Atlantic World. French officials targeted other governments in order to minimize the damage of their defeat by trying to convince these governments that they should be fighting in solidarity for a common cause. The case of the *Lille*, however, reveals that the Dutch Empire had its own specific interests and concerns.

French Pressure at St. Thomas

Arnaud André Roberjot Lartigue, a creole planter from Saint Domingue, had fled the French colony in 1803, and, even after the *Armée Indigène* declared independence in 1804, he continued to hope that the French army would soon regain possession of the entire island. Lartigue was keen to aid the French Empire in this endeavor and wrote energetically and at length to General Jean-Louis Ferrand, as well as to the governors of Guadeloupe and Martinique, in order to voice his opinion and to report on the situation in the Caribbean so as to motivate the reconquest efforts and to inform their planning.

In April 1805, Lartigue was appointed to serve as the "agent pour le Gouvernement de St. Domingue à St. Thomas" (Dominguan agent to St. Thomas).[115] Lartigue's assignment was to supervise issues that had to do with French prize cases or any other French citizens arriving in Danish St. Thomas.[116] Lartigue reported regularly to Ferrand and indeed went beyond the assignments outlined for him by his predecessor. In particular, Lartigue, like Thilorier, badgered the governor of St. Thomas to outlaw trade between St. Thomas and the parts of Hispaniola that were occupied by Dessalines's government.

"Does a foreign nation have the right to support commerce with the revolted of Saint Domingue," Lartigue asked the governor of the island.[117] Instead of waiting for a response, he provided Governor Balthazar Frederik Mühlenfels with an answer of his own. "To answer this question," he argued, "you have to consider the fact that the revolt of blacks in one part of a colony does not interrupt ownership."[118] Lartigue made this claim close to two years after the Haitian Declaration of Independence; he classified the revolution as a "revolt" and tried to undermine the authority of the leadership in Haiti. The status of the island as a French colony, he also emphasized, had implications for foreign merchants trading with Haiti. "The revolt does not abolish the laws that prohibit foreigners from trading with Saint Domingue," he claimed; "it is first an infringement of the treaties with France, and it is furthermore an illegitimate commerce in all other respects."[119] Not only was the trade illegal, from the French perspective, but Lartigue also declared that it was in the Danish government's own interests to help the French. "What then is this government that does not hasten to assign monetary and shameful penalties against this trade?" he asked, and then declared that "what happens today to one government will soon happen to another. Yes, all have the same interest in rigorously prohibiting this illicit commerce, if they do not themselves want to become victims."[120] According to Lartigue, the trade between St. Thomas and Haiti was both illegal and inadvisable. But for two years it continued unabashedly.

Continued Trade

Lartigue encountered similar frustrations to those that Jean-Pierre Gouges had experienced in Curaçao because it was clear that the merchants of St. Thomas were not following the instructions proclaimed by Ferrand. He therefore set out to convince the governor of St. Thomas, Balthazar Frederik Mühlenfels, to prohibit the trade himself. The problem, Lartigue argued, was out of control. For example, on 2 May 1805, just three months after Ferrand's proclamation that condemned merchants trading with Haiti to death, Lartigue reported to Ferrand that "a few days ago, four ships left [St. Thomas] for St. Domingue, going to Au Cap [Cap Français/Cap Haïtien], Aux Cayes, and to Jacmel. . . . This illegal trade continues without fear or regard for your proclamation."[121] Lartigue had done his duty in publicizing the proclamation. "Your order was published and displayed in the city," Lartigue reported to Ferrand; "it is well known to merchants and sailors; but those who hold relations with the revolted are not intimidated." "Ships leave daily," Lartigue complained, "for Le Cap [Cap Français/Cap Haïtien], Les Cayes, [and] Jacmel with supplies of all kinds."[122]

The Danish merchants trading from St. Thomas to Haiti, Lartigue argued, were breaking the rules of neutrality.[123] From his perspective, trade with the "*révoltés*" in Haiti broke the laws that governed international economic relationships during wartime. It is unclear, however, whether Lartigue considered this trade illegal because the Danish merchants were involving themselves in a civil war within the French Empire (between a revolted colony and the metropole) or whether he perceived their actions to be beneficial to the British Empire, France's enemy. In three Admiralty Court cases between 1804 and 1806, the British had declared that trade with Haiti in items considered "contraband of war" (that is, arms and ammunition) was illegal, but the courts highlighted that trade between neutral nations and nations engaged in war was legal as long as the merchants followed the rules delimiting the items allowed for trade (for example, provisions).[124] In his letter to Ferrand, Lartigue did not state that the merchants were supplying the Haitian Government with arms—he just noted "supplies of all kinds." Lartigue clearly held a different perspective regarding what constituted legal trade with respect to neutral nations from the one that had been hashed out in the British Admiralty Courts.

Lartigue also argued for a broader allegiance among Atlantic nations; merchants belonging to nations that allowed slavery, in his opinion, should sympathize with France's plight. Here, Lartigue argued, the United States was the number one culprit. "From the News that I have received, my Research and my own Observations with regard to that

Commerce which is so disastrous for the French merchants and *habitants* of St. Domingue," Lartigue wrote to Ferrand, "I remain informed that all the ports of the United States do it without cover, bluntly, and without Any Regard for The French Empire, this Bad Example for The Nations who have Colonies and Slaves, in order to exploit manufactured goods, is not for them an object of Consideration."[125] The Danish government and merchants from St. Thomas, Lartigue argued, should take greater precaution; they owned the possessions—slaves and colonies—that France had recently lost.

In an effort to help enforce the French proclamations prohibiting international trade with Haiti, Lartigue forwarded to Ferrand and to the governors of Guadeloupe and Martinique any information he could obtain regarding the illicit trade and especially about the parties involved. "I have the honor to send herewith," Lartigue wrote to Ferrand on 29 October 1805, "a list of names of ship owners in St. Thomas who are involved in the trade with the revolted in St. Domingue." "I sent a copy to General Villaret [in Martinique]," he continued, "and another to General Ernouf [in Guadeloupe], so that they will not receive any of these ships in their ports." While knowing exactly which ship owners and which ships were engaged in trade with Haitians, the French were still struggling to convince the international community that the trade was illegal. Furthermore, they were unable to enforce the regulations that they had decreed for other nations. "I could not procure all of the Ship names with their captains," Lartigue conceded in the same letter, "but they are easy to recognize; they are all pilot boats, the crews are all *mulâtres* and blacks of all nations."[126] Economic trade, Lartigue argued, provided openings for inter-island communication and cooperation, and the skin color of the crews made the trade even more dangerous to other Caribbean colonies.[127]

Despite this ongoing trade, Lartigue noted that the population of St. Thomas was divided in sentiment with respect to the legitimacy and rightness of economic partnerships with Haitians. While the merchants, on the one hand, benefited greatly from these relationships, others felt threatened by the success of the Haitian Revolution. "With the exception of those engaged in this commerce here," Lartigue reported to Ferrand at the end of 1805, "everyone applauded the measures of justice and firmness issued in your proclamation."[128] Lartigue hoped that Ferrand's proclamation would help change the policies of other American polities and even saw a connection between the publication of the proclamation and the decision of the governor of St. Thomas to outlaw the trade. "You have put, Mr. General, with your proclamation, the seal on the defense that the [governor] general Mühlenfels proclaimed.... I have no doubt that this commerce will cease entirely here, and that Congress will pronounce the defense of this audacious commerce in the United States."[129] On 29 October 1805, close to ten months after Ferrand issued his proclamation, Governor Balthazar Frederik Mühlenfels bowed to French demands and outlawed trade between Danish merchants and "Saint Domingue."[130]

Lartigue rejoiced at this news and wrote to inform Ferrand. The French representatives in the Caribbean had finally received support from the governor of St. Thomas in their mission to prevent international merchants from trading with Haiti. "I have already informed you of the defense that the Danish governor published against the commerce that the merchants of this city do with the revolted of St. Domingue," Lartigue wrote to Ferrand just over a month after the prohibition; "several have since stopped this commerce, and with surveillance I hope that they will abandon it completely."[131] A few months later, Lartigue wrote again to ensure that Ferrand understood his own role in securing this prohibition on trade. "The surveillance that I always required from the Danish government," he argued, "has been fulfilled in the most loyal manner."[132]

Like Lartigue, the British agent for the Virgin Islands at the time of the Danish prohibition on trade with Haiti thought that the proclamation had effectively eliminated the trade. Patrick Colquhoun wrote a memorial to encourage the British government to reopen Tortola as a free port so that British merchants could capitalize on the economic opportunities in Haiti. "That the Danish Government (under French Influence) has," Colquhoun reported, "by severe Restrictions, prohibited all Commercial Intercourse with that part of St Domingo, under the Government of the Blacks, which strikes immediately at the most lucrative Trade, carried on by St Thomas, and has occasioned a great stagnation of Business."[133] Colquhoun argued that the prohibition on trade with Haiti in St. Thomas created a new opportunity for British merchants, and he encouraged the British government to legalize trade with the island. Drawing on information that he had allegedly received from a resident of Haiti "in the Diplomatic Line," Colquhoun argued that the British occupied an advantageous position with respect to Haiti. The informant from Haiti, he reported, "states that the Trade to the south side of the Island of St Domingo which has for the last two years afforded so valuable a Branch of Commerce to the Danish Island of St Thomas being now prohibited by that Government through the Influence of France, may now with great ease be transferred to Tortola, and be carried on under the British Flag with more safety than under any neutral flag, as the French Government has made it capital, and punishable with Death, where the Traders of any neutral Nation, are found in Intercourse with that Country."[134]

Following Mühlenfels's proclamation, Lartigue received information from an unnamed source about Dessalines's response to this change in policy. "He [Dessalines] decided," Lartigue reported, "and said that since the Danish did not want to recognize them, they would not be received except by special permission from him, [and] he would leave the ports open only for the United States."[135] This reaction, Lartigue hoped, would help end the trade between the two islands.

Lartigue's optimism following the publication of Mühlenfels's ban on trade with Haiti soon proved to be unjustified. Only ten days after his encouraging letter to Ferrand about the decrease in ships leaving for Haiti, he wrote again about the great number of ships engaged in the trade.[136] Lartigue reported that the merchants had slightly changed their trading pattern based on this proclamation rather than actually complying with the goal of isolating Haiti. "Few ships do it [trade] directly from this port," he told Ferrand; "the Danish and the Americans take the flag and sail to Tortola [in the British Virgin Islands]."[137] Merchants in St. Thomas appear to have used similar tactics as those in Curaçao and simply cleared out for legal points of destination.

Mühlenfels's prohibition on trade with Haiti occurred four months before the U.S. Congress similarly banned this trade. Merchants from both places, however, apparently continued to trade with Haiti by sailing under a Danish flag, suggesting the prohibition on trade from St. Thomas to Haiti was something of a joke. "Since the defense issued by Congress, the Americans come here to take the Danish flag and go to visit the rebels," Lartigue complained; "they hide their expeditions and their routes in order to avoid the penalties prescribed by the proclamation of the Danish governor, but the Danish flag flies openly in the ports of the revolted of St. Domingue."[138] If so, this continuing trade also suggests that, contrary to Lartigue's earlier report, Dessalines had not responded to the Danish governor's prohibition on trade by refusing entry to non-U.S. ships. Alternatively, perhaps Dessalines had conceded to trading with places that did not recognize Haiti's independence.

The strategies that merchants developed to circumvent the proclamations issued by the Danish and French governments in the Caribbean left Lartigue without sufficient evidence to convince the Danish governor to convict the merchants.[139] Gouges experienced similar frustrations in Curaçao, but the solution he offered would have required the governors of the islands to contact the destination ports noted in the ships' papers. Lartigue argued that Mühlenfels was not enforcing either the regulations issued by the French governors or those in his own proclamation, and this meant that the Haitians could continue to be supplied with all of their wants. "It is with this same flag [Danish]," Lartigue protested to Ferrand in September 1806, "that the rebels are supplied with food and ammunition, although [they are] enemies of France and of humanity, and although they should not enjoy the benefits of neutrality."[140] It appears as though some merchants were in fact trading war materials or items considered "contraband of war" with the new nation, although Lartigue did not focus on this fact but rather gave as much weight to non-contraband items.

Lartigue hounded Mühlenfels to take additional measures to put an end to trade with Haiti by claiming that his inaction implicitly condoned the trade. This support, he argued, jeopardized the neutrality between the Danish and French governments.[141] Lartigue wrote to Ferrand again several days later and enclosed a letter from Mühlenfels to Ferrand in which he emphasized that the Danish were willing to cooperate. Lartigue recounted that the governor promised to "take new measures to stop the abuses that are done with the Danish flag to go visit the revolted of St. Domingue."[142] These "new" measures included the republication of the initial proclamation.[143] Lartigue implied that the republication of the initial proclamation may have had some influence, since "the Americans who leave from here [St. Thomas] or from St. Barthélemy to go to Haiti, have left to station themselves at Curaçao to better communicate with the revolted of Saint Domingue."[144] The fact that American merchants were willing to use Curaçao as a new trading post, however, highlights the failures of the prohibition on trade by the Curaçaoan governor.

Rumors of Revolution Abroad

"A foreign government whose nation is engaging in commerce with St Domingue, and who does not defend it: what are they exposing themselves to?" Lartigue had rhetorically asked Governor Mühlenfels in a letter in October 1805.[145] By heightening fear of the spread of the Haitian Revolution to other islands in the Caribbean, Lartigue tried to convince the Danish governor to prohibit trade. "The revolution is a common problem for all governments," he answered his own question in the same letter; "it is like a fire, which puts the entire world in danger, and from which everyone must run, as soon as the fire starts."[146]

Is there evidence that Lartigue's warnings were correct and that Haitian leaders did not follow their own promises of nonintervention abroad? French studies scholar Deborah Jenson has recently studied the complaints made by Lartigue about inter-island revolutionary associations involving alleged emissaries sent by Dessalines.[147] Lartigue criticized the trade between Danish merchants and the "*révoltés*" and warned of the potential dangers involved in allowing connections between Haiti and other Caribbean islands. Specifically, he claimed that Dessalines was sending emissaries around the Caribbean with instructions to instigate parallel revolutions on other islands. He argued that plots for rebellion in St. Thomas, Puerto Rico, and Trinidad could be linked directly to Dessalines. As Jenson shows, Lartigue accused Dessalines and the Haitian government of sending emissaries to St. Thomas. Their plan, as Lartigue described in an 1815 report, was "to execute the monstrous project of descending to Martinique and Guadeloupe, to assassinate all the inhabitants, to burn the cities, to raise up the blacks and people of color, free or enslaved, and to form fourteen regiments, to become masters of and to establish the independence of these colonies."[148] Lartigue claimed that this plot made clear how vital it was to protect the French colonies by preventing the introduction of blacks or people of color from Haiti to the Danish West Indies.

Scholars have not come to a consensus on whether these various individuals were in fact emissaries sent by Dessalines or where they intended to instigate rebellion—in the French Caribbean islands, in Trinidad, or in Puerto Rico. "The supposed expedition sent in 1805 by Dessalines to Martinique and Trinidad," historian David Geggus argues, "seems fairly obviously based on a rumor spread by a French colonist."[149] Jenson, in contrast, writes: "Where there is smoke, there is fire—and here there would seem to be an unthinkable amount of smoke for a purely rumored fire."[150]

Lartigue's correspondence with Ferrand reveals inconsistencies and discrepancies in his account that suggest that his claim that Dessalines was starting a Caribbean-wide revolution was either fabricated or exaggerated. And, indeed, Lartigue had personal reasons to insist on how important his role was in protecting the French colonies because some of his colleagues seem to have deeply doubted his abilities. "You told me, general [Ferrand]," Lartigue wrote on 25 September 1805, "that in my capacity as agent I have not been, up until now, of any use; it is possible, general, that I have not been able to fulfill your wishes, despite the zeal with which I undertake the service in which I am in charge."[151] Ferrand's dismissive attitude toward Lartigue could have driven him to either fabricate or exaggerate the extent of a conspiracy in St. Thomas, Trinidad, and elsewhere. Indeed, the evidence about this alleged event, as it was recounted in his correspondence with Ferrand, suggests that Lartigue jumped to conclusions that were far beyond the reality.

In the last four months of 1805, Lartigue accused Dessalines and the Haitian government of sending emissaries to St. Thomas. He appears to have made the connection between Dessalines and the alleged conspirators in St. Thomas from an account told to him by an Englishman, Mr. Yong. Ferrand does not provide any further background information on his informant. Yong, Lartigue recounted to Ferrand, traveled to Jacmel, Haiti, from Jamaica with a Frenchman, Mr. Breda, a former *habitant* of Saint Domingue. Yong was well received in Jacmel by the regional commander, General Moreau, an *homme de couleur*; in contrast, Breda was asked to produce papers justifying his visit since "no Frenchman can set foot on the territory of haity [sic], without incurring the death penalty."[152] Breda, lacking the correct papers, fled on the next boat leaving Jacmel.

Moreau requested another meeting with Yong, and he candidly discussed the war in Europe and other news. Lartigue reported that Yong's "air of complacency" during these conversations led Moreau to unveil Dessalines's plan to ally with the British, "or to have them as protectors." More important, Moreau boasted that they were "expecting at any moment news that in Guadeloupe and Martinique the blacks had revolted, and that already this news should have arrived, and that they were certain that the Slaves in those two colonies were demanding the same regime that Dessalines had set up in haity [sic]."[153]

Moreau's anticipation that a similar revolution would occur in France's other Caribbean colonies inspired fear in Lartigue. He became convinced that the victors in Haiti were scheming to make it happen. "The confession made by Moreau to Mr. Yong," Lartigue concluded in his letter to Ferrand, "suggests that Dessalines is taking measures to carry out this rebellion in your two colonies, and this suspicion I refuse to ignore." "Every day people of color pass here," Lartigue argued, "and they have the air of emissaries for conspiracies, rather than people traveling on personal business. The people of color here have a club, the travelers reunite with them, and there they transmit their projects and their mission."[154]

Lartigue later called this group the "Club Haitien," and he connected the economic relationship between Haiti and St. Thomas to the ability of these alleged emissaries to instigate and spread the revolution.[155] This commerce, he argued, "provided the opportunity for the people of color to disembark easily."[156]

Lartigue made a long leap from the news that Moreau expected the slaves in Guadeloupe and Martinique to revolt to an assumption that Dessalines had coordinated this revolt, but he quickly convinced himself that this was the reality. "I have already informed you, Mr. General," Lartigue wrote to Ferrand, months after his report on Yong's experience, "about the project that Dessalines has to raise up the blacks of Martinique and Guadeloupe."[157] Lartigue also notified Generals Villaret and Ernouf in Martinique and Guadeloupe so that they could prepare for any potential infiltrators. "General Ernouf sent his *aide de camp* here with orders to search for Dessalines's emissaries, and to take, [in coordination] with the Danish governor, all precautions to punish and remove all the authors and adherents of these conspiracies."[158]

Lartigue came to these conclusions despite the claims made in a proclamation in April 1804, in which Dessalines openly declared his desire to assist the slaves of the French Caribbean islands, but in the same breath claimed he was unable to do so. "Unfortunate people of Martinique, could I but fly to your assistance, and break your fetters!" he lamented. "Alas! An insurmountable barrier separates us." He unabashedly encouraged enslaved people within the French Empire to follow his country's lead. "Perhaps a spark from the same fire which enflames us, will alight into your bosoms: perhaps, at the sound of this commotion, suddenly awakened from your lethargy, with arms in your hands, you will reclaim your sacred and imprescriptible [sic] rights."[159] But, at least officially, his support remained rhetorical. There is no extant evidence that Dessalines extended covert support for rebels in the eastern Caribbean nor that he provided direct government backing for such endeavors, despite his promises of "eternal hatred toward France."[160]

Lartigue perceived a general atmosphere of rebellion in the Caribbean and linked these events to what had recently occurred in Saint Domingue. Each new rebellion had the potential to escalate the damage that had already been done to European colonialism and financial investment in the Caribbean. "The insurrections that have recently broken out in Surinam and Cayenne are events that force the increase of policing in all the colonies."[161] Lartigue recognized the influence that events in one colony could have on the rest and encouraged the governors of St. Thomas, Martinique, and Guadeloupe to heighten security.

Lartigue's activism did have some impact on Danish policy in St. Thomas. And indeed the research of historian Neville Hall reveals that the Danish were already wary of the influences of the events in Saint Domingue/Haiti. "Governor General Walterstorff [1787–94, 1802] informed his superiors that year," Hall recounts, "that it would be unreasonable to expect slaves to be unaffected by the developments in St. Domingue and the French islands. Moreover, Walterstoff, who had served in a variety of West Indian posts for some two decades, concluded from his experience that slaves in 1802 were showing, if not outright contempt, certainly less respect for whites than previously."[162] Governor Mühlenfels might have already been conscious of the international influences of the revolution. After Lartigue exposed the alleged plot, Mühlenfels issued orders of arrest and deportation of the suspected revolutionaries. Lartigue reported to Ferrand that these orders were soon executed and that these initial efforts had already discouraged ships departing for Haiti and that he hoped that it would prevent any further conspiracies.[163] It is unclear how the decision was made regarding whom to arrest and deport. In one case, Lartigue recorded a list of people that Mühlenfels had ordered deported. This list might not have been comprehensive or exclusive, but it suggests the kinds of people that the French representatives and the Danish governor perceived as threatening. "Governor Mühlenfels ordered the deportation," Lartigue noted, "of M. Cunningham [an American consul to Haiti], and of the Bernardine family (of which the wife is the sister of Christophe *generalissime* of the army of the revolted of St. Domingue) who resided at St. Thomas, and who have always had relationships with the revolted; he ordered the arrest of M. Loiseau who always held a criminal conduct with the rebels; and also a man Pierre, black, from Grenada residing in St. Thomas, who was the agent of Bernadine."[164] The logic for the arrest of each of these individuals had little to do with specific instructions issued by Dessalines for inter-island revolution but rather with ongoing relationships between these people and those in Haiti.

Even after the alleged emissaries were expelled from St. Thomas, Lartigue continued to feel threatened by their presence in the Caribbean. Officials in Trinidad allegedly uncovered a similar conspiracy at the end of 1805, and Lartigue was quick to connect this plot to the revolution in Saint Domingue. According to a transcription and translation of an article from the *Trinidad Gazette* from 4 January 1806, the members of the Colonial Council at Trinidad had gathered on 20 December 1805 to analyze the alleged conspiracy.[165] According to this article, four slaves were condemned to death for organizing a rebellion in Carenage and *la ville*. The conspirators, the *Gazette* reported, were organized into four regiments, which included ranks such as general in chief, colonel, major, treasurer, and others. In addition to these details, the newspaper noted that the Colonial Council took into consideration local rumor. Apparently, blacks and slaves, including women, were publicly singing about the uprising. The famously quoted song from this rebellion is noted in the *Gazette*'s report: "Bread is the meat of the *béqué*, wine is the blood of the *béqué*, we will eat the *béqué* bread, we will drink the *béqué* wine; and the others responded with the refrain of St. Domingue."[166] The conspirators' plan was to "march on the town to set fire to it and afterward Massacre all the whites, the Free People of Color, and the blacks who refused to join."[167]

Lartigue sent the transcription of this article to Ferrand, and he connected the story to the recent conspiracy that he had allegedly uncovered in St. Thomas by arguing "that a similar discovery has been made at Tobago [Trinidad]." Two alleged conspiracies had been reported in St. Thomas and Trinidad. Lartigue then leapt to a much greater conclusion: "It appears that Dessalines played a large part in this project [in Trinidad], [that is] both monstrous and criminal."[168] Lartigue did not note how he got this information but simply highlighted that "for more than six months I have had suspicions, and since the proofs and the emissaries, I have no doubt."[169] The report from the *Trinidad Gazette* did not mention any information about emissaries from Haiti or instructions from Dessalines; the only mention of "St. Domingue" is in the rumored song sung in the markets. But even this mention suggests only inspiration and not collaboration.

A copy of the *Morning Chronicle* from New York that contained information about the Trinidad conspiracy also reached St. Thomas, and Lartigue again sent a translation to Ferrand. This article stated that 7,000 blacks gathered for a rebellion in the port at Trinidad with the intention of "massacring all the whites." The "King" of the insurgents was taken prisoner along with seventeen other leaders. The article did not mention anything about Haiti, Saint Domingue, or Dessalines.[170] In contrast, Lartigue's cover letter with the extract from the *Morning Chronicle* claimed that this event was a manifestation of Dessalines's plan for international revolution. "I am so well informed," Lartigue wrote to Ferrand, "about

Dessalines's plan to Raise up all the Slaves *en masse* in all of the colonies, to assure his power and his position as Emperor, that I lend my full attention and all of my research so as not to lose the trail of the plan."[171] Fear of an international Caribbean slave revolution consumed Lartigue, and he obsessed about the different ways that Dessalines could destroy the European colonial system in the Caribbean. "Our unfortunate colony is an alarming Example," he argued; "it began by disjointed insurrections, and afterward became irreparable."[172]

Lartigue noted in another letter that a man named George from the Trinidad conspiracy had been identified as a confidant of Dessalines. George, it was said, had been in line to become the king of the insurrection. The source for this information, however, is unnamed, and it is unclear whether the investigators in Trinidad had drawn this conclusion or whether the connection had been made in St. Thomas.[173] Despite the vagaries surrounding the claims Lartigue made regarding Dessalines's alleged international scheme, Lartigue informed Ferrand that, as a result of this information, the governors of the Danish islands, Puerto Rico, Guadeloupe, and Martinique, "refused to let any people of color, free or enslaved, land in their colonies, so that the contagion would not catch among the Slaves of their governments."[174]

Lartigue connected Dessalines's alleged efforts for international revolution to the internal conflicts flaring up in the new country. "The villain Dessalines is so convinced that the end of his reign is near," Lartigue argued, "that he makes every effort to ensure the success of the project of general uprising."[175] A rumor that Dessalines had published printed documents that declared him to be the emperor of Haiti, Cuba, and Puerto Rico, Lartigue reported, further proved the existence of a Haitian-led, Caribbean-wide movement. Lartigue received this information from a Spanish colonel who formerly commanded in the eastern side of Hispaniola and who had recently been to Havana. This man, Don Arata, claimed to have seen these prints, but he did not bring any copies for Lartigue to see. "This outrageous arrogance," Lartigue vented to Ferrand in March 1806, "clearly proves his desire to extend his power in the Caribbean, and he does not renounce the project that he conceived a long time ago to raise up the slaves in all the colonies."[176]

This alleged project, as the previous rumor suggests, also had implications for Puerto Rico. The governor of Puerto Rico, like Lartigue, informed government representatives in neighboring islands about rumors or suspicions regarding slave rebellions. For example, he sent the governor of

St. Thomas a notice regarding a man who had recently been deported from the island for allegedly planning a rebellion. "The government here chased a great villain named Cazeau de franquevill," the notice declared; "he is going to St. Thomas, beware of him, he wanted one time to lead a revolt of the blacks of our island; this man is the most dangerous, he is capable of anything, he was once the secretary of Biassou with the rebels of St. Domingue."[177] Lartigue noted that the governor of Puerto Rico continued to watch out for further disruptions connected with Haiti, and he vetted all suspected persons arriving on the island, especially those of color.[178]

Lartigue remained rather desperate for support from French authorities, and in November 1806 he wrote to a former Saint Dominguan planter and the council of state of the French Empire, Médéric Louis Élie Moreau de Saint-Méry, begging for help in securing the payment of his salary from the governors of Martinique and Guadeloupe.[179] In making this request, he used the conspiracy as evidence of the work that he was doing for all three Caribbean colonies (including Haiti) and for the French Empire. His letter to Saint-Méry in 1806 did not mention anything about the similar conspiracy in Trinidad. Just under a decade later, however, Lartigue printed and published a revised version of this letter in which he directly connected the alleged plot in St. Thomas with the one publicized in Trinidad.[180] In his correspondence with Ferrand in 1805 and 1806, Lartigue claimed that emissaries sent by Dessalines had coordinated both of the conspiracies, but his 1815 report directly linked the two events. According to the later report, unable to get to Martinique and Guadeloupe from St. Thomas, the emissaries decided to land in Trinidad instead, intent on starting a similar revolt somewhere. The discrepancy between reports raises further questions about the veracity of his recounting of the events on the British island.[181] Here, as in several other well-known cases, it is difficult—maybe even impossible—to know for sure whether there was a real conspiracy. What is clear, however, is that Lartigue's reports of such plans played an important role in shaping perceptions of Haiti's influence in the Caribbean in the early independence period.[182]

Lartigue's campaign to inspire fear in the governors of Martinique, Guadeloupe, St. Thomas, and Puerto Rico highlights the opposition that the government of Haiti faced in the early years of independence. State leaders in Haiti had pragmatically promised the international community that they would not instigate rebellion abroad; however, the success of the revolution continued to inspire fear in the Caribbean. An international coalition to isolate Haiti, initiated by former planters like

Lartigue, might have forced the independence movement to fail. Neither the Haitian state nor individuals abroad were successful in implementing their espoused goals: Haiti was not able to secure the complete confidence of the international community, nor was the country uniformly isolated, even after different governors prohibited trade to Haiti.

Conclusion

During the crucial first months and years of Haitian independence, French agents attempted to rupture established networks of trade between Curaçao and St. Thomas and Haiti. Furthermore, they attempted to put external constraints on the lifelines of the islands. Without large-scale plantation economies, Curaçao and St. Thomas had to survive on international trade; this could not be done if their governments were willing to accommodate the wishes of foreign nations. In St. Thomas, the activities of the French agent reveal the desperation with which he campaigned for the international community to prohibit trade with Haiti. Roberjot Lartigue claimed that Jean-Jacques Dessalines was planning a Caribbean-wide revolution, and he argued that to prevent this disastrous event, the international community had to rally together to isolate the island. The evidence presented by the French agent suggests that the conspiracy theory arose from his own investment in regaining the colony and in proving his usefulness as a French agent. Fear mongering did not succeed as a major tactic to corral support for France in its efforts to isolate Haiti.

The tensions and conflicts revealed by Haitian independence between the overlapping spheres of legal and military authority in the Caribbean are well illustrated in a case surrounding the capture of a Danish ship in 1805. Seized by a French privateer in the territorial waters around Curaçao, this ship was brought into the port of Fort Amsterdam. But local authorities balked at French claims that this was a legitimate capture of a vessel trading with Haiti. The case of the *Lille* reveals the limited ability of the French agents to successfully convince the international community to isolate Haiti. The Dutch governor was not willing to compromise Dutch natural rights within the law of nations in order to give the French free jurisdictional reign in the Caribbean.[183] For the Dutch governor of Curaçao, the local priority of maintaining jurisdictional authority trumped the French goal of isolating Haiti. The Dutch governor had prohibited trade, but he was not willing to allow French privateers to police the waters around Curaçao in order to enforce the prohibition.

The frequent and detailed letters between the French agents and the foreign governor and Ferrand help explain why the French were unable to organize the international community to support a general blockade of Haiti. Thilorier, Gouges, and Lartigue did, in fact, try to force the governors of Curaçao and St. Thomas to implement the proclamations issued by Ferrand and other French representatives that prohibited trade with the rebels in Haiti. At times, they also tried to enforce these provisions themselves. The governors of Curaçao and St. Thomas did outlaw trade with Haiti in late 1804 and late 1805, respectively, but the prohibition on trade—like similar prohibitions declared by imperial governments throughout the eighteenth century—remained largely on paper. The governors of Curaçao and St. Thomas accommodated French demands by issuing decrees; but they did little to enforce them. French agents constantly complained that neither governor supervised the activities of the merchants with enough zeal. Merchants from both islands found ways to continue the illicit trade, and the agents found themselves increasingly exasperated by the perceived lack of effort on the parts of the governors to implement stricter regulatory measures. In the end, they could do little to change the situation. Throughout their years of protest and constant campaigning for active prevention of illicit trade, these agents expressed great frustration at the continued trade between Dutch and Danish merchants and the rebel colony, thereby admitting—and exposing—the limits of French power in the Caribbean. Local imperial representatives and merchants largely ignored the French attempt to create a rupture between Haiti and the rest of the Caribbean. As a result, Haiti remained connected in crucial ways to other parts of the Caribbean through the trade hubs of Curaçao and St. Thomas during the first three years after the Declaration of Independence. These connections help explain the finding of economist Mats Lundahl that Haitian exports were quite healthy during the year after the Declaration of Independence.[184]

Gouges's and Lartigue's efforts to prevent merchants in Curaçao and St. Thomas from trading with Haiti were quickly forgotten when the British Empire took control of St. Thomas, St. John, St. Croix, and Curaçao in 1807 as a result of the larger Napoleonic Wars. The takeover of both islands was relatively easy, given Britain's overwhelming naval and military superiority. And indeed, as Linda Rupert reveals, this takeover was even promoted by members of the Curaçaoan ruling class. "Twenty-eight members of the merchant elite," she notes, "signed a petition asking the governor to capitulate to the British; he relented at the end of 1806."[185] This occupation lasted until 1815, when, under the Treaty of Paris, both islands were returned to their previous owners.

In 1830, the first British consul to Haiti published an account of his time in Haiti. He noted that there had been an increase in Danish trade with the island after 1825—the year that France recognized Haitian independence—and he attributed that trade to "the renewed intercourse between Haiti and the Danish colony of St. Thomas."[186] Furthermore, he highlighted that the Dutch also sent a consul to Haiti in 1826.[187] Evidently official recognition of the island's sovereignty had some influence on trade between Curaçao and St. Thomas and Haiti, despite the fact that merchants continued the trade during the period of prohibition.

During the British occupation of Curaçao and St. Thomas, British economic policy applied to both islands. "Curaçao now fell under the British Navigation Act," Rupert notes, "which prohibited trade with any non-British country or colony; similarly, imports were only allowed from British territories."[188] The case of Haiti, however, presents an exception to the British Navigation Acts. Over the course of the first two years of Haitian independence, British representatives figured out a way to incorporate a de facto foreign island into their colonial system. In this sense, British policy with respect to nascent Haiti was dramatically different from every other nation of the Atlantic. An examination of this unique approach is the next step in understanding Haiti's connections with the rest of the Atlantic World following the Declaration of Independence.

2

I, LEADER OF A COUNTRY, TREAT FOR MY CITIZENS

Haiti and Jamaica after the French Defeat

On 23 June 1803, over six months before the Declaration of Independence, Jean-Jacques Dessalines, the general in chief of rebel forces in Saint Domingue, wrote to George Nugent, the lieutenant governor of Jamaica, inviting British merchants to establish commercial relationships with Saint Domingue.[1] With military victory in his sights, Dessalines told Nugent that the French, "treading on the laws of man and humanity," had made "reconciliation" impossible; the people of Saint Domingue, "weary with humiliation," were determined to become independent. Since "all the links that tied Saint-Domingue to France are shattered," Dessalines had begun strategizing about how to incorporate a new independent nation into the Caribbean political economy. Dessalines promised Nugent that "from now on, our ports will be open to all of His Britannic Majesty's ships who will find the security of commerce and good faith in treaties."[2] In particular, Dessalines invited British ships to bring manufactured goods (especially arms and ammunition) to the island in exchange for agricultural products.

But not long before Dessalines's invitation, Nugent had also received letters from Donatien Rochambeau, general of the French army in Saint Domingue, asking for assistance in his war against Dessalines's forces. Rochambeau had published several proclamations inviting foreign nations to trade in "diverse goods for consumption" in the ports of Cap Français, Port Républicain, and Santo Domingo.[3] News from travelers and refugees from Saint Domingue clearly outlined the desperation of these pleas for assistance and noted the urgent need for reinforcements from France, which were expected daily but never arrived in sufficient numbers.[4]

In his pleas for assistance, Rochambeau used racial tensions to play on the British fear of another slave revolution. He made a thinly veiled threat that the British might one day feel the same misery as the French if they did not help to quash the revolution. "I think it necessary to reprimand the Rebellion in St. Domingue so that our neighbors do not feel the same distress," he wrote insistently to General John Thomas Duckworth, a British naval officer who assumed the chief command in Jamaica in 1803. "We are pleading the case of all the planters in the New World."[5]

Significantly, as it turned out, Nugent did not respond in writing to Rochambeau's requests, and he did not send aid. Given how economically important Saint Domingue was within the French Empire, the imperatives of British military strategy led Nugent to report to Robert Hobart, the secretary of state for war and the colonies, that the French demands for assistance were "of course refused."[6] Although Nugent did indeed fear the spread of the revolution, he did not perceive an immediate threat from the island in 1803. Instead, he saw opportunity in the wake of the French evacuation and further economic and security benefits in an agreement with Dessalines. "The Proclamations clearly prove their [the French] Distress," Nugent wrote to John Sullivan, the under-secretary of state for war and the colonies, in January 1803, "and the little Probability there is of their Government's Deriving any Advantage from the Produce of St. Domingo for many many Years to come."[7] Nugent hoped that Jamaica and other British Caribbean colonies would profit from the collapse of Dominguan sugar.

A sugar revival would have been timely, since the Jamaican sugar economy began a sharp decline in 1775.[8] In the end, Nugent was correct in some respects: Saint Domingue/Haiti never regained its superiority in sugar production. Instead, other Caribbean islands, primarily Cuba, shifted focus and entered a sugar boom.[9] By 1840, Cuba took over from Saint Domingue as the world's leading sugar producer.[10] Haitians continued to produce and export other crops, primarily coffee, cotton, and wood, but exports were limited because of strong resistance by Haitian laborers or *cultivateurs*. In the early independence period, Haitian laborers continued the struggles of the Haitian Revolution in order to develop a subsistence economy based on peasant farming. During the first decades of independence, Haitian leaders tried to force formerly enslaved laborers back on the plantations, but the laborers resisted and imposed a transition during the nineteenth century from "plantation colony to peasant society."[11] The result was that exports from Haiti declined after the Declaration of Independence. Significantly, though, a wider array of export products reflected the changing ambitions of Haitian workers. "Some could also harvest secondary export commodities," historian Johnhenry Gonzalez reveals, "including hardwoods, long staple cotton, cacao, leather, beeswax, and tortoiseshell." Furthermore, "instead of intensive plantation cultivation, the coffee, dyewoods, hardwoods, and animal products that the Haitian peasants harvested and sold were either remnants of colonial era plantations or the products of spontaneous, natural growth."[12] Sugar exports halted after the Declaration of Independence, despite the efforts of some leaders to revitalize the plantation economy, but other crops, to a lesser degree, took its place.

Dessalines's letter to Nugent in June 1803 explicitly and implicitly posed profound questions about the interplay of empires, slavery, and economic relationships in the rapidly changing Atlantic World of the early nineteenth century. For the next three years, British leaders debated and negotiated possible answers as Nugent and others came to grips with a new nation founded on the world's first successful slave revolution. The archival record of these interactions provides a strong evidentiary foundation for analyzing both the theory and the practice of international engagement as Haiti made the transition from official colony to proclaimed nation.

Why did Dessalines and Nugent fail to reach a trade agreement? Pivotal decisions changed the trajectory of the negotiations between 1803 and 1806. Jamaican authorities and the British government in London were less concerned about the consequences of dealing with a country governed by former slaves than much of the literature about the Haitian Revolution has suggested. The British engaged in an intricate dance of containment, isolation, and engagement with Saint Domingue/Haiti in an effort to reap the greatest benefit without further disruption to colonialism and slavery. In addition to Nugent's own response to Dessalines's commercial invitation, representatives in London suggested various treaties designed to secure a friendly relationship between the British and the Haitians. During February, March, and April 1804, however, a series of brutal massacres of French whites in Haiti made Nugent and others increasingly hesitant to engage with or even appear to support the Haitian government. Then Nugent became aware of intensifying internal conflicts in Haiti and decided that the British Empire's goals could be better accomplished without a trade treaty. But British officials in London saw events in the Caribbean differently and continued to imagine commercial relations with Haiti through 1806. Despite these differing perspectives, however, Nugent was able to convince representatives in London that British interests could be best served without an official treaty.

Systematically examining the twists and turns of these negotiations illuminates how the development of Haiti was framed by, and helped frame, the larger context of the Atlantic World. Though scholars have convincingly shown that by 1806 Atlantic nations had collectively begun diplomatically isolating Haiti in a clear attempt to minimize the implications of the establishment of a black country in the Caribbean, this strategy was not immediately adopted. During the summer of 1803, when the rebel leaders in Saint Domingue were preparing to declare independence, the French refused to concede their claims on the island, and they exerted pressure on other nations to avoid supporting the rebellion and to continue considering Haiti a French colony. They received the strongest support from their military ally Spain, and French and Spanish privateers aggressively interfered with international trade with Haiti.[13] In the context of their conflict with the British, the French argued that the neutral nations of the Atlantic should not carry on trading with the rebellious colony. Their efforts were partially successful: by 1806 the Dutch and Danish Empires and the United States had all prohibited trade with Haiti. Yet these official prohibitions did not stop the trade, since the Caribbean was teeming with merchants focused on trade rather than politics and laws.[14]

In contrast, Britain, the most powerful naval power of the time, followed its own unique path, one that diverged in important respects from the approach taken by other nations. War between France and Britain was central to British policy toward Haiti, enabling British leaders to see economic opportunity in an agreement with Saint Domingue/Haiti. By the end of the eighteenth century, about 40 percent of imports to the imperial metropole (mainly agricultural goods) arrived from the colonies, with about the same percentage of Britain's manufactured exports supplying the colonies. Since constant warfare in Europe had closed Britain's main export markets at the end of the eighteenth century, British factories were anxious to find other outlets for their goods.[15] In return, the production of cotton textiles in England, which dominated the manufacturing industry, would benefit from agricultural imports from Haiti.[16] With a trade treaty, an independent Haiti could be subsumed into the British mercantilist economy.[17]

Dessalines's 1803 invitation forced Nugent to confront competing economic, military, and security questions and to evaluate how he could reconcile them in order to achieve the best overall results for the British Caribbean. On the one hand, the renewal of war between France and Britain in May 1803, after a brief peace, set the stage for a British alliance with the rebels in Saint Domingue. But how could British officials prevent the spread of the Dominguan revolution to other parts of the Caribbean, especially Jamaica? Could they gain an advantage in the war raging throughout the Atlantic by landing a blow to France's Caribbean investments? And, if they could accomplish these two goals, how could they benefit from trade with Saint Domingue/Haiti? Nugent confronted these questions, and their implications, as the idea of a successful black country quickly evolved from the unthinkable to reality at the outset of the nineteenth century.[18]

For his part, Dessalines had to figure out how to negotiate the new geopolitical status that he was seeking for Haiti. He was determined to avoid relationships that would re-create the island's colonial status; rather, he campaigned for Haiti to participate equally, governed by the same rules that applied to exchanges between the other Atlantic nations and empires. In this sense, Dessalines offered Nugent both familiar opportunities and new challenges within the frame of imperial trade, international warfare, and domestic security. As Nugent and Dessalines confronted these converging goals and aspirations, each seeking to protect the existing regimes in their respective islands, they ultimately produced an uneasy compromise with long-standing implications for the future of Haiti.

Setting a Precedent

The multiple proposals and responses that followed Jean-Jacques Dessalines's invitation to George Nugent in 1803 came about because of Saint Domingue's eighteenth-century reputation as the "pearl of the Antilles"—a nickname assigned because it was the Atlantic's most wealth-producing colony. Saint Domingue's economic significance had made the Caribbean colony a focus of concern and interest throughout the Atlantic World by the end of the eighteenth century. The Haitian Revolution became an international war that brought the occupation of parts of the southern and western provinces as well as Môle Saint-Nicolas by the British from 1793 to 1798. Marcus Rainsford, a British soldier and chronicler of the Haitian Revolution, criticized the British occupation of Saint Domingue in his 1805 book, *An Historical Account of the Black Empire of*

Haiti, and was relieved by the evacuation of the British troops. "The possessions of the English were here given up," Rainsford wrote, "as well as their colonial troops, and some commercial stipulations being entered into, which recognized the island as a neutral power, England resigned all her pretensions to St. Domingo for ever!"[19] Following the British evacuation, the British in Jamaica did indeed sign three commercial agreements with Toussaint Louverture's government; however, none of them recognized Haiti as a neutral power. Nevertheless, it was clear that the political and military upheavals disrupted and confused established lines of authority.

After the evacuation of the British troops, Thomas Maitland, the brigadier-general for the British forces, signed a convention with Toussaint Louverture, the governor general of Saint Domingue (despite the fact that such agreements should have been negotiated with Gabriel d'Hédouville, France's agent and the top civilian authority in Saint Domingue).[20] Maitland signed this convention on his own behalf, and it became known as a "secret convention" because the British were conscious of their international image and were not entirely comfortable with the agreement.[21] Two more agreements between representatives from Jamaica and Louverture's government in 1799 and 1801 expanded British diplomatic power over Saint Domingue.[22] Focused on the security of their Caribbean possessions, the British were willing to aid Louverture's army in exchange for promises of friendship and the containment of the revolution.[23] For Louverture, this friendly relationship set the groundwork for a military alliance in the likely case of a renewal of the war between the colony and the French metropole.[24]

The British in Jamaica felt forced to abandon these agreements when they heard news of the peace protocols—the precursors to the Treaty of Amiens, signed in March 1802—which established a precarious peace between France and Britain.[25] With France no longer officially an enemy, the British government would not aid Louverture because the French metropole considered him a rebel rather than the leader of a colony. In 1802, Napoléon Bonaparte sent an army to deport the rebel leaders and to disarm the population of Saint Domingue.[26] Despite the peace treaty between France and Britain, which had led to the cancellation of the accords with the Dominguan leaders, Nugent rejected direct pleas to help the French army that arrived to reestablish metropolitan control over the colony. Rather than get involved in the conflict, Nugent chose to wait and observe, recognizing that internal conflict in Saint Domingue helped the British Empire. The war in Saint Domingue cut off the supply of sugar, coffee, and other colonial commodities to the French metropole and also redirected French troops that could be used against the British if war resumed. Nugent, therefore, was conscious of how events in the Caribbean affected the British Empire at large.

Though Nugent was attracted to the economic offer that Dessalines extended in June 1803, he did not underestimate the difficulty of the delicate balancing act that a relationship with Saint Domingue would require, since his main goal at the time was to quarantine the contagion of freedom in order to maintain the traditional plantation hierarchy in Jamaica. Throughout the Haitian Revolution, French planters had fled to locations throughout the Caribbean and North America.[27] In the first half of 1803, French planters made up the majority of people arriving in Jamaica because they recognized that the French army was on the verge of defeat and wanted to escape the potential consequences of this loss. French refugees played a complicated role in Jamaican society: they were fellow planters and slave owners in distress, but they were also citizens of an unfriendly nation—most assumed the war between the two countries would soon resume. The British in Jamaica—and certainly the ruling class—characteristically feared that these immigrants would spread republican political thought, thereby challenging their class hierarchy.[28] Furthermore, Jamaicans assumed that the slaves that the immigrants brought with them had been corrupted by ideas of freedom and equality. "As long as we use proper Precautions in Jamaica," Nugent wrote to the secretary of state for war and the colonies in March 1803, "we have in my humble opinion but little to fear from that Quarter . . . but it requires great Vigilance to prevent the interested Inhabitants from introducing improper Subjects into this Island. The French Emigrants at Kingston &c, are constantly importing their Slaves from St. Domingo, who are of the worst Description."[29] Significantly, however, the individuals that Nugent referred to as "slaves" had in fact been freed from slavery in Saint Domingue in 1793; Nugent symbolically and legally denied this freedom by referring to their former status in legal bondage.[30]

In this context, Nugent did not immediately respond to Dessalines's friendly commercial invitation of June 1803. Instead he waited cautiously as merchants, migrants, and other people brought reports to Jamaica of the diseased and starving French troops in Saint Domingue. Nugent was open to the idea of a commercial relationship with a de facto independent Saint Domingue, but only if he could acquire political and military benefits for Jamaica and the British Empire and still respect the Treaty of Amiens. The evidence reveals that Nugent played a key role in assessing these opportunities and challenges and in making crucial decisions based on communications with leaders in the Caribbean and London. He reported regularly to the secretary of state for war and the colonies in London, a position held during this period first by Robert Hobart, 4th Earl of Buckinghamshire, and then John Jeffreys Pratt, 2nd Earl of Camden. But Nugent could not always wait for advice or orders from London, so he often depended on news and suggestions from the navy admirals at the Jamaica station, John Thomas Duckworth and James Richard Dacres, who frequently sailed along the coasts of Hispaniola, and from British merchants visiting or residing in the port cities in Haiti. Nugent never visited Saint Domingue or Haiti, but since his arrival in the Caribbean in August 1801, he had gained considerable experience in the region's political, economic, and military activity. To explore possible responses to Dessalines, Nugent sent two emissaries, Captain James Walker of the navy, and Hugh Cathcart, who had previously served as a British agent in Saint Domingue, to the island in August 1803. He then sent Edward Corbet, who had also previously served as a British agent in Saint Domingue, to propose a trade treaty in January 1804 and to handle subsequent negotiations.

In July 1803, Nugent learned that the Franco-British war had resumed two months earlier, and thus he concluded that Rochambeau had no hope of receiving reinforcements from France.[31] Nugent now began imagining the British as the major power affecting Saint Domingue. In late July, the British naval squadron at Jamaica blockaded Cap Français, one of the island's major trading ports, further ensuring that the French army could not receive any badly needed supplies and hastening its final defeat.[32] Despite this blatant military aid, Nugent suggested that "until the French evacuate the island it may not be politic to treat with them [the rebel leaders] openly." Moreover, he lamented that they could not effectively blockade all Dominguan ports, a limitation that allowed the French some respite through trade with American merchants.[33] The French army was the common enemy of the British and the rebels in Saint Domingue, but Nugent recognized the complicated implications of an explicit alliance between a European empire and an army of ex-slaves and free people of color. British representatives had to balance their military strategy with the preservation of their own colonial interests.

Not surprisingly, Nugent's decision to provide some aid to the independence movement in Saint Domingue was not easy, and some evidence suggests that it was difficult for him and others to separate personal opinion from official policy, since such assistance was clearly contradictory to well-established practice and hierarchy in imperial relations. "Though the Lieut. General [Nugent] like me felt the greatest embarrassement," Duckworth wrote from Jamaica to Evan Nepean of the Admiralty on 29 September 1803, "in promoting the views of the blacks against the whites without any instructions on the subject[,] yet when we reflected upon the enmity the French in all their actions shew towards our country, we thought it our duty to conciliate the minds of the blacks that there might be no disgust to operate against our endeavours in fulfilling His Majesty's intentions when known."[34] Duckworth and Nugent saw the incongruity in helping nonwhite insurgents defeat a parallel European empire, but the conflict between England and France took precedence over racial preoccupations in this case. Duckworth assured his superiors in London that he would follow their orders regardless of his personal feelings, and he waited for instructions on how to respond to the news of the French evacuation. By this point, however, Nugent had already decided to send British representatives Walker and Cathcart on a fact-finding mission to Saint Domingue. As would be the case a few months later, Nugent took the initiative in the decision-making process with respect to Saint Domingue/Haiti.

Nugent imagined a commercial treaty that would not imply British approval of the slave rebellion but would demonstrate that the British government would accept, albeit reluctantly, the island's independence if the safety and security of the Jamaican colonial slave system could be preserved. Nugent clearly recognized that Dessalines's military victory and political break with France enhanced the British advantage over a weakened French Empire. "I have taken the earliest opportunity," Nugent finally responded to Dessalines on 18 August 1803, "of sending two persons to Gonaïves to treat with your Excellency relative to a commercial intercourse etc, between Jamaica and St. Domingo, and we hope that the result will prove advantageous to both parties." As became clear in subsequent exchanges, the "etc." in this sentence included profound issues that ultimately prevented the two islands from establishing a commercial treaty. But at this time, Nugent simply declared that he was "happy at all times to attend to [Dessalines's] wishes, and to improve the good understanding which ought always to subsist between the two islands."[35] In taking this position, Nugent had the support of the king's ministers in London, who sided with the coalition of former slaves and free people of color against the French following the renewal of the Franco-British war.

At this time, official British policy certainly did not seek to isolate Saint Domingue/Haiti from the wider Atlantic World; in fact the British helped the independence movement in the French colony.

But recognition as an independent nation went beyond good understanding between Haiti and Jamaica, and Nugent wanted to get a better sense of the domestic situation in order to decide how the British should react to the French colony's independence. To do this, he sent Walker and Cathcart to the island to "learn [Dessalines's] future Intentions with regard to the white Inhabitants, as well as his Intercourse with this Island."[36] Walker and Cathcart met with Dessalines several times, and they noted that Generals Henry Christophe, Andrew [André] Vernet, and others were also present at the meetings. "The following," Walker and Cathcart later reported to Nugent, "he said was his [Dessalines's] present view: To throw off all allegiance to France, and declare the colony independent, under the government of himself and his officers."[37]

During their meetings in Saint Domingue, Walker and Cathcart argued that a trade agreement with Saint Domingue would be a British favor to Dessalines, and they stipulated that the treaty depended upon two conditions: first, they asked that white inhabitants be permitted to regain possession of their former estates and that Dessalines "bury in oblivion, what had passed during the revolution."[38] The concern expressed by Walker and Cathcart for the white inhabitants suggests that British officials differentiated between French soldiers and French colonists. Nugent had not been willing to aid the French army under Rochambeau in 1802 and 1803, but he now sought to persuade Dessalines to respect the safety and property of white plantation owners. This distinction reflected the fact that Jamaica had been one of the primary destinations for French citizens fleeing the revolution in 1803. If Dessalines guaranteed the security of French planters in Saint Domingue, then those who had fled to Jamaica would no longer be a resident problem for the Jamaican planter class because they could return home. Moreover, a return to white-ruled plantation agriculture in Saint Domingue might demarcate the limits of the revolution and thereby discourage further attempts at rebellion.

Walker and Cathcart's second condition was the British acquisition of military bases on Saint Domingue for the duration of the war with France. Specifically, the British sought to take possession of the military bases at Tiburon and Môle Saint Nicolas, on the southwest and northwest tips of the island, to provide the British with military stations to help minimize or prevent privateering from Cuba. Walker and Cathcart framed this second request within the context of the aid to expel the French army that the British blockade provided for Dessalines's forces. They argued that the bases had been earned by this military aid.

With respect to the first demand, Dessalines reportedly answered that assuring the safe return of white planters to their plantations was "too much to expect." In such a scenario, Dessalines argued, the whites "would possess much influence over their former negroes." The racial dynamic of this power hierarchy, he feared, would re-create a slave-like society. Dessalines concluded that while he could permit whites to inhabit the towns, "the soil should be exclusively possessed by the natives (Blacks and Mulattos)[;] they would never agree to the whites holding property in the soil."[39] Dessalines thus differentiated between categories of white inhabitants; the commercial trade in the towns did not necessarily have the same connections to slavery as did white landownership and plantation agriculture. This decision disappointed those who had hoped for a return to the policy of Toussaint Louverture, who had allowed white inhabitants to reclaim their former plantations during the revolution. Dessalines rejected this policy by insisting that independence required a clean break from France and French rule and more generally a break from white control of plantations.

Dessalines's approach, however, may not have had the support of all of his generals. The evidence suggests that there was some disagreement or at least miscommunication within the leadership in Saint Domingue. When Walker and Cathcart asked General Vernet to renew the policies that Louverture had initiated, Vernet "agreed perfectly[;] he said that unless that measure was adopted it would not be possible to restore confidence, so as to induce Foreign Merchants to trade with them ... and he promised to use his best endeavours to get that point effected."[40] In fact, Dessalines did not allow any whites to return to their former plantations; either Vernet was misleading the British representatives or Dessalines did not follow Vernet's advice. Either way, Dessalines's response set the policy prohibiting white landownership for more than a century to come.

In response to the second request for military bases, Dessalines made clear that he would not allow any kind of foreign landownership or occupation, let alone by military divisions. "He answered it was a proposition he could never come into," Walker and Cathcart reported to Nugent on 27 August 1803, "for to grant it was more than his life was worth[;] the people he commanded were so very Jealous and ignorant they would give way to the idea, he had sold the colony to England, who would reduce them to slavery."[41] Prior experience rather than ignorance might have been the inspiration for such distrust, since the British had maintained slavery during their occupation of part of Saint Domingue from 1793 to 1798.[42] But this argument may have also been a negotiation tactic by Dessalines; he could demonstrate his allegiance to the British, but blame his rejection of the military bases on the unalterable sentiments of the people at large.

It does appear, however, that Dessalines was in fact responding to the wishes of his forces and indeed Walker and Cathcart thought popular opinion had played a role in Dessalines's political strategy. "If he was to give up Tiburon, in the present stage of his Affairs," they reported to Nugent, "he would run the risk of being deserted by his Army. General Rochambeau has given out amongst the negroes, by means of emissaries that he [Dessalines] was entering into a treaty with England to sell them the colony which had caused a number of congo negroes in the neighbourhood of Cape Francois to desert him (2 or 3,000) and enter into a treaty with General Rochambeau."[43] Dessalines believed that the army would not follow his lead if their goals and demands were not taken into consideration. As a result, Walker and Cathcart returned to Jamaica without having secured either landownership for the former French planters or the occupation of the two military bases by the British army.

On 19 November 1803, Dessalines and Rochambeau signed an agreement coordinating the evacuation of the French army in Saint Domingue from Cap Français, thereby signaling that the French army had indeed lost the war and justifying Dessalines's claims that his forces were on the verge of declaring independence. The agreement guaranteed the safety of the white inhabitants who chose to remain on the island but also provided the means for them to leave with the army.[44] On the same day, Dessalines similarly issued a proclamation to the citizens residing in Cap Français promising loyalty and security to inhabitants of all colors.[45]

An Official Treaty Proposal

As the French troops set sail from Cap Français, they had to contend with British ships blockading the ports, which were now seeking to capture the departing French military ships to prevent them from invading Britain's Caribbean colonies.[46] In reflecting on the evacuation of the French troops, Rear-Admiral Duckworth considered two options available to the British. He wrote to Evan Nepean for advice as to "whether upon such Capitulation St Domingo is not still to be viewed as a Colony of France; liable to the Blockade of his Majesty's Ships; . . . or whether it is to be allowed an independent trade with all nations that choose to permit the intercourse."[47] In other words, did France's military automatically signal the independence of Saint Domingue as a country or was it necessary for the metropole to formally acknowledge its loss?

The British answer to this question was that the military defeat of the French was good enough grounds to proceed with plans for securing "commercial intercourse" with Saint Domingue to promote the security of the British colonies. With this goal in mind, Nugent sent Edward Corbet to the island at the start of 1804 to serve as British agent for affairs in "St. Domingo" and, in this capacity, to propose a formal treaty for Dessalines's consideration. Corbet left Jamaica on 3 January 1804 and arrived in Saint Domingue to find that Dessalines had just issued an official Declaration of Independence on 1 January. In this document, the island was renamed "Hayti"—its name prior to the arrival of Christopher Columbus in 1492.[48] Nugent had already acknowledged in the proposed treaty carried by Corbet that Dessalines had broken all ties to France, but the publication of the Haitian Declaration of Independence officially forced nations and citizens across the Atlantic World to confront the first nation born of slave rebellion. Corbet brought back to Jamaica a printed copy of the Declaration of Independence in the third week of January 1804; given its importance, Nugent then sent it directly to London.[49]

While proclaiming universal freedom, Haitian leaders were convinced that the success of their antislavery movement hinged on its geographic containment on the island because disruption to foreign slave systems might instigate invasion or isolation. Antislavery in Saint Domingue/Haiti fused with an independence movement that created a new country, and thereby made the boundaries of the nation the limits of the general freedom.[50] But rather than confining Haitians to their territory, as Nugent would propose in early 1804, Dessalines assured the international community that his citizens would not instigate rebellion elsewhere in the Caribbean. "Let us take care however," Dessalines proclaimed in the Declaration of Independence, "that we are not converted from our purpose, let our Neighbours, remain in Peace let them live quietly under the Laws which they have made and let us not go as incendiaries, erecting ourselves legislators of the Antilles, constituting our Glory in disturbing the tranquility of the neighbouring Islands."[51] Dessalines pragmatically hoped that these promises would reassure foreign governments and therefore prevent the invasion of the free territory created by the

Declaration of Independence. Dessalines made one important exception to this promise to the international community: "peace to our neighbors, but anathema to the French name."[52]

Corbet's records reflect that, just as when Walker and Cathcart visited the island, other Haitian generals actively participated in meetings with Dessalines. After witnessing the interactions among Haiti's leaders, Corbet reported on the internal dynamics of the Haitian state. "He [Dessalines] pays or appears to pay, a considerable degree of deference to his Officers of Colour," he noted in a letter to Nugent, "but altho' they contributed to elevate him to his present situation of 'Governor General of Hayti for Life,' I entertain great doubts of there being much sincerity on either side." Corbet had indeed observed one of the most important conflicts in independent Haiti, the politics of the skin. The lighter-skinned, or *mulâtre*, generals in the army became known as the *anciens libres*, those who had been free before the revolution, while the darker-skinned generals were known as the *nouveaux libres*, those freed by the abolition of slavery in 1793.[53] Corbet remarked, however, that while Dessalines might have to consider the wishes of the other leading generals, "the Government of the Island . . . is perfectly despotic under the chief Dessalines."[54] Although this assessment would soon change, Dessalines was seen to be in charge for the moment.

The treaty Nugent proposed to Dessalines included fourteen articles designed to renew the peace agreement between the two islands while also creating an alliance against enemy nations and privateers. Nugent bargained for regulating power over Haiti's marine navigation and tried to set guidelines for the ships of other independent nations that carried out trade with Haiti. The treaty sought to confine Haitians to their territory so as to prevent communication between the "brigands" and the enslaved people of the British Caribbean. In return, the British would provide protection for Saint Domingue's coastal trade, although regulations would limit ships' tonnage and crews. To secure maximum economic advantage, Nugent vied for exclusive trade in British manufactured goods in exchange for agricultural products. When trading with Haitians, British ships would sail under a flag of truce and would carry a trade license from the British government. Since flags of truce implied that the two nations were at war, this article assumed some degree of continued French authority over the island. At the same time, the treaty would demonstrate a greater amount of British influence there. The Jamaican governor's proposal was thus an attempt to secure firm British control over Haitian trade and to provide for a close watch over other international trade.

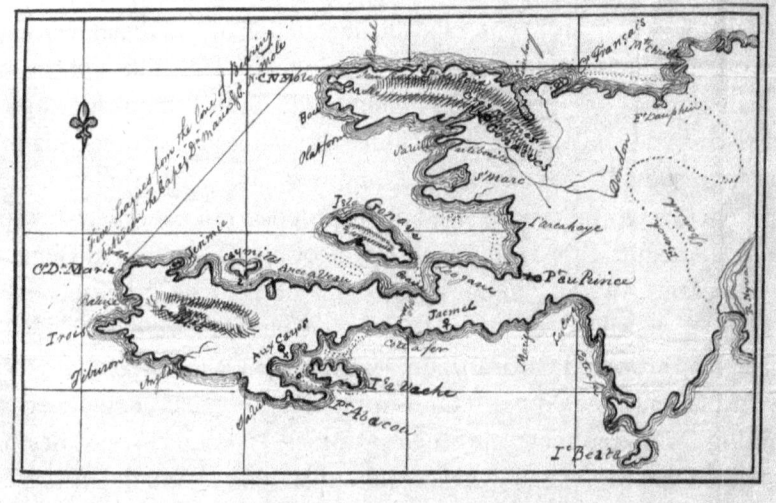

FIGURE THREE Draft map from the 1801 accord between Joseph Bunel on behalf of the British and Toussaint Louverture. (Courtesy of The National Archives of the United Kingdom, CO 137–111.) This image outlines the restricted area for Haitian shipping—a boundary that Nugent attempted to reinforce in his 1804 treaty proposal.

In addition to discussing the formal treaty proposals, Corbet reiterated the British desire to acquire a military post on the island for the duration of the Franco-British war; he requested possession of Môle Saint Nicolas. Dessalines rejected this request as an unacceptable compromise of the island's political autonomy, but Corbet reported that Nugent felt "a strong confidence" that he would come to a different conclusion if he reconsidered the proposal. "The possession of this part [of the island]," Corbet explained to Dessalines, "is neither wished nor asked for as a place of arms ever to be used hostily [sic] against the Inhabitants of Saint Domingo but merely as a desireable [sic] situation for a depot of Naval Stores for supplying our ships of war cruising in those seas for the protection of our Commerce against the corsairs of the Enemy." This occupation, Corbet calculated, would also benefit Haiti's economy, because the British would "check" the privateers from Cuba that "infect your coast."[55] Dessalines clearly saw through the altruistic presentation of this request. He

Haiti and Jamaica after the French Defeat   75

responded that he had ordered the destruction of the base, and since it would not be any good to the British army, the issue was moot.⁵⁶ Dessalines took the high road by reassuring Corbet that "the demand by the British Government did not inspire any distrust of its Loyalty and good faith" and thus that he was ready to continue the negotiation of an official treaty.⁵⁷

Corbet returned to Jamaica after meeting with Dessalines on 15 and 17 January 1804 and presented Nugent with a French-language copy of a revised trade agreement that included Dessalines's reactions, his proposed amendments to each article, and two additional articles. Corbet reported that Dessalines's revised treaty proposal did not reflect any special relationship with Great Britain. "One of his [Dessalines's] Generals then present, a man of colour of the name of Gerin," Corbet recounted to Nugent, "having been pleased to observe that they were perfectly disposed to act towards Great Britain, 'comme une nation favorisée' [as a most favored nation] I could not refrain from remarking that I could discover nothing favored in what they then proposed."⁵⁸ Earlier Dessalines had explained that he wanted to give preferential treatment to the British but that he would not do so at the expense of trade relationships with other nations. "It is my responsibility," Dessalines declared in a letter to Corbet on 16 January 1804, "to offer protection to all (the French rigorously and rightfully excepted) who want to establish amicable relations and trade relationships with the indigenous People [Haitians]." Dessalines did not elaborate on the potential content of any official "treaties for commercial intercourse" or a political and military partnership; instead he promised that "all diplomatic and commercial measures on the part of the British that would not prove detrimental to the sacred independence in these lands, nor to the exclusive privilege of rights, will be taken into consideration by me."⁵⁹

On 25 January 1804, Nugent's wife, Maria, recorded in her diary that her husband met with a group of men to discuss the "proposals for a treaty of commerce, &c. to His Excellency General Dessalines, the black Emperor."⁶⁰ "Then came the Admiral," she wrote, "the Commissioner, and several Navy men, Mr. Corbet, and Doctors Robertson and Edgar. In short, our little front drawing-room was so full, that many sat in the veranda." The scene described by Lady Nugent suggests that Nugent's decisions were made in conversation with other British officials in Jamaica. "Mr. C[orbet] has not succeeded in his negotiation," Lady Nugent recorded in her diary. "General Dessalines," she wrote, "wishes to make some terms on his own part, that certainly will not be acceded to by General N[ugent]."⁶¹ Lady Nugent was keenly aware of the disagreements between Dessalines and Nugent.

In the revised treaty proposal that Corbet brought to Nugent, Dessalines agreed to peace and to a coordinated effort to prevent enemy piracy, but he emphasized that he would not tolerate any interference with or supervision of Haiti's trade relationships with other foreign nations. In response to Nugent's attempts to regulate Haiti's international relationships and to imprison Haitians within their borders, Dessalines made clear that "the 'independence of Hayti and the dignity of its Government' was opposed to them" and therefore his government would set the rules for Haiti's international commerce.⁶² Dessalines flatly rejected Nugent's proposed integration of Haiti into the British colonial system, particularly the restrictions on the trade of other foreign nations such as the anticipated American re-export trade, which would allow him to play the British and the Americans against each other. Overall, Dessalines insisted that "Hayti" be treated as an independent nation.

Dessalines's first additional article requested that the British agents residing in Haiti make arrangements for the importation of, first, arms and ammunition for the defense of the country and, second, individuals being held as slaves to help repopulate the island. His second article obliged the governor of Jamaica to repatriate any Haitians on board British ships or in British prisons.⁶³ These articles reflect Dessalines's recognition that the restoration of the island's agricultural economy required a large labor force. Corbet estimated that the population in Haiti after the revolution was between 150,000 and 160,000 men, women, and children.⁶⁴ Presumably the people bought through the slave trade would then be freed since the 1804 Declaration of Independence had reaffirmed the 1793 abolition of slavery on the island. Dessalines's proposal followed the example set by Toussaint Louverture, who had requested that Jamaican slave traders sell people in Saint Domingue where they would then become *cultivateurs* [cultivators].⁶⁵ The requests issued by Louverture and Dessalines highlight the difficult decisions that each had to make. Furthermore, they show how the two leaders reconciled seemingly contradictory goals—supporting general slave emancipation and purchasing people through the slave trade—to advance the larger project of postrevolutionary reconstruction.

The leaders of Haiti in the early independence period did not wish to support or instigate revolution throughout the Caribbean; however, the territory that they commanded could become a haven for slaves aspiring to freedom. Dessalines sought to repatriate many of the ex-slaves that French colonists had taken with them when they fled the island at different points during the revolution. Dessalines published a note in American newspapers in order to secure the safe return of formerly enslaved residents of Saint Domingue: "The Governor-General [Dessalines,] considering that a large number of blacks and men of color endure, in the United States, all sorts of deprivations, because they do not have the means to return to Haiti, decrees that each American ship captain will be reimbursed forty dollars for every individual that they return to the country."[66] Dessalines also demanded that Governor Nugent in Jamaica return all Haitians on British territory as part of the trade negotiations between the two islands. The governor of Jamaica obliged, despite the fact that no treaty was signed.[67]

Dessalines also extended these invitations to blacks and people of color in the French colonies of Martinique and Guadeloupe. Merchants took advantage of these calls, and French Chargé d'Affaires Louis-André Pichon complained that merchants often had on board fifty to sixty men "of which the majority are Blacks and people of color for whose return Dessalines has promised up to forty dollars per person."[68] Finally, in October 1804, Dessalines also issued a law prohibiting foreign merchants from transporting any "*indigènes*" (natives) from the island. If a foreign captain was caught with a Haitian citizen on board his ship and his intention was to take that person to a foreign country, the captain would be imprisoned for ten months and then banished from the country forever. The Haitian would be shot in a public place.[69]

These early policies might have been a genuine attempt to help people secure their rights as Haitian citizens; however, early Haitian leaders also perceived the urgent need for population growth, since many of the laborers on the island had been killed during the revolution and the particularly brutal War for Independence in 1802–3. Once these individuals returned safely to Haiti, they could then be integrated into the labor force as *cultivateurs* on plantations.

The calls for nonwhites to come join the nation might raise questions about the promises by Haitian leaders not to instigate rebellion abroad, since migrations to Haiti would detract from the slave populations of the islands or U.S. states from which they fled. Such migrants, however, would only become free citizens once they reached Haitian territory; Haitian leaders, therefore, could maintain that the revolution was still contained within the borders of the island. These policies suggest a clever way to pragmatically implement the national ideals of universal freedom without directly intervening in the colonial and slave systems of neighboring territories.[70]

A Second Treaty Proposal

After considering the comments and amendments made by Dessalines, Nugent sent Corbet back to Haiti with the power to sign a treaty if Dessalines agreed to a slightly modified version of his original proposal. Corbet arrived in Jérémie, Haiti, on 10 February 1804, this time equipped with "presents to Dessalines and his principal officers, to the value of several hundred pounds, chiefly composed of hats, gold lace, epaulettes and sabers."[71] While waiting in Jérémie, Corbet wrote to Dessalines to question his rejection of Nugent's previous proposal. Corbet claimed that Dessalines should be favoring the British, who had provided aid to ensure the evacuation of the French army. "At some of the interviews I was honored with when I was last in this quarter," he noted, "it was observed that you were disposed to act towards Great Britain as a favored nation. The Governor of Jamaica can discover nothing of this in what you propose. You offer to us only what you seem equally disposed to grant to every other nation and from whom you have not in any shape received the smallest benefit." Nugent and Corbet recognized that Dessalines was trying to promote free trade for Haiti, but they claimed to be shocked that the British were not offered partial control over the governance of the island in return for having supported the rebels through the military blockades of key ports.[72] From their perspective, the British should be given a share of trade and diplomacy since they had helped Saint Domingue achieve de facto independence from France.

In discussing the new version of the proposed treaty, Dessalines and Corbet quickly came to terms regarding the articles that did not concern British regulation of other foreign merchants and of Haiti's maritime movement. Most notably, Nugent had agreed to omit the article requiring British ships to trade under a flag of truce and therefore implicitly conceded that Haiti was no longer a French colony, although, as soon became clear, he was not ready to officially recognize national independence. In addition, Nugent had readily accepted Dessalines's request regarding expatriated Haitians, and the British quickly returned 154 prisoners "belonging to this Island." Nugent did modify Dessalines's demands for military supplies since, as he explained, it was not the duty of the British agent to promote the arms trade in Haiti; "every thing of that sort must be left to private merchants, who will, with permission of the Governor of Jamaica, be allowed to import to this Island a reasonable quantity of ammunition and as the public service of that Island may admit of."[73] Dessalines achieved one of his main objectives in the new proposal, since the British would not only allow but also encourage a limited arms trade with Haiti for the purpose of internal security.

In contrast, Corbet explained to Dessalines that the second half of the article, "respecting the importation of negroes for sale," was "inadmissible and of a tenor which was not within His Excellency's [Nugent's] comprehension."[74] Undaunted, Dessalines asked Nugent to submit the proposed article for review in London. This request revealed an astute recognition that perspectives in Jamaica and in London could differ significantly, and, as events unfolded, such differences became crucial for Haitian-Jamaican relations. In this case, Nugent did not explain his aversion to this article, but given his concern that Haitians might instigate rebellion elsewhere in the Caribbean, he could not actively support population growth because it could bolster military manpower. The movement of Haitians beyond the island's boundaries was still Nugent's primary concern, and he did not accept Dessalines's rejection of the articles limiting coastal navigation. He also remained firm in his efforts to secure a monopoly on trade with Haiti for British manufactured goods.

Nugent's reluctance to concede to such demands reflected the debates in the British Parliament regarding the abolition of the slave trade. Indeed, in considering William Wilberforce's Bill to Abolish the Slave Trade, many members of Parliament connected the slave trade to the revolution in Saint Domingue. "A good deal had been adduced in favour of the abolition," Robert Deverell argued in the House of Commons on 13 June 1804, "from the present situation of the island of St. Domingo, and the dangers which would, necessarily, result from fresh importations of negroes."[75] Deverell and others argued that they should abolish the slave trade to preserve slavery.[76] One representative who opposed abolition, however, connected the debate directly to the treaty negotiations between Nugent and Dessalines. "Mr. Fuller spoke against the principle of the bill," the records report for 13 June 1804, "and asserted that if we should surrender this valuable branch of trade it would be immediately taken up by other nations." Fuller not only argued that the trade would continue elsewhere in the Atlantic but also anticipated its expansion as a result of the Dessalines-Nugent negotiations: "He mentioned . . . the negotiation which was understood to have lately taken place between General Dessalines and the agent for Jamaica, in which the former is stated to have offered to sell slaves to our colonies."[77] In making this argument, Fuller misinterpreted the article proposed by Dessalines, which in fact called for the importation of slaves to Haiti rather than to the British colonies; nonetheless, five days earlier, he had referenced an alleged treaty between Nugent and Dessalines in which "the government of St. Domingo might import slaves from Africa."[78] Such evidence makes clear that representatives in London connected their arguments regarding the Bill to Abolish the Slave Trade to the events in Saint Domingue/Haiti. Nugent undoubtedly had to consider the broader context in which he was negotiating with Dessalines. He therefore could not have supported the expansion of the slave trade at a moment when Parliament was debating its complete abolition. A few months later, government representatives in London rejected Dessalines's proposed article but justified this rejection based on regulations prohibiting merchants from selling slaves outside the empire.[79]

On 30 January 1806, the *Gazette Politique et Commerciale d'Haïti* published a translation of a report on the debate about William Wilberforce's proposed Bill to Abolish the Slave Trade; the article included a translated excerpt of a speech given by Wilberforce on 8 June 1804 in the British House of Commons. The article outlined the importance of "preserving Jamaica from the winds of contagion that blow from Saint Domingue" by forming an alliance with Dessalines.[80] The article noted that Wilberforce's speech supported this approach. Wilberforce argued that in order to prevent rebellion in Jamaica, Parliament should abolish the slave trade, announce the slaves' impending enfranchisement, and disavow the poor treatment that they had suffered. Forming an alliance with Dessalines was also part of his strategy for preventing rebellion in the British Caribbean. He argued that Dessalines was a "dangerous neighbor" but suggested that the British "flatter his pride; make him believe that we have embraced the same dreams as he has; announce to his subjects that we are the only power in the world who can live on good terms with them, who want to ratify their independence, and to recognize them as good and worthy allies."[81] This alliance would help ensure the security of the British colonies in the Caribbean from the winds of contagion from Haiti. Despite the perceived benefits of a trade treaty, the British were not willing to agree to many of Dessalines's amendments.

As a result of Dessalines's response to Corbet's 10 February letter and the subsequent discussion, the revised treaty proposal was left unsigned.[82]

After his second visit to Haiti, Corbet returned to Jamaica and reported to Nugent that Dessalines had rejected the treaty proposal, largely because it would limit his autonomy. "Our refusing also to acknowledge the independence of Hayti," Corbet wrote to Nugent, "by declining to treat with him as Governor General thereof, but merely as General in Chief of the Army Indigene of Saint Domingo, also experienced his strongest objection and he expressed himself in terms to a rejection of those parts of our proposals altogether."[83] Corbet had told Dessalines that he had not been instructed to address him as anything more than "General-in-Chief of St. Domingo." Corbet's refusal to call Dessalines by his new political title on his second visit after the Declaration of Independence makes it clear that the question of sovereignty was at the heart of the negotiations for a trade treaty. Dessalines's insistence on recognition as the leader of an independent nation indicates that he wanted more than implicit acceptance that Haiti was no longer a French colony.

Such recognition was not forthcoming. "I have not sent Mr. Corbet again to St. Domingo," Nugent wrote to Dessalines on 8 March 1804, "because the Alterations which you have been please[d] to make in the Articles in question would if carried into Execution so materially affect the British Interests, and are altogether so inadmissible, that I rather chose to wait [for] a [more] favorable Change in your sentiments in respect of them, which I make no doubt upon your mature reflection will soon take place."[84] Despite this assertion of confidence, Nugent reported to Hobart on 19 March 1804, "I am extremely concerned to say, that Dessalines by no means appears to be inclined at present to agree to my Propositions."[85] He assured Hobart, however, that "I will keep a very watchful eye upon St. Domingo, and should a favorable opportunity offer of requiring Mr. Corbet's services there, he shall be sent without Delay." But all was not lost. "I consider Jamaica much more secure from any attempts from St. Domingo," Nugent concluded, "than when the French were in possession of it."[86]

As Nugent feared, Dessalines was not inclined to sign the treaty. He was not willing to submit to Nugent's restrictive clauses, since they did not reflect Haiti's new political reality. "First off, your Excellency will allow me to recount," Dessalines explained in his final response to Nugent, "that the general Toussaint treated with the British Government as a subject or official of the French government, [but] that under these circumstances, I cannot nor do I have to, treat but as ruler of the people that I command. . . . I, leader of a country, treat for my citizens, I do not owe anything to any power nor am I seeking to be attached to any government or to comply with any accommodations or treaties."[87] By making clear how he differed from Louverture, Dessalines challenged British officials in Jamaica and London to come to grips with a new sovereign nation in the Caribbean. In return, Dessalines offered promises of nonintervention abroad to reassure the British that the revolution would remain within the borders of Hispaniola. From Dessalines's point of view, Jamaica and Haiti could coexist peacefully; a free state could be a good neighbor to a slave colony. "The intention of my Government," Dessalines explained in his response to Nugent's final letter, "is solely to defend itself from the French Government and their allies, to fight against oppression and to attempt nothing against the powers who are charitable enough to see the French government as treacherous, regicidal, and tyrannous."[88] Non-intervention abroad, Dessalines hoped, would ensure that other nations would not invade Haiti, thereby protecting the legacy of the revolution at home. In fact, Dessalines's calls for a peaceful relationship with the British reassured Nugent during the period between Walker and Cathcart's August 1803 visit to Saint Domingue and Corbet's first visit to Haiti in January 1804. Dessalines's promises soon lost their credibility, however, as graphic reports of white French citizens being massacred in Haiti began arriving in Jamaica.

Massacres in Haiti

On 22 February 1804, Dessalines issued a proclamation that ordered military leaders in Haiti to collect individuals who were known to have taken part in the campaigns commanded by French generals Charles Victor Emmanuel Leclerc and Donatien Rochambeau in the final stages of the Haitian Revolution.[89] According to a document reproduced in Marcus Rainsford's 1805 account of the Haitian Revolution, "The names and surnames of persons executed [in Dessalines's massacres], shall be inscribed and sent to the General in Chief, who will make them public. This measure is adopted in order to inform the Nations of the World, that although we grant an asylum and protection to those who act candidly and friendly towards us, nothing shall ever turn our vengeance from those murderers who have delighted to bathe themselves in the blood of the innocent children of Hayti."[90] This proclamation highlights a theme articulated in the Haitian Declaration of Independence in which Dessalines had declared that "the name French overclouds our Country" and asked the population to "swear at last to pursue eternally the Traitors and Enemies of the Independence."[91] By the end of April 1804, Dessalines had ordered his troops to kill the few thousand remaining white French citizens on the island. This massacre reportedly reduced the white population "to a token presence."[92] In addition, Dessalines proclaimed in a public document that was reprinted in the *Times* (London) on 26 September that his government would "swear an eternal hatred, destruction and death" to the "White slaves of Buonaparte [sic]."[93]

British accounts of the massacres during the first months of 1804 emphasized the grotesque nature of the killings. These descriptions heightened British fears that a relationship with Haiti was far too risky, since British lives might be lost along the way. The massacres altered the trajectory of the discussion about Haiti in the Atlantic World. Corbet wrote to Nugent on 23 March 1804, about a month after his second trip to Haiti, and notified him that the information received from Port-au-Prince "is upon the score of humanity extremely distressing. Almost the whole of the white Inhabitants of the Grande Ance [sic] have been, by the express orders of Dessalines, destroyed."[94] Days earlier, Captain John Perkins of HMS *Tartar*, a free man of color, wrote to Duckworth about a massacre that had occurred at Jérémie in mid-March. "The evening we came to an anchor," he wrote on 17 March, "several bodys [sic] got entangled in it, in fact such scenes of cruelty and devastation have been committed as is impossible to imagine or my pen to describe."[95]

Perkins recounted another massacre at Port-au-Prince at the end of March that highlighted the benefits Dessalines reaped through such violence. "The plunder Dessalines is supposed to have collected by the sacrifice of so many lives," he wrote to Duckworth, "is calculated at no less a sum than one million of dollars."[96] Further, after the massacre at Jérémie, Dessalines was said to have traveled to Port-au-Prince followed by eighty-five mules loaded with goods and treasures stolen from the dead.

The massacre of the remaining white French plantation owners reportedly allowed Dessalines to confiscate more than goods and money; now he was able to seize their plantations as state property.[97] "The whole settled part of the Island," Corbet described after his first trip to Haiti, "it is intended shall be in this manner leased out and it is from this source and the duties levied upon imports and exports that the General in Chief means to defray the expenses of Government and of his military Establishment, which he intends shall be at least for a time, not inconsiderable." Indeed, the day after Dessalines had issued the Declaration of Independence, he published an *Arrêté* that declared all leases on plantations void.⁹⁸ This measure opened the door for the state to confiscate the majority of the land on the western side of the island. Less than three weeks later, Dessalines again published another *Arrêté* regarding the plantations. In this, he proclaimed that all market vendors would have to apply for special licenses without which they would be sent back to "the plantation to which they belonged." Soldiers' wives would also be sent back to the plantations.⁹⁹

Corbet also believed that land acquisition had been a primary objective in the massacres and one that was reportedly promoted by people of color. "I am not without my apprehensions," Corbet told Nugent, "that they [the people of color] are urging Dessalines to the total destruction of the white people now in this power, so that whatever may happen hereafter there may be no claimants to many of those properties of which they may now get possession."¹⁰⁰ The emphasis on the importance of land proved to be consistent with Dessalines's 1805 constitution, which declared that "all property that was previously owned by a white Frenchmen, is, and unquestionably of right, forfeited to profit the State."¹⁰¹

The massacres led British officials on both sides of the Atlantic to recalculate the moral and economic equation of trade with Haiti. But these recalculations generated surprisingly inconsistent results. On 9 March 1804, in the midst of the massacres, Corbet's assistant, W. L. Whitfield, wrote from Jamaica to the British ministers in London to ask whether they should continue negotiating with Haiti. "Having detailed pretty exactly what has passed," he wrote, "I leave you to judge whether it is consistent either with humanity or policy to enter into a Treaty with a hord of ferocious banditte, and expose the lives and properties of British Merchants to the Caprice of these Barbarous Chieftains."¹⁰² Nugent himself concluded that the massacres ended any possibility of a friendly relationship with Dessalines and reported to London accordingly. "The Indiscriminate massacre of the white Inhabitants of St. Domingo," Nugent wrote to Hobart on 10 June 1804, "will prevent me from maintaining any correspondence with Dessalines[.] I have therefore not written him since the 8th of March last which was Previous to our knowledge of those transactions."¹⁰³

The negotiations between Nugent and Dessalines stopped, but British ministers in London continued drafting other versions of a treaty in the hope that they could secure a "commercial intercourse" with Haiti—one that included certain British political regulations as well as protection for the white inhabitants of Haiti. From their own vantage point, British officials in London remained convinced—even after news of the massacres reached them—that Nugent could sign a trade treaty with Dessalines and develop a friendly relationship between Haiti and Jamaica.[104] Indeed, key officials remained determined to sign a treaty to ensure the security of the British colonies in the Caribbean. The difference of opinion might have stemmed from the information available to those in the Caribbean versus those in the metropole. British representatives in Jamaica would have been bombarded with information about events in Haiti, most notably from French refugees and defeated military personnel. This information would have heightened their fears and made them more convinced that the revolution would spread. Jamaica's proximity to Haiti, therefore, might have influenced the priorities of Jamaican officials and made them more wary than British officials in London. Their lives were the ones in danger.

Dessalines, however, appears to have been aware of the fear that his actions might inspire among British citizens in Haiti, elsewhere in the Caribbean, and in Europe. According to a British merchant who witnessed some of the massacres, Dessalines was careful to protect their property and personal safety. "Being on the *spot* during the unfortunate repeated massacres of the French white Inhabitants," British merchant Robert Sutherland later recounted, "the utmost attention and respect was paid to the persons and property of our subjects, and guards placed over them for protection of both one and other while their sanguinary s___ were acting."[105] The vengeance that Dessalines initiated was intended specifically for the French, and he hoped that his protection for the merchants of other foreign nations would reassure them that they would be safe in Haiti. Nugent was not convinced, but officials in London appear to have been willing to overlook the events.

On 31 August 1804, John Jeffreys Pratt, 2nd Earl of Camden, the new secretary of state for war and the colonies, wrote to Nugent to propose a revised trade agreement to submit to "General Dessalines." Because of the "unsettled" state of Haiti, Pratt suggested that it would be more prudent if Nugent himself, rather than the King George III of the British Empire, entered into a trade "convention" with Dessalines.[106] This type of convention would have followed the same pattern as the three accords between Jamaica and Saint Domingue under Louverture during the Haitian Revolution. Pratt did not instruct Nugent to keep the convention "secret," as Maitland had done in 1798, but his tactic would have allowed the British Crown to keep some distance from such a controversial policy. A week later, after the *Times* (London) published its second and more graphic report on the massacres in Haiti, Pratt clarified the rationale for his decision: "As that government," he wrote, "has been supported by means so abhorrent to Humanity and may possibly afford an evil example to our Colonies. I cannot advise his Majesty to suffer his name to be used as himself entering into a Treaty with a Chief established in government by all the circumstances which have marked the elevation of General Dessalines."[107]

The massacres in Haiti occurred after Dessalines and Rochambeau had signed an evacuation treaty and after Dessalines promised the safety and security of the white inhabitants on the island. These events, therefore, had violated what historian Eliga Gould calls the "rules of war as understood in Europe."[108] This violation seems to have impacted Secretary Pratt's perspective about whether Haiti could participate as an equal to the metropole, but his instruction that Nugent sign the convention suggests that he was willing to consider Haiti at the level of a colony.[109] Agreements with Haiti, however, might have been possible because there was not only a sense that the colonies were subject to different rules than the metropole but that "slavery also had its own laws and customs."[110] What happens, then, when slavery is abolished? Would the former slaves still be subject to different laws? The three agreements before the Haitian Declaration of Independence and the proposed treaties afterward suggest that the British officials indeed considered Haiti within a different set of laws or customs.

Despite the wariness of the British government in London to officially engage with Haiti, they still sought to pursue economic measures that would allow them to profit from Haiti's break with France. Some, however, saw even economic engagement as a dangerous path. "By trading with them," W. L. Whitfield, Corbet's former assistant in Saint Domingue/Haiti, claimed, "we not only expose the lives and properties of our merchants, who may venture to settle among them, and perhaps involve the nation in a connection which may in some measure interfere with any further arrangements with France, but also hold up a bad example to our own colonies, by tacitly acknowledging their independence, which we should certainly do by trading with them." Whitfield understood that there was a precedent for such a treaty, but he argued that the Haitian Declaration of Independence had dramatically changed the circumstances. "It may be said the same example existed during Toussaint's time," he conceded, "but such was not the case, as we treated with him as commander in chief of the forces of the French Republic."[111] The British ministers in London, however, continued to pursue alternative options for a commercial agreement with Haiti and disregarded any warnings about violent or diplomatic repercussions.

Pratt recognized that the British did not possess all the "commercial advantages to offer to Dessalines" since Haiti was developing international trade successfully in 1804, according to Nugent and others. Despite the recognition that they could not sway Dessalines's decisions with commercial incentives, Pratt still counseled that they should "not . . . relax in the smallest degree in those Articles, which are to watch over and regulate his [Dessalines's] maritime conduct."[112] As was characteristic of British officials, Pratt clearly underestimated the importance for Dessalines of political autonomy beyond official diplomatic recognition.

"His Majesty's Ministers," Pratt reported, "have considered it the wisest line to resort to a policy wholly liberal as the best means of securing the friendly disposition of that Island and preventing those ill consequences to Jamaica, which might flow from a different temper." If the British officially recognized Haiti's independence, Pratt reasoned that the "brigands" would be reluctant to encourage slave rebellion in the British colonies. In addition, Pratt proposed that British merchants trade with Haiti directly from Europe, rather than through Jamaica. He concluded, without local knowledge of the web of relationships in the Caribbean, that this course of action would prevent "intercourse between the Black Inhabitants of the two Islands."[113]

Although there is no evidence that Dessalines was ever presented with these proposals, they make clear that the security of whites in Haiti had become a central British concern on both sides of the Atlantic. Furthermore, the new proposal reflected the key role that diplomatic recognition had assumed over the course of the negotiations. "If it should occur to General Dessalines," Pratt wrote in the same letter, "that no mention is made in this convention of the Independence of Hayti you will acquaint him that the circumstance of treating with him is the proper acknowledgement of that Independence and that it is not usual to make a formal recognition in such cases."[114] A week later, Pratt explained to Nugent that formal recognition of independence was only needed in cases where the new country was a former colony of that nation, and Haiti had never been a British colony. Pratt even offered a precedent to support his perspective: "You may give him [Dessalines] as an instance, that tho' it was necessary that America should require this Country to acknowledge her Independence before she treated with us, that when she treated with France, who had never had any Dominions over her, there was no formal Article making that acknowledgement."[115]

In contrast, the actual proposed convention between Jamaica and Haiti that Pratt sent to Nugent explicitly acknowledged Haiti's independence in the first article: "That there shall be perpetual Amity between His Majesty and the Government of Hayti and that a Treaty shall be made between the two Governments for establishing the security and Independence of Hayti and for protecting the Trade and Possessions of His Britannic Majesty." The article illustrates the contradictions inherent in a convention designed to promote a friendly relationship between "his Majesty" and the government of Haiti, yet intended to be signed by Nugent so that the king would not have to "suffer" placing his name on a document with that of Dessalines. Pratt was obviously trying to protect the British king's reputation by distancing him from Haiti, while at the same time hoping to show Dessalines that he had an agreement with the British Empire. The proposed convention also stipulated that the British would support the importation of military supplies to provide for Haiti's defense (but not so many as to support foreign expeditions) and would "guarantee the Independence of Hayti from the Attacks of France."[116]

When Pratt sent this revised proposal to Jamaica in August 1804, he instructed Nugent to notify Dessalines that his country's independence would be recognized by the British Empire. Nugent did not act on these instructions and, in fact, refused to send Dessalines the proposed convention. "Should Civil Wars arise in that Island," Nugent explained to Pratt on 12 October 1804, "of which there is every appearance, we shall not in that case be bound to support any particular Party, but act as may be most advantageous to our interests at the Moment."[117] The internal rivalries and divisions that Corbet and others reported had convinced Nugent that the turmoil on the island meant that Haitian military forces would be occupied at home and therefore unable to attack foreign islands. Nugent described for Pratt the internal divisions that he perceived to be most pertinent. "The People of Colour from their Insignificance will fall an easy Prey," he predicted, "but the Creole and African Classes are sufficiently equal in Numbers, to be most formidable Enemies to each other. Dessalines is at the Head to the latter and Christophe is considered as the Leader of the former."[118] Nugent anticipated that the internal difficulties in Haiti would eventually afford the British opportunities for a more favorable trade agreement, and, therefore, he did not submit Pratt's proposed convention to Dessalines.

Internal divisions and the expectation of civil war might also have influenced Nugent's perception of Haiti as a "treaty-worth nation."

Eliga Gould's research on the search for international recognition after the American Declaration of Independence highlights the importance of internal unity for framing the identity of the nation for foreign audiences. Unity and cohesion would have ensured that foreign merchants would have been subject to the same regulations and protections in all of the ports of the country. With the perception of inevitable conflict, Nugent could not guarantee that British merchants would be safe. As this moment passed, the negotiations between Haiti and Jamaica that had been launched by Dessalines's initial letter to Nugent in June 1803 ended.

Conclusion

Despite the fact that Dessalines was not able to sign a treaty with Nugent, he continued to pursue his nation-building project in Haiti. The ongoing threat of reinvasion by French forces led to a concentration of authority in Haiti and compromised the new country's revolutionary ideals.[119] The military apparatus formed the basis of the Haitian government in the early years of the country's independence and led to the militarization of the state. By 1804, Dessalines, along with a select group of generals, was making all the important decisions for the Haitian state. On 8 October 1804, he took on the title of Jacques 1er, Emperor of Hayti, and he declared the Empire of Hayti.[120] On 20 May 1805, he issued the first national constitution of Haiti. In this constitution, Dessalines attempted to define Haiti as a distinctive nation by focusing on citizenship, political organization, and culture. As both anthropologist Michel-Rolph Trouillot and historian David Nicholls have argued, Haiti became a symbol of black equality and freedom in this period. While the success of the revolution provided the basis for this reputation, Dessalines's constitution offered one form of a symbolic re-racialized nationalism by putting restrictions on who could be considered "Haitian." The constitution followed the precedent set by his negotiations with the British and the nationwide massacres in 1804 and prohibited landownership for whites.[121] Another article, however, allowed some significant and surprising exceptions to this rule, including white women, Germans, and Poles who had been naturalized by the Haitian government.[122] The institution of the policy against white landownership is important in Haitian history because it was reinforced in national constitutions, almost without exception, for the next hundred years. As historian Claude Moïse has remarked, "All the constitutions up to that of 1918, adopted under American occupation, with the exception of those of Christophe (1807 and 1811), repeat these prohibitions with more or less subtlety. Beginning in 1867, the purely racial formulation was abandoned in favor of the more generic term foreigner."[123] The development of Haiti as a nation was therefore associated with race and color, in keeping with the colonial history of the country and with policies instituted after independence, such as those that forbade white males from ownership of slaves or property.

A second way that Dessalines restricted who would be included in the nation can be seen in article seven of the constitution. This article states that "the quality of citizen of Hayti is lost by emigration and naturalization in foreign countries and condemnation to corporal or disgrace punishments. The first case carries with it the punishment of death and confiscation of property."[124] In contrast to Toussaint Louverture's 1801 constitution, which allowed for absentee owners, Dessalines's constitution not only restricted citizenship but also made this citizenship conditional. In terms of nationality, this policy was designed to strengthen an individual's allegiance to the state by forbidding citizenship ties to another country. It may have also been an attempt by Dessalines to keep the Haitian population within the borders of the island and thereby support his promises to foreign nations that Haitians would not disrupt their colonial and slave systems.

While the British were reluctant to fully accept the demands made by Haitian leaders, a feeling that friendship might be the best protection for the British Caribbean circulated in the British Empire. Marcus Rainsford claimed that they would have nothing to worry about if they engaged in an (unequal) relationship with the Haitian government. "The negroes, though sufficiently warlike and vindictive," he wrote in 1805, "when roused by revenge, court quiet, and are ardent in all the relations of life, when kindly treated by superiors."[125] He also suggested that the British could expect to treat with them as they would the government of any other less powerful country. "They are not to be compared with the Maroons, or the Charaibs," he continued, "as they possess a territory with an organised government, and sufficient resources of their own, all which they must lose in proportion to the success of any project of ambition."[126] While Haitian leaders expected to be able to join the community of the Atlantic World as equals, the British, as Rainsford's statements suggest, continued to explore ways that Haiti could remain independent from France but not entirely independent of foreign influence and control.

A commercial treaty with the governor of Jamaica would have signaled the recognition of Haiti's independence by the most powerful empire in the nineteenth century. This recognition would have lessened French claims to

Haiti's colonial status and would have provided protection for the country in the case of a French reinvasion. At the same time, however, the articles of the treaty restricted Haitian sovereignty and allowed the British Empire to dictate domestic and foreign policy. Had Dessalines signed a commercial treaty with George Nugent, it would have been the first in a series of treaties that allowed the British Empire control over newly independent countries in the Americas. The treaty that Nugent submitted to Dessalines in early 1804 was much more than simply a commercial agreement. It instituted regulations that would satisfy British needs—mainly economic exclusivity and the containment of the revolution. In the decades following the Haitian Declaration of Independence, the British again tried to capitalize on the independence of a rival empire's colonies. "British recognition of Independence in the 1820s," historian Matthew Brown argues, "was the 'highpoint' of British informal political influence in Latin America, where the treaties of recognition were specifically designed with British interests in mind."[127] Brown was building on the work of historians John Gallagher and Ronald Robinson who argued in 1953 that "British governments sought to exploit the colonial revolutions to shatter the Spanish trade monopoly, and to gain informal supremacy and the good will which would all favour British commercial penetration."[128] To do this, the British often signed commercial treaties that had broader implications. In Haiti, however, they had been unsuccessful in accomplishing this goal.

After the crucial years between 1803 and 1806, the British government reached a strange compromise with lasting consequences for Haiti. It resisted formally acknowledging Haitian independence but sought alternative ways to capitalize on Haiti's break from France. By this time, some of the restrictions on Haiti's foreign commerce that the British sought to obtain through the commercial treaty had already been put in place by other foreign governments. The governors of Curaçao and St. Thomas had succumbed to French pressure and had prohibited trade with Haiti. The U.S. Congress had also prohibited all trade with "St. Domingo" in 1806, and therefore British merchants were the only group who were legally permitted to trade with merchants in Haiti. Because of this, in 1806 the British no longer needed to sign a commercial treaty restricting Haiti's foreign commerce; other foreign governments had accomplished this goal for them. At the same time, however, profound questions continued to swirl around Haiti's place in the Atlantic World and, not surprising, became the focus of international law.

3

LEGISLATORS OF THE ANTILLES
British Regulation of Trade with Haiti

Britain's policies during the first years after the Haitian Declaration of Independence magnified the complexity of decisions regarding who constituted a legitimate actor on the international stage at the start of the nineteenth century.[1] The British government initially remained silent on the question of whether it would recognize Haiti as a sovereign state, but when the question came before judges in the Admiralty Court system, they could not sidestep the issue.

Law, especially admiralty law, was a crucial part of state building and was—to some degree—outside the control of government officials in either London or Port-au-Prince. Beyond the official rulings of the British government, there existed a world of admiralty jurisprudence in the Atlantic that made certain assumptions about what constituted a good prize and what constituted a neutral nation. While the Haitian leadership promised that they would not try to change the laws of foreign islands, that they would not be "legislators of the Antilles," the British, in contrast, were quite willing to impose their own laws on the merchants of other nations. For this reason, admiralty jurisprudence also reveals the broader implications of British policy, since the Admiralty Courts applied British law to foreign merchants.

This chapter studies four maritime prize cases that, taken together, reveal the multiple layers of possession and recognition that were possible in the early nineteenth-century Atlantic World. Sovereignty and statehood were constructed in a number of ways outside of formal recognition. Indeed, these cases show how the status of Haiti's national legitimacy depended upon intertwined interpretations of diplomatic, economic, and legal relationships and definitions.

The following analysis of these four cases builds on the work of historian Lauren Benton, whose research highlights the importance of maritime law in the late eighteenth and early nineteenth centuries by revealing the multiple layers of power and sovereignty in Atlantic empires. She also shows how the nearly continuous warfare of the period infused prize courts with an unusual degree of political and economic power, including the ability to change the trajectory of events in order to serve the interests of individuals in the colonies.[2] But exercising this power was not straightforward. While judges considered cases involving the capture of vessels coming from the United States, they also had to consider the context of international European war, Britain's dominance on the high seas, and the benefits to Great Britain in obtaining a monopoly on trade with Haiti. Foreign ships captured by the British would, according to the common understanding between European empires, be brought to British Admiralty Courts.[3] There, the captors and claimants would have the opportunity to argue their cases and present supporting evidence. "Prize courts were broadly assumed," Benton notes, "to operate on the basis of customary practices of the law of nations while observing stipulations of treaties."[4] The evidentiary basis for an Admiralty Court decision had to come from the ship itself, either the papers found on board the captured ship or the depositions of those who witnessed the capture. The judge could, however, make exceptions to this rule and include additional material such as treaties or proclamations. The result is that these sources combine to support new insight into the unprecedented discussions and debates that Haiti's declared independence forced on the rest of the Atlantic World. The "law of nations" formed the basis of much of this discussion in the Admiralty Court system; however, this concept was not clearly defined in the rapidly changing Atlantic of the early nineteenth century. Individuals drew on "customary practices," as well as precedent and the analyses of various legal thinkers, most notably Emer de Vattel, a Swiss philosopher and diplomat who published his influential *The Law of Nations* in the mid-eighteenth century. One result was that the ambiguous concept of the "law of nations" could be strategically deployed to support diverse and sometimes opposing perspectives.

Neutral shipping was an especially contentious issue in the early nineteenth century since it could differentially affect warring countries and empires. Indeed, during times of military conflict, Benton points out that "neutrals stood to gain a much larger share of rich Atlantic commerce; weaker belligerents hoped to profit from the use of neutral shipping; and Britain sought to protect its growing advantages in naval warfare by limiting the scope of neutral shipping."[5] The official silence of the British government after the Haitian Declaration of Independence meant that the actors in the courts had to consider the island in light of the evidence they could gather from before 1804. In turn, British dominance on the high seas meant that British policy often extended to regulate the actions of others. It should be kept in mind, therefore, that the four prize cases relating to Haiti under study in this chapter unfolded at a time when Admiralty Courts had a significant degree of power in shaping Atlantic policy and when international Atlantic warfare significantly determined the ways that the British perceived neutral shipping.[6]

The cases of the *Happy Couple* and the *Dart* were heard at the same time in two separate courts, and both ships were condemned for trading in items considered contraband of war with a belligerent nation; the judges considered Haiti a belligerent nation because they argued it was still a French colony. The later cases of the *Manilla* and the *Pelican* referenced these two earlier decisions, but the courts ordered both of these ships to be returned to their owners. The key event in between these two pairings was the issuing of an Order in Council by King George III that permitted British merchants to trade with Haiti. The new British economic policy meant that the Admiralty Courts had to reevaluate Haiti's diplomatic status in the Atlantic World economy.[7]

The four cases were brought to court after Lieutenant-Governor George Nugent of Jamaica had ended economic and diplomatic negotiations with Jean-Jacques Dessalines in March 1804, and during a period when the British government did not pass any new legislation or issue any executive decrees regarding Haiti. This silence created additional diplomatic and economic confusion and left the British courts with little policy guidance as to how to judge prize cases. The British government left it to the courts to address the question of how the international community should integrate or exclude this new polity in the context of Atlantic commerce. Could Haiti participate in the Atlantic economy as a sovereign power? How would this decision impact the existing economic systems? Although the British government did not offer its own answer to these questions, the circumstances meant that the questions would be answered in practice, if not in theory. When the question was posed in the Admiralty Courts because of the capture of prizes, the judges had to rule on the issue despite the fact that the diversity of the international actors invested in this question complicated the decision-making process. Merchants, political leaders, judges, lawyers, newspaper editors, newspaper readers, and others talked about and participated in the debate about

Haiti's right to sovereignty. In addressing this issue, interested parties primarily considered international relationships and military strategy. For example, the Franco-British war meant that Haiti's success aided the British war effort. In addition, the United States and Denmark were both neutral nations, and, according to common practice within the law of nations, their citizens could not trade items considered "contraband of war" (that is, arms or ammunition) with belligerent nations. In this contested context, Admiralty judges had to make a decision regarding Haiti's status. Was the island independent and therefore able to be considered a neutral nation? Or was it still a French colony and therefore part of a belligerent nation? Interestingly, while discussions about Haiti's place in the Atlantic World in political and public settings often centered on questions of moral legitimacy or illegitimacy, the courts stayed away from these debates and focused on the relationship between economic and diplomatic policy within the common practices of the law of nations as they applied to other nations of the Atlantic.

In evaluating the questions posed by Haiti's Declaration of Independence, interested parties considered diverse frames of reference. Merchants, lawyers, and judges introduced as evidence political and economic treaties, Orders in Council, constitutions, national laws, writings on the law of nations, and the actions of individuals during the international debate about Haiti's status as a sovereign nation. Taken together, Haiti's national legitimacy and international status depended upon intertwined interpretations of diplomatic, economic, and legal relationships and definitions.

The capture of a vessel was one step in a series of events in which variously qualified individuals defined Haiti's place in the Atlantic. Sailors in the Caribbean acted on their own interpretations of national and international maritime law and policed the seas around Haiti. Indeed, British sailors took it upon themselves to control the trade of others. These actions were not unique in the Caribbean, and French and Spanish privateers and ships of war also patrolled the waters surrounding Haiti. This unusual cooperation among belligerent powers implied some degree of (accidental) international cohesion, if only temporarily, in an attempt to limit the revolution in Haiti.

The court records show how the British government's silence after 1804 left it to British ship captains and the Admiralty Courts to make decisions regarding the legality or illegality of trade with Haiti. Individuals creatively used the sparse documentation produced by the British and

French governments to evaluate the legitimacy of trade with Haiti and to decide whether the island should still be considered a French colony or whether they could treat it as a sovereign nation. These British Admiralty cases highlight the changes that occurred in British policy as a result of rulings that connected economic policy and diplomatic power as the courts made use of the material in front of them.

The *Happy Couple* and the *Dart*

Elias Kane and John B. Murray, residents of New York and citizens of the United States, sent the *Happy Couple* to Gonaïves, Haiti, on 19 October 1804. Elias Kane's brother Archibald was managing a trading house and residing in St. Marc, Haiti. Together, these merchants had entered into a contract to furnish Jean-Jacques Dessalines, emperor of Haiti, with a large supply of gunpowder.[8] The ship carried 3,105 kegs of gunpowder, as well as beef, pork, flour, and other goods.[9] The *Happy Couple* was armed "for her defence against the French and to protect [the] convoy from their cruisers to the port of her destination."[10] The ship arrived in Gonaïves on 12 November 1804 and then proceeded to the city of St. Marc, where it remained until 22 February 1805. After the ship sailed from St. Marc, it was soon captured by His Majesty's Ship (HMS) *Cambria* for trading in contraband of war (that is, arms or ammunition) with a colony of His Majesty's enemies. The *Cambria* escorted the ship to Nova Scotia for the case to be heard in the Prize Court of the Vice-Admiralty in Halifax.

At about the same time as the *Happy Couple* sailed to Haiti, the American schooner the *Dart*, owned by a Baltimore merchant, also sailed from the United States to the newly independent nation. On 3 January 1805, the *Dart* left Baltimore destined for Cap Haïtien (formerly Cap Français) carrying flour, pork, fish, tobacco, dry goods, and "100 quarter casks of Gun Powder."[11] On the ship's voyage to Haiti, the British private vessel of war (privateer) the *Sarah Ann* captured and seized the ship. The *Dart* was carried into the Port of Nassau in New Providence (Bahama Islands) in the first week of February 1805.[12]

The Admiralty records at The National Archives of the United Kingdom contain little about the court hearing after the capture of the *Dart*; however, the *Royal Gazette and Bahama Advertiser* published a detailed report on the case. "At a Court of Vice Admiralty for these islands, held on Wednesday last," the newspaper announced on 12 March 1805, "a cause came on for trial, quite novel in kind, and in consequence highly interesting."[13] The admiralty courts of the Bahama Islands and Halifax heard the cases of the *Dart* and the *Happy Couple* concurrently, so neither court could draw on the decisions of the other. The two judges nevertheless came to the same conclusion. What is interesting, however, is that they reached this same conclusion by citing different evidence and by using different reasoning.

The records for the case of the *Happy Couple* reflect the diverse considerations that influenced the judge's decision. Deborah Jenson has studied the decision of the case of the *Happy Couple* in the context of other instances in which foreign merchants were prohibited from trading with Haiti. She argues that "although it is not yet clear whether there was any direct bearing of these legal arguments on Haiti's actual independence, it is difficult to imagine that they did not indirectly circumscribe the ability of Haiti to assume a place in the international order economically, politically, and psychologically."[14] And indeed, in the British case, this appears to have been true, at least until 1806.

The originality of the cases of the *Happy Couple* and the *Dart* magnified the complexity since there was no legal precedent. The lawyer presenting the case for the captors of the *Happy Couple* argued that they had captured a neutral ship involved in trade in articles that were considered contraband of war with an enemy nation. The captors recognized that the island was in a "peculiar state" but claimed that they had no "official evidence" to prove that the island was no longer a colony of France. Because there was no official recognition offered by the French or the British of the fact that "St Domingo" was no longer a French colony, they had to consider that "the insurrection of the negroes may be a temporary event of no permanence." The illegality of the voyage, therefore, was obvious because trading in contraband of war was an "infringe[ment of] one of the most important rules of national law."[15]

The master of the *Happy Couple*, Thomas Story, filed a claim on behalf of the ship's owners. In contrast to the captors' focus on "official evidence," he countered that the island "appears to have been completely wrested from the power of that country [France]." Rather than looking for documentation of this independence, he focused on the reality of the situation and claimed that the power was clearly in the hands of the Haitian government. Furthermore, he argued, the point of the voyage was to sell the Haitian government arms so that it could firmly secure its sovereignty. He claimed that no "official evidence" was needed since "the *fact* upon which his [Dessalines's] rights exist, is clearly ascertained, and not even disputed." The claimants engaged in commerce with the island because of the "actual state of the belligerent country"; they did not wait for official recognition or the signing of treaties.[16] Story recognized that the European powers had not issued a treaty or proclamation recognizing Haitian independence, but the voyage was based on the fact that the French no longer controlled the western side of the island. Military defeat provided good enough justification for commercial relationships. It is interesting to note that George Nugent, the lieutenant-governor of Jamaica, used this same logic when he sent two emissaries to Haiti in 1803 to research the possibility of a trade agreement.

Alexander Croke presided as judge for the case of the *Happy Couple* and considered a variety of evidence and arguments.[17] The preparatory testimony included depositions taken from the ship's master, Thomas Story, the carpenter on board the ship, and the steward of the brig. In addition, the court used letters and other documents included in the ship's papers. Judge Croke's first order of business was to consider the fact that the ship had been armed for the voyage. He recognized that the armament of a ship for its own defense was not unlawful and that this was "one of the most sacred and imprescriptible rights of mankind."[18] While Croke was willing to accept the armament of merchant vessels as a general rule, he argued that it must be ascertained why the ship was armed in such a way. The evidence presented on the side of the *Happy Couple* focused on the number of French privateers that swarmed the coasts of Hispaniola.[19] In the end, the judge conceded that "the depredations committed by the French upon American commerce are notorious."[20] The ship's papers, he noted, contained ample evidence to support this statement: "Amongst the letters on board, the danger and number of French privateers is a prominent feature in the greater part of the different correspondence."[21] This evidence included the examination of Thomas Story as well as extracts from letters from Port-au-Prince and Gonaïves that were part of the ship's papers.[22] Furthermore, according to Story, the voyage of the *Happy Couple* from New York to Gonaïves was interrupted by a quick stop at Turks Island (Bahama Islands) so that he could gather information regarding the French privateers around Hispaniola.[23] Finally, the examination of Story and a letter that he wrote to the ship's owners noted that the ship fell in with two French privateers off Léogâne, Haiti, before the *Cambria* captured it.[24] Taken together, the diverse evidence assured the judge that the ship was armed for protection from French privateers. He concluded that the vessel was clearly not armed to cause injury to the

British Empire, and therefore the arming of the vessel was not grounds to condemn the ship.[25]

The judge then turned to the contract entered into between the American merchants and the government of Haiti; a deal that he considered to be "no ordinary transaction in the usual course of mercantile affairs."[26] The contract was for the supply of gunpowder to the Government of Haiti.[27] Elias Kane & Co. and John B. Murray had entered into a contract to supply Dessalines "with a large quantity of Gun powder to enable him to prosecute a war in which he then was and now is engaged with the French Government."[28] Therein lay the problem—gunpowder was contraband of war. Neutral nations were only allowed to trade with enemy nations in articles not considered contraband of war, by a British Royal proclamation of 24 June 1803.[29]

The nature of the materials that the *Happy Couple* brought to Haiti required the court to consider whether Haiti was part of an enemy nation. This same issue arose during the case of the *Dart* because that ship also attempted to bring items considered contraband of war to Haiti. The newspaper report from the *Bahama Gazette* highlighted the significance of the ship's cargo in the sentencing of the *Dart*. "Part of her cargo being *articles* universally deemed '*contraband of war*,'" the *Gazette* reported, "the only question to be decided was, whether they were destined for the *supply of an enemy*?" Similarly, the judge in Halifax argued that it was necessary to determine the "national character of St Domingo." Was "Hayti" an independent country and therefore neutral? Or was "Saint Domingue" still a French colony and therefore part of a belligerent nation?[30]

Since the British government did not issue an executive decree or other legislation answering this question after the Haitian Declaration of Independence, Judge Croke in Halifax turned to the international treaties that had previously established ownership over the territory. First, he cited the transfer of ownership of the western part of the island from Spain to France with the Treaty of Ryswick in 1627. He also noted that the Treaty of Basel in 1795, during the French and Haitian Revolutions, surrendered the rest of the island to France. He argued that these two documents firmly established French control over the entire island. Interestingly, the judge then considered the 1801 constitution of Saint Domingue as an express acknowledgement of French authority.[31] Toussaint Louverture's constitution reiterated French control over the entire island, and it was promulgated just two months after his forces invaded the east to secure and affirm this control.[32] Louverture, leader of the "rebel" army for much of the 1790s, wrote this constitution when he was the French-appointed governor-general of the island. The French metropolitan government did not itself recognize this constitution, and instead Napoléon Bonaparte ordered his army to reinvade the colony. The constitution, according to Bonaparte, gave the colony too much independent authority.[33] Nevertheless, the judge considered this document to be an official statement of allegiance to France from the colonial authorities, and therefore he argued that the constitution helped prove that the island was a part of the French Empire.

Given these three affirmations of French authority over the island, the judge declared that nothing of the same style had been signed or published reversing France's claims. Judge Croke argued that the rebel army had won the war but that this did not mean that they were the legitimate rulers: "Might does not constitute right; and if France has a just title to the dominion of St Domingo, no acts done by revolting negroes can divest it."[34] According to this logic, the rebels in Haiti did not have the power to assert their own sovereignty; only international powers could give them that distinction. The French had not yet recognized Haitian sovereignty, and in fact, the judge argued, the French still claimed to hold title to the island and had actionable plans for its reconquest.[35] He concluded, therefore, that the military victory could not be complete if the former colonial power did not concede defeat.

The judge, however, offered another route by which Haiti could be recognized as a sovereign nation: by a British admission. In order to conclude that the island was independent from France, the judge argued, the courts would require a British "declaration, treaty, or other public act" that declared that Haiti was not considered part of the enemy nation.[36] In this scenario, a British declaration of recognition would have trumped the claims made by the French government to continued colonial authority over the island. It appears as though British diplomatic might may have been able to constitute right, while Judge Croke declared that the military victories of rebel armies in Haiti were—at the moment—an illegitimate form of authority. It is unclear, however, whether this was because only a sovereign nation had the ability to admit another power into that category or whether Haiti's colonial and revolutionary history resulted in parallel perceptions of international hierarchy after independence. Either way, the British government had not issued such a document.

The actors in the case of the *Happy Couple* filled the gap in British policy with historical references to French claims over the island. In contrast, the claimants for the case of the *Dart* put forward a different argument to support their actions. They too searched for historical references but instead turned to British treaties and agreements with Saint Domingue/Haiti, both signed and proposed. "The claimants maintained," reported the *Bahama Gazette*, "that the soi-disant Haytians were the open and avowed enemies of France—that though Great Britain had not acknowledged them as an independent state; yet from a former treaty entered into with them by General Maitland [in 1799], and from another lately attempted by Governor Nugent [in early 1804], it was evidently her intention not to consider them as *enemies*; and in point of *fact*, that France *really* was the common enemy of both countries."[37] It was clear to these American sailors that the British had engaged in treaties and negotiations with the island in order to support the rebellion against France. Furthermore, the U.S. government had not yet issued legislation prohibiting the trade. Maitland and Nugent had both sought to establish friendly relationships with the Dominguan and Haitian governments, and these American merchants interpreted these acts of friendship as signs of support and cooperation; they argued that this support demonstrated an alliance.

The judge presiding over the case of the *Dart* did not immediately rule on the question, but he gave the claimants another opportunity to make their case: he needed "further proof as to the fact of any agreement between the British Government and the inhabitants of St. Domingo (previous to the present capture) excepting them from the general state of Hostility." This judge argued that the conventions between Jamaica and Saint Domingue did not reflect the current situation and were not sufficient evidence of a British-Haitian alliance. The judge gave the claimants three months to produce the additional proof.

The judge presiding over the case of the *Happy Couple* also felt that he needed additional evidence to support the past treaties admitting French authority over the island and the absence of a decision on the part of the British. He therefore considered whether there might be "private forms of evidence" that would supplement the official government documents and actions in order to clarify whether Haiti was in fact independent from France. By this, he meant documents that were not part of the official political and legal spheres but rather evidence such as personal correspondence and depositions. The judge gathered this source base from the ship's papers and the examinations done by the courts. From this evidence, two key arguments came into play: first, that Dessalines and his armies were at war with France, and therefore Haiti could not or should not be considered part of the French Empire; second, that the British themselves were friendly with Haiti, and that they were engaging in commercial and military alliances with the new nation.[38] Again, the two relationships between France and Haiti and Britain and Haiti demonstrate the centrality of foreign powers in the decision-making process regarding Haitian sovereignty.

Thomas Story, master of the *Happy Couple*, argued that his ship was sailing under convoy and was destined for Gonaïves, "in the Island, of St Domingo, now called the Empire of Hayti. And for the purpose of supplying the army of Dessalines (Emperor of Hayti) with powder against the French."[39] The primary attack on the French would occur at the city of Santo Domingo on the eastern side of the island, formerly the Spanish colonial capital. "The Indigene Army take the field next week against St Domingo," Archibald Kane wrote to his brother Elias from St. Marc, Haiti, "headed in person by His Majesty. Dessalines is truly a man of *strong mind and prodigious firmness*. I like him on account of his quick decision."[40] Numerous other letters on board the captured ship supported the claims that Dessalines's army, about 20,000 strong, was marching against the small French force at Santo Domingo.[41]

The evidence also contained information regarding British involvement in the conflict between Dessalines and the French and even suggested that the British themselves were collaborators in this attack. "I have no new material to communicate," a merchant wrote from St. Marc, "except the Emperor marching against the city of St Domingo with an army of twenty thousand men, there is little doubt of their taking it when every soul is to be put to the sword without mercy. Some English ships of war are cruising off the harbour to prevent their [the French] escape by sea."[42] The British navy had previously aided Dessalines's army in order to ensure the evacuation of General Rochambeau's troops from Cap Français in the second half of 1803, and evidently the British admirals had again agreed to support another attack on the French on the other side of the island. Thomas Story also emphasized this point in his examination at the Vice-Admiralty Court in Nova Scotia. The "deponent [Thomas Story] was informed by the interpreter and aid de Camp of General Dessalines that he had received a letter from the British Naval Commander named Duckworth informing him that he had sent three Frigates to Blockade the city of Saint Domingo and to co-operate in the reduction of that fortress."[43] William Ely, another merchant in Haiti, corroborated these statements in a letter that was submitted as evidence. Ely argued that before he marched on Santo Domingo, Dessalines received "dispatches from Admiral Duckworth at Jamaica assuring him of his determination to cooperate with him by sea in the reduction of the city of St Domingo, which the Emperor intends to raze to the ground, blow up its fortifications, burn its buildings and bring off the black inhabitants to cultivate what was formerly called the French part of the Island."[44]

The British, the claimants put forward, also collaborated with Dessalines on the western side of the island. "During the time this deponent was at Gonaives [sic]," Thomas Story argued in his testimony, "His Majesty's schooner *Superior* commanded by a lieutenant of the Royal Navy came into the said port for the purpose of getting refreshments, which was supplied to them by the permission of Dessalines."[45] Furthermore, he argued, the British themselves were engaging in similar trade with the Haitian government since "Dessalines had[,] a short time before[,] exchanged a number of anchors with Admiral Duckworth for a quantity of small arms."[46] Haitians were providing British sailors with provisional supplies when they landed on shore, and members of the British navy were supplying the Haitian government with items considered contraband of war. According to Story, this evidence proved that, by comparison, his ship was not engaged in illegal activity.

The judge, however, discounted these arguments and stated that they were "mere belief, hearsays, reports, and suppositions."[47] He argued that none of this amounted to evidence of the recognition of Haiti's independence by Great Britain. "That there should be some interchange of reciprocal civilities, and even occasional limited co-operations, between parties engaged in war against a common enemy, is extremely natural; but all these circumstances fall very short of proving what is necessary in this case, that an alliance subsists between Great Britain and the Emperor of Hayti, to such an extent as would authorize such an immense supply of ammunition, in support of the establishment of an independent government in that island."[48] The judge recognized that some support was possible in the interest of bringing down the common enemy; but this small-scale collaboration did not amount to official recognition of the island's independence from France. This rationale may have also taken into consideration the perceived benefits for Great Britain of continued civil war within the French Empire. Civil war would not only cut off a large source of income for the French but it would also require the metropole to spend additional resources in their efforts to reconquer the island.

Without any formal concession from the French government recognizing the independence of its former colony and without proof of an alliance between Haiti and Great Britain, the judge presiding over the case of the *Happy Couple* argued that "St Domingo" had to be considered a French colony.[49] Because the ship *Happy Couple* had carried gunpowder to Haiti, he concluded that the confiscation of the ship was legal.[50] Similarly, a 4 April 1806 *Supplement to the Royal Gazette* reported that the claimants for the *Dart* had failed to supply the courts with sufficient evidence to prove Haiti's independence from France.[51] The records of the High Court of Admiralty note that the *Dart* was condemned in the Court of Vice-Admiralty of the Bahama Islands on 16 July 1805. The claimants appealed the decision on 5 May 1806, but the High Court of Admiralty upheld the Vice-Admiralty Court's decision.[52]

News of the British Vice-Admiralty Courts' decisions quickly reached the United States, and at least one American newspaper reflected on the ambiguities of British policy toward the Caribbean island in an article about the capture of the *Dart*. "In their courts of admiralty," the *Aurora General Advertiser* (Philadelphia) reported on 9 March 1805, "the British have not yet recognized his majesty the emperor Dessalines." The article warned merchants venturing to Haiti that "all vessels carrying military stores to those ports will be condemned as going to a *French port*." The writer for the *Aurora General Advertiser* noted the distinction between mercantile adventure and government recognition and argued that "it is one thing for the traders to St Domingo to acknowledge a negro chief, and another to persuade the British of their being engaged in a lawful trade; when their privateers deem it to their advantage to make use of their knowledge, or to seize our merchant vessels when cleared out for that island."[53] This newspaper article highlights the diverse people and interests in discussions surrounding Haitian independence. Many merchants were willing to accept Haitian independence since this status allowed for new economic opportunities. In contrast, the British Empire remained silent on the diplomatic legitimacy of the island. This newspaper argued that this might have been a strategic financial decision since the British won prize money in court cases such as those of the *Happy Couple* and the *Dart*.

The French agent in St. Thomas interpreted these actions within the framework of the French attempts to unify foreign powers in an effort to isolate Haiti. He saw these captures and condemnations as evidence of support for French efforts to prevent international trade with the island. "The English bring to Jamaica and Tortola the ships that come and go from Hayti," he reported to the French general Jean-Louis Ferrand in Santo Domingo; "they condemn some, and ransom the others; there is general disapproval of this kind of commerce."[54] The French agent in St. Thomas considered these captures in light of French proclamations prohibiting trade with Haiti and concluded that the British supported this policy.

In referring to the capture of the *Dart*, James Stephen, a lawyer for the prize appeal court of the Privy Council, wrote from the Bahama Islands to the Admiralty authorities in London to ask for guidance as to how Haiti should be considered by the British. "The claimant is required to produce within a limited time, proof of some actual convention between our Government and Dessalines, intitling him to the privileges of neutrality; and that in default thereof, the Ship and Cargo, which I understand are of considerable value, will be condemned." To help answer this question, Stephen asked for more information on the king's intentions with respect to Haiti: "It would be great presumption in me to enquire what are the views of His Majesty's Ministers in relation to St Domingo," but he argued that he had to ask the question since the issue was so important in terms for the Franco-British war. "Captures like this [of the *Dart*] will be highly acceptable to the Government of France," Stephen argued, "for it is I believe a certain fact, that Gen. Ferrand and the Governor of Guadaloupe [sic], have lately declared their resolution of putting to death all the neutrals whom they may take in their exercise of this obnoxious commerce." Stephen thought that this punishment was out of the ordinary and assumed that it would have other consequences for France's international relationships. "Extremities like these might be dangerous to the good understanding between the American People and France," he calculated, "especially as the Government of the former was barely strong enough to carry in Congress a law for restraining the trade in armed vessels with the negroes, and was even left in a minority on some of its more vigorous clauses." Stephen assumed that the United States had no interest in curtailing the trade between American merchants and Haiti and figured that the French needed Britain's help in preventing the trade. "It is therefore every way convenient to Buonaparte [sic] that the British Navy should assist him in the suppression of this trade," he concluded, "and thereby divide with him the murders of the American Merchants, and the indignation of the negroes."[55] Stephen wanted no part in being a pawn of the French in the Caribbean.

According to Stephen, the British should have considered their policy toward Haiti in the context of France's efforts to convince the international community to prohibit the trade. Stephen highlighted the American inclination to support and continue the trade, although that would soon change, and argued that the British should not side with the French in these circumstances. The records from the Bahama Islands do not contain a response to Stephen's letter, but the Privy Council soon came to a conclusion regarding British economic policy toward Haiti.

The Privy Council and the Orders in Council

British policy on trade with Haiti changed in 1806, and international merchants, lawyers, and Admiralty Court judges used the new economic policy to situate Haiti in the broader Atlantic diplomatic system. The Privy Council for Trade and Foreign Plantations had, even before Haitian independence, been debating ways for the British Empire to ensure the friendly disposition of the Haitian government as a way to protect its own colonies. Even though the Jamaican governor's initial attempt to secure a trade treaty with Dessalines in 1804 had failed, the Privy Council continued to discuss the economic value of trade with Haiti, and it considered how the British Empire might profit from this enterprise while still considering the security of the British colonies in the Caribbean. Could they devise a plan that would benefit British merchants and manufacturers and prevent communication between the "brigands of St. Domingo" and the slaves held in the British Caribbean? Their answer, in contrast to the Jamaican governor's conclusion in March 1804, was yes.

On 8 July 1806, the Privy Council assigned a representative of the Lords of the Committee for Trade, His Majesty's Advisor General, to prepare a draft of an order that would allow "British subjects to Trade to that Part of the Island of St Domingo not in the Possession of the French or Spaniards from such Ports and Places in such Articles and in such Ships as by Law they can be done without the Interposition of the Legislature."[56] This draft, the committee argued, should be modeled on an Order in Council issued in 1799 that opened the trade between Jamaica and Saint Domingue in conformity with an accord signed between the British general Thomas Maitland and the then governor-general of Saint Domingue, Toussaint Louverture. Just as the Jamaican governor had looked for British precedents with respect to trade agreements with Saint Domigue/Haiti, so did the Privy Council. This previous Order in Council, issued on 9 January 1799, stated that "it would be expedient to allow certain articles, under certain restrictions, to be exported from Jamaica, to certain Ports in the Island of St. Domingo, and to import the produce of the said Island in return for such articles."[57] The 1799 Order did not comment on the status of the island since the colonial leaders had not yet attempted to officially break from France. In 1806, however, the British king introduced new language to restrict the places where British merchants could trade. The drafting of the order led to an official Order in Council made by the king on 21 July 1806:

> His Majesty by and with the Advice of His Privy Council, is pleased to order, and it is hereby ordered, That Licences shall be granted to British Ships to go from any Port of the United Kingdom to such Ports and Places in the island of St. Domingo as are not, or shall not be under the immediate Dominion and in the actual Possession of France or Spain, laden with such Articles as shall be expressed in such Licences; and to bring back from such Ports and Places the Produce of the said Island directly to any Port of the United Kingdom subject to the same Duties, and under the same Regulations and Restrictions as the like Articles not being the Produce of His Majesty's Colonies and Plantations are subject to, on being brought to any of the Parts of this Kingdom.[58]

This Order in Council did not recognize Haiti as a sovereign nation, but, at the same time, it acknowledged that France had lost control over the island. The ambiguous language allowed British merchants to trade with Haiti, but it withheld judgment on Haiti's sovereignty.

Merchants could apply for a trade license from the Privy Council by stating the ship(s) and cargo that they planned to take to Haiti and what goods they hoped to receive in exchange. The British merchants MacKenzie and Glennie, for example, were allowed to bring to Haiti the following: "an assorted Cargo of British Manufactures to the amount of £50,000 Sterling, and consisting of the following Articles viz Hardware and Cutlery, Needles, Plated Wares and Plantation Utensils, Tin Plates, Iron Wire, Sein[e] and sewing Twine, Leather Gloves, Silk, Thread, and Cotton Hose, Threads coloured and plain, Cottons, Muslins, and Calicoes, printed, dyed and plain Irish and British Linens, Checks and Stripes, Canvas and Bunting, Castor and Felt Hats, Woolen Manufactures, Earthen and Glass Ware, Gold and Silver Laces, German and Russian Linen, Cheese Ale and Porter, and other British Manufactures."[59] In return, MacKenzie and Glennie were permitted to import "Specie,

Bullion, Coffee, Sugar, Cocoa, Cotton, Dye Woods, Mahogany and any other Articles of colonial Growth and Produce."[60]

The licenses that the merchants received provide some additional information regarding Haiti's status since they altered the language of the Order in Council to include both a colonial and an independent status for the island: "the Island of St. Domingo or Hayti."[61] The additional two words represent the first reinterpretation of the economic legislation and demonstrate a perceived connection between economic and diplomatic policy. The Order in Council maintained the island's colonial name; however, the licenses included another possibility: the island might be a colony and it might be a sovereign nation.

In the nine months after this Order in Council, the Privy Council issued at least eleven licenses that allowed British merchants to sail one or more ships to Haiti. Some merchants made multiple applications and return voyages.[62] Shortly after the first Order in Council of July 1806, the king granted the governors of the Bahama Islands and the Leeward Islands the power to issue licenses to British merchants as a way to facilitate this trade. Then again, in July 1807, the king authorized the governor of Nova Scotia to issue trade licenses to British merchants for voyages to Haiti.[63]

In 1807, the British also applied their policy of limited economic engagement with Haiti to the captured islands of St. Thomas and Curaçao, and the British governors there were allowed to issue licenses to merchants wanting to trade with Haiti. In 1807, at least thirteen merchants from Curaçao successfully applied for licenses to trade with Haiti. The licenses signed by these merchants, however, highlight the continued danger in such voyages, dangers for which the British government was not willing to assume the risk. "I further freely and voluntarily acknowledge, testify, and declare," read one license, "and do also hereby promise and engage that in Case of Capture or detention of the said vessel, or her Cargo, in any manner whatsoever, or by any person or persons whomsoever either during the prosecution of her said voyage or otherwise howsoever that I shall bear pay suffer and sustain all losses Costs Charges Damages and Expenses whatsoever, that may accrue."[64] The licenses issued in London, in contrast, did not regulate the course of action in the case of the ship's capture by a foreign vessel. Instead, the license made clear that if a British ship of war captured the merchant vessel and "brought [it] to Adjudication in any of Our Courts of Admiralty or Vice Admiralty[,] the said Property shall be forthwith released upon a Claim being exhibited and sufficient Bail being given to answer the Adjudication thereof." The merchants did have some responsibility, since they would have to bring forth evidence of their compliance with the license: "But it shall lie upon the said James MacKenzie and Alex'r Glennie to make due Proof of the Circumstances herein stated and that every thing was had and done according to the true Intent and Meaning of this Our Licence."[65] The difference might have been because of the different people issuing the licenses, the Privy Council and a colonial governor. Alternatively, it might have been a result of the different merchants applying for the licenses. The merchants applying in London would have been British merchants; however, the British had only recently assumed control of Curaçao, and it is likely that the merchant community remained the same. Perhaps the British administrators in Curaçao did not feel responsible for merchants who were not British subjects.

Some merchants continued to pressure the Privy Council to take its decision even further and to recognize Haiti as a sovereign state. "The people [in Haiti] are more attached to the English, than to any other Nation," John Downie, a British merchant, wrote to William Fawkener, the clerk of the Privy Council, on 3 January 1807; "this feeling arises 1st from our Conduct during the period we had possession of the Country, in the last war, 2ndly from an Idea (which, I hope well founded), of our trading on more liberal Terms than any other State but chiefly from the repose they enjoy, the consequence of our Maritime Superiority, by which alone they conceive themselves secure from the French."[66] According to this logic, the continued support for Haitian opposition to France meant that the British might secure even more favorable terms. Furthermore, this trade would not only benefit the Haitian state, but could provide great benefits to the British. What Downie did not know at the time that he wrote this letter was that the British economic decree would have implications for Haiti's diplomatic status because the Admiralty Courts would use the decree as evidence of the government's intentions toward Haiti.

British ships were now formally allowed to trade with Haiti, and this new development changed the discussion about whether the island could be considered to be in the possession of Britain's enemies. An economic agreement might have been able to prove an alliance between the British and Haitian Empires; however, the language remained ambiguous with respect to Haiti's sovereignty. The Orders recognized that France did not have control over certain places in the island, but they did not define who had legal title of these places. The British were, nevertheless, willing to work around this technicality in order to secure trade advantages.

When the claimants for the case of the *Happy Couple* appealed the decision of the Admiralty Court of Halifax, they cited the Order in Council allowing British trade with Haiti. The judge concluded, however, that the laws could not be applied retroactively. The capture had been made before the Order, and so, on 17 March 1808, the High Court of Admiralty upheld the decision from Halifax. "The Judge . . . pronounced the brig *Happy Couple* and cargo to have belonged at the time of capture and seizure thereof to Enemies of the Crown of Great Britain and as such or otherwise Subject and liable to confiscation . . . and Condemned the same as good and lawful prize." The justification for this decision, however, acknowledged that the Order in Council would have an impact on future decisions. "The trade to St Domingo was placed upon a new footing by the orders in council," the judge concluded; "after these orders, such ports of that island as were not in possession of the enemy were considered as not within the principle of the *Happy Couple*."[67]

Individuals around the Caribbean observed the behavior of British privateers and ships of war and commented on the decisions handed down by the Admiralty Courts. The French agent at St. Thomas, André Arnaud Roberjot Lartigue, reported with satisfaction on the restrictions these British ships initiated with regard to international trade to Haiti. "I have the honor to report to you," he wrote in October 1806 to French general Jean-Louis Ferrand at Santo Domingo, "that the English who watch over the coast of St. Thomas take all Ships coming from Haiti, both Danish and American."[68] In the same letter he argued that these ships had been instructed to capture ships trading with Haiti, although he did not suggest who issued these orders.

However, just as the judges in the cases of the *Happy Couple* and the *Dart* saw inconsistencies within British policy toward Haiti, Lartigue also thought that these actions were contrary to the spirit of Britain's relationship with Haiti. "Dessalines will be surprised by this," he continued in his letter to Ferrand, "particularly because the King of England has permitted merchants to engage in commercial relations with Dessalines."[69] It appears that some British sailors ignored the Orders in Council and took their chances by capturing foreign ships engaged in trade with Haiti. The British government had implemented policies allowing trade with Haiti; however, British sailors did not necessarily follow these guidelines. According to Lartigue, at least some continued to capture foreign ships going to or leaving Haitian ports. This fact, however, is not altogether surprising. Lauren Benton's research on maritime legal systems and practices in the Atlantic suggests that a significant portion of sailors found ways to circumvent or manipulate the system. "An inter-imperial Atlantic legal regime existed by the beginning of the eighteenth century," Benton argues, "but it was not a regime of well-ordered practices. Shippers and their sponsors gamed the system in myriad ways."[70]

Despite the inconsistencies between British policy and individual action, Lartigue concluded that this matter might be advantageous to France's efforts. If the British continued to capture foreign vessels trading with Haiti, he argued, "the Danish and the Americans will no longer go to Haiti."[71] Even after the Orders in Council permitted trade, some British ships either intentionally or unwittingly went against the new policy. This may have been either to secure financial gain or to enforce their own interpretations of British policy with respect to Haiti. Lartigue observed this trend and reported to Ferrand: "The English," he noted, "continue to stop the [foreign] ships coming from the [ports controlled by the] rebels of Saint Domingue, and they only free them for a large sum."[72] Some took this illegal strategy even further and threatened to denounce them to the French or Danish governments if they refused to pay.[73] If they had done this, the French punishment for trading with Haiti would have been death.[74] British sailors could continue to use foreign laws to threaten merchants trading with Haiti; however, another case in the British Admiralty Courts, that of the Manilla, clarified British legal policy with respect to this trade and made it difficult for sailors to capture prizes within the laws of the British Empire.

The Manilla and the Pelican

The ship Manilla, owned by Abraham and Jacob Barker of New York, sailed from Port-au-Prince to Gothenburg, Sweden, and on 11 December 1807 the British sloop Halifax captured the ship. The ship was brought before the Vice-Admiralty Court at Portsmouth (Bahama Islands) and freed. The decision was appealed in the High Court of Admiralty on 1 April 1808. For the captors, the king's advocate, Sir Christopher Robinson, argued that the precedents set by the cases of the Dart and the Happy Couple determined that "notwithstanding the unsettled state of St Domingo, it was still in the point of law under the dominion of France, and must be considered as an enemy's colony."[75] The lawyers for the claimants, however, highlighted that the situation in 1808 was drastically different from 1804 because of the Orders in Council. "If by these orders

British subjects are permitted to frequent such parts of the colony," they argued, "they ascribe a distinct character to the places excepted, of which neutrals are entitled to avail themselves equally with the subjects of this country."[76] According to this logic, British ships could not prevent neutral ships from trading with the places that were open to British merchants. The act of legalizing trade with a place charged the port with further meaning, a "distinct character."

Judge Sir William Scott had received the Orders in Council directly from the Privy Council. In a letter dated 1 December 1806, the Privy Council informed Scott that "the Governor of the Bahama and the Leeward Islands [is] to grant Licences to British Vessels to trade, under certain Restrictions, to such Ports and Places in the Island of St. Domingo as are not or shall not be under the Dominion, and in the actual Possession of His Majesty's Enemies."[77] The fact that the Privy Council sent this information directly to Scott suggests that it was its intention that the executive decrees should influence the rulings in future prize cases.

To rule on the case, Scott dissected the Order in Council that opened the trade with Haiti for British merchants.[78] "In construing public acts," Scott argued, "every word must be taken as expressive, and the words 'dominion and actual possession' must mean something more than the mere fact of possession." The ambiguous wording of the Order avoided a decision regarding the diplomatic recognition of Haiti, and, as a result, it did not provide much guidance for the court systems: "What is the legal meaning of *dominion*? Its legal meaning implies rightful possession and authority; as applied to private property it signifies not merely possession but possession with rights of property." Again, the judge considered the concept that "might does not constitute right." "That of which the person is *dominus*," he continued, "as applied to public possession it is the right of legal authority."

Another Order in Council issued in February 1807 expanded the terms of the 21 July 1806 Order to allow ships that had previously cleared out for Buenos Aires and Rio Plata to proceed directly to Haiti to dispose of their cargoes.[79] This Order was translated and published in the *Gazette Officielle de l'État d'Hayti* (published in the north of Haiti) in May 1807 in order to notify both Haitian and local British merchants.[80] This Order modified the original decree and included additional language that described a country's rights over the territory. "In His Majesty's instructions of the 11th Feb. 1807," Scott offered as an alternative, "the expression made use of is, 'under control,' a word of less definite meaning, and which may have a more or less restricted signification, but when I find 'dominion' used in two instances, I must take it rather as interpreting and enlarging the meaning of the word 'control,' than as in any manner restricted by it."[81] The key conflict in the language used by the Orders in Council was "dominion" versus "control." One constituted ownership on paper, and the other was ownership in practice.

From the inconsistently and ambiguously worded Orders in Council, the judge concluded that they represented a "positive declaration of the state that parts of St Domingo are neither in the possession nor in the dominion of France." However, the break from France did not imply that the British recognized Haiti's sovereignty. "It is not necessary," the judge declared, "that this should amount to a perpetual recognition of the independence of these places as in the case of a formal and permanent cession. It is sufficient that there is a rightful and acknowledged suspension of the authority of France." The British recognized the temporary sovereignty of certain parts of Hispaniola, but they were not willing to concede that this amounted to diplomatic recognition. The recognition of temporary sovereignty, however, allowed both British and foreign merchants access to the financial benefits available because of the island's de facto independence from France.

The ruling on the case points to the multiple layers of possession and ownership that the British recognized on the island. "Ports and places of St Domingo not in possession of the French," Scott concluded, "[are] excepted out of the general character of the island as an enemy's colony since the Orders in Council recognised them as open to British trade."[82] From this perspective, the French maintained legal authority over the island since they had not conceded defeat in the war and they had not signed an agreement with the colony acknowledging the island's independence. But, at the same time, it was clear that the French had lost control of certain parts of the island. Therefore, American merchants as well as British merchants who had received licenses to trade with Haiti could not be condemned for trading with an enemy nation. In consequence of this ruling, the *Manilla* was restored to the claimant.

The British king's Orders in Council limited the abilities of British sailors to regulate international trade with Haiti. Furthermore, these documents ushered in a new era of British trade with Haiti. Despite the fact that the British government refused to recognize Haitian independence or the national sovereignty of the country, British merchants flocked to the island to take advantage of the economic opportunities available.

The French agent in St. Thomas reported that, because of these Orders in Council, a British convoy of seventeen ships arrived there in October 1806. It was Britain's intention, he noted, to form an exclusive trade relationship with Haiti.[83] Lartigue further argued that this new economic relationship between the British Empire and Haiti would result in "consequences that are disastrous for all of their own colonies."[84] Lartigue, like Governor Nugent in Jamaica, perceived the potential dangers involved in economic relationships with Haiti because it meant that the free people of color and slaves in other Caribbean colonies would be in contact with the successful revolutionaries in Haiti. Nevertheless, the British opened up a commercial relationship with the new country.

Some interested parties, however, continued to complain about the complications of halfway recognition. "I have revealed to you the incoherence and the contradictions that the uncertainty regarding the state of Haiti, that are occasioned by the judgments in your admiralty courts," Jean-Gabriel Peltier, an unofficial emissary of the Haitian government and a French citizen exiled in London, wrote to the under-secretary of state for war and the colonies. "I beg you again," he pleaded, "to establish in the end a fixed order of things; to establish a uniform system of politics and jurisprudence; and thus to prevent any conflict in the future."[85] Peltier wanted the British ministers to issue an official statement of recognition respecting Haiti's independence. Although this statement was not forthcoming, the Orders in Council continued to influence Haiti's legal status in the Atlantic World.

The Orders in Council, as the case of the *Manilla* illustrates, were not clear in their implications for the economic activities of foreign merchants. Judge Scott thought carefully about the different meanings that stemmed from the specific language of the Orders. The case of the *Pelican*, however, reveals that the Orders were not immediately integrated into the discussion surrounding neutral trade with Haiti. The Orders successfully provided evidence for the legality of the trade only when the claimants appealed the decision in the Court of Appeal in Cases of Capture of the Admiralty.

The Danish ship *Pelican* sailed unarmed in October 1806 from St. Thomas to New York with a cargo of sugar, rum, mahogany, logwood, bark, sarsaparilla, and fustic and with instructions to have repairs done to the ship. Because of a debt owed on the ship's account from the repairs, the master of the ship, Walter Burke, received permission in April 1807 from the ship's supercargo to charter the ship to Aaron Lidman, a

Swedish merchant from St. Barthélemy, for a voyage from New York to Port-au-Prince with a cargo of salt provisions, flour, tobacco, wine, oil, soap, fish, and lumber. The ship, however, despite not being an American vessel, could not in 1807 clear out from an American port for a voyage to Haiti because, on 28 February 1806, U.S. president Thomas Jefferson had signed a bill to prohibit all trade from the United States with the island.[86] The parties involved in the charter of the *Pelican* easily found a way around this legislation: since "no vessels are suffered to be cleared out from the United States of America to any port in Saint Domingo, the voyage stated in the Charter-party was for Saint Jago de Cuba [Santiago] instead of Port au Prince, though the fact the latter was her intended port of destination, and was so agreed upon at the time of the said charter-party."[87] This strategy appears to have been a common tactic for merchants in the United States and elsewhere. Danish merchants, as the French agent in St. Thomas pointed out, similarly cleared out for other Caribbean destinations.[88]

The *Pelican* arrived in Port-au-Prince and exchanged the goods on shore with a house of trade under the American firm of Jacob Lewis and Company. The Notary Public at Port-au-Prince stated that "no person, either friend or enemy of the Belligerent powers, hath the least share or interest in his said Cargo which deposition is taken in writing at his request."[89] According to this Haitian representative, the United States, St. Thomas, and Haiti all held neutral status. Burke then sailed for New York. On its return voyage, the British ship of war the *Lark* captured the *Pelican* off St. Marc, Haiti, on 4 September 1807, and escorted it to Kingston, Jamaica.

On 2 October 1807, at a hearing in the Vice-Admiralty Court in Jamaica, the judge condemned the cargo and awarded the master's adventure as prize to the captor. The claimants interposed an appeal to request the reversal of the sentence, and it was heard in the Court of Appeal in Cases of Capture on 6 May 1809—after the ruling on the *Manilla* and after another key piece of economic policy. This appeal demonstrates a keen awareness on the part of merchants and sailors of the changing status of Haiti in Atlantic networks of trade. On 14 December 1808, King George III issued another Order in Council eliminating the need for British merchants to secure licenses from the Privy Council before trading with Haiti. The Order declared "that those ports and places of the Island of St. Domingo, which are not in the Actual possession of France, and from which the British Flag is not excluded, shall be considered as not being in a State of Hostility with His Majesty, and that His Majesty's Subjects, and

Officers, are at Liberty freely to trade thereat, in the same manner as they may trade at neutral Ports and Places."[90] This declaration removed the restrictions on trade with Haiti and allowed merchants to treat the ports of Haiti as they would any other neutral nation.

The British government, however, was clearly aware of the diplomatic implications that this Order in Council might have for current cases and tried to limit its impact, even though two years earlier, on 1 December 1806, it had expressly sent the initial Orders in Council to Sir William Scott in the High Court of Admiralty in London. Perhaps the British government in London was wary of the impact that its economic policy was having on perceptions of the relationship between the British Empire and Haiti. "Provided nevertheless," the 1808 Order stated, "that nothing herein contained shall be construed to affect any Questions now depending in His Majesty's Tribunals respecting the character of the said Ports and Places, but such Question shall be decided in the same manner as if this Order and Declaration had not [been] issued." This statement, however, did not eliminate the possibility that British officials could use the previous Orders to determine the "character" of Haiti. Future cases could also reference this Order.

Despite these efforts, however, it seems as though the 1808 Order may have suggested to some onlookers that Haiti's diplomatic status was in fact changing. According to the unofficial emissary of the Haitian government, Jean-Gabriel Peltier, news of the British Order in Council that opened and regulated the trade with Haiti was good news for Haitian merchants. "The Order in Council of His Majesty that announced that the ports of Haiti are no longer in hostility with Great Britain," Peltier reported to the British secretary of state for war and the colonies, "and that the commerce is free like with all other countries, caused great fanfare, and the greatest enthusiasm among the inhabitants of Haiti. They are filled with gratitude for His Majesty and his ministers for this act."[91] Peltier suggested that the elimination of the restrictions on the trade with Haiti raised Haiti's status in the international economic sphere—it was now "like all other countries."

The records from the Court of Appeal for the *Pelican* state that the lawyers for the claimants put forward two reasons for the appeal: first, "the property is sufficiently proved to belong as claimed"; second, "because by various Orders in Council antecedent to the Date of this Transaction, Port au Prince was in effect declared to be not in the possession or under the control of the enemies of Great Britain, and in consequence of such declaration, as well as the actual political state of Saint Domingo, was open to Neutral Trade without restriction."[92] The claimants argued that the British king had produced decrees recognizing Haitian sovereignty (if only temporarily), and, therefore, the cases of the *Happy Couple* and the *Dart* could no longer be used as precedents. Furthermore, they drew on the new Order in Council from 1808 to emphasize that the British government had declared that Haiti was not an enemy nation, even though the text of the Order expressly stated that they could not.

The judges for the case, Sir William Grant, the Master of the Rolls, Sir William Wynne, Sir William Scott, and Sir John Nicholl, agreed with the arguments presented by the claimants. "Although it was matter of notoriety," Grant reported in the judgment, "that a considerable part of St. Domingo had been emancipated from the dominion of France, yet, when the former cases ("*Dart*" and "*Happy Couple*") were decided, we thought there was no sufficient ground to authorise the Court to presume a change in its national character. It always belongs to the Government of the country to determine in what relation any other country stands towards it; that is a point upon which Courts of Justice cannot decide."[93] Prior to the Orders in Council, the judges argued that the government had not given the courts any reason to think that there had been a "change in the national character." In the present situation, however, they did in fact take the new 1808 Order into consideration and argued that "the Orders negative a hostile character applying to certain parts of the colony; and it was not contended in argument, that the port from which this vessel sailed was not one of those to which these subsequent Orders would apply." The hostile character of the island had been erased by the new British economic policy that allowed merchants to engage in an unlicensed trade with the island. "We are therefore of opinion," Grant concluded in his report, "that this property must be restored; but as the question is altogether new, we think the captors ought to be reimbursed in their expenses."[94] The judges showed some sympathy for the British captors since they had been trapped in uncharted legal territory.

Robert Sutherland, a British merchant residing in Port au Prince, however, felt that British merchants who had been captured while legally trading with Haiti had suffered even when their ships and goods were restored. "Several of your memorialists," Sutherland and twenty other merchants wrote to the Board of Trade in September 1810, "altho they have had their property given up to them on appeal to the Court of Vice Admiralty, have suffered greatly from the manner in which their property in Jamaica was exposed to Public Sale (in the same manner that French property was sold) as well as from the detention and expenses attending the claiming such property."[95] The British merchants in Haiti were constantly advocating for broader recognition of Haitian independence in order to facilitate trade and to protect their investments in the country.

Consistent Rulings in the Common Law Courts

The Admiralty Court records for the cases of the *Happy Couple*, the *Dart*, the *Manilla*, and the *Pelican* document how economic policy impacted Haiti's diplomatic status in the Atlantic World between 1804 and 1809.[96] International trade during times of war infused these legal decisions with economic and diplomatic implications. Along with great interest and activity in trade with Haiti, debate continued regarding the legality of these voyages. The decisions of the Admiralty Courts also impacted civil cases, and the cases of the *Manilla* and the *Pelican* were used as proof that this trade was legal. Two cases, one in the Court of Common Pleas and one in the Court of the King's Bench, in which British ships were seized for trading outside the stipulations of their licenses, gave the courts the opportunity to further expand the implications of the Orders in Council allowing trade with Haiti. The records from the Court of Common Pleas in May 1810 discuss the capture of the British ship the *Ben Lomond* in March 1808. The plaintiff had chartered a vessel to sail to Haiti to exchange a cargo from Portsmouth. He sued the defendant, the ship owner, for breach of contract; one of the alleged breaches being the improper acquisition of a license to trade with Haiti, which led to the ship's capture. The conclusion of this case solidified the rulings issued by Scott with respect to the *Manilla*, but the judges also considered the new issue of licenses. The initial Orders in Council issued by the British king required British merchants trading with Haiti to procure licenses from the Privy Council for their voyages, but the December 1808 Order eliminated that requirement and permitted British merchants to engage in a free and neutral trade with Haiti. One of the judges for the case of the *Ben Lomond*, Janes Mansfield, declared that the ports not in the possession of France must be considered under the category of "neutrality." In this case, he argued, ships trading with these ports would not require licenses to trade. "Those ports of St. Domingo which are under the domination of Christophe and the negroes engaged in hostility with France, are neutral ports," Mansfield argued, "and no license is necessary to legalize a trade with them."[97] The voyage did not involve the exchange of items considered contraband of war; instead, the ship intended to trade a "cargo from Portsmouth," mainly composed of coffee sacks, for a cargo of "coffee, cotton, indigo, and other lawful goods." After the Order of 1808, however, British merchants were not required to obtain licenses to trade with Haiti, and therefore it did not matter whether the cargo on board matched the merchant's license.

Two years later, the British ship *Elizabeth and Mary* was captured for having items on board that were not specified in the license. It was condemned in the Vice-Admiralty Court of Jamaica, but the decision was reversed in the High Court of Admiralty. The case was then transferred to the Court of the King's Bench to resolve a dispute regarding insurance.[98] This case referenced the proceedings of the Admiralty hearings and drew on the cases of the *Manilla* and the *Pelican* and also used the case of the *Ben Lomond* in order to support the legality of the ship's voyage to two northern ports in Haiti that were under the control of Henry Christophe. The judges ruling on this case declared that the ports considered open for trade by the Orders in Council would fall within the guidelines for relationships between British subjects and neutral nations. The arguments put forward to support the legality of the actions of the *Elizabeth and Mary* included references to the decision handed down by Judge Scott, the statements made by the Master of the Rolls for the appeal of the *Pelican*, and the statements of the neutrality of certain ports in "St. Domingo" made during the decision process for the *Ben Lomond*. The case of the *Elizabeth and Mary* hinged on the regulations surrounding licensing specifications, but the judges concluded that "the licence itself not being necessary, the carrying of goods not included in it was no legal cause of seizure." They referenced the new Order in Council from 14 December 1808 (after the capture of the *Elizabeth and Mary* and the *Ben Lomond*) that "opened to the British trade in general all the ports of St. Domingo not in the possession of France in like manner as to any neutral country." Not only that, but a letter printed in the *Morning Chronicle* (London) under the title "Free Trade with Hayti," noted that his Majesty declared "that those ports and places of the Island of St. Domingo which are not in the actual possession of France, and from which the British flag is not excluded, shall be considered as not being in a state of hostility with his Majesty." This backhanded recognition of Haiti's independence was addressed to "J. Peltier, Agent of Hayti," and suggests that the British government was responding to the diplomatic pressure that Peltier had been exerting since 1807.[99]

Despite the fact that this Order in Council could not be applied retroactively, in considering the case of the *Elizabeth and Mary*, Judge Le Blanc argued, "I consider the last Order in Council as meant to remove all doubt." According to this interpretation, the Order did not represent a change in British policy but a mere clarification of past policy. The court ruled, therefore, that the British government had decreed the neutrality of Haitian ports in practice, and this declaration had been solidified in the British Admiralty Court system. Another judge hearing the case, Judge Bayley, agreed with these interpretations and noted that, as per the decisions of Judge Scott and the report from the Master of the Rolls for the appeal of the *Pelican*, "the ports in question were not hostile."[100] The *Elizabeth and Mary*, therefore, fell within the rules governing trade with neutral ports, and these voyages did not require any specific licenses.

The Admiralty Courts followed the British government's lead on issues surrounding the temporary recognition of Haitian sovereignty and France's loss of control over specific places on the island and these decisions had further implications in the civil courts. While the judges for the cases of the *Happy Couple* and the *Dart* both looked for historic diplomatic precedents in order to evaluate the nationality of the ports of Haiti, the Orders in Council issued by the British king ushered in a new era of trade with Haiti by allowing ships to treat the ports controlled by the Haitian government within the regulations governing relationships between neutrals.

Conclusion

In the first years after Haitian independence, British and Haitian leaders creatively developed a controlled economic relationship in which British merchants were issued special licenses to trade with the regions on the island that were under the control of the Haitians. In one sense, the Order in Council issued by the British Crown on 21 July 1806 implicitly acknowledged the independence of Haiti because it declared that the French did not have control over areas of the island despite the fact that they still claimed that it was their colony. Furthermore, the licenses issued to British merchants altered the language of the Order in Council to include both a colonial and an independent status for the island: "the island of St. Domingo or Hayti."[101]

While continuing the British diplomatic ambiguity about Haiti's status, this Order in Council created new legal relationships between British merchants and the government of Haiti. These relationships increasingly pressured the British to implicitly acknowledge Haitian sovereignty. In August 1807, for example, a group of British merchants wrote from Jérémie, Haiti, to the commander in chief of Jamaica, Rear-Admiral James Richard Dacres, to ask that British naval ships respect the "common usages and rights of *nations*" in Haitian ports. They argued that if British ships of war acted in a hostile manner, it might endanger the "several hundreds of British subjects, and an immense amount of property, that has been sent here under the guarantee of National Honor and good faith." "You are of course aware," they wrote to Dacres, "that we have adventured our persons and property in the island of Hayti, under the sanction and protection of our Government, and consequently every act that places at hazard our lives and funds must be deprecated as contrary to the spirit of that Government and Flag."[102]

The British merchants in Haiti advocated for their own interests and corresponded with the Board of Trade, the Admiralty, and the secretary of state for war and the colonies because the British did not appoint a commercial agent to Haiti until 1826. The merchants, therefore, often served as de facto agents in order to protect their own interests. One British representative, Mr. Hallam, saw the need for a commercial agent and volunteered his services. Mr. Hallam had been sent to Jamaica to replace Edward Corbet in the event that the British required the services of an agent in Haiti, but he had not been sent to the island. Hallam wrote to the under-secretary of state for war and the colonies in February 1808, observing that he might be able to fix the administrative gap that he saw in Britain's relationship with Haiti. "Perceiving by the London papers that a considerable Commerce is now carried on direct from England to Hayti apparently with tolerable ___rity and advantage to the British Merchants speculating to that Island. I beg leave to bring myself to your recollection as having been through your kindness nominated by Lord Camden as the Agent, should any be found necessary, to be employed by the Governor of this Island in ___ have actions with the Government of Hayti." Despite these commercial relationships, he assumed that the current policy of the British government would not take advantage of his position. "Hitherto I have not been called upon by Mr. E Coote [the governor of Jamaica] nor do I imagine it is likely he will do so, it appearing to be the policy of the Government, or House of Assembly rather, to avoid all possible Communication with that Island." Nevertheless, he expressed his willingness to travel to Haiti if the government changed its policies. I have not found evidence that Hallam was ever sent to Haiti, and instead the British merchants continued to act as unofficial agents.[103]

The British merchants in Haiti were experiencing the general contradictions of Haiti's diplomatic and economic status as the British continued to juggle their intertwined security, military, and commercial interests. The rulings of the Admiralty Courts had profound significance for Haiti's place in the early nineteenth-century Atlantic World by infusing the British economic policies with a degree of diplomatic authority, despite the continued refusal to overtly recognize Haiti as a sovereign nation. The balancing act of both diplomatic distance and economic opportunism understandably puzzled the merchant community as well as the Admiralty Court system. The positive development for Haitian leaders was that, by 1806, they now had a regulated and legal system of trade with the British Empire. The difficulty was that, after a two-year period of possibility in which Haiti's leaders could imagine official treaties and commerce with many different powers, Haiti's fortunes were increasingly tied to British connections despite their refusal to grant official recognition.

The ill-defined British policy in the first years after Haitian independence highlights the difficulty with which governments made decisions regarding who constituted a legitimate actor on the international stage of the turbulent Atlantic World in the early nineteenth century. Furthermore, these policies engaged other foreign powers and connected British definitions of sovereignty and legal rights to other imaginaries and spheres of influence. These maritime cases show the multiple layers of possession and recognition and the diverse actors that contributed to the judicial decisions. They also reveal a layered system of decision making involving merchants, sailors, judges, statesmen, and lawyers within the British Empire. These groups and individuals engaged each other as they considered foreign legal systems and the guidelines outlined in public proclamations and treaties. The different imaginings and conceptualizations of how Haiti fit into the Atlantic World's political and economic systems shaped Haiti's postindependence experiences and made for a diversity of foreign interactions with the new country. Each of these layers of influence affected the early independence years in Haiti, during which national sovereignty reflected intertwined diplomatic, economic, and legal relationships and definitions. In this context, Haiti's curious connections to Britain became more important than ever, especially as the United States increasingly made clear its refusal to recognize a second declaration of independence in the Americas.

4

AIMING A BLOW AT THEIR VERY VITALS

U.S. Interdiction of Trade with Haiti

"I cannot help thinking," American merchant Jacob Lewis wrote from Port-au-Prince to U.S. Secretary of State James Madison in October 1804, "that if... the policy of our Government is to Encourage the Trade to this Island, it would be well to Communicate with the Emperor [Dessalines], *if not directly*, let him have the assurances of our Friendship and our determination to Support our Commerce with them while the property and Citizens of the U.S. are respected and favoured in this Island." Lewis had learned that the British had tried to sign a formal trade treaty with Dessalines in early 1804, and, although he knew that that effort had failed, he still feared that the British might succeed in achieving a monopoly over Haiti's foreign trade. Lewis worried that if the U.S. government did not establish its own friendly relationship with the Haitian government, American merchants would lose the profitable trade opportunities that they were enjoying in 1804. On the other hand, if the U.S. government did establish contact with Jean-Jacques Dessalines, Lewis argued, "this would encourage them [the Haitians] and render our Commerce hither much more advantageous than it now is, and prevent them from taking any arrangement with the British Government which they otherwise may do."[1]

Beginning in 1941, several studies have focused on the United States' diplomatic response to Haiti's independence during the first years after 1 January 1804. These studies provide a valuable point of departure for understanding the multiple and competing interests of diverse Americans who engaged with Haiti, including merchants like Jacob Lewis.[2] Based on the historical records of the U.S. Congress as well as diplomatic correspondence among American, British, and French representatives, these studies have emphasized how the United States contributed significantly to Haiti's diplomatic and political isolation in the years following the Haitian Declaration of Independence. Rather than welcoming a successor to its own recent initiative to break free from imperial ties, the United States officially oscillated between explicit and implicit policies that did not support Haiti's claim to follow in its footsteps. While recognizing to some extent that certain merchants, congressmen, newspaper editors, and other interested individuals supported Haiti's independence, researchers have emphasized the fact that the United States was the last Atlantic nation to recognize Haiti, doing so only in 1862.

At the same time, the established research on Haitian connections with the United States leaves significant questions unanswered or addressed in limited ways. If the United States is appropriately understood to be part of a larger official isolation of Haiti, why was trade only legislatively banned in 1806, two full years after the Haitian Declaration of Independence? And why was such trade approved again by 1810 despite the continued official policy of non-recognition? Moreover, and beyond formal positions, how did connections between Haiti and the United States evolve over the course of the first years of Haiti's independence? In order to address these questions, this chapter builds on the previous studies by first focusing on the crucial period between 1804 and 1806 before the U.S. Congress outlawed trade with Haiti and when American merchants like Jacob Lewis were actively and legally engaged in commerce with their Haitian counterparts. By examining specific examples of merchant activity, we can gain a better understanding of how and why this trade was so significant, as well as of the impact of its official banning in 1806. This background then leads to a focus on the robust debate that accompanied the legislative proposal to end trade between Haiti and the United States. In particular, the following analysis pays detailed attention to the substantial and sophisticated defense of American trade with Haiti, offered most compellingly by Senator Samuel White from Delaware in a speech that Senator John Quincy Adams called "one of the most powerful and beautiful speeches I have ever heard made in Congress."[3] This chapter then turns to the implications of the 1806 prohibition on trade by analyzing how the U.S. court system interpreted the link between economic ties and diplomatic non-recognition. Taken together, a detailed analysis of Haiti's interactions with the United States reveals the ongoing challenges of reconciling competing priorities of ideology, especially racialized identities and freedom, with economics, local and international law, and politics. The evidence highlights the complicated and layered process through which decisions were made as well as the fact that the outcomes did not always add up coherently. Rather than inspiring isolationism, Haitian independence launched a profound and unprecedented debate, just as evident in the United States as elsewhere in the Atlantic World.

United States–Haiti Trade

When Jacob Lewis wrote to Secretary of State James Madison, he reported that Haitian leaders anticipated that the French would successfully persuade the U.S. government to prohibit trade with Haiti. In contrast, Lewis emphasized that he remained convinced that the United States would not succumb to foreign pressure, for two reasons: the attractiveness of economic opportunities and concern about the safety and security of Americans and their property. "They [the Haitians] appear to be very ignorant of our strength and policy," he wrote to Madison, "and should they be taught to believe (*as they fear*) either by Circumstances, or British policy; they would at one blow take every american ship in their ports, which are in great number, great value and extraordinary well armed and manned generally with forty to one hundred men."[4]

For Madison, the letter from Lewis was only one part of a growing file of correspondence involving relationships between Haiti and the United States. Indeed, on the same day that he first made contact with Lieutenant-Governor George Nugent of Jamaica in June 1803, Jean-Jacques Dessalines had sent a similar letter to President Thomas Jefferson to advise him that American ships would find safety and profit in Saint Domingue's ports.[5] Jefferson had never responded to this letter, but clearly Lewis was implying that Madison should take Dessalines up on his offer. As Lewis's letter illustrates, American merchants began to pressure the U.S. government to establish some form of connection with the new Haitian government soon after the Declaration of Independence. In opposition to this trade, French representatives, as they did in St. Thomas and Curaçao, tried to convince American officials that Haiti was still a French colony, and, therefore by allowing trade, they were supporting a rebellious colony.

The efforts of both Haitian leaders and American merchants to promote trade after the Declaration of Independence built on a long history dating back into the eighteenth century during which American merchants from ports like Baltimore, Philadelphia, and New York visited the Caribbean regularly. Even during the Haitian Revolution, these merchants found economic opportunities in relationships with both the French forces as well as the rebel armies. As Toussaint Louverture consolidated his power in the French colony, the U.S. government and American merchants supported the increasing independence of Louverture's government from the French metropole. In 1799, with a Federalist majority, the U.S. Congress passed an amendment to a bill known as "Toussaint's Clause" that allowed American merchants to trade with Saint Domingue, despite a renewal of the embargo on trade with the French Empire.[6] While the U.S. government intended the bill to simply facilitate trade with Saint Domingue, historian Gordon Brown argues that "it would, in practice, allow the United States to take sides in a foreign civil war and encourage the colony's leaders to reach for independence."[7] The evacuation of the French troops in late 1803 did not cut off the trade networks established during the revolution, and merchants from the United States continued to visit Haitian ports to bring provisions and matériel in exchange for coffee, cotton, and mahogany. In the two years after the Haitian Declaration of Independence, American merchants were some of Haiti's most important trade partners.[8]

When Congress banned trade with Haiti in 1806, the prohibition interrupted the commercial activities of many U.S. merchants, but as the French agent in St. Thomas constantly complained, American merchants found ways to circumvent the new law and continued to trade with Haiti, by either lying on their papers about their destinations or sailing under different flags.[9] New Yorker Archibald Kane, in partnership with his brother's company, Elias Kane & Co., set up a trading house in St. Marc, Haiti, in the years after Haitian independence. Archibald Kane lived in Haiti on and off until his death in Port-au-Prince in 1817.[10] The records relating to Kane's time in Haiti are sparse, but a number of personal and business letters shed light on the economic benefits that American merchants enjoyed in Haiti after the Haitian Declaration of Independence while also revealing their close business relationships with the Haitian community and even Haitian leaders.[11] "The arguments made use of by His Majesty [Dessalines] and Minister with their Privy Council," Archibald Kane wrote from Haiti to his brother in February 1805, "convince me that even among the *blackest of Creation, Wisdom and Correctness of View* are to be found." "I never was more surprised," he continued; "I expected to treat with Men who knew little of Financing and Government, but I found Men who had been Educated in France, and who would be thought Brilliant Men in the United States."[12] The personal connections that these merchants established on the island present a significantly different picture from the often sensationalist representations of independent Haiti and the Haitian leaders that appeared in newspapers across the Atlantic. For example, less than a year before Kane wrote about his experiences in Haiti, the *National Intelligencer and Washington Advertiser* published an account of Dessalines's massacres that emphasize the racial characteristics of the killing. "After assassinating these unfortunate men," the newspaper reported, "they pillaged their houses, and threw their corpses into the sea. The following day the city was comparatively tranquil, but there is reason to suppose that the negroes will ultimately butcher all the French whites within their power."[13] Kane's experiences in Haiti offer a different picture of Dessalines and of the population as a whole. Moreover, his positive experiences and his appreciation for the expertise of the Haitian government had earned Kane respect in the Haitian political sphere. "At present no one in this Island stands better at *Court* than *I do*," Kane again wrote to his brother a few days later. "*His Midnight Majesty*, is really partial to me."[14]

Another merchant, William Ely, wrote from St. Marc to a business associate, J. Catling, in Litchfield, Connecticut, at the same time. He recounted the scene of a ball, thrown by the Haitian emperor and his wife. "I neither Dined or Danced with their *Majesties*," he reported, "the Americans here were all disappointed of that *Honor*, his Majesty being ill and continuing only one night in the place I had but a transient view of him." But the experience was not a complete disappointment. "[I had] a better one [view] of her [Madame Dessalines]," he wrote with great admiration, "as I had the honor of delivering a Letter *immediately* into her *fair hand*. She rec'd me in a Stile of easy Gentility peculiar to the French and those who have been long in the Habit of seeing and imitating their manners. She is a large genteel, sociable, affable, agreeable African, and drives a large Trade with the Americans to whom she is quite polite."[15] These merchants appear to have cultivated close and friendly relationships with Haitian leaders, and their letters intimate a high level of respect.

When Haiti divided in civil war in late 1806, however, the American merchants—who were more interested in financial gain than the internal politics of the country—inadvertently entangled themselves in the conflict by trading with different ports. While Jacob Lewis had been a strong proponent of supporting the trade with Haiti, he was subjected to Henry Christophe's public outrage because of his alleged affiliation with Alexandre Pétion in the South. "What confidence can you have in this fraudulent and broke adventurer named Lewis," Christophe announced in a proclamation published in the *Gazette Officielle de l'État d'Hayti*, on 13 August 1807, "who disgraced himself both by his bankruptcy in New York and by the harm he did to the Haitian government by sneaking out of the harbor of Port-au-Prince without paying the export costs."[16] Christophe also condemned Lewis's "collaborators," Kane and Windsor, because they had lent their ships to the "revolted" who were using them to propagate their cause in foreign countries. Christophe regretted that these few individuals were ruining the reputations of the honest American merchants in Haiti and sought to publicize their wrongdoings in order to emphasize the good work being done by the majority of the "respectable" ones.[17] Evidently, the relationship between the American merchant community and the Haitian government evolved over time as internal and foreign relations became increasingly complicated. It is noteworthy that Christophe published this proclamation and his condemnation of these merchants after the American prohibition on trade with Haiti, highlighting that the trade continued illegally.

In 1804, American merchants took advantage of the U.S. policy of tacitly permitting trade with Haiti, despite the objections launched by French government representatives. They set up trading houses in various port cities and received contracts from the Haitian government for supplies and money. When Archibald Kane and his brother Elias formed the New York West India Company, they saw Haiti as a good investment. Kane also argued that this economic venture was partly inspired by an ideological connection between the United States and Haiti. "The Contract for Supplying all the wants of Government for 5 Years," Archibald Kane reported to his other brother, James, with whom he owned a store in New York, "was made merely to convince the Gov[ernment] that the *New York West India Company* wished to embrace the Commerce of the Island. And that their Capital was equal to it." "I represented to the Government," he continued, "that the Spanish Minister had offered our Company immense advantage in the South America Business, but from the proximity of this Island to the United States, and a desire to lend a helping hand to the Establishment of the Independence of this Island, our Comp[any] was induced first to make them the offer."[18] According to Kane, he entered into a trade contract with the Haitian government because it was both profitable and morally just. Perhaps this was because he identified with Haitians as revolutionaries and as members of a sister republic. He might also have been anti-French.

The contract that Archibald Kane entered into was an agreement between the New York West India Company and the Haitian minister of finance, General André Vernet. On 24 January 1805, Kane submitted a letter to Vernet noting that "the Trading West India Compan'y propose purchasing from the Government of Haiti, all the *Coffee, Sugar, and Cotton* that they will have for Sale for *five Years* to commence from date of Contract, and to supply the Government with every Description of Articles, that they may require during the said term, and to be delivered at such City in the Island of Haiti as the Government shall say."[19] The contract, entered into on 4 February 1805, reveals that the merchants were well aware of the dangers in trading with Haiti since it outlined the ways that they were prepared to overcome these obstacles.[20] "The Company propose in order to Insure the regular Delivery of their Articles and Dollars, to have the Ships belonging to the 'Trading West India Company' Convoyed by two Armed Ships of 36 Guns each under such Colours as shall be deemed most prudent and proper."[21] The merchants of the West India Trading Company were prepared to militarily defend their voyages from New York to Haiti and were also prepared to evade legal constraints by changing the colors under which they were sailing. The practice was evidently so frequent that the governor of Jamaica noted that "the trade between America and St. Domingo is now carried on in well armed vessels mounting from 12 to 18 guns each and manned for the French Privateers from Cuba."[22]

The risks, however, were sure to be worth it, since "the undersigned wishes His Excellency General Vernett clearly to understand that the Convention contemplated by the 'Trading West India Company' is Bottom'd on the principle of the Governments allowing them the exclusive privilege of Supplying all the wants of the Government of Haiti, and receiving the whole of the Sugars, Coffee and Cotton, and the said Company will be bound on their part not to purchase or trade with any Individuals of the Island of Haiti during the continuance of the said Convention."[23] Archibald Kane was clearly concerned with the exclusivity of the agreement because so many others had ventured to the island for economic opportunity. "The Island is over run with Americans and the Ports are crowded with American Vessels," Archibald reported to his brother James; "trade is now very Dull and some Voyages will sink heavy Sums."[24] Production levels in Haiti had dropped significantly over the course of the war for independence (1802–3), and it appears as though Haitian exporters were not able to match the demand. The contract that he had entered into with the Haitian minister of finance, however, provided a guarantee that this would not be the case on the voyages taken by his ships, since the West India Company would have exclusive trading rights with the government.

One of the primary arguments for the U.S. government's decision to continue trade with Haiti during 1804 and 1805 was the balance of power in Europe. If this trade ceased, then the British would have a virtual monopoly on the Haitian market, which would then fully support France's enemies. Perhaps more important, however, was the issue of piracy or privateering and the arming of merchant vessels. The French, unable to mobilize a force large enough to attack Haiti, began attacking American vessels that supplied Dessalines's army with provisions and matériel.[25] After Haitian independence, the conflicts between French and Spanish privateers and American merchants in the Caribbean amounted to unofficial war. Within this context, the issue of trade in articles considered contraband of war (that is, arms or ammunition) was central to the debate surrounding the arming of merchant vessels and their legal capture by foreign privateers. The possibility that the arms on board American merchant ships would be sold to the Haitian government made the arming of merchants' vessels the central point of contention in the U.S. Congress in the first year after Haitian independence. The trade as a whole, however, was not under discussion, and U.S. Secretary of State James Madison had argued in 1804 that American merchants could legally trade non-contraband items with ports that were not under blockade, since Haiti was de facto independent from France.[26] Again, the distinction between independence on paper versus independence in practice came into play. In this case, French paper—their continued claim to legal title over Haiti—was seen to be worth more than Haitian paper—the official Haitian Declaration of Independence.

During the first year after the Haitian Declaration of Independence, the U.S. government did not challenge the ongoing trade between the United States and Haiti, although U.S. leaders were conscious of the tension that this merchant activity created between their government and that of France. French representatives in the United States, as they had done in Dutch Curaçao and Danish St. Thomas, considered all neutral trade with Haiti to be a breach of a country's neutrality and tried to convince the U.S. government to initiate official prohibitions on the trade. One British representative, Anthony Merry, the minister to the United States, also exerted pressure on the U.S. government to prohibit the trade and sought to create an alliance in isolating Haiti, despite the fact that other members of his government in Kingston and in London were in the process of figuring out how to capitalize on the trade opportunities.[27] This approach differed significantly from that undertaken by Governor Nugent of Jamaica in 1804, and it suggests that officials of the British Empire from different administrative offices viewed the situation in Haiti with contradictory interests and goals. Each had particular local concerns and each had a degree of independence in the decision-making process. The evidence reveals that the U.S. government assumed that British policy was supportive of Haitian independence, in line with Governor Nugent in Jamaica, rather than following the goal of isolation that Merry proposed, and therefore U.S. officials did not seek to create an international alliance against Haiti, as France would obviously have welcomed. Neither the British nor the Americans attempted to forge such an alliance while the United States remained wary of French pressure on its policy making.

International politicking and diplomacy clearly affected how foreign governments reacted to news of Haitian independence. The United States was not willing to go to war with France in order to support Haitian independence.[28] During the Napoleonic Wars, American neutrality limited the ability to form relationships with Haiti, and for this reason, the government was willing to negotiate with the French representative in the United States, French Chargé d'Affaires Louis André Pichon. The first proposal that Secretary of State Madison offered was an agreement that American merchants would be prohibited from carrying articles considered contraband of war, a stipulation already agreed upon under the common practices of the law of nations for relationships between neutral and belligerent nations.[29] If Madison considered Haiti to be a belligerent nation, this concession would have already been implied by the traditions of international law, and so the fact that Haiti required a special agreement highlights the ambiguity of the country's status on the international stage. Madison's concession, however, might have also been used to signal that he did indeed consider Haiti to be a belligerent and was simply explicitly including Haiti in the existing law. The French representatives did not interpret Madison's actions to signal any kind of concession—they expected him to go beyond the established practices between neutral and belligerent nations.

Not surprisingly, the French continued to pressure the U.S. government to find an alternative. Madison agreed, since the conflict between French privateers and American merchants was affecting all of the United States' Caribbean trade.[30] The ambiguity of Haiti's international status allowed navy ships and privateers to capture any ships in the Caribbean that they suspected—or claimed to suspect—of trading with Haiti. From the American perspective, the problem was rampant privateering in the Caribbean. From the French perspective, France "could not tolerate this kind of 'private war' that American citizens were waging against France" by allowing merchants to trade in armed vessels.[31]

The U.S. government initially attempted to find a solution within the established law of nations and was willing to treat Haiti as it would any other newly independent country. Pichon, however, argued that the United States could not possibly trade with Haiti under the customary practices of international law since Haitian independence presented a unique situation; the existing labor regimes and socio-racial hierarchies in the Americas were at the heart of the discussion. "The United States could not place herself on a level with Negroes," Pichon told Madison; "their position required that the United States as well as all other powers recognize a difference in the application of the law of nations according to the difference in persons and places."[32] Even if trade with Haiti fell within the parameters of typical interactions between nations, Pichon argued that this case had to be considered special. He claimed that the fact that slavery existed in the United States demonstrated that "negroes" should be considered under a different set of laws.

The U.S. government did indeed consider this a special case, since its decision to appease the French was also influenced by its desire for French support in the United States' acquisition of the Floridas.[33] This land acquisition, completed in 1821, was more valuable to the United States than trade with Haiti, and President Thomas Jefferson calculated that the Spanish would only relinquish the Floridas if the French used their alliance to secure the transfer.[34] Historian Tim Matthewson also attributes the change in American policy to the massacres initiated by Dessalines in April 1804.[35] It is conceivable that both of these reasons inspired Jefferson to initiate the change in U.S. policy toward Haiti since both land acquisition and the fear of the spread of the Haitian Revolution were influential factors in American policy making.

Armed Merchant Vessels

Haiti's ambiguous status continued to pose problems both within the United States and between U.S. officials and French representatives in the country. American merchants continued to visit Haiti, but their voyages became risky because of the rampant privateering that the French and Spanish focused on this trade after the Declaration of Independence. Furthermore, as they had been in Curaçao and St. Thomas, French officials were relentless in their efforts to convince the U.S. government to prohibit the trade. The initial problem-solving efforts in the U.S. government focused on the "unofficial war" being waged in the Caribbean. The issue was the fact that American merchants were arming their vessels like warships. The arming of merchant vessels was "common practice," but the specificity of the trade relationship involving a rebel colony of former slaves and the nature of the goods exported to Haiti (war matériel) meant that southern slaveholders opposed the practice.[36] Governor Nugent in Jamaica encountered similar opposition in Jamaica, but he remained convinced that a friendly relationship with Haiti would prevent the spread of the revolution. The U.S. government, however, could not act on this concern immediately since there was no law forbidding the arming of merchant vessels. The French would have to wait until Congress could pass such a law.[37]

At the beginning of the 8th session of Congress, on 8 November 1804, President Thomas Jefferson made it clear to the members of Congress that they had to take action in order to stop the unofficial war in the Caribbean. He noted an increase in illicit behavior on the high seas by foreign ships, including unacceptable actions by American merchants. "While noticing the irregularities on the ocean by others," he stated, "those on our own part should not be omitted, nor left unprovided for. Complaints have been received that persons, residing within the United States, have taken on themselves to arm merchant vessels, and to force a commerce into certain ports and countries, in defiance of the laws of those countries." This statement implies that Jefferson still recognized French control over Haiti since he assumed that French law applied to the island. "That individuals should undertake to wage private war, independently of the authority of their country," he concluded, "cannot be permitted in a well ordered society."

Just four days after this address, the House of Representatives created a committee to find a solution to the problem of Haiti's status, especially the legality of trade with the new country. On 23 November 1804, the committee read a proposed bill for the first and second times; the bill did not actually prohibit merchants from arming themselves or from trading with Haiti. Rather, the bill simply stipulated that the owners of armed vessels would have to post bond with two sufficient sureties in the sum of double the value of the vessel on the condition "that such vessel shall not make or commit any depredation, outrage, unlawful assault, or violence, against the vessels, citizens, subjects, or territory of any nation in amity with the United States." France was not at war with the United States, and therefore the bill implicitly prohibited trade with Haiti, since the trade might be considered an "outrage" against France. The proposed bill received a mixed response from the House. One representative clearly took issue with this regulation. "What! Shall it be permitted to every man," Representative John W. Eppes from Virginia argued, "who can execute a bond, to wield the arms of the nation?" Indeed, opponents of the bill challenged it on the grounds that it promoted criminal activity for those who could afford it. Financial wealth provided the means for merchants to continue this trade and the unofficial war. Eppes, therefore, "thought the bill [was] founded on erroneous principles. Instead of permitting our merchantmen to arm and afterwards punishing them for the abuse of those arms, he conceived it would be infinitely more prudent and politic to restrain them altogether from arming."[38] This proposed amendment would leave no doubt as to the good faith with which the U.S. government was implementing this new law.

Similarly, Representative Thomas Lowndes of South Carolina acknowledged the halfway measure of the proposed bill. He argued that the bill postponed making a decision regarding trade with Haiti and only partially conceded to French pressure. "[I] should think it the best and fairest mode of proceeding," he argued, "either to declare the trade to St. Domingo to be a lawful trade, and in that case protect commerce by a public force, or suffer the private shipping to defend themselves. Or say, that the trade to that island is unlawful, and interdict it at once, and altogether."[39] His argument highlights that he assumed that Jefferson had implied the latter in his message to Congress, and so he concluded that this bill did not provide an adequate solution to the problem because it did not actually prohibit the trade.

Others members of the House, however, opposed the bill because it interfered with American economic interests. If merchants could not arm their vessels, Representative William Eustis of Massachusetts argued, it "would be to deprive them of the capacity of trading to St. Domingo—not to St. Domingo alone, but to Cuba, and many other of the West India islands, as well as the Spanish Main." This, he argued, would severely impede U.S. commercial interests. "The interdiction of the trade," he claimed, "would be followed by a loss to this country, which existing circumstance did not call upon us to make."[40] In his opinion, the current debate in the House jumped the gun; why should the American government take the initiative to ban this trade?

Another opponent of the bill declared that any decision taken by the U.S. government would not have the ability to change the entire system of trade in the Atlantic and in the Caribbean and therefore the measure was pointless. "Were America to suspend her intercourse with St. Domingo," Representative Joseph Clay of Pennsylvania argued, "the evil of having the present inhabitants for our neighbors would not be lessened." Haiti, he concluded, would continue to thrive as an independent nation, "for, whilst the rich productions of that island are in such universal demand, they will find their way to market, and their want of military stores or contraband of war will be equally supplied to them, not by Americans, but by British vessels, from the Danish or other neutral islands; the trade will continue, and either neutral or belligerent nations will reap the benefit."[41] In 1805, only the Dutch government had outlawed trade with Haiti, but the trade continued illegally. Indeed, American, British, Danish, and Dutch merchants sought to capitalize on Haiti's independence, and Clay did not anticipate that an American prohibition on trade would induce them to stop. Merchants had devised strategies for circumventing the laws implemented by their own governments as well as by others, including sailing under different flags and misrepresenting their destinations when they cleared out from port. From Clay's perspective, the measure prohibiting merchant vessels from arming themselves would not achieve the desired result, and he wondered why the United States should lose out on the lucrative trade.

The most vocal contributors to the discussion about the bill to prohibit the arming of merchant vessels argued that the bill either did not go far enough in prohibiting the trade with Haiti—as they interpreted President Jefferson's message to Congress to require—or that the bill went too far in restricting merchants' rights. Representative John Lucas of Pennsylvania concluded that the bill did not have much to do with trade with Haiti at all. "He [Lucas] thought the object of the bill was not so much to preclude the continuation of the trade to St. Domingo," the records report, "as to give a kind of half-way satisfaction to France in excuse for the iniquity of that trade, as it had for some time past been carried on."[42] French representatives in the United States had actively tried to convince the government to prohibit the trade with Haiti, and the members of Congress were well aware of the pressure that they exerted on their government.

The Federalists were outnumbered in Congress, but the popular press was particularly vocal on the topic of trade with Haiti. "The black people of Hayti," reported Boston's *Columbian Centinel*, "having solemnly declared themselves a sovereign, free and independent nation, having adopted a constitution, and having by their strength and valor demonstrated their power to maintain their Independence, ought to be considered and treated by neutral nations, as an Independent State." The newspaper article then connected Haiti's independence struggle to the American Revolution: "Their condition is not dissimilar to that of the people of the United States in 1778."[43] Despite the emphasis on the moral obligation of the U.S. government, the newspaper also made sure to emphasize the economic benefits of continuing the trade with Haiti.

In the end, the bill passed in the House of Representatives by a vote of seventy-seven to thirty-three and was sent to the Senate for concurrence. In the middle of the two-month Senate discussion of the bill, Senator George Logan of Pennsylvania asked permission to bring forward a bill "to suspend trade and intercourse with the island of St. Domingo." At this point in time, however, the members of the Senate were not willing to expand the restrictions outlined in the current bill, and Logan was not given leave to even propose a new bill.[44] In 1805, it seems, it was out of the question to ban all U.S. trade with Haiti. After the Senate had signed the bill regulating the arming of merchant vessels, however, Logan was able to garner support in a protest vote against the decision. Despite the fact that the initial bill had passed by a vote of twenty to eight, the protest vote ended in a tie; Vice President Aaron Burr's vote defeated the protest.[45]

At some point during the debates in Congress, the Chamber of Commerce of Philadelphia presented a memoire in opposition to the passage of the bill, and an excerpt of the memoire was published in the *Gazette Politique et Commerciale d'Haïti* in March 1805. Thomas Fitzsimons, the president of the Chamber, argued that immediately after the evacuation of the French from Saint Domingue, French privateers, operating out of the eastern side of Hispaniola and Cuba, "were constantly harassing our commerce, and even capturing our ships, even though they are employed in a normal and legal trade."[46] If Americans were not allowed to arm their vessels on commercial voyages to Haiti, Fitzsimons argued, then the Haitians could not receive the supplies that they needed and they would be forced to acquire and arm their own merchant vessels—they would then become the "Algerians of our hemisphere."[47] The *Gazette* reported that it regretted to inform its readers that the protest on the part of the Chamber of Commerce had not been successful.

The Act to Regulate the Clearance of Armed Merchant Vessels passed in the Senate, and President Jefferson signed the bill into law on 3 March 1805. Historian Rayford Logan's analysis of this bill suggests that the sole reason for its passing was pressure from French and British agents. Evidently, the British agent had more influence than Madison's earlier reaction suggested.[48] The law did not in fact prohibit merchants from sailing in armed vessels, since it simply limited this traffic to individuals who could afford to post the guarantee. Furthermore, merchants only had to declare that they would not sell any armaments on board the ship to the Haitian government. Finally, unarmed merchant vessels were free to continue trading with Haiti, although this would have been a risky venture since French and Spanish privateers would have been waiting to capture them. This solution to the problem, however, did not last long.

Prohibiting Trade with "St. Domingo"

On 26 June 1805, the *Albany Register* published an account of a celebration on a ship in the harbor of New York. "Yesterday an elegant dinner [was] given on board the *Indostan*, by Capt. [Jacob] Lewis, Samuel G. Ogden, and Washington Morton, Esq. to a select party of one hundred of the most respectable characters in this city."[49] This report did not describe the reason for the gathering, but additional details were given in the newspaper coverage from other cities. On 4 July 1805, the *City Gazette and Daily Advertiser* of Charleston, South Carolina, published news of the event that it had received from Boston. "Now let us enquire what was the intention of this nautical gala," the writer for the *City Gazette* asked; "we answer, with sorrow and surprise, that it was, according to the evidence and circumstances, a display of mischievous resistance to the wise decrees of the Executive Authority, in regard to the forbidden trade with the brigands of St. Domingo."[50] Indeed the *Aurora General Advertiser* (Philadelphia) expanded on this information and noted that Rufus King, a Federalist vice presidential candidate, who was on board the ship, toasted "the government of Hayti, founded on the only legitimate basis of all authority: the *people's choice!* May it be as durable as its principles are pure!"[51]

This public banquet renewed French fury at the ongoing trade between the United States and Haiti and inspired the resumption of the debate in the Senate in late 1805. Senator George Logan of Pennsylvania made another motion to present a bill interdicting all trade between the United States and Haiti. The *Gazette Politique et Commerciale d'Haïti* printed news of Logan's proposed bill, but the news received no further comment.[52]

The motion received considerable resistance. Despite the fact that Congress was strongly Republican, some northern Republicans sided with their Federalist opponents since their interests focused on maritime trade. At the same time, however, "the perennial debate over slavery, which was becoming more acute as a result of the revolution in Haiti, the cotton boom, and the impending ban on slave imports, also divided the party."[53]

The hesitancy of Congress to pass a bill that completely prohibited the trade the first time around was proof that this trade was too valuable to sacrifice simply because of complaints lodged by foreign agents. "Its purpose is totally to prohibit a branch of our commerce," Senator John Quincy Adams of Massachusetts argued, "which at the last session of the Legislature was proved to be of great importance to the country."[54] Why, therefore, would the U.S. government again take the initiative to cut off a lucrative branch of trade? "How great will be the surprise," Senator James Hillhouse of Connecticut agreed on 20 December 1805, "if the first step taken by the Senate of the United States is found to be a further restriction, or a total prohibition, of a lawful and lucrative branch of our commerce." Hillhouse then argued that the United States should go on the offensive and aggressively protect the trade with Haiti. "A more proper and dignified course he thought would be to send armed ships into those seas, to capture or demolish those bucaniers [sic] and pirates, who rob us of our property, and insult and murder our citizens." The French and Spanish privateers were the problem, and they had instigated the unofficial war in the Caribbean. "Virtually everyone involved in the legislation," Gordon Brown argues, "realized that it offered too many loopholes to be able to stop the armed trade. And even if it had done so, the French persisted in considering the entire trade with the rebels, armed or not, contraband or not, an unfriendly and perhaps even illegal practice."[55]

Other senators made protests based on resistance to foreign pressure. Regardless of the issue, the senators did not like the idea that the U.S. government would base its foreign policy on the demands of another government. Given the recent American war for independence, it would seem counterproductive to then start taking orders from other foreign governments. Senator Samuel L. Mitchill from New York instead claimed that the United States should not be expected to comply in any degree with the demands made by the French chargé d'affaire. "I am very far from approving the means by which it [the trade with Haiti] has been carried on; but I dislike the idea of forbidding it, at the mandate of a foreign Power. Like our Revolutionary patriots, let us put our foot here, and hence refuse to budge. It is not for us to legislate at the nod or bidding of any nation."[56] Mitchill's opposition to the bill may have been influenced by the fact that some of his constituents were heavily involved in the arms trade with Haiti.[57] The issue of bowing to foreign pressure also had economic motives.

Logan presented letters from Merry and Pichon and argued that according to these documents the measure adopted on 5 March 1805 was not sufficient. The foreign agents continued to be dissatisfied with the U.S. government's response to Haiti's independence. The protesters, however, noted that this evidence was not new and that Jefferson had signed the previous bill that was based on the same criticism. They had no reason to suppose, therefore, that the British and the French were not satisfied with the legislation enacted during the previous session involving the regulation of armed merchant vessels. Because of this opposition, Logan made another motion to ask Jefferson to give the Senate copies of all documentation in his possession relating to French complaints against American commerce to Haiti. The motion passed, and on 10 January 1806, the members of the Senate were able to see the continued objections launched by the French government.

The evidence that Jefferson submitted was sufficient to convince the Senate to allow Logan to move forward with the new bill to prohibit all trade between the United States and Haiti. Logan was given leave to bring in the bill, and it was read for the first time on 15 January 1806. The arguments in this debate mirror the debate in the House during the previous session of Congress. "The United States, by affording them succor, arms, ammunition, and provisions," argued Senator James Jackson of Georgia on 20 December 1805, "must be considered by them as their allies—their supporters and their protectors." This support, he continued, could have a disastrous impact on the American South: "This was a melancholy subject for South Carolina and Georgia, and one of those brigands introduced into the Southern States was worse than an hundred importations of blacks from Africa, and more dangerous to the United States." Just as Governor Nugent of Jamaica had been wary of the dangers that economic relationship might facilitate, Jackson also knew that economic partnerships meant the movement of people and ideas. Both white and nonwhite former residents of Saint Domingue had been arriving in the United States throughout the Haitian Revolution. The nonwhite and enslaved émigrés from the French colony made southern slaveholders extremely nervous, and they worried that the new residents would organize or inspire similar rebellions or revolutions in the United States.[58]

Senator Samuel White's Speech

The bill (with amendments) passed in the Senate by a vote of twenty-one to eight. Out of the eight voters who opposed the bill, one particularly vocal senator made a lengthy speech in Congress, and this speech deserves special attention for what it reveals about the character of political debate during this crucial period.[59] Samuel White was a lawyer from a plantation close to Whiteleysburg in central Delaware but moved to Williamsburg while in public life.[60] As a Federalist politician, he served as state senator from Delaware from 1801 until his death in 1809. White's father manumitted his twenty-one slaves in his will and declared, "I think it wrong and oppressive and not doing as I would be willing to be done by, to keep negroes in bondage or perpetual slavery."[61] Between 1799 and 1804, White also manumitted four slaves. In the Senate, in addition to voicing his strong opinions against the prohibition on trade with Haiti, White had also vocally opposed the Louisiana Purchase in 1803 and American expansionism more generally.[62]

White's lengthy speech argued that Senator Logan's bill should not pass, and to support this claim he referenced the work of legal theorists, public proclamations, and treaties. This intellectual and emotional case for the continuation of trade with Haiti deserves special attention because it supported the independent economic interests of American merchants and investors. In a debate about the law of nations, White highlighted the implications that economic policy could have on international warfare and argued that merchant activity should remain neutral. Furthermore, he argued that independent American investment should not be sacrificed to the dictates of foreign governments.

In this speech, White drew on legal scholarship and past treaties, in an appeal to American identity designed to convince the other senators that prohibiting trade with Haiti was contradictory to the common practices of the law of nations. From this perspective, any further action would only show a willingness for the U.S. government to bend to foreign will, setting a very bad precedent. White's keen knowledge of the customs of international law and his emotional rejections of French-dictated policy offer a striking and lucid analysis of the situation. His speech articulated a sophisticated examination of what he thought should have been the United States' course of action with respect to Haiti according to the common practices of the law of nations and the best interests of the country, and it highlighted the silences on the part of the bill's supporters. White strategically drew on theories of international law, and his speech illustrates the ways that the law of nations could be used to serve different interests. His denunciation was not matched or refuted, and yet the bill passed in the Senate and was sent to the House of Representatives for concurrence before it received Jefferson's signature. It was clear that Congress considered Haiti to be a special case and that it was willing to make an exception in order to appease the French and accommodate the demands of American slaveholders.

White addressed his speech to the president and asked him to fully consider the implications of the bill. His strategy was twofold. First, White argued that prohibiting trade with Haiti was contrary to the law of nations, and, second, that folding under French pressure was against American policy and identity. To set up these two arguments, White cited proclamations, letters, and rumored stories to argue that the French abolition of slavery was legal and was not done under constrained circumstances. "I cite these papers to shew that the French have now no claim, either in right, in justice, or in law, to any portion of the people of St. Domingo, as slaves . . . in order to rebut a fallacious idea that has been taken up, and urged by some that our merchants are conducting this commerce with slaves, the property of freemen, and not with freemen themselves." This false claim, he argued, was intended to set Haiti apart, "thus ingeniously endeavoring to draw a distinction between the situation of St. Domingo and that of any other colony that has ever heretofore attempted to separate itself from the mother country."[63] Because the people of Haiti were free men, he argued that "their case does form a distinction from any other, and in this it consists—the people of St. Domingo are fighting to preserve not only their independence as a community, but their liberty as individuals."[64] Because the people of Haiti were free men, White concluded, their country should be considered within the laws that govern interactions between other nations.

The status of Haitians as free men also had implications for the type of war that they were waging against France. White argued that the battle between Haiti and France was not a "rebellion" but instead a "civil war."

He cited the Swiss philosopher and diplomat Emer de Vattel in support of this argument. "Custom appropriates the term of civil war," White read from Vattel's writings, "to every war between the members of one and the same political society. If it be between part of the citizens on the one side, and the sovereign, with those who continue in obedience to him, on the other; provided the malcontents have any reason for taking up arms nothing further is required to entitle such disturbance to the name of civil war, and not that of rebellion."[65] Did the people of Haiti have good reason for taking up arms? White emphatically argued yes. "I will submit with confidence to the high and honorable feelings of this Senate," he declared, "whether the human mind is capable of conceiving a stronger reason to induce a people to take up arms, than to resist those whose known object it is to reduce them not only to political, but to personal slavery."[66] The just cause for resistance launched by free citizens of the French Empire, White concluded, categorized the conflict as civil war. While he was not willing to concede that Haiti was independent, he prioritized the conflict with France in interpreting the island's status.

Once he established that the conflict should be considered a civil war, White argued that in such scenarios neutral nations were to treat both parties equally; prohibiting trade with either side would affect the balance of power so as to make the United States active in the war rather than neutral. White argued that it was not the place of foreign nations to decide which party should win the civil war. "And now let me ask," he posited, "if the United States, or any other power upon earth, is competent to decide this great controversy between them?"[67] His own answer was that they were not. A civil war was not the business of the international community. "It is exclusively an affair of their own," he concluded, "and it behoves the rest of the world to stand aloof, the silent and impartial spectators of the conflict, treating in their commercial relations each of the parties with like civility."[68] The present bill would force the United States to take sides in the conflict. "It is a neutral's withholding from one of the parties," White proclaimed, "what she grants to the other."[69] Prohibiting trade with Haiti would help France's effort to reclaim possession of their lost colony; as a result, the United States would not be neutral in the conflict.

"From all these cases, Mr. President," White summarized, "I am well warranted in the following deductions: 1st. That when the bands of government among a people, by means of civil war, become broken, or for a time suspended, the two parties are to be considered, at least during the contest, as two distinct powers, as two independent nations who, being otherwise unable to settle their disputes, make a solemn appeal to arms." This vague statement provided some space for U.S. recognition of Haitian independence, but in this scenario trade with the island did not require diplomatic recognition. White's second conclusion expanded this provision but maintained that the island's new status might be temporary: "That a revolted colony or province, whilst holding and exercising the rights of sovereignty, is to be treated by neutral nations as an independent people, without regarding the legality or illegality of their claim to such independence." Independence in practice, White argued, meant "that in the disputes of such belligerents, neutrals have no right to interfere, either commercially or otherwise, to the injury of either"[70] Because of these claims, White argued that the United States could not in good conscience prohibit the trade.

White declared that the French themselves had proved the obligation of neutral nations to trade with both parties of a civil war just three decades prior. "After these colonies had revolted against the authority of Great Britain," he claimed, "France continued uninterruptedly her commerce with them, other than such as was contraband."[71] Why now, White asked, when it was the French who were under fire, should the law of nations be thrown out? "It clearly appears France then considered herself as not only having a right to trade, but publicly to enter into a commercial treaty with the revolted colonies of Great Britain, upon the ground that they were, for the time at least, holding and exercising the rights of independence."[72] There is an important reference to the temporary nature of Haiti's independence in this quotation. Indeed, Rayford Logan notes an important distinction in White's lengthy speech: "Even he, however, did not demand that the United States recognize the independence of Haiti, although he asserted that she was *de facto* independent."[73] "Holding and exercising the rights of independence" did not, according to White, necessarily mean that Haiti was independent.

White argued that prohibiting trade between the United States and Haiti would only show a willingness to accommodate the wishes of a few—and from his perspective, delusional—French authorities in the Americas. In this second argument, he focused on the attempts by the French general Jean-Louis Ferrand in the city of Santo Domingo to prohibit this trade. "General Ferrand[,] shut up in the city of St. Domingo," he mocked, "with scarcely the power of conveying his proclamation beyond the redoubts of his garrison, undertakes to prescribe, to all the neutral nations of the earth, the extent of their rights, and the manner in which they shall conduct their commerce."[74] Ferrand was waging a "war of proclamations," and White challenged the Senate to resist conforming to these outrageous demands. "As if the navigation, the commerce, and all the rights of neutral nations depended now, upon the caprice of a French officer, and were, like the police of a camp, to be settled by general orders."[75] In thinking about the proclamations issued by Ferrand that declared trade with Haiti illegal for all and condemned those who dared continue the trade to death, White dismissed the laws as madness. "Sir, I can liken this proclamation," he derided, "to nothing but the idle vapourings of a fettered maniac, menacing, from the grates of his cell, the overthrow of the world."[76]

Finally, White suggested that a decision to pass the bill would jeopardize the security of the United States. Taking sides with the French and breaking American neutrality would open the door for the Haitians to declare war on the United States—an event that White acknowledged would be within their rights. White warned the southern senators that they should be particularly wary of such repercussions. "Only restrict or embarrass your commerce with them; only pass a measure like the present, and you wound them in the tenderest part: they will see you, without provocation, aiming a blow at their very vitals; and will consider you as having abandoned your neutral ground, and sided with their enemies."[77] The real threat for the South would not be ignited by friendly commercial relationships. Instead, White argued that it was through a withholding of the natural rights owed to the island: "Those people are now content to stay home, to till their own fields, to fight their own battles, and to depend upon us for supplies." Indeed, many Haitian proclamations reinforced this conclusion. "I do not wish to see their views extend further," White continued, "I do not wish to see them navigating the ocean, or tasting the sweets of maritime plunder."[78]

White's speech in the Senate did not attract a rebuttal. The bill passed by a vote of twenty-one to eight and was sent to the House for concurrence.[79] Members of the House debated the length of time stipulated in the bill (one year) and the punishments to be meted out to violators. The discussion was brief, however, in keeping with a sense of urgency. Representatives William Ely of Massachusetts and John Smilie of Pennsylvania concluded the debates with the two opposing arguments. "Have the Haytians no rights?" asked Ely, "If they were once subjects of a Government that can no longer hold them, has that nation any right to call on us to starve them out; to starve these people into subjection to that Power?" Smilie countered: "I deny that the inhabitants of St. Domingo are a nation. Has the United States, or any other nation acknowledged them so? No. How, then, are they to be considered other than part of France?" The bill was supported by a vote of ninety-three to twenty-six, thereby securing its passing.

Just as in early 1805, the evidence makes clear that foreign agents influenced the decision to prohibit trade with Haiti.[80] Despite the best efforts of Senator White and others, the prohibition was not based on the common understandings of the law of nations but instead on strategic politicking and fear. Even Secretary of State James Madison acknowledged the unusual nature of the bill. "Madison admitted this interpretation in a letter of 15 March 1806, to Armstrong," historian Rayford Logan reports, "in which he declared that the law went 'beyond the obligations of the United States under the law of nations; but the measure was deemed expedient for the present and the eventual welfare of the United States.'"[81] This statement shows that the law of nations acted as optional guidelines rather than compulsory rules, especially when they conflicted with immediate political or strategic priorities. The research of Tim Matthewson led him to the claim that "it arose from the triumph of racism occasioned by Saint Domingue-Haiti and the Southern belief that they were seriously menaced by slave insurrection."[82]

Congress renewed the 28 February 1806 bill the following year for a term lasting until the 10th session of Congress (October 1807 to April 1808).[83] But such legislating masks the extent to which American merchants continued to focus on trade relations with Haiti. This ongoing interest is illustrated by the case of the American-owned *Manilla*, which cleared out from Nantucket, Massachusetts, on 7 March 1807, just one week after the planned expiry date of the bill prohibiting trade.[84] Congress had passed an act renewing the bill on 24 February 1807, but the agents for the *Manilla* claimed that news of the renewal of the bill had not yet reached Nantucket before it raised anchor and set sail for Gonaïves, Haiti. These merchants were clearly aware of the changing laws of the United States with respect to Haiti, and they seized the opportunity to engage in trade on the day when the bill was expected to have expired. When the ship arrived in the harbor at Port-au-Prince, the captain waited, because news had arrived that the collector of the port of Nantucket had "noted his intention to seize the vessel and cargo, on her return from the voyage, for the purpose of having them condemned, as forfeited for infraction of the last mentioned act of 24th February, 1807."[85] In response, the agents for the *Manilla* applied to Congress for relief, which they received without difficulty; their knowledge of the system had allowed them to successfully plead their case.

At the end of the renewed bill, the declining support for the policy was reflected in the decision by Congress to end the prohibition on trade with Haiti on 26 April 1808. This change of policy may have been due to the increase in Federalist representation and a reactionary move against the pro-French policy of the administration.[86] The expiration of the bill prohibiting trade with Haiti reopened the trade to American merchants. In 1809, Representative Edward Livermore of Massachusetts proposed a bill that explicitly reopened the trade with Haiti, but the bill received no support.[87] There appears to have been a clear distinction between permitting trade implicitly and explicitly condoning and regulating the trade. Perhaps the members of Congress knew about the diplomatic implications that the British trade licenses had had in the British Admiralty Court system.

In his seminal work, Rayford Logan concluded that although trade with Haiti became legal after 1808, few American merchants took advantage of it. Tim Matthewson has subsequently argued, in contrast, that a general embargo and "similar prohibitions on commerce" continued to make trade with Haiti illegal until 1810. In order to resolve this question, we can turn to a series of court cases in the United States that provide substantial evidence about the extent to which the general embargoes did prohibit trade with Haiti.

Is "St. Domingo" Still French?

In August 1806, the American ship *General Pinkney* cleared out from Alexandria, Virginia, for a voyage to St. Jago de Cuba (Santiago). The ship did not follow the planned route and instead sailed for Cap Haïtien (formerly Cap Français). The ship was seized on 17 November 1806 on its return voyage. The *General Pinkney* was condemned in the District Court of Maryland, and the ruling was confirmed by the Circuit Court. The claimants appealed the decision to the Supreme Court, and the case was heard in February 1808. According to the 28 February 1806 law signed by Jefferson, the ship was liable for confiscation (and indeed that is why the ship had been seized). By the time the claimants appealed the decision to the Supreme Court, however, the law justifying the ship's condemnation had expired. Supreme Court judge John Marshall delivered the opinion of the Court and argued that the ship could not be condemned "under a law not in force at the time of pronouncing such sentence."[88] The ship, therefore, could not be condemned as good prize. The result was that the expiration of these laws in the United States signaled an opening of the trade with Haiti. The abandonment of the 1806 law prohibiting trade in combination with the sentencing of the *General Pinkney* clearly legalized trade with Haiti.[89]

The case of the ship *Helen* provides another example of the keen awareness of merchants and sailors from the United States about these issues. The ship was seized in September 1808 after the act prohibiting trade had expired. The records report that the judge concluded that "a vessel having violated a law of the United States, cannot be seized for such violation, after the law has expired. Unless some special provision be made therefore by statute."[90] The law specifically prohibiting trade with Haiti had expired, and therefore the courts interpreted that trade to be legal. What is interesting, however, is that the Supreme Court issued the rulings for the *General Pinkney* and the *Helen* during the time of the Embargo Act. On 22 December 1807, Congress had prohibited trade between the United States and foreign nations. The fact that the Supreme Court rulings freed the *General Pinkney* and the *Helen* reveals the inconsistencies with respect to foreign trade.

The rulings for the *General Pinkney* and the *Helen* and the expiration of the law prohibiting trade between the United States and Haiti might have ushered in a new era of trade between the two countries; however, a new law that specifically prohibited trade with the French and British Empires had a different impact on American court rulings. The new law did not explicitly prohibit trade with Haiti, but the courts interpreted this law with consideration for the 1806 prohibition and assumed some diplomatic intention in the previous economic policy. In 1809, the Non-Intercourse Act replaced the Embargo Act and modified the restrictions to British and French ports. This new law, signed on 1 March 1809, prohibited the importation of goods "from any port or place situated in France, or in any of her colonies or dependencies."[91] While the 1806 law stated specifically that trade with Haiti was illegal, this new legislation left unanswered the question as to whether Haiti was included under this prohibition.

The case of *Clark v. The United States* presented the opportunity for this question to be tested. "The question is, whether the island of St. Domingo, in October 1809, when the importation charged in this information was made, was a colony or dependence of France, or not?"[92] This case involved the American ships the *Sea Nymph* and the *Emma*. The initial case was heard in October 1809 in the District Court of Eastern Pennsylvania, and the decision was appealed in 1811 in the Circuit Court of Pennsylvania on the grounds that the trial should have been by jury and not under admiralty jurisdiction. The silence on the part of the U.S. government gave the Circuit Court judges the power to interpret whether Haiti was still a French colony and therefore whether trade with the island was legal or illegal. "On the part of the United States, it is contended," the records report, "that in point of fact, this island, at the time above mentioned, was, and still continues [to be], a dependence of France; and that even if this were not the case, according to the principles of the law of nations, still, it is not for this, or any other Court, to decide on the ground of her independence, until the government of the United States has so declared, or France has relinquished her claim."[93] Since the U.S. government had not expressly acknowledged the independence of Haiti, the courts, argued the defendants, had to assume that the island remained a colony of France.

In contrast, the claimants argued in 1811 that the Haitian government had demonstrated that the island was independent and that it should therefore be treated as such. "On the part of the claimant, it was insisted," the records report, "that the people of this island had not only declared themselves independent, but have thus far shown themselves able to maintain it; having, ever since the declaration, exercised without interruption from the armed force of France, the rights and powers of self-government, under a constitution framed by themselves."[94] Since the island was independent, it was their duty to treat them as they would all other neutral nations: "That neutral nations are bound, by the law which ought to govern nations, to consider St. Domingo as a government separate from, and independent of France; and the war, if any there be between them, as being equally just on both sides."

In thinking about this case, the Circuit judges considered Vattel's analysis of civil war in the context of international trade but argued that it was not applicable since Vattel's guidance was intended to inform the actions of governments, not court systems.[95] This conclusion contrasts with the British Admiralty Courts' use of Vattel's work in its decision-making processes, but at the same time, the British judges were reluctant to act without additional evidence issued by their own government. In the American case, however, it appears as though Vattel's conclusions had less influence on policy outcome, since even when Samuel White had proposed this argument in Congress, the government was not willing to concede. "It is for governments to decide," the judges argued, "whether they will consider St. Domingo as an independent nation; and till such decision is made, or France shall relinquish her claim, Courts must consider the ancient state of things as remaining unaltered, *and the sovereign power of France over the colony as still subsisting.*" The question then remained: had any government acknowledged Haitian independence?

The judges cited the 1801 constitution under Toussaint Louverture as proof of French authority over the island, as had Judge Croke in the British Vice-Admiralty Court in Halifax, Nova Scotia, in 1805. He then noted that since this overt declaration of French authority, the island had been consumed by civil war until 1809, when General Ferrand's troops evacuated the city of Santo Domingo. During that period of civil war, the rebel armies had declared national independence under the leadership of Jean-Jacques Dessalines. On the part of the United States, the judges cited the February 1806 bill that prohibited trade between the United States and "St. Domingo," which lasted until March 1808. This law, however, overlapped with the "embargo laws," which were then replaced with "a non-importation law, as to those nations [Britain and France], and their colonies, and dependencies, and places within their actual possession," to take effect from 20 May 1809.

In the judges' opinion, Haiti possessed the characteristics of an independent nation. "When the non-intercourse law passed, in February 1806," they argued, "the island of St. Domingo was in a state of open public war with France; having declared herself independent, framed a Constitution of government, and shown herself able to maintain that independence." Because of these characteristics, they concluded that "as an independent nation, the United States had an unquestionable right to carry on a commercial intercourse with that island." But only the U.S. government, they argued, could make this decision independently and without foreign influence. "The attempt of any foreign nation to interdict such commerce, and still worse, a demand upon the government of the United States," they railed, "to enforce such prohibition by law, would have been an insult, to which no nation ought, and to which our government most certainly would not have submitted." They recognized, nevertheless, that such had been the case and that the U.S. government only prohibited the trade because of French pressure. While the judges did not believe that the government was required to have done so, the fact that it conceded to French demands changed the ability for American merchants to trade with Haiti.

"We view the law of 1806," reported the chief justice for the case, "under the circumstances which produced it, as a clear acknowledgment of the sovereignty of France over the island, which no subsequent act of our government, has in any respect impaired." The judge assumed that the law prohibiting trade with Haiti in 1806 had been implemented because the U.S. government had decided that the island was still a French colony. The 1806 law did not explicitly state that the trade had been prohibited because of the island's character as a rebellious French colony, but trade was only prohibited with those ports and places that were not under French control. "All commercial intercourse between any person or persons resident within the United States," the act proclaimed, "and any person or persons resident within any part of the island of St. Domingo, not in possession, and under the acknowledged government of France, shall be, and is hereby prohibited."[96] The reference to France's lost control over certain places implied that it was because of this conflict that U.S. merchants could not trade with Haiti.

The judges ruling in *Clark v. The United States* also saw this connection. "When congress," the judges argued, "by the law on which this information is founded, interdicted the importation into the United States, of goods, &c., from the colonies and dependencies of France, we feel ourselves compelled to say, that St. Domingo was considered by that body as included." "So that the government has not only not acknowledged the independence of this island," they concluded, "but has very plainly declared the contrary."[97] From this perspective, the prohibition on trade with the island signified that Haiti could not be considered independent from France.

The economic legislation in the United States focused on banning trade with Haiti and therefore set a precedent for non-recognition. In contrast, the positive declarations in the British Orders in Council that permitted and regulated trade with Haiti allowed the Admiralty Courts to interpret the neutrality of the ports and places on Hispaniola under the control of the Haitian government. In both cases, the court systems interpreted the economic policies of the national governments as having implications for the island's diplomatic and legal status. When the government prohibited trade, the courts considered the island to be a French colony; when the government permitted trade, the courts saw the island within the category of a neutral nation.

Conclusion

Two years passed after the Haitian Declaration of Independence before the United States officially prevented trade with Haiti; this prohibition only lasted four years. The discussions surrounding the embargo on trade reveal that the bill prohibiting trade received engaged and articulate resistance. Furthermore, the resistance, compellingly argued by Senator Samuel White, used the law of nations to claim that prohibiting the trade contradicted common custom. It is noteworthy that White's speech was published as a twenty-seven-page pamphlet. Clearly this perspective did not disappear when trade was legally prohibited.

Similarly, the rulings in the various courts of the United States highlight the negation of the law of nations in the U.S. government's decisions. From this perspective, Jefferson and Congress overlooked their obligations under the law of nations in order to appease the French, to gain an upper hand in securing the Floridas, and to help assuage the fears of southern slaveholders.

The Supreme Court and Circuit Court cases demonstrate how interpretations of the embargo on trade with the French Empire had implications for Haiti's status as a country or colony. The prohibition on trade led the Circuit Court judge in Pennsylvania to conclude that, from the perspective of the United States, Haiti was still a French colony. Again the relationship between the government and the court systems influenced the practical nature of Haiti's place as an independent country in the Caribbean because it expanded the implications of the government's economic policy. The U.S. court system interpreted diplomatic status through economic policy, and the prohibition on trade with Haiti resulted in a denial of Haiti's sovereignty.

These various prohibitions on trade, however, had a limited effect on U.S. trade with Haiti since American merchants did not want the British to secure a monopoly.[98] After the prohibition ended in 1810, trade again resumed, and within a decade American merchants were supplying close to half of Haiti's imports.[99] In 1813, the United States appointed commercial agents to Cap Haïtien and Port-au-Prince, despite withholding official diplomatic recognition.[100] One important result of such ongoing connections with the United States after 1804 was Haiti's enhanced ability to leverage more explicit support from Great Britain. This larger context became more important than ever as internal challenges moved the focus of attention from the independence of Haiti to the future "States of Hayti."

5

THE "STATES OF HAYTI" AND THE BRITISH EMPIRE

Throughout Jean-Jacques Dessalines's rule in Haiti—first as governor-general for life and then as emperor—he faced continued political resistance from various factions. According to nineteenth-century Haitian historian Thomas Madiou, Dessalines's demise was inevitable because of his "excesses" while in office and because of his violation of the sacred rights of the citizens, the soldiers, and his supporters.[1] In mid-1806, political resistance turned violent as town after town turned to armed revolt and many of Dessalines's own generals turned against him. On 17 October 1806, rebel officers assassinated Emperor Jacques Ier at Pont Rouge, just outside of Port-au-Prince. The killers are said to have hacked Dessalines's body to pieces in order to parade their victim around the city.

Alexandre Pétion would later claim that the assassins had complete support from Henry Christophe. He explained that he had in fact written to Christophe to notify him of the plot and that Christophe had agreed not to interfere—a claim that Christophe would later deny.[2] In any event, there is no evidence that either leader tried to prevent Dessalines's demise. Leaders in Haiti were still aware that foreign officials were keeping track of events in Haiti, and they did not want Dessalines's assassination to negatively influence foreign opinion. General Laurent Férou, commander of the region of Grande Anse in the South of Haiti, wrote to the governor of Jamaica, Eyre Coote, to justify Dessalines's inevitable removal from power. "As soon as he [Dessalines] was sure of his power," Férou argued, "he hastened to make himself the hero of the revolution of St. Domingo; drawing on his natural ferocity and proud nature, he only saw the state in himself, without disguise. . . . He believed that the art of government consisted of nothing but his tyrannical will and he indulged in the most villainous debauchery."[3] The letter then outlined a plan in which troops from the South would march on Port-au-Prince to meet troops from the North in order to capture Dessalines. At that point, the "revolution" would install Henry Christophe as head of state. Férou reassured Coote that the current revolution was simply an effort to restore order and morals in the country, and he noted that the internal violence that Haiti was experiencing was nothing to worry about, and in fact that the revolution would create a more stable and friendly relationship between Haiti and the British Empire. He also asked for aid and supplies.[4] But just as Férou was finishing his composition of this letter, he learned that Dessalines had been assassinated just three days earlier. He decided to send it anyway (mentioning Dessalines's death in the postscript), undoubtedly convinced of the need to emphasize the larger importance of Haitian connections with Britain.

Coote responded to Férou to remind him that he was not authorized to allow any exchange of goods between Jamaica and Haiti. But he also sent Férou's letter to the secretary of state for war and the colonies in London with the commentary that "in the divided and unsettled form of government, which much necessarily exist, at present, in that ill-fated island, I should have considered myself as very culpable in suffering any commercial intercourse between the two colonies."[5] Coote also reported that he had read the earlier correspondence of his predecessor, George Nugent, regarding a trade treaty with Haiti. His conclusion from this correspondence was "that it was not the wish of government, that a direct intercourse should take place between Jamaica and St. Domingo, but betwixt the latter island and Great Britain."[6] He therefore felt that his role in the matter was limited since Jamaica had been taken out of the equation.

Scholars have clearly shown how, in the immediate years after Dessalines's assassination, serious internal divisions added significantly to the initial challenges of establishing Haiti as a viable independent country by undermining Haiti's credibility as a nation worthy of foreign recognition in the Atlantic World. Numerous documents suggest that diverse foreign onlookers used the internal conflicts as justification to withhold support and diplomatic recognition. In addition, researchers have shown how the struggles between Henry Christophe and Alexandre Pétion worked against nation building by contributing to the continued militarization of Haitian society and by using valuable resources for the conflict.

This scholarly emphasis is, however, incomplete and, in fact, misleading. Internal divisions certainly added to the challenges facing Haitian leaders in the immediate years after the Declaration of Independence, but they did not prevent continued efforts to secure stabilizing connections in the Atlantic World. This conclusion is based on a systematic study of previously overlooked correspondence relating to the treaty proposals made by the Haitian governments and their unofficial agents to British representatives in London. This correspondence reveals the central goals of the Haitian presidents in the first year of civil war in Haiti, especially when analyzed alongside internal nation-building processes by the presidents, evident in their respective national constitutions. Both Christophe and Pétion used foreign delegates to communicate and negotiate with British ministers in London because the government had not recognized Haitian independence and therefore could not receive Haitian agents or diplomats. Henry Christophe and his secretary of state, Rouanez, *jeune*, wrote to the British secretary of state for war and the colonies, Robert Stewart, Viscount Castlereagh, and they also wrote to two unofficial agents whom they employed to negotiate on their behalf. Thomas Richardson, whose nationality is not noted in the correspondence but who was likely a British merchant, teamed up with a royalist French émigré in London, Jean-Gabriel Peltier, to submit Christophe's proposed treaty and to advocate for the benefits of an agreement with Christophe's government. Pétion and his secretary of state, Bruno Blanchet, also wrote to Stewart and similarly tried to enlist Peltier's help in their effort to sign a trade treaty with the British government.

Based on such evidence, the following analysis of the post-Dessalinian "States of Hayti" focuses on the ways in which Henry Christophe and Alexandre Pétion sought to establish effective economic and diplomatic connections with the British Empire. Like Dessalines, Christophe and Pétion recognized the value of an economic relationship with the British Empire and the potential diplomatic and military security that the British could provide. But Christophe and Pétion did not have the same perceived options that Dessalines had had in 1804. The situation in 1807 was significantly different from that in 1804 because the United States, Curaçao, and St. Thomas had all prohibited trade with Haiti by that time. The two Haitian presidents no longer felt the same confident optimism that Jean-Jacques Dessalines had expressed during his negotiations with George Nugent in Jamaica in 1803 and 1804. Nonetheless, they did not give up, and understanding their efforts further contributes to the reinterpretation of the crucial first years of Haitian independence.

To begin with, there is no doubt that the broader context of the States of Hayti was not promising for establishing security or achieving recognition. Not only did the Haitian presidents have to contend with the continued and consistent threat of a French reinvasion—immediately visible in Jean-Louis Ferrand's constant harassment of foreign ships visiting Haitian ports (either legally or illegally) with privateers based in Santo Domingo and in Cuba—but they also had to contend with each other. Agricultural laborers had to join the army, which prevented them from producing the exports crops that the states could have traded for matériel. Indeed, according to the 1805 constitution under Dessalines, Haitian citizenship (for men) was defined by military service.[7] Nevertheless, British merchant Robert Sutherland claimed in late 1806 that although production had dropped significantly since 1801, the country was producing 15 million pounds of coffee, 10 million pounds of cotton, and 4 million pounds of cocoa per year.[8] Sutherland also predicted that the production levels would increase in the coming years. This was in part because Dessalines had promoted the use of female laborers to continue the agricultural production, and indeed, the British agent Edward Corbet noted in early 1804 that "the cultivation of the plantations is chiefly carried on by women."[9] This measure had been one of his first acts after the Declaration of Independence, when, on 20 January 1804, Dessalines had published an ordinance declaring that all agricultural laborers would have to obtain a special license in order to become *marchand(e)s* (hucksters). The ordinance noted that too many people—primarily creole women—had been leaving the plantations to escape to the cities and towns. The new licenses would limit and regulate the number of people who were allowed to leave the plantations.

By 1807, the internal and external threats and the absence of trade partners left the British as the Haitian presidents' only option. In this context, to varying degrees and in different ways, Christophe and Pétion both pursued an official trade treaty that would signal British diplomatic recognition of Haiti and would enhance the existing trade relationship between the two jurisdictions. A treaty would also secure British aid for protection against the French and against the opposing government in the Haitian civil war. From this perspective, British support in the form of a trade treaty would guarantee Haiti's independence, both on paper and in practice, and would have decided the civil war in order to reunite the country under one president.

In 1807, the Haitian presidents specifically sought to secure French émigré Jean-Gabriel Peltier's aid in their efforts to sign a trade treaty because they aligned themselves with his anti-Napoleonic activism. In London, Peltier published an antirevolutionary newspaper called l'*Ambigu*; in 1803 he was tried for and convicted of libel against Napoléon Bonaparte in a British court.[10] According to Pétion's secretary of state, Bruno Blanchet, Haitians were big fans of Peltier. "An enemy of Bonaparte as fearless as you are," he wrote, "is necessarily one of our friends. Your newspaper is the favorite among Haitians and has become required reading for them."[11] Haitians certainly had access to newspapers from London since so many British merchants were arriving in Haiti directly from England. The *Gazette Officielle de l'Etat d'Hayti*, published in the north, noted on 20 August 1807 that several copies of *l'Ambigu* had arrived in the country. The article included an excerpt from an issue of *l'Ambigu* and promised that more would follow. The excerpt noted that Peltier had reprinted Christophe's 1807 constitution, and the article applauded the contents of the document. In particular, Peltier highlighted Article 36, "in which the government of Haiti announces to the powers who have neighboring colonies, its unwavering determination not to disturb the system by which they are governed."[12] In his correspondence with the British ministers in London, Peltier energetically advocated for British recognition of Haitian independence on the basis of common enemies and mutually beneficial trade relationships. The evidence makes clear, however, that nothing would be straightforward in these contested years.

Civil War

During the decade after the Declaration of Independence, British merchants in the various port cities of Haiti made sure to keep their government officials apprised of any events that they felt might support or jeopardize their investments. In the weeks leading up to Dessalines's assassination, Robert Sutherland, a vocal British merchant and someone who served as an unofficial agent in Haiti, was in London, unaware of the plans to remove Dessalines from power. Sutherland wrote to George Shee, the under-secretary of state for war and the colonies, in support of an official relationship with Haiti. He claimed that the Haitian Revolution was an immense boon to the British Empire since it had reduced the available quantities of colonial produce, which thereby helped British planters in the West Indies. He also reasoned that the Haitian Revolution had actually increased the safety of the British colonies because the outcome had discouraged any rebellion among the free people of color. "The Mulattoe Men in the British West India Islands are far from being a satisfied Race of People," Sutherland argued, "although their Rights privileges and comforts are superior to their merit."[13] The failure of the *gens de couleur* (people of color) in Haiti to take the place of the whites as the ruling class, Sutherland concluded, "completely damped the Rising ambition of that Class of Colonists in all the Islands in the western world and pointed out to them the necessity of keeping well with the whites."[14] Because of these facts, Sutherland argued that the British should support Haiti's independence.

The British king had expressly permitted trade between British merchants and Haiti with an Order in Council in July 1806, and for his part, Dessalines had actively worked to strengthen the relationship between the two countries. "I invite you to make known to the English Merchants my good intentions in their favour," Dessalines wrote to British merchant John Downie, "that I am disposed to receive them with distinction and to offer them the most extensive protection for those sent by them their Ships and Merchandise. You have been an Eye Witness of the resources the Empire affords, they will be still more considerable next year in consequence of my having lately taken the most vigorous measures for promoting the prosperity of agriculture."[15] Dessalines hoped to increase the trade, while British merchants hoped to secure additional protection for their economic initiatives. Many merchants advocated not only for the placement of an official British agent in Haiti to protect their interests in the case of a conflict but also for official recognition of the independence of the country. "I presume to think a trade with Hayti an object of National Importance," Downie argued in a letter to the clerk of the Privy Council, "and I have no doubt of our securing it, almost exclusively, merely by recognizing them as a nation and giving them some consideration and Civility."[16]

Despite the fact that trade was flourishing by the end of 1806, British merchants continued to advocate for a trade treaty between the Haitian and British governments. Some British ministers who perceived advantages for the British Empire shared their advocacy. Shee notified Sutherland in early 1807 that a trade treaty might in fact still be an option. "In answer to your question," he wrote, "how I thought any overture on the part of the Emperor of Hayti respecting a commercial Intercourse and arrangement with this Country would be received by His Majesty's government[,] I have not any hesitation in acquainting you that I am of opinion any such overture would be well received and I have not any doubt but that an arrangement might be formed highly advantageous to both countries."[17] Almost three years after the Haitian Declaration of Independence, and after Dessalines's death, some British ministers were still considering an official trade treaty with Haiti.

On 16 November 1806, the commander in chief of the British navy in Jamaica reported that he had heard "of the Death of the Black General Dessalines calling himself the Emperor of Haity (supposed by murder) and that Christophe succeeds to the Government of the Brigands under the said Title."[18] As the leader of the north, the country's wealthiest region, Christophe had a loyal following. After Dessalines's death, Pétion, then in the position of general of the West, and Étienne Gérin, the minister for war and the navy, both wrote to Christophe to ask him to "to take the reins of government, and let us enjoy the fullness of our rights, and our freedom, for which we have fought for so long, and to be the custodian of our laws that we swear to obey, since they will be fair."[19] Pétion and his supporters were, however, determined to limit the power of the new national leader to avoid the "excesses" that they had experienced under Dessalines. When a constitutional convention was called in December 1806, Pétion and his supporters formally limited the powers of the president by establishing an elected senate.[20] Christophe rejected this proposed constitution, and he marched on Port-au-Prince to disband the committee and assert his own authority. Christophe's forces, however, were not able to defeat Pétion's armies, and the country divided in civil war, with Pétion leading the South and the West while Christophe retreated to the North.

In February 1807, Christophe issued his own national constitution that named him president and general of the army.[21] The next month, Pétion was also elected president under the constitution that he and his committee had themselves drafted in late 1806. The country now had two presidents, both of whom claimed to be the sole legal authority on the island. Their respective jurisdictions in practice only covered a portion of the country, and neither had the military capacity to defeat the other, but both argued that Haitians and foreigners should consider them to be the true president of the entire country.

Both Pétion and Christophe continued to actively pursue foreign relationships in order to secure favorable trade relationships and official diplomatic recognition. They both desperately needed the support of the British in their efforts to sustain their victory against France, as well as to secure diplomatic recognition from the community of nations in the Atlantic World and to become the sole ruler of the entire country. Since the governor of Jamaica had removed himself from the discussion about a possible agreement between the British and Haitian governments, both Haitian presidents separately sought to make distinct agreements directly with the British ministers in London; each proposal claimed to be made on behalf of the entire country. Even though Eyre Coote in Jamaica had refused to engage in treaty negotiations, Pétion and Christophe both knew that the ultimate decision would come from London.

States' Formation

As Henry Christophe and Alexandre Pétion each worked to consolidate his own leadership, they had to focus on internal nation-building processes and on foreign relations. These two goals were related, since proving their ability to participate in the community of nations of the Atlantic World meant establishing a stable government based on recognizable and approved institutions and customs. Despite the civil war and the existence of two self-professed national governments between 1806 and 1820, these two Haitian leaders consistently argued that the country was composed of a unified national community based on the principles of antislavery and anticolonialism. "Happily (General Christophe excepted)," Pétion wrote to British abolitionists William Wilberforce and James Stephen in December of 1806, "the cause of all Haitians is the same and despite the separation of the family, all know to appreciate that. There exists, despite the difference between Governments, an implicit and tacit alliance against all enemies of our liberty and our independence." "For the defense of the territory," he continued, "I do not recognize any difference of country, and my heart does not see any abstraction but Haiti."[22] The wars within the border, according to Pétion, were secondary concerns when compared with international encroachments and the unity of the national community.

Christophe expressed a similar sentiment as he reflected on the civil war a decade later in a letter to British abolitionist Thomas Clarkson. "They [the Haitians under Pétion's command]," he wrote on 18 November 1816, "are no more disposed to resume the yoke of slavery than are the inhabitants of the Northern, Eastern, or Western parts of the kingdom. It is a consolation to me to see that the great majority of Haitians have reached an understanding, and that a common danger has tacitly united us all, from one end of the island to the other, for we all abhor the French and their oppressive Government."[23] Just as Dessalines had explained in the Declaration of Independence, opposition and "eternal hatred" toward the French were the basis for Haitian identity.

Both Christophe and Pétion believed that Haitian citizens now formed one people, united by the principles of the Haitian Revolution. In turn, they each viewed themselves as the better leader to build on the revolution's success for the entire new country. Despite the conflict surrounding the constitutional convention in 1806, the two presidents of Haiti did establish independent governments that shared some of the same basic principles. For example, they both reaffirmed the abolition of slavery in the first article of their national constitutions.[24] Both leaders tied the unification of the Haitian people to freedom, and according to Christophe and Pétion, their common history and experiences during the revolution created a common national identity. Most important for the British, both Christophe and Pétion repeated Dessalines's promises not to instigate rebellion abroad, and Christophe's constitution even contained a section heading titled "Guarantee to Neighboring Colonies," which included the following article: "The nation of Haiti shall not in any way make conquests outside the Island, limiting itself to conserving its territory."[25] This article vowed not to instigate rebellion beyond Haitian borders and to focus on the preservation of achievements at home. Territorial conservation was the primary objective in the early years of Haitian independence; the state would not jeopardize its hard-won achievements.

Despite some overarching similarities, however, the two constitutions set up remarkably different governments. In contrast to the previous political structures in Haiti, Pétion's republic attempted to create a less authoritarian society. While the constitution dispersed some of the power of the leader, the structure of the government was far from democratic. In the end, the results proved to be a variation of the authoritarian government that Pétion and his supporters claimed to have overturned. "In the [Pétion's] republic," historian David Nicholls argues, "a careful reading of the constitution as well as an examination of the practice, would reveal that despite talk of sovereignty of the people, real power was in the hands of a small self-perpetuating elite."[26] Systematic study of the constitution of 1806 does in fact reveal contradictions to the assertions of a democratic state. Political power in the Republic of the South was placed in the hands of a senate and a president. While the president was considered the head of state and of the army, the senate was also in control.[27] The senate was composed of a select group of people "who serve or have served a civil or military function with integrity and honor," and they had the ability to control all legislative aspects of the state.[28] Pétion had been named by the Constituent Assembly, but all future presidents would have had to have served in the senate, and the senate was given the ability to choose which member or former member was to become the next president.[29] The senate and the president essentially held all of the power in Pétion's republic. Power was intended to remain in the hands of a small group of elite, even though the republic claimed to be a less authoritarian state.

Just over a month after Christophe attacked Pétion's forces in Port-au-Prince, he issued his own national constitution, again claiming that it applied to the entire country. Christophe announced the publication of his constitution with two proclamations, the first of which was addressed to the *habitants et cultivateurs* (inhabitants and cultivators)—both of the proclamations were printed by the government's printing press and sent to the British. "That the union, labor, trade and industry of all citizens," Christophe hoped, "providing the Government's capacity to support with dignity and to honorably fulfill its commitments, also give him the power to make you happy and to save you from the traps of our Enemies."[30] These enemies were external (the French) and internal (the rebels under Pétion). In his view, internal cohesion and hard work could save the country from France and from Pétion.

To accompany his constitution, Christophe issued a second proclamation addressed to the army and the people. In this proclamation he condemned the "rebels" under Pétion because they rejected his authority. He also emphasized the importance of foreign connections and promised that all but their enemies would benefit from a political or commercial relationship with Haiti: "Those who want to create political relations or enjoy the benefits of our trade, [will] find fair reciprocity; let us offer only death and war to others."[31] While political and commercial relationships are posited as a one or the other option, this was at the heart of the conflict between the British and Haitian governments during the entire period of non-recognition. In fact, Haitian governments wanted political and commercial relationships, not trade without politics.

Christophe's constitution of 1807 created a state with a political structure that was significantly different from that of the South, but the outcome was quite similar. Christophe was both president and general of the army, and he held almost complete political and military control. The president was to be aided by a Council of State, which he had the power to name. He would also have the right to name his successor after serving a life term as president.

In the constitution of 1807, economic policies continued to play an important role in how the country was officially defined. Henry

Christophe followed a similar line to that of Dessalines by declaring that "agriculture, as the first, noblest, and most useful of all the crafts, shall be fostered and protected."[32] But Christophe did not ignore the importance of commerce in the newly independent nation. While agriculture was to be valued and promoted, foreign merchants were to be welcomed and protected.[33] Again, Christophe proposed a twofold strategy: the first was to develop and promote agriculture and the second was to promote international commerce based on the export of agricultural products.

Pétion and Christophe both included constitutional articles designed to reassure foreign readers that they should not fear any further repercussions in their Caribbean colonies. The rebuilding of the country's agricultural production also played a prominent role, and both presidents knew that they needed foreign trade partners in order to capitalize on the current and future production on the country's plantations. Pétion and Christophe both sought to reopen the negotiations with the British Empire and to succeed where Jean-Jacques Dessalines and George Nugent had failed in 1804.

Treaty Proposals to the British Ministers

Promises of peace and friendship in both Christophe's and Pétion's constitutions did not succeed in encouraging foreign relationships, and both leaders soon concluded that they had to exert more pressure on the British government in London in order to secure diplomatic recognition. Christophe and Pétion each contacted British ministers in London about possible treaties that would give Haiti diplomatic recognition, would encourage trade with Haiti, and would create an alliance in case of any French attacks.

The Haitian presidents could not send official agents to London since the British government had not recognized Haiti's independence, and so they enlisted pro-Haitian foreigners to negotiate on their behalf. Christophe and Pétion both approached Jean-Gabriel Peltier for help in securing diplomatic recognition from the British Empire, but from the outset Peltier chose to support Christophe's efforts to secure recognition for himself and for the country. On 5 April 1807, Christophe's secretary of state, Rouanez, *jeune*, wrote to Peltier to accept his offer to serve as a mediator between Christophe and the British ministers in London. "The President was pleased to see the offer that you made to the Government of Hayti," Rouanez wrote to Peltier, "and your good intentions to her.

There is nobody better than you who can fulfill its purpose, and work effectively to bring the British Government to enter into a treaty with the State of Hayti. You know the extent of the benefits that the commerce of Great Britain can derive from creating Trade relations with us."[34] It is unclear why Peltier would have had extensive knowledge about Haitian-British trade relations, but it appears as though he was particularly willing to advocate on Haiti's behalf because of their mutual enemy, Napoléon Bonaparte.

On 8 June 1807, Peltier wrote to Robert Stewart, Viscount Castlereagh, the secretary of state for war and the colonies, announcing that it was Christophe's desire for him to discuss with the British ministers what kind of relationship might be beneficial to both Haiti and the British Empire. Over the course of the next two years, Peltier wrote to Stewart thirteen times to highlight the benefits of signing a treaty with Christophe. Peltier cited the "immense trade relations that exist between England and the State of Haiti" as a reason why Stewart should consider a trade treaty and claimed that "His Excellency President Christophe is perfectly worthy of benevolence, esteem and patronage of H.M. [His Majesty's] Government."[35]

Peltier forwarded to Stewart letters that he received from Rouanez and Christophe in order to convince him of the good intentions that Christophe's government had toward the British. But, while the relationship between the two countries would be favorable, he would not concede that it would be an exclusive relationship. "The recognition of the Independence of this State by the British Government," Rouanez wrote to Peltier, "would perhaps encourage others to imitate its example: but the advantage of such an act would be to the benefit of England. Its business, its navy always finds in our ports a government that is disposed to offer them all kinds of hospitality and preference over the subjects of other nations."[36] The British would enjoy preferential treatment but not exclusive trading rights. In reality, in 1807 the distinction would not have meant much; trade between all other nations and Haiti was illegal. This did not mean, however, that the trade had stopped completely, since foreign merchants continued to circumvent the laws of their nations in order to continue trading with Haiti illegally. A treaty with the British, however, would have limited Haiti's ability to capitalize on the illegal trade, since they would have been committed to a preferential relationship with the British.

Rouanez reminded the British ministers that the Haitian government had no intention of spreading the revolution beyond the boundaries of the island of Hispaniola. "The Intention of the people of Hayti," he claimed, "is far removed from causing concern among nations who have possessions in the neighborhood. . . . It is one of the main articles of the new constitution and we welcome the English to frequent our ports to judge for themselves."[37] Christophe had translated previous Haitian promises not to export the revolution into constitutional law. Pétion had made a similar promise in his 1806 constitution, and perhaps the presidents assumed that this act would carry more weight with a foreign audience because—in theory—they would have had to rewrite the Haitian constitution in order to undertake any foreign expeditions. It is unclear, however, whether foreign audiences believed that Haitian domestic policy would in fact check any international ambitions.

The secretary of state under Pétion, Bruno Blanchet, also wrote a letter to Peltier at the end of July 1807, a few months after Peltier had agreed to serve as the representative of Christophe's government in London. Blanchet tried to convince Peltier that Christophe was in the wrong and that he should support Pétion and broker a deal with the British on Pétion's behalf rather than on Christophe's. "After the death of Dessalines," Blanchet argued, "in which Christophe cooperated not by military force, he was too afraid to, but by proposals skillfully communicated to Generals Pétion and Gérin to get rid of the Tyrant [Dessalines], Christophe was temporarily declared Head of Government."[38] While Dessalines's assassination is usually attributed to Pétion and his supporters, Blanchet made sure to emphasize that Christophe had been a willing co-conspirator in the plot. He also argued that after Dessalines's death, Pétion thought that it would be more politic to put a black man at the head of the country, which is why Christophe was initially selected as Dessalines's successor. But it turned out that Christophe—from Pétion's and his supporters' perspective—had become a tyrant just like Dessalines. "He seized all of the food from the residents and farmers," Blanchet reported, "by giving them a large one time payment, that is to say, paper in exchange, most of the members from the North in the constituent assembly who had the imprudence to find themselves in their Communities no longer exist, all men of color that he could find no longer exist, women and children were the victims of his ferocity."[39] Blanchet suggested that the people of Haiti were on Pétion's side and opposed to tyranny: "The tragic end of Dessalines should have proved that Haitians know how to reject tyranny in whatever form and whatever color it presents itself."[40]

Blanchet wanted to use Peltier to secure British recognition, but he also wanted to use him to sway internal allegiances in Haiti. He knew how valuable Peltier's newspaper could be in terms of shaping international and local opinion, and he asked him to write a critique of Christophe and his government. "Now continue with the weapon of ridicule that you wield so deftly. In moments of respite from your address to the Emperor Napoleon," he requested, "I recommend you spend some time on the Emperor Christophe, who describes himself as the natural and legitimate successor of Dessalines."[41] According to Blanchet, being the legitimate heir of Dessalines simply meant a continuation of the authoritarian tradition. About a month later, however, the *Gazette Officielle de l'État d'Hayti* notified Haitians that Peltier had done just the opposite and had published an article in *l'Ambigu* promoting Christophe's constitution and warning foreign audiences against Pétion's government.

Not knowing that Peltier had already made up his mind, Blanchet argued that Pétion was the natural ally of Great Britain since they were both fighting against tyranny (the British against Bonaparte and Pétion against Christophe), and he also condemned President Thomas Jefferson for remaining neutral while Bonaparte "walked with giant steps toward universal domination."[42] By 1807, however, Jefferson had also taken sides in the battle by prohibiting American merchants from trading with Haiti. Blanchet argued that Jefferson's supposed neutrality suggested "cowardice With regard to France, and perhaps an inveterate hatred With regard to Great Britain."[43] By prohibiting trade with Haiti and withholding diplomatic recognition, Blanchet argued that the American government was implicitly supporting Bonaparte, and since the British and French were at war, he encouraged Peltier to consider this move to be an act of war by the Americans against the British. By aligning Christophe and Bonaparte, Blanchet tried to swing Peltier's favor toward Pétion.

Peltier, however, had already agreed to support Christophe's government, and his letters do not reveal why he refused to support Pétion since the records do not contain a response to Blanchet's letter. Following this decision, Peltier assumed the role of advocate for the recognition of the independence and sovereignty of Haiti, and for the recognition of Christophe as the legitimate ruler of that country in the position of president and general of the Forces of Land and Sea. In his role as mediator, Peltier set out to secure a diplomatic and commercial treaty between Haiti and Great Britain. In this endeavor, he encountered some problems: "Your Lordship has informed me by Mr. Cooke," Peltier wrote to

Stewart, "that because of civil unrest that has recently arisen in this country [Haiti], or for other reasons, the Government of His Majesty did not think fit to take these overtures into serious consideration."[44] At the end of 1806, George Shee had been optimistic about the prospects of a trade treaty between Haiti and the British Empire, but the civil war in Haiti seems to have changed the opinion of the British ministers in London. Governor George Nugent in Jamaica had previously anticipated the outbreak of civil war in Haiti and suggested that it would be advisable to wait so that the British government would not be tied to one side or the other. Perhaps, in 1807, the British ministers wanted to gather more information about the two leaders in order to make an informed decision as to which side they would support. Additionally, civil war in Haiti occupied the military strength of the country and would have prevented any serious external expeditions.

Nevertheless, Peltier tried to convince the British ministers that Christophe's government should in fact be taken seriously. To do this, he emphasized three key points. First, Peltier argued that Christophe was the legitimate ruler of all of Haiti and that he had superior military power; he was not using this superior military power at the moment to defeat Pétion, however, because he did not want to kill more Haitian citizens. Peltier argued that he only needed a bit of British help in the form of blockades to prevent Pétion's forces from gaining access to matériel, food, and manufactured goods. Second, Peltier promoted Haiti as a valuable trade partner; Haiti would provide agricultural products and a market for British manufactured goods. Nugent had already made this argument when he was advocating for a trade treaty in 1804, and the large number of merchants keen to trade with Haiti also supports the suggestion that a trade relationship with Haiti was valuable for the British economy. Finally, Peltier emphasized the natural alliance created by the war against Napoléon Bonaparte. Haiti was "a country proud to be the best island in the world after England," Peltier argued, "and asks her older sister to take her under her protection; a country which, alone with you, defeated Bonaparte, and alone wants to continue the fight with you; a country, naturally your ally, can it still continue to be treated as a colony of the enemy?"[45] Peltier created a familial relationship between Haiti and Great Britain with the British as Haiti's big sister, its protector.

Peltier teamed up with Thomas Richardson, an envoy from Christophe, to convince the British ministers to sign a trade treaty. Richardson arrived in London from Haiti carrying specific instructions and articles for a proposed treaty. His instructions from Christophe noted that he should first "propose to His Majesty's Ministers to recognize the island of Haity as a free and independent state, and its government as a sovereign government under the protection of England."[46] The relationship that Christophe proposed mirrored the one that Toussaint Louverture had introduced in his 1801 constitution. Louverture had secured near-complete autonomy for his government in Saint Domingue, but he still professed allegiance to the French Empire. The relationship that Louverture envisioned was not in place long enough for us to completely understand the practical implications of this diplomatic affiliation, but the evidence suggests that Christophe wanted to re-create this relationship with the British Empire. In this situation, his government would have almost complete autonomy but would also benefit from an economic and military alliance with the British Empire.

Second, Christophe instructed Richardson to secure the recognition of his authority as the "supreme and legitimate" ruler under the title of president and general of the Forces of Land and Sea of Haiti. Furthermore, to help secure this status, he required the cooperation of the Jamaican admiralty for the defeat of the "rebels" (under Pétion) by blockading the ports that they occupied. In addition to helping remove the threat from the South, Christophe wanted help from the British in his effort to eliminate the continued threat from the East. Richardson requested that the British blockade the port of Santo Domingo in coordination with Christophe's planned march across the island to defeat Jean-Louis Ferrand's army. Finally, Christophe instructed Richardson to remind the British of all the advantages of trading with Haiti and to assure them that their merchants would receive preferential treatment over those of other nations.[47] Preferential treatment would have meant favorable rates on duties and perhaps higher import quotas. Richardson's instructions emphasized that each of these goals would be mutually beneficial for Haiti and for Great Britain.

Richardson and Peltier wrote to Stewart to remind him that British government officials had either signed accords with previous governments (Thomas Maitland with Toussaint Louverture) or attempted to sign treaties (George Nugent with Jean-Jacques Dessalines). Their proposal, therefore, simply followed a precedent, and the British ministers should not feel squeamish in treating with Christophe's government. According to Richardson and Peltier, Christophe was proposing the same articles that the British themselves had signed and suggested to leaders in Saint

Domingue and Haiti. They argued for the benefits of having a treaty of alliance and commerce but also highlighted the potential dangers of not signing the treaty. "It is easy to sense that the British traders and settlers, in both London and Jamaica," they argued, "would rather see in Haiti 60 thousand farmers [cultivateurs], hoe in hand, than 60 thousand soldiers, bayonet at the end of their gun; in the eyes of philosophers, the spirit of industry is much more desirable for the progress of civilization than the military spirit."[48] The only way to disarm the population was to eliminate the military threats against Christophe's government, and only an alliance between Haiti and Great Britain could save the country from internal threats (Pétion) and external threats (France). A treaty of alliance would have also had the key benefit of allowing the former soldiers to return to the plantations, thereby increasing agricultural production so as to provide more products with which to supply the British merchants.

The economic benefits of a treaty, Richardson and Peltier argued, would be maximized by the fact that the British would not be responsible for the governance of the island. British merchants, therefore, could enjoy the benefits of a colonial relationship, but the state would not have the burden of colonial government. "This trade could one day earn you as much as all of your colonies together," they argued, "and it would not cost you government fees, or administration and military fees[;] a treaty, a minister resident, and three consuls is enough to assure you the benefits."[49] The relationship that Richardson and Peltier were proposing on behalf of Christophe very closely resembles the relationship that the British Empire established with a number of Latin American states just a few decades later. This relationship, which scholars have labeled "informal empire," has typically been criticized for being designed to favor British over local interests. "Treaties of recognition [between the British and Latin American countries in the 1820s]," historian Matthew Brown argues, "were specifically designed with British interests in mind, such as the prohibition of the slave trade and guarantees of beneficial British trading rights."[50] Perhaps Christophe's government did not realize the potentially disastrous effects of this kind of relationship, but the fact that he was the one offering the benefits of colonialism without the administrative responsibility suggests a degree of desperation in his attempt to forge international alliances.

The treaty that Richardson proposed to the British secretary of state for war and the colonies on behalf of Christophe contained twenty-two articles.[51] It would establish a relationship of friendship in which the British

Crown would recognize Haiti as a free, independent, and sovereign state under the presidency of Henry Christophe. The new country, however, would be placed under British "protection." Richardson and Peltier's correspondence suggests that the emphasis here was on military protection. The treaty explicitly called for an alliance to defend Haiti from external threats as well as internal threats to Christophe's government. Pétion and Ferrand were both challenging Christophe's rule from within the boundaries of the island—and Christophe claimed that the entire island was Haitian territory under his authority. He further feared another invasion from the French metropole, and so British military support was essential for the survival of the country and of his government. In the immediate context of the treaty, this meant a coordinated effort to expel Ferrand from Santo Domingo and Pétion from the South and West of Haiti.

Under the proposed treaty, the two nations would have free and open commerce; British merchants would enjoy a reduced tariff on importations while the British would waive the "auction duty" for Haitian goods and put them on the same footing as British colonial goods. The British Crown would send a minister, consuls, and vice-consuls to Haiti to help regulate the trade, and Christophe would send a minister to London. Christophe's treaty ensured that a jury composed of both Haitian and British citizens would hear any conflicts between British subjects or between British and Haitian subjects in a Haitian court, as was typical for foreigners being tried in local courts.

Christophe, unlike any other leader between 1804 and 1918, was willing to allow white foreigners to own land in Haiti. Neither of his constitutions, in 1807 and in 1811, included an article prohibiting white landownership; all other Haitian constitutions did so, until the 1918 document written under American Occupation. Instead, Christophe's treaty proposal included provisions that would allow British subjects to own land and would also allow the British military to temporarily occupy three military bases on the island. Christophe was willing to allow the British to occupy—for the duration of Great Britain's war with France—Môle Saint Nicolas in the Northwest, Samaná in the Northeast, and either Tiburon or Fort Saint-Louis in the Southwest. He also included an article that would allow British subjects who formerly owned land in Haiti (during the British occupation of the South and West during the revolution) to reclaim that land by applying to the Haitian courts. George Nugent had requested the use of the military bases at Môle Saint Nicolas and Tiburon in his negotiations with Dessalines in late 1803 and early 1804, but Dessalines had vehemently rejected the request because it would have given the Haitian population the impression that he had "sold the colony to England."[52]

While promoting a relationship with Great Britain, Christophe supported all British measures to prevent contact between Haiti and the British West Indies. He also noted that it was illegal for Haitians to board British ships without a license that he himself had issued; the British certainly would not have objected to this stipulation. Christophe reserved the right to have a few small boats for coastal navigation but accepted that Haitians would not be sailing beyond the territorial waters of the island—about three miles from the coast. Nugent had previously proposed a similar article in 1804, and it is likely that in 1807 Christophe's willingness to prevent Haitian ships from leaving the territorial waters of Haiti would have been even more appealing. Over the course of the first three years of Haiti's independence, Haitian ships had sailed beyond a few miles from the coast and had intercepted and captured foreign ships. Most notably, historian Ada Ferrer's research reveals, Haitian ships began to retaliate in early 1804 after receiving news of Spanish support for French attacks on Haiti's economic livelihood.[53] British Admiralty captains from the Jamaica station also kept detailed lists of Haitian ships belonging to both Christophe's and Pétion's navies and worried that they were amassing too much maritime capital.[54]

Finally, British subjects would be free to practice their own religions. This policy was in line with the constitutions of both Christophe and Pétion, who professed that Roman Catholicism would be the official state religion but allowed citizens to practice other religions. An article in Pétion's constitution stated that, "if in the future, other religions are introduced, no one will be prevented, if they abide by the laws, from practicing their chosen form of worship."[55] In terms of popular religious affiliation, the North did not differ significantly from the South, and the constitution did allow for some deviation from a singular Catholic adhesion. An article in Christophe's constitutions stated that "the [apostolic and Roman Catholic] is the only one recognized by the Government. The exercise of others is tolerated, but shall not be done publicly."[56] This article suggests that Haiti was to have two religious components; the first was to be a public and formal religious affiliation to the Catholic Church, while the second was to be a private and informal practice. The duality of religious affiliation in Christophe's constitution allowed for the development of domestic religious realities, while the state could claim allegiance to the Catholic Church. Both constitutions would have allowed foreign merchants to practice their respective religions without government interference, and Christophe's treaty proposal simply reaffirmed that ability.

As Richardson and Peltier suggested, the treaty proposed by Christophe very closely resembled the one that Dessalines had rejected in 1804. The situation in 1807, however, was dramatically different from 1804. The British were the only nation that had not prohibited trade with Haiti, and in fact they had explicitly allowed the trade. Illegal trade continued, but foreign governments would not allow the trade to flourish as the Haitian government had hoped. The British were now its only legal option and the only way that the Haitian government could secure diplomatic recognition. Christophe, therefore, was willing to concede to the restrictive treaty articles that Dessalines had confidently rejected. This treaty called for Haiti to become part of the British "informal empire."

To help support his efforts to convince the British ministers to recognize Haiti's independence, Peltier wrote a three-part memoire and submitted it to Stewart.[57] In this memoire, he acknowledged the uniqueness of the present situation and sympathized with the British minsters. "The recognition of a new state form," he wrote, "and whose territory not only was a dependent of a great European power, but whose people were, for the most part the slaves of subjects of this power, [was] surprising at first sight, and the novelty of the situation at first elicited a host of objections that we believe we can easily dissipate."[58] Peltier hoped to confront these objections in order to overcome the barriers to recognition. The most important factor was that Haiti had succeeded in achieving its independence. "The Independence of Haiti is a matter of fact," Peltier argued, "that already exists, and that will always exist."[59] The last part of the statement was perhaps wishful thinking, since it was clear that the Haitian governments continued to fear another French invasion and a return to their previous colonial status. But their current de facto independence, Peltier argued, should have made the decision for the British easier since it was a fait accompli. The fact that Haiti was the product of an "insurrection" should not have deterred its recognition, since other countries founded on the same basis, including Switzerland, Holland, and the United States, were "recognized by all of the sovereigns of Europe and were currently regular members in the society of States [société des États]."[60] Furthermore, as had arisen in the discussion of recognition when Dessalines was in power, Peltier pointed out that the British did not have to wait for the

French to recognize Haiti's independence since France had not waited for the British to recognize the independence of the United States.

In addition to the revolutionary manner in which Haiti had achieved its independence, Peltier realized that the racial composition of the Haitian population and the Haitian government was a factor in preventing the British from recognizing Haiti's independence. But race, Peltier argued, should not pose a problem, since the British had treaties with other nations of black people. "It would be a waste of time to respond by objecting because of the dangers of recognizing the sovereignty of a new people," he argued, "of which three quarters were randomly assembled from all parts of Africa while all of the governments of Europe have treaties with several African or Mohammedan rulers."[61] Even though they had signed treaties with these governments, the British, Peltier argued, had less to fear in signing a treaty with Christophe since Haiti had the advantage of having a European-style government, religion, and society. "Today, it [Haiti] aspires to account for something." Peltier explained to Stewart. "It has raised its institutions to the level of European Governments. It has courts, churches, priests, ministers who would not be out of place in any European cabinet, a mint, concert halls, forts, citadels, public schools, an army of 70,000 men organized in the style of Europe." The civil war, he argued, did not suggest that Haiti did not deserve recognition but that it simply needed "a strong and powerful hand to guide its path and ensure its existence."[62] They needed British help, Peltier pleaded.

Rather than simply emphasizing the benefits of an official relationship with Haiti, Peltier's memoire also focused on the potential dangers of not signing the treaty. First, he integrated the conversation about Haiti into the discussion of "amelioration" in the British Caribbean. He noted that the very abrupt French abolition of slavery during the revolution had resulted in the deaths of 100,000 whites and the same number of blacks, as well as costing an enormous sum of sterling and the eventual loss of the colony by France. By recognizing Haiti, he argued, the British would show the enslaved populations in their Caribbean colonies that it was possible to be free under British rule. At the end of the eighteenth century, West Indian planters, the West Indian Committee, and the abolitionist community began to discuss a gradual improvement policy on the colonial plantations that became known at "amelioration." Inspired by Enlightenment and Evangelical movements, the rising cost of enslaved laborers from Africa, and fear of slave revolts after Tacky's Rebellion in

1760, amelioration was designed—depending on the perspective—either to maintain colonial slavery in the face of increasing opposition or to prepare enslaved laborers for eventual freedom.[63] Peltier argued that recognition of Haiti was in line with the British policy of amelioration and that it would be helpful "because we would show the blacks that they are not destined to be slaves forever."[64] But, although Peltier emphasized that recognizing Haiti's independence would demonstrate that the British were willing to (eventually) permit universal freedom in their Caribbean colonies, he also highlighted that it was important to reassert British political control. He argued that this treaty of amity and commerce would assure European power over the island and therefore control its potentially damaging influence on the British Caribbean: "It would replace under European influence a population that has sworn to avoid it."[65] According to this logic, while the enslaved people in the Caribbean should hope for eventual freedom, they should not ever expect self-rule.

He also—perhaps a bit dangerously—warned of the risks of not becoming friendly with Haiti. "There is no need to search for what may be the moral influence of the recognition of the independence of Haity on your colonies," he argued. "Consideration should be given," he continued, "for precautions against the dangers of a state of affairs that is more hostile than friendly, that you created or at least that you tolerate."[66] Peltier's warning was a reminder of a British fear that Haitian leaders had worked hard to assuage. Neither of the Haitian presidents wanted to give the international community the impression that they would initiate foreign expeditions, and Peltier was treading a fine line with this threat since it might bring British fears to the forefront of the discussion.

Finally, Peltier undertook a detailed character description of Christophe to emphasize his good qualities while condemning Pétion and his followers. Peltier highlighted Christophe's favorable disposition toward the British and argued that the British should appreciate this to a greater degree since not all Haitian leaders felt the same way. "Toussaint and Dessalines died, without the death of either having elicited any regret in England," he reported, "[and] neither of the two were favorably disposed to her. Toussaint never showed a frank desire to ally with England who fought him without success. Dessalines in turn sent an agent to propose to the United-States a treaty of alliance and exclusive commerce between America and Haiti."[67] Peltier did not take the time to consider whether Christophe would have also tried to negotiate an alliance with the United

States had the American government not recently prohibited trade with Haiti. Instead, he focused on the reasons why Christophe was favorably disposed toward the British. A key feature, in Peltier's mind, was that Christophe was a "*nègre Anglaise*" (English negro) and was therefore willing to give the British preferential treatment.[68] Christophe had been born in the British Caribbean—in either Grenada or St. Christopher— but Peltier's claim that Christophe's experience as a slave in a British colony meant that he had a special alliance with the British was a bit of a stretch.[69] Perhaps he was relying on additional information to make this claim, because later Christophe would in fact develop close ties with the British abolitionist community, and through these connections he received aid in manufacturing and religious and educational expertise.[70]

Peltier finished the memoire by criticizing Pétion in an attempt to undermine his legitimacy as president of Haiti. He argued that Pétion was not disposed to treat the British more favorably and in fact had been harmful to their persons and property. Furthermore, Peltier claimed that Pétion was allied with Ferrand and that he was republican. Christophe had not yet established a kingdom in the North (he would in 1811), but unlike Pétion, who established the *République Haïtienne* with his constitution, Christophe ruled l'*État d'Hayti*. Peltier continued to offer comparisons between Christophe and Pétion in subsequent letters to Stewart, in which Christophe figured as the legitimate ruler of Haiti in addition to being the better choice. "I gave to the Government innumerable letters and proof that Christophe was a man of honor," Peltier reported, "a man of good intentions, a thinker, in a word a grand man in a time when we find so many small men at the head of the affairs of this poor world. In other letters I proved that Pétion and his adherents were murderers, cowards, parricidal, republicans, Bonapartists, in the end."[71]

Unresponsive Ministers

The archival records do not include the British response to this memoire, but based on Jean-Gabriel Peltier's later correspondence, it seems that Robert Stewart offered his opinions in person. "I know that you have repeated in this respect," Peltier wrote, "that a government does not have the right to interfere in the internal quarrels of another country. This axiom might be correct, when you do not go to that country; but when you trade as you will continue to do in St. Domingo, the neutrality between a legitimate ruler, and the rebels, is not practical."[72] By trading with Haiti,

Peltier argued, the British had necessarily involved themselves in the conflict. Furthermore, they had a duty to protect the lives and property of the British merchants—allowing them to trade with a nation embroiled in civil war necessarily put them in danger.

Peltier bolstered his own arguments by submitting a second memoire to Stewart, written by Christophe's secretary of state, Rouanez, jeune.[73] In this memoire, Rouanez compared Christophe and Pétion by making some of the same points that Peltier had made, but also by highlighting the good economic opportunities in Haiti for British merchants. The more urgent goal of the memoire, however, was to garner support for a coordinated effort to expel the French from the island. As had been clear in Christophe's treaty proposal, the French were still a threat to the country's survival, and Christophe wanted to eliminate his two opponents on the island. Rouanez provided information about Ferrand's holdout at Santo Domingo and proposed a joint offensive to rid the island of the French once and for all. To do this, however, Rouanez noted that it was essential to end the civil war in Haiti (with Christophe as the victor). He requested maritime support from the British and military supplies to outfit the march on Santo Domingo.

Not only did the British ministers not respond to Peltier and Thomas Richardson, but it seems that the government issued a new law on 11 November 1807 that would severely damage the trade relationship between British merchants and Haiti. Peltier claimed that the government had instituted a 14 shilling duty on each quintal of foreign coffee.[74] Peltier argued that this would essentially ruin the commercial relationship between the two countries since the price of coffee was only 85 shillings.[75] To prove this point, Peltier compiled a report on the state of commercial relations between British merchants and Haiti between September 1806 and December 1808, when trade was legal and regulated. During this time, at least 80 ships traveled to Haiti from London, Liverpool, Bristol, Whitehaven, and Guernsey carrying all kinds of manufactured goods.[76] If the British subjected Haiti to this new duty, Peltier warned that British merchants might feel the repercussions since the Haitian government could put a similar duty on the importation of British manufactured goods.

In explaining why Haiti should be exempt from this new duty, Peltier pointed to the hierarchical relationship that he perceived between the British Empire and Haiti. "Haiti is," he argued, "if not nominally, at least in reality, because of its needs, by the relations that it currently has with Great Britain, a veritable English Colony."[77] This statement was an exaggeration, but it reflected the relationship that Christophe and Pétion had proposed following the outbreak of civil war in Haiti. The one-sided negotiations for a trade treaty between Christophe and the British government had clearly broken down, and Peltier appears to have switched to a new tactic. He had previously been arguing that Haiti's independence was a fait accompli, but now he argued that the "informal empire" of the British in Haiti was already the current status of the relationship. The benefits of the "informality" of this type of imperial relationship, however, would undermine the need for a trade treaty between the British Empire and Haiti. But Peltier had not given up on the possibility of a formal treaty between the two. This new conflict, he argued, demonstrated how "much each day and in every event to come, makes known the need to finally establish the existence of the State of Haiti, in recognizing its independence, and by sending official agents."[78] British recognition would secure the "existence" of the State of Haiti.

Peltier was relentless in his attempt to secure diplomatic recognition for Haiti. In June 1808, a year after he first broached the subject with the British ministers in London, he continued to write to Stewart's office. "Mr. Canning [the foreign secretary] said the day before yesterday in the House of Commons," Peltier argued to the new under-secretary of state for war and the colonies, Edward Cooke, "that 'all countries who rebel against the general oppressor of the world, and the enemy of Great Britain, would by that action become, under whatever circumstances it finds itself, the ally of England!' I invoke this sentiment for my *commettants* the Haitians."[79] As he had done before, Peltier used British policy and British arguments to advocate on behalf of Haitian recognition. It seems, however, that the British were willing to continue making an exception.

While Robert Stewart did not officially respond to Peltier's letters, he did make some efforts to find a solution to the problems presented by Peltier. "Lord Castlereagh [Robert Stewart] had asked me, last January," Peltier wrote to Cooke, "if I would have any objections to the Government of His Majesty recognizing the independence of the two Governments of Haiti."[80] This solution would prevent the British from having to interfere in the internal affairs of the country. When presented with this option, however, Christophe's secretary of state, Rouanez, noted that he would not tolerate the acknowledgment of a divided Haiti: "I am obliged to announce to you that it is not in the ability of any foreign power or government to *morceler* [break up] that of Haiti. If Pétion put himself in a state of revolt against his authority, the President possesses the means to reduce him with force."[81] Christophe and his emissaries continued to argue that he had the military power to defeat Pétion but that he did not want to kill Haitian citizens, even if they did support the "rebel" government. Because of this, they would not agree to let the British recognize the country under two separate governments, since doing so would undermine Christophe's authority and legitimacy.

The negotiations between the Haitian governments and the British ministers in London did not end in an official agreement of any kind. Four years after he initially tried to enter into a trade agreement with the British, Pétion's government tried yet again to establish an official diplomatic relationship: "I beg leave to acquaint Your Lordship," John Goff, perhaps another British merchant, wrote to Robert Jenkins, the new secretary of state for war and the colonies, in 1811, "that, on the part of General Pétion, I am authorized to treat with His Majesty's Ministers on subjects relating to the Island of Hayti. General Pétion is very desirous for the reestablishment of Tranquility in that Island, and anxious to enter into such alliance with this Country as may best conduce to mutual advantage and enable him effectually to exclude the French from obtaining any footing again in Hayti."[82] Pétion's government never submitted an official treaty draft to the British government and simply emphasized that they were willing to accommodate British interests.

Pétion was even willing to have Haiti's independence acknowledged under the leadership of two governments. "General Pétion's wish is," Goff continued, "that the mediation of His Majesty may interpose between the Belligerents Pétion & Christophe. As a basis for Peace between them, He proposes that each party shall retain His present possessions (neither having made any acquisitions). Whatever other conditions may be recommended by this Government, tending to confirm, and establish Peace, will readily be subscribed by General Pétion."[83] The specific articles of any treaty between Haiti and Great Britain, Goff argued, were secondary to the primary goal of preventing any military incursions by France. This could only happen, he argued, if internal warfare ceased. Goff concluded that "it is General Pétion's most ardent desire, that relatives of Amity and Commerce may be as closely drawn as possible between this Country and Hayti."[84] The new secretary of state for war and the colonies did not respond to Goff's request.

Conclusion

Jean-Gabriel Peltier asked Robert Stewart for a response to his and Thomas Richardson's letters on 10 November 1807 and 18 June 1808.[85]

Richardson in turn asked for a response on 29 November 1807 and 14 January 1808.[86] None was forthcoming. The British ministers simply ignored the many letters that the Haitian leaders and their agents delivered to them or only responded orally in person in order to avoid any paper trail that could be used by the Haitian governments to claim that the British had acknowledged their independence. Peltier requested that Stewart at least discuss with Christophe the specifics of their relationship. It was not fair, he argued, to leave him hanging: "It is necessary at least to explain to the leader of Haiti under what title you recognize that state and his government, or if you consider them as an abstraction, a *non-descript*."[87] The British ministers never responded to Christophe's treaty proposal or to Peltier's and Richardson's many letters. Haiti was to remain, in Peltier's words, an "abstraction," a "non-descript."

Three years after his first letter in mid-1807, Peltier still expressed shock at the unequal treatment that Haiti suffered at the hands of the British ministers. He compared Christophe favorably to the Persian envoy, Mirza Abul Hasan Khan, who was sent to London in 1809 to encourage and develop British interests in the Persian silk trade. "The black chieftain which a Series of Revolutions has placed at the head of Haity, may and is willing to render to this Country all possible services, and I make no doubt but that he is much more able to contribute to the Security of the British Possessions and to the prosperity of the British Trade in the West Indies, than the Constituent of Mirza Abdul Hassan, can ever do in behalf of your Eastern Empire."[88]

In 1807, the Haitian presidents badly needed British support in order to achieve diplomatic recognition and military protection. Every other Atlantic power had prohibited trade and the British were their only potential ally. British merchants traded with Haiti legally under the regulation of licenses issued by the British Privy Council and therefore helped to sustain Haiti's break from France. The presidents, however, hoped to secure full diplomatic recognition from the British government in London because they felt that the British were not treating them like they treated other countries. Pétion's secretary of state, Bruno Blanchet, wrote to Stewart in April 1807 and argued that the relationship that currently existed between the two was highly unusual and declared that "it is rare, Sir, that commercial relations between two peoples do not encourage some kind of political relationship."[89] Many of the British merchants trading with Haiti also shared this opinion—they felt that their interests would be better served through official and traditional diplomatic channels.

Almost two years after they initiated contact with the British ministers in London, the Haitian presidents tried to capitalize on the news of the Napoleonic invasion of the Iberian peninsula in order to form a foreign alliance with France's newest enemy. In late 1808, Christophe wrote to authorities in Cuba to announce his support for the deposed Spanish king. He also proposed to open trade between Haiti and Cuba. "What he wanted above all, he said," historian Ada Ferrer reveals, "was peace and union to reign between Haiti and Spain, his neighbor."[90] Cuban officials, however, like the British ministers in London, were reluctant to reply. Christophe also made overtures to Spanish officials on the eastern side of Hispaniola and contributed to the expulsion of the French forces from Santo Domingo in 1809—a combined Spanish, Haitian, and British effort. Spanish metropolitan officials, Ferrer highlights, instructed the governor of Havana, by a Royal Order issued by the Junta Suprema, to "cultivate relations of friendship with said black chief [Christophe] by sending a person in your confidence to his residence."[91] Governor Someruelos in Havana—like Governor Nugent in Jamaica four years earlier—refused to act on these instructions.

Pétion had similarly contacted the Cuban governors and had even sent a ship to collect the exiled Haitians who had left with the French (forcibly or otherwise). The governor of Santiago, however, refused to allow Pétion's men on shore and did not return any exiled Haitians. "He had no power," Ferrer reports, "to receive vessels or enter into agreements with 'foreign colonies,' he said."[92] Governor Kindelán's choice of words reveals the ongoing diplomatic resistance to Haitian independence in Spain's Caribbean colonies. According to Ferrer, the civil war in Haiti provided justification for Cuban authorities to resist engaging with either Haitian leader. As they had in 1804, the Spanish did their best to remove themselves from the conflict. This removal, from their perspective, also had the supposed benefit of preventing communication between the two islands—a lofty goal that they certainly did not achieve. When Napoléon Bonaparte invaded Spain in 1808, however, Cuban authorities exiled the French refugees on the island in 1809 and they stopped supporting France's efforts to capture merchant ships trading with Haiti.[93]

Nevertheless, in 1809, it was clear that neither of France's enemies was willing to concede diplomatic recognition to either Haitian government. Cuban authorities, despite instructions from the metropole to establish a friendly relationship with Christophe, resisted both diplomatic and economic contact. The recent Cuban sugar revolution made officials extra wary of the potential influences, support, or inspiration that Haitians might provide to their own slaves. The British, on the other hand, were eager to support a legal trade with Haiti, but establishing formal diplomatic relations was beyond what they were willing to concede. Meanwhile, Christophe and Pétion continued their civil war in a stalemate since neither army could militarily or politically defeat the other. The civil war lasted until 1820, when Pétion's successor, Jean-Pierre Boyer, reunited the country following Christophe's suicide.[94]

CONCLUSION

Haiti's Declaration of Independence on 1 January 1804 marked the end of the world's only successful slave revolution by proclaiming a spectacular triumph over unimaginable adversity. But whether or not this triumph would endure was not at all clear. The documentary reconstruction of Haiti's declared independence reveals the unprecedented and unique challenges and opportunities that were perceived, debated, rejected, and seized during the initial vulnerable years after 1804. The evidence shows how the intertwined and distinct economic, legal, and ideological currents that characterized the volatile Atlantic World did not flow consistently in any one direction, as France learned in its failure to garner support for Haiti's isolation. The many and diverse connections between Haiti and the surrounding countries, colonies, and empires in the first years after the Haitian Declaration of Independence reveal that there was no straightforward or uniform response to the challenges and opportunities that Haiti afforded to foreign governments and individuals during the Age of Revolution. The close analysis of Haiti's interactions with the rest of the Atlantic World emphasizes the value of looking beyond official policies as articulated in the metropolitan centers in order to understand the meaning of the Declaration of Independence for Haiti's standing in the international community. The years after 1804 do clearly reveal that Atlantic empires and nations helped sustain Haitian independence without extending full diplomatic recognition.

Rather than collectively undermining Haiti's ambitions, government representatives and merchants immediately began calculating how they could capitalize on Haiti's declared independence while also protecting their own priorities. These calculations involved distinct and often competing factors. Along with perceived economic opportunities, foreign onlookers feared that the slave revolution in Haiti would spread throughout the Americas, unleashing severe economic challenges to the status quo. It became urgent, therefore, to find ways to prevent the contagion of rebellion or Haitian military units from reaching other colonies or territories.

Haiti's local, regional, and metropolitan interactions call into question the established scholarly emphasis on the supremacy and singularity of race in the dominant thinking of the early nineteenth century. The evidence of the first years after the Declaration of Independence leads to the conclusion that foreign governments did not collectively and uniformly stigmatize the new country because they could not imagine a "black republic" in their midst. Neighboring nations, while refusing to fully recognize Haitian independence, were eager to take advantage of trade opportunities and to use Haiti to their own advantage in influencing the balance of power in European warfare. The relationship, however, was not completely devoid of racism; foreign officials consistently tried to forge hierarchical relationships with the Haitian government and sought to allocate the island a status somewhere between colony and country. Nevertheless, the multiple connections between Haiti and the Atlantic World after 1 January 1804 help explain how the Declaration of Independence launched international debates about racial hierarchy, the relationship between freedom and sovereignty, and the intertwining of ideological and political relationships with economic ambitions. Understanding these debates helps explain why events in Haiti were pivotal rather than marginal in the Age of Revolution.

The Haitian Declaration of Independence inextricably linked independence and sovereignty (or liberty). Over the course of the following years, however, foreign powers divided the two concepts. At times, foreign officials could imagine a situation in which they would recognize Haitian independence but also assume a level of control over internal and external affairs that compromised the Haitian government's sovereignty. At other times—and in ways that would become the dominant policy of foreign governments after the initial years following 1804—governments withheld official recognition of Haitian independence while treating Haiti as sovereign from France. Diplomatic non-recognition did not discount economic recognition; moreover, the line between the two layers of recognition was blurry. Legal and illegal trade with Haiti helped materially sustain the island's break from France while also politically violating France's claims over the island. On the other hand, non-recognition prevented the Haitian government from entering into economic, military, or political treaties, and it meant that the traditional and established methods of international diplomacy could not be applied to foreign connections with the new country.[1]

While the Declaration of Independence was officially addressed to the "People of Hayti," it was also a public statement to the rest of the world, which the Haitian government printed and distributed to foreign officials and newspapers around the Atlantic. Part of the message of the Declaration, therefore, was clearly articulated for a foreign audience. Haitian leaders understood that the policies of the new state—mainly universal freedom on Haitian soil—would not be welcome news in other territories in the Americas, and so they sought to assuage the fears of foreign readers by promising nonintervention and by trying to cultivate economic and political alliances wherever possible. While not successful to the extent that they hoped, Haitian leaders found the international community willing to negotiate their status in the Atlantic World, because economic, military, and political interests often proved to be more important than concerns about the spread of revolutionary ideas. The various spheres of influence, therefore, meant that Haiti's place in the Atlantic World was ambiguous and often came with qualifications and a lack of clarity. In keeping with historian Lauren Benton's research on "layers" within empires, systematic study of the archival record reveals multiple layers of recognition and non-recognition rather than comprehensive diplomatic isolation. Different foreign governments extended partial or temporary recognition of Haiti's independence in the years after 1804. Furthermore, governments were willing to extend economic recognition to Haiti even while they withheld official diplomatic recognition. Foreign recognition, like sovereignty in the early nineteenth century, was a divisible characteristic that could be portioned within and between economic, diplomatic, and legal spheres.

Diverse individuals at different levels both within and outside of government structures decided to what degree Haiti's independence and sovereignty would be recognized. Central to these decisions was the context of the Napoleonic Wars. One approach was to use Haiti to advance war efforts, as was the case with the British Empire. A second approach, undertaken by the governors of Curaçao and St. Thomas and the U.S. government, was to carefully balance the benefits of trade with Haiti with the politicking that was necessary to remain neutral in the international war. In each case, the potential economic benefits of trade with Haiti encouraged merchants to continue to visit Haiti—either legally or illegally—and these merchants pressured their government representatives to support their interests.

Lawyers and judges further contributed to debates about Haiti's place in the Atlantic World when private or admiralty ships captured merchants trading with Haiti. Did Haiti fit within the customary practices of the law of nations? Had their respective governments recognized Haiti's independence despite their continued silence on the issue? Addressing these questions meant dealing with multiple considerations ranging from the theoretical to the personal. Since Haiti overtly challenged colonialism and slavery, the existence of an independent state ruled by black and mixed-race people made foreign officials worry about the security of their own economic, political, social, and cultural systems. Judges and lawyers sometimes treated Haiti within the customary practices of the law of nations, but they also used the economic policies implemented by their governments to interpret Haiti's proclaimed diplomatic status. In the case of the British Empire, this led to an implicit recognition of Haiti's diplomatic independence from France. In the case of the United States, the prohibition on trade led the courts to conclude that Haiti was still a French colony.

After the initial period, between 1804 and 1810, foreign governments continued to stop short of welcoming the new country into the community of recognized nations of the Atlantic World, but they also embraced innovative compromises that allowed merchants to trade with Haiti. This trade strengthened the foundation upon which Haitian leaders were able to continue beating the odds against sustaining independence. Haiti's economic relationships helped secure independence, despite continued opposition by the French government during the first decade after the Haitian Declaration of Independence.

Although Haiti was able to maintain its independence during the period of official diplomatic non-recognition by foreign governments, the cost of this non-recognition was substantial, for both material and psychological reasons. The threat of a French reinvasion remained real. "For Haiti," historian Brenda Gayle Plummer argues, "diplomatic recognition was the only safeguard against French attack."[2] Such recognition was only given in 1825. Diplomatic recognition may have ensured protection from French reinvasion, and non-recognition also impacted two key features of Haiti's standing in the Atlantic World: first, non-recognition hurt the "dignity" of the government, and, second, non-recognition prevented Haitian leaders and citizens from engaging in the customary practices that governed foreign relations and thereby encouraged a domestic emphasis on military security. The importance of dignity was emphasized as early as 29 November 1803, after the evacuation of the French troops, when Dessalines, Christophe, and Clervaux announced that "the independence of St. Domingo is proclaimed. Restored to our primitive dignity, we have proclaimed our rights: we swear never to yield them to any power on earth: the frightful veil of prejudice is torn to pieces, and is so forever."[3] Similarly, Christophe highlighted the need for the government to "support [the citizens] with dignity and to honorably fulfill its commitments," in announcing the publication of his 1807 constitution.[4]

These claims, however, were undermined by the refusal of the international community to recognize the characteristics that the Haitian leaders asserted. When Dessalines refused to sign the trade treaty with Nugent in early 1804, Edward Corbet rightly perceived that the Haitian governor-general for life felt that it would have undermined the "independence of Hayti and the dignity of its Government."[5] Nugent's proposal, while offering official diplomatic recognition, would have created a hierarchical relationship between the two countries and would have allowed British control over Haiti's foreign relations. At the same time, the evidence also makes clear that non-recognition, in the end, created a version of the relationship that Nugent had proposed, since it limited the ability of Haitian leaders to negotiate, treat, and connect with their counterparts in the Atlantic World. Christophe and Pétion, for example, had to use French and British citizens to communicate with the British secretary of state for war and the colonies. While Haitian leaders were in constant contact with Jamaican admiralty captains and with merchants who served as unofficial agents for their governments, non-recognition also meant that government mail could be simply ignored. When Haitian leaders sent letters to the governors of Cuba and to the president of the United States, they did not receive a response.

Even after France and Great Britain had recognized Haitian independence, their participation was still limited by the United States' holdout. For example, as a result of American influence, Haiti was excluded from the Panama Congress of 1826, a meeting of the newly independent states of Latin America.[6] While economic recognition secured Haitian sovereignty and ensured that France did not succeed in reclaiming its most profitable colony, there is no doubt that diplomatic recognition would have significantly enhanced Haiti's integration into the community of nations and empires in the Atlantic World.

The external pressures associated with official non-recognition also cultivated the roots of militarized authoritarian regimes whose main focus became the maintenance of national independence and sovereignty rather than the individual rights of the nation's citizens. The Haitian

Declaration of Independence assured the abolition of slavery in the country, but at the same time, it limited individual freedom in the name of national independence. By inextricably linking national independence and the abolition of slavery, the Declaration of Independence subsumed individual freedom within the authority of the state. The abolition of legal enslavement was the driving force behind the war for independence in Haiti, unlike the precedent of the United States, where "freedom" referred to the metaphorical or political slavery of colonialism.[7] Dessalines well understood that Haitian independence would come under attack, and the threat of reinvasion led to a concentration of authority in Haiti under military rule and limited the expansion of individual rights and political participation. In order to safeguard its coasts and defend its borders from foreign attack, the Haitian government began creating a society dominated by military needs and security. The defense of national independence proved to be more important than individual freedom.

The association between national independence and freedom meant that the boundaries of the nation (claimed to be the entire island of Hispaniola) demarcated the free society.[8] Dessalines's counsel to Haitians not to disrupt the existing systems of the neighboring islands was a direct promise to the governors of the surrounding islands and their superiors in Europe. By promising not to become "legislators of the Antilles," Dessalines hoped to avoid wars with other countries that might usurp Haiti's independence and re-enslave the population, and he sought to demonstrate that the Haitian government was willing to participate in the established customary practices of the law of nations. Haitians would respect the jurisdictional boundaries of the Atlantic. In connecting with the nations and empires of the Atlantic, Haitian leaders did what they felt was necessary to become a "treaty-worthy nation" in the community of European empires and the United States of America.[9]

As a result of their ongoing trade relationships with Haiti, the British, most importantly, and the Americans, secondarily, took on a central role in Haiti's experience during the first decade of diplomatic non-recognition. While the British were unwilling to officially recognize Haiti as a country, their economic and unofficial diplomatic relationships helped sustain Haiti's independence. The war between France and Britain meant that the British were well positioned and motivated to support Haitian independence, which cut off the French from their main source of wealth in the Americas. Military strategy allowed the British to ignore French claims to the title over the territory and to effectively support Dessalines and his army by allowing British merchants to travel to Haiti with government licenses between 1806 and 1808 and thereafter under the guidelines regulating trade between neutral nations. The war between France and Britain, therefore, opened the door for an exceptional relationship between Haiti and the British Empire.

For their part, the U.S. Congress and the governors of Curaçao and St. Thomas briefly caved under French pressure and prohibited trade with Haiti. But after a period of prohibition between 1806 and 1810, trade between the United States and Haiti became legal under the supervision of commercial agents stationed in Cap Haïtien and Port-au-Prince. Additionally, the British occupied the islands of Curaçao and St. Thomas between 1807 and 1815 and legalized trade under the same rules governing the rest of their colonies. Significant foreign trade with Haiti continued, therefore, despite the fact that foreign governments did not extend official diplomatic recognition to the new country.

The British Orders in Council of 1806 and 1808 established an enduring policy, which the British Empire would maintain until 1826. It first allowed for a regulated and then a free economic relationship but did not offer official diplomatic recognition.[10] British merchants were also able to secure favorable terms of trade. "By 1814," historian Erin Zavitz reveals, "the British had achieved a preferential trade duty of 7% compared to 12% for other nations, which, along with French and American embargos, led to 'a near monopoly of Haitian commerce.'"[11] One American merchant perceived a degree of coercion in the favoritism shown to the British by the Haitians. "I find a great disposition in the officers of the Government [of Haiti] to impose on Americans," New Yorker Jacob Lewis argued in 1818. "There is evidently a preference given, and partiality shewn to Englishmen, not so much from respect as from fear; the Admiralty on the Jamaica Station is in the regular habit of sending frequently ships of war hither, and enquiring of the English residents in what manner they are treated."[12]

Lewis suggested that the British patrolled the waters around Haiti in order to secure economic advantages for their merchants, but the admiralty captains also ensured that Haitians did not stray too far from shore. Indeed, James Richard Dacres, the chief commander of the Jamaica station, asked for further instructions in mid-1805 as to whether he should continue the current policy, which ordered the cruisers "to treat the blacks with civility and attention, but on falling in with their armed vessels at sea to send them to Jamaica."[13] Not only did they protect the investments of their merchants, they also tried to physically contain Haitians within their borders in order to prevent contact with the enslaved populations in the British Caribbean and to prevent Haitian privateers from capturing foreign ships at sea. The senior admiralty officers at Jamaica continued to keep a close eye on events in Haiti and sometimes corresponded with local officials and national leaders. They constantly monitored the safety and security of the British merchants and were prepared to help them in the event of any disturbances. By 1808, the British were unilaterally implementing the articles of the treaty that Jean-Jacques Dessalines had rejected in early 1804 and that Henry Christophe had proposed in 1807.

While a great deal remains to be learned about the years after the first period of Haitian independence, various studies of the subsequent decades suggest the enormous potential of continued systematic research on the complex and contested history of Haiti during the prolonged years of official non-recognition. For example, scholars have shown that once peace was established in Europe, the British were no longer willing to challenge French claims to ownership of Haiti. During the Congress of Vienna in 1814–15, the French and British signed a "secret agreement" that would allow the British to continue trading with Haiti, but in the event of a French attack on the island, the British promised that they would not support Haitian military defense.[14] This secret agreement emphasizes the importance of military strategy in determining the British response to Dessalines's invitation to British merchants in 1803. When the wars ended, the British lost the military motivation to support Haitian independence; their agreement with France illustrates how the larger context of the Atlantic World affected the responses of foreign empires to the Haitian Declaration of Independence.

The end of Napoleonic Wars also changed the relationship between Spain and Haiti, even though the Spanish Empire continued to withhold diplomatic recognition until 1855—the same year that Spain recognized the independence of Santo Domingo (Dominican Republic). In 1817, Spanish officials in Santo Domingo asked for advice regarding how they should treat citizens from Christophe's and Pétion's states—without official recognition, they needed special instructions since they had constant contact and communication with their neighbors.[15] Dominican officials requested permission to tacitly acknowledge the Haitian leaders in order to establish a practical relationship to deal with day-to-day issues. They suggested using a loophole in colonial law that allowed officials in the colonies to establish local relationships while still maintaining the official diplomatic distance of the broader empire. Dominican officials sought to use this loophole because they were hesitant to extend official or even implicit recognition for fear of antagonizing the French. In a letter to the Duke of Richelieu on 8 March 1817, Dominican officials promised that they would not extend official recognition to the Haitian states but stressed the need to establish some kind of informal connection with King Christophe and President Pétion.[16]

Despite the secret agreement with France in 1814, trade continued between British and Haitian merchants, and, fifteen years after the Declaration of Independence, the question of Haiti's sovereignty remained loosely coupled with the reality of British trade. "These activities and mutual interchanges are in fact equivalent to a tacit, if not a formal, recognition of our independence," argued Christophe's foreign minister, Julien Prévost, in a letter to British abolitionist Thomas Clarkson, on 20 November 1819; "nothing then remains for the Haitian government but to see solemnized by treaties an independence which has already been implicitly recognized by the nations."[17] As the British Admiralty Courts had concluded in 1808, Prévost interpreted British economic policy to have diplomatic implications.

But this recognition was not forthcoming. The British implicitly acknowledged Haiti's independence by sending a consul to the island in 1826, but the relationship was still not formalized until 1839. The British had waited for France to acknowledge Haitian independence in 1825. Over two decades after the Haitian Declaration of Independence, France extended a qualified recognition that depended on the payment of an enormous indemnity to compensate former French planters for their losses during the revolution and a 50 percent tariff reduction on French trade.[18] The deal would haunt Haiti's treasury, and therefore its government and population, throughout the nineteenth century. "Towards the close of 1825 M. Malter, the first French consul-general," British Consul Charles Mackenzie wrote, "arrived in Haiti. Early in the following year I followed: Prussia, Lubeck, Hamburgh, Holland and Sweden also sent agents, the three first consuls-general, and the two last consuls. . . . Whether other functionaries from countries [other] than these named have since gone to the republic I do not know."[19] France's recognition of Haitian independence in 1825 opened the door for other foreign powers to engage in diplomatic relationships with the island. In her research, Zavitz has found that the British foreign secretary instructed Mackenzie, in addition to his duties as consul, "to record information on the internal state of Haiti, its relations with France, and the status of agricultural production, especially in regards to the use and control of free labor. This data would help Mackenzie in his larger mission of drawing up a treaty with Haiti."[20] Mackenzie's arrival, therefore, signaled an implicit rather than formal diplomatic recognition of Haitian sovereignty. During his time in the country, he was not able to sign a treaty with the Haitian government. Nevertheless, this was the first step toward the official recognition of Haitian independence by the British.

In 1838, close to three and a half decades after the Haitian Declaration of Independence, the French removed the qualifications on their recognition, reduced the indemnity payment, and fully recognized Haiti's sovereignty.[21] This recognition once again inspired the British to conclude a "Treaty of Amity, Commerce and Navigation."[22] But their efforts butted up against the preferential trade relationship that the French had negotiated with Haiti.[23] It was not until 1844 that Britain and Haiti signed their first commercial treaty.

In 1839, however, Britain and Haiti signed a treaty that incorporated Haiti into Britain's campaign to outlaw the transatlantic slave trade. John Henry Temple, Viscount Palmerston, the principal secretary of state for foreign affairs, wrote to the British consul in Port-au-Prince, George William Conway Courtenay, pressuring him to find a way to include Haiti in the international coalition against the slave trade, a group that included France and the independent states of Venezuela, Chile, and Buenos Aires. "Her Majesty's Government hopes," Temple wrote, "that Hayti will not be the last state in the New World to concur with their fellow Christians in the Old, in putting an end to a system of crime, which has so long continued to disgrace the character of civilized nations."[24] On 9 December 1839, Noel Viallet, on behalf of Haitian president Jean-Pierre Boyer, signed a treaty with Courtenay for the suppression of the slave trade, and it also committed the Haitian state to the conventions signed between the French and British in 1831 and 1833.[25] This treaty, signed between the "Republick of Hayti" and "Great Britain and Ireland," was the first formal and unequivocal British recognition of Haitian independence.

Finally, in 1844, the two countries signed a trade agreement, known as the "Treaty of Commerce and Navigation between Her Britannic Majesty and the Republic of Hayti." The preamble to the treaty emphasized that both nations were "equally animated by the desire of extending the commercial relations between the dominions of her majesty and the territories of the republick." Article 1 described a completely different relationship than the treaty that Jamaican governor George Nugent had proposed in 1804: "That there shall be reciprocal freedom of commerce between the United Kingdom of Great Britain and Ireland and the Republic of Haiti. The subjects of the two countries respectively shall have liberty freely and securely to come with their ships and cargoes to all places, ports, and rivers in the United Kingdom and in the Republic of Haiti, to which other foreigners are or may be permitted to come, and to enter into the same, to remain, and reside in any port of the said territories respectively."[26]

Between 1825 and 1844, the British undertook a series of measures that led from an implicit recognition of Haitian independence to official treaties between the two governments that signaled official recognition. The period between 1825 and 1844 added additional layers of recognition and built upon the period between 1806 and 1825, during which British ships traded with Haiti with the permission of the British government.

Britain's active engagement with Haiti during the war with France made their bilateral relationship unique in the Atlantic World. Indeed, the relationship between Haiti and Britain parallels some of the characteristics that Latin Americanist scholars describe as "informal empire." Historian Matthew Brown argues that informal empire, "in its simplest form, evokes a powerful nation managing to control a territory over which it does not exercise full sovereignty."[27] British hesitancy to recognize Haitian independence resonates with Britain's later actions in relationships with new Latin American states. "Even as British diplomats were undercutting Spanish diplomacy and destroying that country's best prospects for restoring its authority in America," historian Rafe Blaufarb argues, "Britain endeavored to postpone the inevitable recognition of independence."[28] In their considerations for how to deal with the newly proclaimed republics in Latin America, the British appear to have learned from their connections with Haiti and concluded that they could maintain a relationship somewhere in between recognition and non-recognition. "Of the value of the recognition of Spain to the new states," the British foreign office instructed Edward James Dawkins, the British commissioner at the Panama Congress in 1826, "it is not for Gt. Britain to form an estimate. Unquestionably their independence may be practically maintained without that recognition."[29] In helping Haiti maintain its independence from France while also withholding recognition, the British learned a lesson that they carried forward in their dealings with Spain's former colonies in the 1820s. Just as the ambiguous status created by multiple layers of recognition and non-recognition had allowed the British to capitalize on new opportunities in Haiti, this approach appears to have helped Britain jockey for power in South America without "polarizing the international community."[30]

The United States was the last Atlantic World nation to extend official diplomatic recognition to Haiti, and the prohibition on trade between Haiti and the United States from 1806 to 1810 had allowed the British to become Haiti's primary trade partner. "The island had become simply another supplier of tropical products [for the United States]," historian Gordon Brown notes, "where, with the exception of the risky munitions business, profits were average."[31] Nevertheless, in the early 1820s, trade with Haiti still accounted for 3 percent of the total of American trade.[32] The prolonged period of non-recognition, therefore, also saw active economic engagement between American merchants and Haiti.

After it legalized trade with Haiti in 1810, the United States sent commercial agents to Cap Haïtien and Port-au-Prince to help regulate trade and to advocate on behalf of U.S. merchants. The agents acted as intermediaries between the Haitian government and the U.S. government, a position that both U.S. merchants and the Haitian government attempted to use to foster closer diplomatic relationships.[33] In 1815, Alexandre Pétion wrote to the U.S. agent in Port-au-Prince, William Taylor, to appeal to American enlightenment principles in order to secure diplomatic recognition. "All revolutions have one *goal* and an *ending*," Pétion argued. "Ours was founded on the most sacred law of nature, it is just and cannot confront an enemy except those of humanity and reason. It is to the governments enlightened by philosophy and philanthropy to put above the prejudices of the skin and the nuances that are the unjust pretext which are of service to our enemies, and to see in men nothing but the merit and virtue that alone should distinguish them."[34] Pétion's efforts were not successful, and, in fact, resistance to extending official recognition to Haiti heightened after the initial period of negotiation, during 1805 and 1806, as southern planters gained the upper hand in congressional debates about Haiti's place in the Atlantic World. Brown attributes this shift to the decline of American trade with Haiti after the British became Haiti's primary trade partner, but it is clear that Haitian leaders continued to be persistent in securing recognition from their neighbor to the north. Three years after the reunification of the country under Jean-Pierre Boyer, Secretary General B. Inginac wrote to Secretary of State John Quincy Adams and reported that "the government of the United States, *monsieur* Secretary of State, is the first of all governments to which that of Haiti officially communicates the current political situation, and in doing so asks that an act of the legislature of her big sister recognize her independence that is currently in its nineteenth year." Inginac's statement reveals that, from his perspective, Haitian independence was a fact from the moment of the proclamation of the Declaration of Independence, despite the fact that foreign governments had withheld recognition of that independence. Inginac argued that their shared history should have encouraged the United States to support Haiti's independence. "The Haitian people," he concluded, "do not think that the American people, having previously found themselves in the same position and who felt the same need, can refuse them the justice that they are due."[35]

To help foster a better relationship with the United States, President Boyer undertook an aggressive campaign in the mid-1820s to encourage and support the migration of free people of color from the United States to Haiti. Boyer hoped that the emigration plans would encourage diplomatic recognition from the United States. Thousands of black and mixed-race Americans migrated to Haiti in the mid-1820s, but the program did not succeed in achieving Boyer's goal. Most of the emigrants returned home, historian Sara Connors Fanning argues, because of "unforeseen hardship, disease, and a clash between reality and what they had been led to believe."[36] Boyer had been hopeful that he could secure U.S. recognition in the early and mid-1820s but his failed efforts instead had the reverse effect. "Diplomatic relations between Haiti and the U.S.," Fanning argues, "hit a low point in the late 1820s, as revealed in the wrangling over the Congress of Panama, a meeting in 1826 of all the independent nations in the New World. . . . U.S. policy was clearly swayed in this case by southern demands."[37]

Finally, in 1862, in the midst of the American Civil War, the United States extended diplomatic recognition to Haiti. "It took the shock of secession," Brown argues, "to break the stalemate. With no southerners left in Congress who could block such a proposal, President Lincoln offered to send American diplomatic representatives to both Haiti and Liberia."[38] Two years later, Haiti and the United States signed a treaty of amity and commerce. The treaty favored American commercial interests since "the agreement rested on the false premise that commercial goods were at par with agricultural commodities when in reality the latter had less value."[39] The treaty also included articles relating to American, Haitian, and foreign privateering, with the goal of protecting American commercial interests and preventing Haitian and foreign privateers from interrupting American trade.[40]

Haitian connections in the Atlantic World after the Declaration of Independence unfolded in the related context of reactions and interactions between the government of the United States and those of the former Spanish and Portuguese colonies in Latin American in the early nineteenth century. While the independence movements of the Age of Revolution shared complicated processes of foreign recognition, Haiti's experience contained a key difference that suggests a broader policy of exceptionalism and raises further questions about the intertwining of ideology, economics, and politics in the revolutionary Atlantic. Haiti was the only nation to declare independence in the late eighteenth and early nineteenth centuries to be recognized first by its former metropole. Every other Atlantic nation and empire waited until France extended recognition before they diplomatically recognized Haiti as a country. In contrast, in the midst of the American Revolution, France quickly extended recognition to the United States in 1778 with the Treaty of Alliance. In Latin America, the British recognized Brazilian independence in 1824, just two years after Brazil declared its independence from Portugal and a year before Portugal recognized Brazil's independence. The British also recognized the independence of Mexico, Gran Colombia, and Rio de la Plata in 1825 through treaties of amity and commerce. The United States had already recognized these countries in 1822, as well as Chile and Peru. Britain and the United States extended recognition to other Latin American states in the 1820s. Spain, however, only recognized the independence of its Latin American colonies by fifteen treaties between 1837 and 1895, the first of which was with Mexico.[41] The chronology of recognition reflects the unique racial and labor implications of Haitian independence, but the evidence makes clear that racism and slavery were not the only considerations that factored into the decision-making processes of foreign governments. Indeed, the protracted process of foreign recognition of Haiti shares important characteristics of international reaction to revolutions and independence movements, beginning with the American Revolution and continuing during the decades after the Haitian Declaration of Independence, which witnessed numerous declarations throughout Latin America. As Blaufarb has shown, Latin American independence movements occurred in a similar context of international warfare and rivalry as those of the late eighteenth and early nineteenth centuries.[42] In this sense, the case of Haiti became an important precedent for international reaction to subsequent independence movements.

While it is tempting to extrapolate from the early years of declared independence to the following decades, the reinterpretation of initial

Haitian connections in the Atlantic World demonstrates the importance of a comprehensive and inclusive approach to the documentary record of all those who engaged with Haiti both conceptually and materially. This record of Haiti's initial independence experience reveals the multiple ways in which diverse groups, such as government leaders, merchants, and judges, came to grips with the need to confront and make decisions about the relative importance and geopolitical significance of racialized ideologies, economic ambition, and legal calculation. For this reason, the study of the immediate years after 1804 implies that the historical record of the entire independence period of official non-recognition must be defined in terms of diverse sources, ranging from official government documents and diplomatic communication, to legal records and merchant correspondence located in local and metropolitan archives throughout the Atlantic World.

Perhaps the most surprising conclusion of the documentary reconstruction of the initial years after the Declaration of Independence concerns Haitian connections to the British Empire. Indeed, it was Britain, not France, that played the lead external role in Haiti's initial independence experience. International merchants came to the conclusion that Haitian commercial connections with the British did in fact implicitly signal a political relationship. Similarly, the British Admiralty Court system infused economic policies with some degree of diplomatic authority. At the same time, it remained significant that the British government refused to overtly recognize Haiti as a sovereign nation, since this refusal limited Haiti's ability to participate in the community of recognized nations in the Atlantic World and prevented the Haitian government from signing treaties and from sending official delegates to London. In the end, the multiple layers of recognition that took shape in the first years after the Declaration of Independence help explain both Haiti's success in establishing a place in the Atlantic World and the limitations of this success for building an independent and sovereign nation. In hindsight, this result is understandable. Indeed, Haiti's declared independence posed questions relating to human rights and the interplay of economic, political, and legal priorities that have continued to stymie the international community more than two centuries later.

Notes

ABBREVIATIONS USED IN THE NOTES

AGI	Archivo General de Indias, Seville, Spain
AN	Archives Nationales, Paris
JNA	Jamaican National Archives, Spanish Town, Jamaica
NARA	National Archives and Records Administration, Washington, DC
NAM	National Army Museum, London
NLJ	National Library of Jamaica, Kingston
TNA	The National Archives of the United Kingdom, London
ADM	Letters from Senior Admiralty Officers
CO	Colonial Office
HCA	High Court of Appeals for Prizes
MFQ	Maps and plans extract to flat storage from various records of various departments
PC	Privy Council Registers
PRO	Public Records Office
WO	War Office

INTRODUCTION

1. Two other declarations of independence, by Vermont (1777) and by the Flemish estates (1790), were issued before the Haitian Declaration of Independence, but neither succeeded in establishing a lasting nation-state. Armitage, *The Declaration of Independence*, 115; Armitage and Gaffield, "Introduction: 'We Must Live Independent or Die.'"

2. Jenson, "Dessalines's American Proclamations," 72–102; Jenson, "Before Malcolm X, Dessalines," 329–44; Jenson, "From the Kidnapping(s) of the Louvertures," 162–86.

3. See, for example, Blackburn, "The Force of Example," 17.

4. See, for example, Nesbitt, *Universal Emancipation*, 11; and Stinchcombe, "Class Conflict and Diplomacy," 2.

5. For an extensive discussion on the "isolation thesis," see Burnham, "Immigration and Marriage," 9–22. Burnham's research focuses on Caribbean, European, and North American migration to Haiti during the nineteenth century by analyzing marriage records. He reveals that the population in Haiti after 1804 was of diverse nationalities and therefore undermines the scholarly emphasis on isolation.

6. See, for example, White, Encountering Revolution; and Ferrer, Freedom's Mirror.

7. Bellegarde-Smith, "Haitian Social Thought," 12.

8. For example, the Archives Nationales d'Haïti (established 1860), the Bibliothèque Nationale d'Haïti (established 1939), the Bibliothèque Haïtienne des Pères du Saint-Esprit (established 1873), the Bibliothèque Haïtienne des Frères de l'Instruction Chrétienne (established 1912), and the Musée du Panthéon National Haïtien (established 1983) all have rich archives.

9. Gould, Among the Powers of the Earth, 11.

10. Ibid., 7.

11. Ibid., 13.

12. Armitage, The Declaration of Independence, 84.

13. Ibid., 18.

14. Bellegarde, "Alexandre Pétion," 169.

15. Rainsford, An Historical Account of the Black Empire of Hayti, 216.

16. Ferrer, Freedom's Mirror, chap. 5.

17. Vattel, The Law of Nations.

18. Armitage, The Declaration of Independence, 85–86.

19. Ibid., 112–13.

20. For more on metaphorical slavery in the American Revolutions, see Christopher Leslie Brown, Moral Capital, chap. 2.

21. Armitage, The Declaration of Independence, 21.

22. Julius Scott, "The Common Wind."

23. "St. Domingo," Dessalines, Christophe, Clervaux, Done at the Head-quarters, Fort Dauphin, 20 November 1803, Times (London), 6 February 1804, 3.

24. Times (London), 30 May 1804, 2.

25. "Affairs of St. Domingo," Times (London), 23 July 1804, 3.

26. Jean-Jacques Dessalines, "The General in Chief to the People of Hayti," TNA, ADM 1/254.

27. Benton, A Search for Sovereignty, 31. In using this term, Benton draws on the work of Cooper, "Alternatives to Empire"; and Bose, A Hundred Horizons.

28. Benton, A Search for Sovereignty, 5.

29. Benton, "Strange Sovereignty," 5.

30. Ibid., 3.

CHAPTER 1

1. "Proclamation," Jean-Jacques Dessalines and Donatien Rochambeau, 19 November 1803, NLJ, MS 72, Box 2, 717N.

2. Matthewson, A Proslavery Foreign Policy, 121.

3. Nessler, "A Failed Emancipation?" 275–76.

4. Ibid., 276.
5. Picó, *One Frenchman, Four Revolutions*, 37.
6. Jenson, *Beyond the Slave Narrative*, 145.
7. Lubin, "Les Premiers Rapports de la Nation Haïtienne," 297.
8. Ferrer, *Freedom's Mirror*, 201.
9. Edward Corbet to George Nugent, 29 February 1804, NLJ, 665N.
10. George Nugent to Robert Hobart, 20 May 1804, NLJ, 504N; George Nugent to John Sullivan, 14 April 1804, NLJ, 615N.
11. Ferrer, *Freedom's Mirror*, 201.
12. Ibid.; Edward Corbet, "No 1 Report," 25 January 1804, NLJ, 784N.
13. Ferrer, *Freedom's Mirror*, 234.
14. Nessler, "A Failed Emancipation?" 301.
15. Miller, "Forget Haiti," 39.
16. Stein, "From Saint Domingue to Haiti," 190.
17. Brière, *Haïti et la France*, 19–26.
18. Ibid., 20.
19. In 1764, Denmark declared that the Caribbean islands of St. John and St. Thomas were "open to the ships of all nations." Bulmer-Thomas, *The Economic History of the Caribbean*, 38. Curaçao had been a free port and a regional trade center since the seventeenth century. Rupert, *Roots of Our Future*, 91.
20. For more on Ferrand's own efforts to prevent the international community from trading with Haiti, see Jenson, "States of Ghetto, Ghettos of States," 156–71.
21. The case of *Rose v. Himely* notes that there was a French agent from St. Domingo in Cuba as well. HeinOnline, 8 U.S. 241 (1807), 8.
22. Lundahl, "Defense and Distribution," 77–103; Lundahl, "Toussaint L'ouverture and the War Economy of Saint-Domingue," 122–38; Gonzalez, "The War on Sugar."
23. "No 2 Report," Edward Corbet to George Nugent, 25 January 1804, NLJ, MS 72, Box 3, 349N. For more on Haiti's shift away from sugar production after independence, see Sheller, *Democracy after Slavery*, 46–50; and Gonzalez, "The War on Sugar."
24. Robert Sutherland to William Fawkner, 1 October 1806, TNA, WO 1/75.
25. Dubois, *Haiti: The Aftershocks of History*, 117.
26. George Nugent to John Jeffreys Pratt, 2nd Earl of Camden, 15 December 1804, NLJ, MS 72, Box 3, 511N.
27. For more on the use of "brigand" in the international community, see Jenson, "States of Ghetto, Ghettos of States," 159.
28. "Les Corsaires de la Guadeloupe arrêteront tous les bâtiments destinés pour les Ports de St. Domingue occupés par les brigands, ainsi que ceux qui en sortiront. . . . Les Bâtiments dont la destination sera prouvée pour les ports, ou ventant des ports occupés par les révoltés, seront considérés comme ennemis de la France. Ils seront en conséquence déclarés de bonne prise et condamnés d'après les règlements sur la course." A[ugustin] Ernouf, "Arrêté, concernant les bâtiments destinés pour les ports de St. Domingue occupés par les brigands," 16 Prairial an 12/5 June 1804, AN, C7a63.

29. "Tous les individus, quels qu'ils soient, qui seront trouvés sur des bâtiments alliés ou neutres, expédiés pour les ports de Saint-Domingue, occupés par les révoltés, seront punis de mort." "Arrêté," Louis Ferrand, 5 February 1805/16 Pluviose an XIII, Danish National Archives, Generalguvernementet, Breve fra fremmede autoriteter, 1774–1807, A–C, #2.18.1.

30. Rupert, Roots of Our Future, 17, 77.

31. Ibid., 126.

32. Jordaan, "Patriots, Privateers, and International Politics," 152.

33. Rupert, Roots of Our Future, 39.

34. Ibid., 40.

35. Ibid., 41.

36. Edward Corbet to George Nugent, 29 February 1804, NLJ, MS 72, Box 3, 665N.

37. Rupert, Roots of Our Future, 43–44.

38. Ibid., 40.

39. Ibid.

40. Ibid., 43.

41. Hall, Slave Society in the Danish West Indies, 21, 70.

42. Ibid., 126.

43. Knox, A Historical Account of St. Thomas, 101. The British held St. Thomas for ten months in 1801–2.

44. Taylor, Leaflets from the Danish West Indies, 54.

45. George Nugent to John Jeffreys Pratt, 2nd Earl of Camden, 15 December 1804, NLJ, MS 72, Box 3, 511N.

46. "Mulâtres ou nègres de cette colonie, et les brigands de Saint Domingue." J. Thilorier to Donatien Rochambeau, 18 Brumaire an XII/10 November 1803, AN, CC9a41.

47. Ibid.

48. Ibid.

49. Ibid.

50. Ibid.

51. Rupert, Roots of Our Future, 41.

52. Ibid.

53. "N'attender rien de Curaçao sans argent comptant ou marchandises." J. Thilorier to Louis Ferrand, 24 February 1804, AN, CC9a41.

54. "Une méfiance générale, et elle existe entièrement parmi ceux en état de nous être utile." J. Thilorier to Louis Ferrand, 24 February 1804, AN, CC9a41. For more on the failure of the French to repay loans to neighboring islands, see Girard, The Slaves Who Defeated Napoleon, 237.

55. J. Thilorier to Donatien Rochambeau, 23 Frimaire an XII/15 December 1803, AN, CC9a41.

56. Ibid.

57. "Curaçao peut être considéré comme un repaire de mauvais sujets de toutes le couleurs, et de toute les nations." Ibid.

58. Garrigus, Before Haiti, 283–84.

59. "Sont-ils les bons amis de nos rebelles a qui ils sont très utiles par les différents envois qui leurs sont faits journellement, et que le gouvernement d'ici ne surveille, et ne veut surveiller que pour la frome, il semble ne pas devoir se mêler de la querelle de leur voisins." J. Thilorier to Donatien Rochambeau, 23 Frimaire an XII/15 December 1803, AN, CC9a41.

60. "Les ressources qu'y trouveront toujours nos révoltés, surtout sous l'autorité des deux commissaires composant aujourd'hui le gouvernement de Curaçao, lesquels n'ont d'autres vues que l'argent, et d'autres guides que la bassesse et l'ignorance." J. Thilorier to Louis Ferrand, 5 Pluviose an XII/26 January 1804, AN, CC9a41.

61. J. Thilorier to Louis Ferrand, 20 Ventose an XII/11 March 1804, AN, CC9a41.

62. J. Thilorier to Louis Ferrand, 14 Germinal an XII/4 April 1804, AN, CC9a41.

63. J. Thilorier to Louis Ferrand, 25 Prairial an XII/14 June 1804, AN, CC9a41.

64. "Saint Domingue perdu je n'ai plus aucune ressource dans les colonies et je donc profiter de la possibilité qu'il me reste de me rendre au sein de ma famille en Europe." Ibid.

65. Ibid.

66. "Le tribunal de St Domingue était le seul compétant pour juger les bâtiments prise en contreventions sur les cotes de St Domingue." Jean-Pierre Gouges to Louis Ferrand, 1 Vendemaire an 13/23 September 1804, AN, CC9a41.

67. Picó, *One Frenchman, Four Revolutions*, 39.

68. Pierre-Jean Changuion to Louis Ferrand, 2 March 1804, AN, CC9a41.

69. Pierre-Jean Changuion to Louis Ferrand, 23 October 1804, AN, CC9a41.

70. For more on Ferrand's situation in Santo Domingo, see Nessler, "A Failed Emancipation?" chap. 5.

71. "Le Gouvernement d'ici vient d'être change il est arrive un gouverneur d'hollande qui s'appelle Mr. P. J. Changuion ce changement pourrait peut être vous mettre a même de faire cesser un commerce presque ouverte (quoiqu'il soit masque par le Pavillon Espagnol et Danois) qui se fait d'ici avec les rebelles." Jean-Pierre Gouges to Louis Ferrand, 7 September 1804, AN, CC9a41.

72. "Je vois avec horreur que ce commerce ce fait sans y mettre même aucun mystère que celui de dire qu'on vient de Cuba et il apportent une quantité de lettre des Cayes ou Jacmel." Jean-Pierre Gouges to Louis Ferrand, 7 December 1804, AN, CC9a41.

73. "Je déteste ces relations avec ces nègres révoltés, de toute mon âme, sachant bien a quelle horreurs elles ont souvent donne lieu." Pierre-Jean Changuion to Louis Ferrand, 30 December 1805, AN, CC9a41; Jean-Pierre Gouges to Pierre-Jean Changuion, 20 Frimaire an 14/11 December 1805, AN, CC9a41.

74. "De vaisseaux Hollandais (ou Bataves) entrant dans ce port que s'ils étaient convaincus, de venir de quelque ports ou endroits de l'Isle de St Domingue qui sont actuellement en possession des nègres rebelles, ou d'y avoir fait quelque commerce avec les revoltés leurs bâtiments et la cargaison qu'on y trouvera seront confisques." Pierre-Jean Changuion, "Traduction Publication," 18 December 1804, AN, CC9a41.

75. "L'arrivée d'un goélette dans ce port chargée de café venant des Cayes, m'a décidé de voir Mons. De Changuion . . . je lui ai donne connaissance du commerce illicite qui se fait de cette place avec les rebelles je l'ai instruit de toutes les manœuvres

dont on se sert pour vouloir prouver que les bâtiments viennent de Couba [sic]." Jean-Pierre Gouges to Louis Ferrand, 26 December 1804, AN, CC9a41.

76. Ibid.

77. "Je crois que Mr. De Changuion a de très bonne intentions et qu'il empêchera la continuation de ce commerce non pas peut être avec autant d'activité qu'il l'aurait fait si j'avais été reconnu comme délègue en cette qualité j'aurais pu lui donner des preuves." Ibid.

78. "Le dit général le plaint, que les habitants de Curaçao plus intéressés que tous autres, de s'opposer aux progrès du Brigandage sur l'Isle de St Domingue alimentent cependant ce brigandage, en fournissant des moyens aux Révoltés, et ou il nous sollicites avec instance de faire savoir a nos administrés, qu'il lui en contera de les premier, mais qu'il fera pendre tous ceux qu'il trouvera en relations avec les rebelles de Ste Domingue, et qui seront arrête par les croisières que le dit General a stationner, le long des cotes des Révoltés." Pierre-Jean Changuion, "Traduction, Notification," 28 December 1804, AN, CC9a41.

79. "Nous rendons dont chacun responsable pour toutes les calamités et tous les malheurs qui par sa faute pourraient résulter, profluer et s'étendre sur cette Isle (de Curaçao) a la suite d'un commerce aussi dangereux." Ibid.

80. "Je vous annonce avec plaisir que je ne crois pas qu'on fasse d'autre expédition de cette place pour les rebelles, mons. De changuion n'est pas connu et il est craint, ensuite j'ai mis la peur dans le cœur de ceux qui ont fait ce commerce en leur disant qu'ils seraient rechercher même a la paix attendu que notre empereur ne laissera pas impuni les méchant qui aura traite avec ses rebelles." Jean-Pierre Gouges to Louis Ferrand, 28 December 1804, AN, CC9a41.

81. "Je prend donc la confiance de vous inviter, au nom du Gouvernement français, a donner des ordres tels que toute communication cesse, entre Curaçao et les cotes de St Domingue occupées par les révoltés. J'ai l'honneur de vous adresser y inclus, six exemplaires d'un arrêté, que j'ai rendu le 16 de ce mois." Louis Ferrand to Pierre-Jean Changuion, 24 Pluviose an XIII/13 February 1805, AN, CC9a40.

82. "Tous les individus, quels qu'ils soient, qui seront trouves sur des bâtiments allies ou neutres, expédiés pour les ports de Saint-Domingue, occupés par les révoltés, seront punis de mort." "Arrêté," Louis Ferrand, 16 Pluviose an XIII/5 February 1805, Danish National Archives, Generalguvernementet, Breve fra fremmede autoriteter, 1774–1807, A-C, #2.18.1.

83. Pierre-Jean Changuion, 20 February 1805, AN, CC9a41.

84. Jean-Pierre Gouges to Louis Ferrand, 5 March 1805, AN, CC9a41.

85. "Je suis fâché de devoir vous informer qu'une petite altercation ait eu lieu, entre Monsieur Gouges, que vous m'avez recommande dans votre dernier lettre, dont vous m'avez honore et moi, au sujet d'une prize qui a été conduite ici." Pierre-Jean Changuion to Louis Ferrand, 18 January 1806, AN, CC9a41.

86. "A clerk of the admiralty was assigned to every privateer, with power to receive the papers of all captured ships and seal up their cargoes to await trial." Stark, *The Abolition of Privateering*. According to the San Remo Manual (1995), Article 100, "After a vessel has been searched and considered subject to capture, the officer of the capturing vessel must inventory and seal the ship's papers, inventory the vessel and the goods

on board, account for all persons on board the ship and either provide a crew for the vessel or leave on board sufficient crew to operate the ship." Kraska, "Prize Law."

87. "Les personnes intéressés a la continuation de ce commerce avait vu avec plaisir que le gouverneur n'avait pas voulu me reconnaître comme délègue du gouvernement français, (d'après les ordres de son gouvernement) il ont trouve bien extraordinaire qu'il m'est écoute quand je lui ai porte des plaintes a ce sujet, un des chef de ce pays, c'est même permis de dire que s'il avait été a la place du gouverneur, il m'aurait fait sortir de la colonie." Jean-Pierre Gouges to Louis Ferrand, 5 March 1805, AN, CC9a41.

88. "Qu'un gouvernement qui est en Europe sous la dépendance du gouvernement français." Ibid.

89. Pierre-Jean Changuion to Jean-Pierre Gouges, copy, 15 January 1806, AN, CC9a41.

90. Pierre-Jean Changuion to Louis Ferrand, 18 January 1806, AN, CC9a41.

91. "Mon principe fondamental est d'obéir et d'être exactement fidèle a mes instructions et aux ordres du Gouvernement Batave." Ibid.

92. "Les bons principe exigent que l__ conforme aux loix du pays ou l'on y trouve . . . je suis très persuade que le gouvernement français ne permettrais jamais aux Bataves d'exercer la jurisdiction de donner la liberté de faire des actes d'autorité sur son territoire sans son ____, parce que cela serait contraire aux règles de saine raison." Pierre-Jean Changuion to Jean-Pierre Gouges, copy, 16 January 1806, AN, CC9a41.

93. "Mr. Le fiscal me dit d'un ton ironique et insultant qu'il ne reconnaissait pas d'agent français a Curaçao, et qu'il devait faire respecter le pavillon Batave." Jean-Pierre Gouges to Louis Ferrand, 20 January 1806, AN, CC9a41.

94. "Tout le monde de terre criait contre les français, qui était des pirates et qu'on devait les pendre." Jean-Pierre Gouges to Louis Ferrand, 31 January 1806, AN, CC9a41.

95. "La triste obligation du Gouvernement français du se voir oblige de prononcer contre des bâtiments, et des particuliers des puissances amis et allies que l'appas du gain apportée a des égarements au point de soutenir cette monstrueux rébellion, en les approvisionnant de tous les moyens et serons tout envivres, qu'en munitions de guerre qui les maintenir dans un état a pouvoir opposer résistance aux force, que S.M. y dirigera contre eux." Jean-Pierre Gouges to Pierre-Jean Changuion, 30 January 1806, AN, CC9a41.

96. "Il parait que vous favorisez plus les bâtiments qui viennent de chez les révoltées, que les bâtiments de la nation française." "Précis verbal du Capture, nous soussignons capitaine, officiers, marinier, et non marinier, du corsaire l'Eulalie de Sto Domingo, Capt. Roullit." 29 January 1806, AN, CC9a41.

97. "Il me dit que je voulais donner des lois dans son pays." Ibid.

98. "Sous le feu des canons du fort de ce nom." "Extrait du registre du conseil de civile et criminelle justice de l'Isle de Curaçao." 4 February 1806, AN, CC9a41.

99. "La résolution fondées principalement sur la publication express du gouvernement Bataves au sujet de prises qui ont été faites dans l'enceintes du territoire qui ne laisse aucune doute[?] sur la justesse de son application dans le cas présent, a été conclu." Pierre-Jean Changuion to Louis Ferrand, 22 February 1806, AN, CC9a41.

100. "Puis que le territoire avait été notoirement viole et que la prise avait été faites *sans notre aveu . . . et sous notre canon.*" Ibid.

101. "*La violation de notre territoire.*" Ibid.

102. "Le conseil n'avait aucune intention de vouloir s'arroger le jugement sur la *condammabilité ou non condammabilité du bâtiment en vertu des loix françaises.*" Ibid.

103. "Il ne sera pas difficile de prouver le contraire, il y a abord environ 70 millier de caffé, du vois de teinture, des ignonce, et des poix, la cote de Ste Marthe ne produit aucun de ses articles." Jean-Pierre Gouges to Louis Ferrand, 31 January 1806, AN, CC9a41.

104. "On n'a qu'a envoyer un exprès a Cuba et a Porto Rico, pour savoir si dans tel tems on a expédié tel bâtiment charge de caffé on aura bientôt la preuve du contraire." Jean-Pierre Gouges to Louis Ferrand, 1 February 1806, AN, CC9a41.

105. "Jusqu'ici il n'en existe pas la moindre preuve." Pierre-Jean Changuion to Louis Ferrand, 2 February 1806, AN, CC9a41.

106. "Le résultat en a été, que tous les individus qui le composaient et deux passagers, ont déclarés sous la foi solennelle du serment que le bâtiment venait de *Baracoa* sur la cote espagnole et qu'ils n'avaient ni touche ni vu même Sto. Domingo." Pierre-Jean Changuion to Louis Ferrand, 22 February 1806, AN, CC9a41.

107. "Extrait du registre du conseil de civile et criminelle justice de l'Isle de Curaçao." 4 February 1806, AN, CC9a41.

108. "D'après la certitude que j'ais que la goélette conduite dans ce port (par le corsaire français l'Eulalie) vient de traiter avec les révoltés de St. Domingue, au mépris des loix du gouvernement français établis a se sujet, je croirais manquer aux devoirs de ma place donc j'ai été honorée par Monsieur le Capitaine General Ferrand, si je ne dénoncer a V.E. la ditte goélette pour avoir traite et fait le commerce défendu par nos loix avec les révoltés de la colonie de St. Domingue." Jean-Pierre Gouges to Pierre-Jean Changuion, 14 February 1806, AN, CC9a41.

109. Pierre-Jean Changuion to Capt. Roullit, copy, 14 February 1806, AN, CC9a41.

110. "Sont personnellement *intéressées dans le commerce avec les révoltés!*" Pierre-Jean Changuion to Louis Ferrand, 24 March 1806, AN, CC9a41.

111. "Je vous invites donc avec *toute l'instance* possible de me *dénoncer nominalement ces riches particuliers ces membres du conseil,* et de me faire porter les preuves non équivoques de leur conduit infernale." Ibid.

112. "La considération politique de l'intérêt des colonies exige indubitablement, que toutes les puissances qui possèdent des colonies le réunissent d'un commun accord, pour exterminer a jamais jusqu'aux moindre traces de cette rébellion détestables!!" Ibid.

113. "De l'aveu du Gouvernement et du conseil de Curaçao, le Gouvernement français est le *seul juge compètent* au sujet de la *condamabilité* du bâtiment qui a été capture." Ibid.

114. "Je suis prêt a céder a votre proposition a l'égard de Mr. Gouges et a le recevoir comme votre fonde de pouvoir personnel et spécial, et a admettre en cette qualité comme partie intéressé sur le fait des prises." Ibid.

115. He was temporarily replacing Mr. Lothon in that position. Arnaud André Roberjot Lartigue to Louis Ferrand, 21 Germinal l'an 13/11 April 1805, AN, CC9a41.

Ferrand confirmed this appointment on 11 Floreal an 13/1 May 1805, Arnaud André Roberjot Lartigue to Louis Ferrand, 23 Floreal l'an 13/13 May 1805, AN, CC9a41.

116. Arnaud André Roberjot Lartigue to Louis Ferrand, 21 Germinal l'an 13/11 April 1805, AN, CC9a41.

117. "Une nation étrangère a-t-elle intérêt de défendre le commerce avec les révoltés de St Domingue?" Arnaud André Roberjot Lartigue to Balthazar Frederik Mühlenfels, 15 October 1805, AN, F3/284.

118. "Pour répondre a cette 1re question, il faut considérer que la révolté des nègres dans une partie d'une colonie n'en interrompe pas la propriété." Ibid. Independence.

119. "La révoltée n'abolit pas les loix qui prohibent aux étrangères de faire la commerce a St Domingue c'est d'abord une contravention ceux traités des nations avec la france, et c'est encore un commerce illégitime sous tous les rapports." Ibid.

120. "Quel est dont ce gouvernement qui ne s'empressera pas de prononcer contre ce commerce des peines pécuniaires et infamantes? Ce qui arrive aujourd'hui à un gouvernement arrivera dans un autre temps à un autre. Oui, tous ont le même intérêt de prononcer rigoureusement contre ce commerce illicite, s'ils ne veulent pas en être victimes à leur tour." Ibid.

121. "Il est partie depuis peu de jours 4 bâtiments d'ici pour St Domingue, allant au Cap, aux Cayes, et a Jacmel. . . . Ce commerce illicite se continue sans crainte et sans égard pour votre arrête." Arnaud André Roberjot Lartigue to Louis Ferrand, 12 Floreal an 13/2 May 1805, AN, CC9a41.

122. "Votre arrête a été publie et affiché dans cette ville. Il est parfaitement connu des négociants et des marins; mais ceux qui pratiquent des relations avec les révoltés ne font point intimidé. . . . Il part journellement des bâtiments pour le Cap, les Cayes, Jacmel et avec des approvisionnement et de toutes espèces." Arnaud André Roberjot Lartigue to Louis Ferrand, 30 Floreal an 13/ 20 May 1805, AN, CC9a41.

123. Arnaud André Roberjot Lartigue to Louis Ferrand, 1 August 1806, AN, CC9a41.

124. For more, see Chapter 3.

125. "Par les renseignements que me procurent, mes recherches et ma surveillance a l'égard de ce commerce si désastreux pour les négociants français et les habitant de St Domingue, je demeure très instruit que tous les ports des Etats Unis le font sans mystère, sans ménagement et sans aucun égard pour l'empire français, ce mauvais, exemple pour les nations qui ont des colonies et des esclaves pour exploiter les manufactures, n'est pas pour eux un objet de considération." Arnaud André Roberjot Lartigue to Louis Ferrand, 26 Prairial an 13/15 June 1805, AN, CC9a41.

126. "J'ai l'honneur de vous remettre ci joint l'état des noms des armateurs de St Thomas qui font le commerce avec les révoltés de St Domingue. J'en ai envoyé une copie au Général Vilaret et une autre au général Ernouf, afin qu'ils ne reçoivent pas dans leur ports aucune de ces Bâtiments"; "Je n'ai pu me procurer tous les noms des bâtiments et des capitaines; mais ils sont faciles a connaître; ce sont tous des pilotes bots[?], les équipages sont tous mulâtres et nègres de toutes nations." Arnaud André Roberjot Lartigue to Louis Ferrand, le 7 Brumaire an 14/29 October 1805, CC9a41.

127. Ada Ferrer similarly shows that the governors of Cuba tried to prevent access to information about the Haitian Revolution for fear that the enslaved population would similarly rebel. See Ferrer, *Freedom's Mirror*, chaps. 2 and 4; see also Blackburn, "The Force of Example."

128. "A l'exception de ceux qui fessaient ce commerce, ici, tout le monde a applaudi ceux mesures de justice et de fermeté que vous avez prononce par votre arrête; en mon particulière, je l'ai lu avec la plus grande satisfaction." Arnaud André Roberjot Lartigue to Louis Ferrand, le 22 Frimaire an 14/13 December 1805, AN, CC9a41.

129. "Vous avez mis, monsieur le général, par votre arrête le sceau a la défense que le général Mühlenfels a prononcée; vous avez si bien et si rigoureusement tout prévu, que je doute que ce commerce ne cesse entièrement ici, et que le congrès se refuse a prononcer la défense de cet adieux commerce dans les états unis." Ibid.

130. "Publication," Balthazar Frederik Mühlenfels, 29 October 1805, Danish National Archives, Dep. For de Udenlandske Anliggender, Gruppeordnede sager: Vestindien: Sager Vedr. Vestindien, 1820–21, #1320.

131. "Je vous ai déjà instruit de la défense que le gouverneur danois a faite publie contre le commerce que les négociants de cette ville font avec les révoltés de St Domingue; plusieurs ont cessé ce commerce depuis, avec de la surveillance j'espère qu'ils l'abandonneront tout a fait." Arnaud André Roberjot Lartigue to Louis Ferrand, le 12 Frimaire an 14/3 December 1805, AN, CC9a41.

132. "La surveillance que j'ai toujours requise du gouvernement danois a été remplie de la manière la plus loyale." Arnaud André Roberjot Lartigue to Louis Ferrand, 28 May 1806, AN, CC9a41.

133. "Extract from a memorial of Patrick Colquhoun esq Agent for the Virgin Islands," 13 February 1806, TNA, PRO 30/42/12/2.

134. Ibid.

135. "Sur la connaissance que Dessalines a eue de la défense du gouverneur danois de faire le commerce de St Domingue, il s'en est formalisé, et a dit que puisque les danois ne voulait pas les reconnaître, qu'il n'en recevrait qu'après une permission obtenue de lui, il ne laisse les port libres que pour les états unis." Arnaud André Roberjot Lartigue to Louis Ferrand, le 12 Frimaire an 14/3 December 1805, AN, CC9a41.

136. "Voilà bien des jours que j'ai des entretiens fréquents avec m. le commandant de St Thomas, au sujet du pavillon Danois qui sert à faire, plus que jamais, le commerce avec les révoltés de st Domingue." Arnaud André Roberjot Lartigue to Louis Ferrand, 1 August 1806, AN, CC9a41.

137. "Peu de bâtiments le font directement de ce port; les Danois et les Américains prennent le pavillon et vont a Tortole s'expédier." Ibid.

138. "Depuis la défense du congres, les américains viennent ici prendre le pavillon Danois et vont chez les révoltés; ils masquent leur expéditions et leur route, pour se garantir de peines portées par l'arrête du gouvernement danois; mais reste toujours que le pavillon danois flotte ouvertement dans les ports des révoltés de St Domingue." Ibid.

139. Ibid.

140. "C'est par ce même pavillon que les révoltés se trouvent approvisionnées de vivres et de munitions de guerre quoique ennemis de la France et de l'humanité et quoiqu'ils ne doivent pas jouir du bénéfice de la neutralité." Arnaud André Roberjot Lartigue to Louis Ferrand, 17 September 1806, AN, CC9a41.

141. Arnaud André Roberjot Lartigue to Louis Ferrand, 1 August 1806, AN, CC9a41.

142. "Prendre de nouvelles mesures pour faire cesser l'abus qui se fait du pavillon danois pour aller chez les révoltés de St Domingue." Arnaud André Roberjot Laritgue to Louis Ferrand, 8 August 1806, AN, CC9a41.

143. Arnaud André Roberjot Lartigue to Louis Ferrand, 17 September 1806, AN, CC9a41.

144. "Les américains qui partaient d'ici ou de st Barthelemy pour aller a haity [sic], se disposent a aller se fixer a curaçao pour communiquer plus librement avec les revoltés de St Domingue." Arnaud André Roberjot Lartigue to Louis Ferrand, 30 January 1807, AN, CC9a41.

145. "Un gouvernement étranger, dont la nation fait le commerce avec les révoltés de St Domingue, et qui ne le défend pas: a quoi s'expose-t-il?" Arnaud André Roberjot Lartigue to Balthazar Frederik Mühlenfels, 15 October 1805, AN, F3/284.

146. "La révolte est une cause commune a tous les gouvernements: c'est comme le feu, dont tout le monde doit en prévenir le danger, et au quel tout le monde doit courir; lorsque l'incendie éclate." Ibid.

147. Jenson, *Beyond the Slave Narrative*, 162. See also Jean-Baptiste, *Le Fondateur Devant l'Histoire*; Fouchard, "Quand Haïti exportait la liberté aux Antilles," 41–47; and Ferrer, "Speaking of Haiti," 236.

148. "Rapport de la conduite qu'a tenue M. Roberjot Lartigue, au sujet de l'entreprise formée par Dessalines, pour soulever la Martinique, la Guadeloupe et Marie-Galante . . . daté de St-Thomas, île Danoise, du 26 Mai 1806" (Dubray, Imprimeur, Rue Ventadour, No. 5, 1815). Bibliothèque Nationale de France, Département Philosophie, Histoire, Sciences de l'Homme, 8-LK12-36.

149. Geggus, "The Slaves and Free Coloreds of Martinique," 296.

150. Jenson, *Beyond the Slave Narrative*, 176.

151. "Vous m'observé, monsieur le général, que mes fonctions d'agent n'ont été, jusques a ce jour, d'aucune espèce d'utilité: il est possible, monsieur le général, que je n'aye pas pu remplir tous vos désirs, malgré l'exactitude et la zèle que je mets dans le service dont je suis chargé." Arnaud André Roberjot Lartigue to Louis Ferrand, 25 September 1805, AN, F3/284.

152. "Parce qu'aucun français ne peut mettre le pied sur le territoire d'haity [sic], sans encourir la peine de mort." Arnaud André Roberjot Lartigue to Louis Ferrand, 26 Fructidor an 13/13 September 1805, AN, CC9a41.

153. "Moreau a fait part aussi a Yong qu'ils attendaient a chaque instant la nouvelle qu'a la Guadeloupe et a la Martinique les nègres se soient révoltés, que déjà ils auraient du en avoir la nouvelle, et qu'il étaient certains que les esclaves de ces deux colonies demandaient la même régime que Dessalines a établie a haity." Ibid.

154. "Cet aveu de moreau a M. Yong ferait croire que Dessalines prend des Mesures pour opérer ce soulèvement dans vos deux colonies, et je ne me refuserai pas au soupçon; il passe tous les jours ici des gens de couleur, qui ont plus l'air d'émissaires

pour des complots, que des gens voyageant pour affaires particulières. Les gens de couleur ont ici un club, on se réunissent les voyageurs, et la ils confèrent de leurs projets et de leur missions." Ibid.

155. Arnaud André Roberjot Lartigue to Louis Ferrand, 15 February 1806, AN, CC9a41.

156. "Cela fournit des moyens aux gens de couleur de descendre facilement." Arnaud André Roberjot Lartigue to Louis Ferrand, 26 Fructidor an 13/13 September 1805, AN, CC9a41.

157. "Je vous ai déjà instruit, Monsieur le General, du projet qu'avais Dessalines de soulever les nègres de la Martinique et de la Guadeloupe." Arnaud André Roberjot Lartigue to Louis Ferrand, le 15 Vendemaire an 14/7 October 1805, AN, CC9a41.

158. "Général Ernouf a envoyé ici son premier aide de camp, avec des ordres positifs pour rechercher les émissaires de Dessalines, et prendre avec le gouverneur Danois toutes les précautions pour punir et éloigner tous les auteurs et adhérents des complotes." Ibid.

159. "Affairs of St. Domingo," *Times* (London), 23 July 1804, issue 6082, 3.

160. "Haine éternelle a la France." "Liberté ou la Mort," TNA, CO 137/111, 113.

161. "Les insurrections qui viennent d'éclater à Surinam et à Cayenne sont des événements qui doivent faire redoubler de surveillance dans toutes les colonies." Arnaud André Roberjot Lartigue to Louis Ferrand, le 15 Vendemaire an 14/7 October 1805, AN, CC9a41.

162. Hall, *Slave Society in the Danish West Indies*, 28.

163. Arnaud André Roberjot Lartigue to Louis Ferrand, le 3 Brumaire an 14/25 October 1805, AN, CC9a41.

164. "Le gouverneur Mühlenfels, a ordonné la déportation de M. Cunningham, et de la famille Bernardine (dont la femme est sœur de Christophe généralissime des armées des révoltés de St Domingue) qui résidait a St Thomas, et qui ont toujours eu des relations avec les révoltés; il a ordonné l'arrestation de M. Loiseau qui a toujours tenu une conduite criminelle avec les révoltés; et aussi du nommé Pierre nègre de la Grenade résidant a St. Thomas, qui était l'agent de Bernardine." Arnaud André Roberjot Lartigue to Louis Ferrand, 10 Brumaire an 14/1 November 1805, AN, CC9a41.

165. "Extrait de la Gazette de la Trinite, du 4 Janvier 1806." Arnaud André Roberjot Lartigue to Louis Ferrand, attached to a letter dated 28 January 1806, AN, CC9a41.

166. "Pain c'est viande béqué, vin c'est sang béqué, nous va mange pain béqué, nous va boire sans béqué; et les autres répondent par le refrain de St Domingue." "Extrait de la Gazette de la Trinite, du 4 Janvier 1806," Arnaud André Roberjot Lartigue to Louis Ferrand, attached to a letter dated 28 January 1806, AN, CC9a41.

167. "Marché a la ville pour la mettre a feu et après quoi massacrer tous les blancs les gens de couleur libres et les nègres qui refusaient a les soumire." Ibid.

168. "Il paraît que Dessalines a une grande part dans ce projet, aussi monstrueux que criminel." Arnaud André Roberjot Lartigue to Louis Ferrand, 28 January 1806, AN, CC9a41.

169. "Il y a plus de six mois que j'en avais des notions positives, et depuis les preuves et les émissaires, ne m'ont pas permis d'en douter." Ibid.

170. "Extrait du Morning Chronicle de New York, 22 Janvier 1806." Arnaud André Roberjot Lartigue to Louis Ferrand, attached to a letter dated 15 February 1806, AN, CC9a41.

171. "Je suis si bien informé du plan que Dessalines a formé de faire soulevée tous les esclaves en masse dans toutes les colonies, pour assurer sa puissance et son caractère d'empereur, que je prête toute mon attention et toutes mes recherches pour ne pas perdre le fil de la trame formée." Ibid.

172. "Notre malheureux colonie en est un exemple alarmant, cella a commencé par des insurrections partielle, et par suite s'est devenue irrémédiable." Ibid.

173. "On a reconnu a la trinité un nègre nomme George confident de Dessalines, qui était désigné pour être le Roi des révoltés, dans le soulèvement qui a déjà eu lieu a la trinité." Arnaud André Roberjot Lartigue to Louis Ferrand, 8 March 1806, AN, CC9a41.

174. "Les gouverneur des iles Danoises, de Puerto Rico, de la Martinique et de la Guadeloupe, ne laissent aborder de leur colonies aucune espèce de gens de couleur, libres ou esclaves, pour éviter que la contagion ne gagne chez les esclaves de leur gouvernements." Arnaud André Roberjot Lartigue to Louis Ferrand, 8 March 1806, AN, CC9a41.

175. "Le Scélérat de Dessalines est si persuadé que la fin de son règne n'est pas loin, qu'il met tout en œuvre, pour faire réussir le projet du soulèvement général." Ibid.

176. "C'est une arrogance outrée, qui manifeste clairement le désir d'étendre sa puissance sur les antilles, et qu'il ne renonce pas au projet qu'il a conçu depuis longtemps de soulever les esclaves dans toutes les colonies." Arnaud André Roberjot Lartigue to Louis Ferrand, 22 March 1806, AN, CC9a41.

177. "Le Gouvernement d'ici a chasse un grand scélérat nommé Cazeau de franquevill, il va a St Thomas, prenez garde a lui, il a voulu une fois faire révolter les nègres de notre ile; c'est l'homme le plus dangereux, il est capable de tout, il a été secrétaire de biassou chez les révoltés de St Domingue." "Avis de Puerto Rico a Mr le Commandant de St Thomas" [19 May 1806, date derived from cover letter], AN, CC9a41.

178. Arnaud André Roberjot Lartigue to Louis Ferrand, 15 April 1806, AN, CC9a41.

179. Arnaud André Roberjot Lartigue to Médéric Louis Élie Moreau de Saint-Méry, 30 November 1806, AN, F3/284.

180. "Rapport de la conduite qu'a tenue M. Roberjot Lartigue, au sujet de l'entreprise formée par Dessalines, pour soulever la Martinique, la Guadeloupe et Marie-Galante . . . daté de St-Thomas, île Danoise, du 26 Mai 1806" (Dubray, Imprimeur, Rue Ventadour, No. 5, 1815), Bibliothèque Nationale de France, Département Philosophie, Histoire, Sciences de l'Homme, 8-LK12-36.

181. Arnaud André Roberjot Lartigue to Médéric Louis Élie Moreau de Saint-Méry, 30 November 1806, AN, F3/284.

182. Jenson, *Beyond the Slave Narrative*, 176. For other cases in which scholars have struggled to determine whether conspiracies were real or imagined and for how these conspiracies allow scholars to learn more about the societies, see, for example, Johnson, "Denmark Vesey and His Co-Conspirators," 915–76; Jordan, *Tumult and Silence at Second Creek*; and Gaspar, *Bondmen and Rebels*.

183. According to Vattel, sovereignty and independence meant "that it [the sovereign state] govern itself by its own authority and laws." Vattel, *The Law of Nations*, 2.
184. Lundahl, *Peasants and Poverty*, 180.
185. Rupert, *Roots of Our Future*, 41.
186. MacKenzie, *Notes on Haiti*, 180.
187. Ibid., 88.
188. Rupert, *Roots of Our Future*, 42.

CHAPTER 2

1. This chapter is an updated version of Gaffield, "Haiti and Jamaica in the Remaking of the Early Nineteenth-Century Atlantic World."
2. "Foulant aux pieds les loix de l'homme et de l'humanité . . . brisant le sceau de la réconciliation." "C'est au nom de ce peuple lassé d'humiliation, que j'ai l'honneur d'instruire votre excellence, que tous les liens qui attachaient Saint Domingue à la France sont rompus" and "Nos ports seront désormais ouverts à tous les bâtiments de sa majesté Britannique qui y trouveront la sûreté du commerce et la bonne foi dans les traites." Jean-Jacques Dessalines to George Nugent, 23 June 1803, NLJ, MS 72, Box 2, 846N.
3. "Proclamation," Donatien Rochambeau, undated [late 1802], TNA, CO 137/109; "Proclamation," Donatien Rochambeau, 16 December 1802, TNA, CO 137/111; "Arrête," Donatien Rochambeau, 28 December 1802, TNA, CO 137/110.
4. It was reported from Saint Domingue, "that unless the French receive in the course of 6 weeks or two months very powerful reinforcements, they will be forced to abandon the island altogether." Edward Corbet to George Nugent, 6 November 1802, TNA, CO 137/110.
5. Donatien Rochambeau to John Thomas Duckworth, 30 January 1803, TNA, CO 137/110.
6. George Nugent to Robert Hobart, 9 August 1803, TNA, CO 137/110.
7. George Nugent to John Sullivan, 30 January 1803, TNA, CO 137/110.
8. Mintz, "Labor and Sugar in Puerto Rico and in Jamaica," 276.
9. Knight, *Slave Society in Cuba during the Nineteenth Century*, 28; Curry-Machado, *Cuban Sugar Industry*, 6. See also Ferrer, *Freedom's Mirror*.
10. Paquette, *Sugar Is Made with Blood*, 29.
11. Gonzalez, "The War on Sugar," 4.
12. Ibid., 8; "Mercantile Relations, Arrivals in the Port of Curaçao since the 28th Ultimo" and "The English Schooner, John, Anthony Mathey, Master, from Aux Cayes, with Corn and Rice," *Curaçao Gazette and Commercial Advertiser*, 11 December 1812, nos. 1, 4.
13. For more on France's relationship with Haiti, see Brière, *Haïti et la France*; and Blancpain, *Un Siècle de Relations Financières entre Haïti et la France*. For more on the Spanish Empire during and after the Haitian Revolution, see Ferrer, *Freedom's Mirror*.
14. The Dutch were not allied with the French, but they were in the French sphere and therefore had a status somewhere between neutrality and ally. Enthoven, "An Assessment of Dutch Transatlantic Commerce," 401.
15. Nash, "The Organization of Trade and Finance," 95, 117.

16. Ibid., 96.

17. "The general strategy of this development was to convert these areas into complementary satellite economies, which would provide raw materials and food for Great Britain, and also provide widening markets for its manufactures." Gallagher and Robinson, "The Imperialism of Free Trade," 9.

18. Michel-Rolph Trouillot explored the idea of the Haitian Revolution as an unthinkable event in *Silencing the Past*.

19. Rainsford, *An Historical Account of the Black Empire of Hayti*, 130.

20. Philippe Girard highlights that the British chose to sign this accord with Louverture in the hope of creating a conflict between the military and civilian leaders in Saint Domingue so that they could secure an agreement that was more in line with the British interest. Girard, "Black Talleyrand," 94; Laurent Dubois, "Toussaint Louverture, Jean-Jacques Dessalines, and the Quest for Haitian Sovereignty," presented at Haitian Revolution in Global Context Conference, Cornell University, 16–17 April 2004; Conventions Secrètes [illegible] entre le Colonel Harcourt, Député Adjudant Général des Forces de la Majesté Britannique au nom de son Excellence l'Honorable Brigadier Général Maitland, commandant en chef les dites forces, et Mons. Falinger, Adjudant Général Chef de l'Etat Major de l'Armée Française au nom du Général Toussaint L'Ouverture," 31 August 1798, JNA, 1B/5/3/21.

21. For more on the secret convention, see Geggus, *Slavery, War, and Revolution*, 381.

22. For copies of these treaties, see "Jamaica Minutes of the Council, May 1799–May 1805," JNA, 1B/5/3/21; "Copy of Articles agreed upon between Edward Corbet acting by the direction of Major General Nugent and Joseph Bunel acting in behalf of General Toussaint Louverture being a sequel to and explanation of the secret convention of l'Archaye between General Maitland and General Toussaint of 13th June, 1799," 16 November 1801, BNAM, 6807–183–1, 132; Duffy, *Soldiers, Sugar, and Seapower*, 310. Philippe Girard's research suggests that this accord was never finalized because the peace treaty between the British and the French prevented the governor of Jamaica from signing an agreement with France's enemy. See Girard, "Black Talleyrand," 120–21. These changes reflect the shifting power dynamic of the Haitian Revolution. For more on the Haitian Revolution, see Dubois, *Avengers of the New World*, 238.

23. Saint-Louis, *Aux Origines du drame d'Haïti*, 136.

24. Dubois, *Avengers of the New World*, 223.

25. For more on the peace protocols, see *Official Papers, Relative to the Preliminaries of London and the Treaty of Amiens, Published at Paris by Authority of the French Government* (London: Printed for J. Debrett, 1803), Part II.

26. For more on this war, see Dubois, *Avengers of the New World*, 254–55; and Girard, "Napoleon Bonaparte and the Emancipation Issue in Saint Domingue," 587–618.

27. For more on the waves of migration to Jamaica, see Dessens, *From Saint-Domingue to New Orleans*, 15–18.

28. Bryan, "Emigrés: Conflict and Reconciliation," 17.

29. George Nugent to Robert Hobart, 4 March 1803, TNA, CO 137–110, 57.

30. For details on the process of abolition in Saint Domingue and in the French Empire, see Stein, "The Abolition of Slavery in the North, West, and South of Saint

Domingue," 47–55; and Dubois, *Avengers of the New World*, 168–70. The British had previously maintained slavery in Saint Domingue in their zones of occupation from 1793 to 1798. For more, see Geggus, *Slavery, War, and Revolution*. Nugent was not the only government official to disregard the abolition decrees issued in Saint Domingue in 1793 and in the entire French Empire in 1794; in 1807 the territorial governor of Louisiana, W. C. C. Claiborne, issued a statute that required testimonies or certificates to prove the free status of an individual of color from the island of Hispaniola; otherwise, the individual would be considered a "fugitive slave." Both governors chose to limit the geographical scope of the 1793/94 emancipation and invalidated the decree once an individual had passed into another jurisdiction. Rebecca J. Scott, "'She . . . Refuses to Deliver Up Herself as the Slave of Your Petitioner,'" 120–21; Peabody, "Free upon Higher Ground." For more on the complexities surrounding the 1802 maintenance of slavery in the French Empire, see Girard, "Napoleon Bonaparte and the Emancipation Issue in Saint Domingue," 587–618. Louis Ferrand also elided the 1793/94 emancipation decrees in Santo Domingo; see Nessler, "A Failed Emancipation?" chap. 5.

31. Dubois, *Avengers of the New World*, 297.

32. George Nugent to Robert Hobart, 21 July 1803, BNAM, 6807–183–4, 191; Dubois, *Avengers of the New World*, 297.

33. George Nugent to Robert Hobart, 9 August 1803, TNA, CO 137/110, 160.

34. John Thomas Duckworth to Evan Nepean, 29 September 1803, TNA, ADM 1/253.

35. George Nugent to Jean-Jacques Dessalines, 18 August 1803, NLJ, MS 72, Box 2, 935N.

36. George Nugent to Robert Hobart, 9 August 1803, TNA, CO 137/110, 160.

37. "Narrative of the proceedings of Captain Walker and Mr. Hugh Cathcart, on their mission to the Brigand Chiefs from the Government of Jamaica," James Walker and Hugh Cathcart, 27 August 1803, NLJ, MS 72, Box 2, 493N.

38. Ibid.

39. Ibid. For more on the value of land in Saint Domingue and Haiti, see Fick, "Emancipation in Haiti," 11–40. This sentiment was put into law in Dessalines's 1805 constitution, and this clause was included in all Haitian constitutions, except Christophe's two constitutions in 1807 and 1811, until the 1918 constitution written under the American Occupation, at which point the article was dropped. Gaffield, "Complexities of Imagining Haiti," 89.

40. "Narrative of the proceedings," James Walker and Hugh Cathcart, 27 August 1803, NLJ, MS 72, Box 2, 493N.

41. Ibid.

42. For details on re-enslavement during the British occupation during the Haitian Revolution, see Geggus, *Slavery, War, and Revolution*, 99, 109; and Dubois, *Avengers of the New World*, 167.

43. "Narrative of the proceedings," James Walker and Hugh Cathcart, 27 August 1803, NLJ, MS 72, Box 2, 493N.

44. "Proclamation," Jean-Jacques Dessalines and Donatien Rochambeau, 19 November 1803, NLJ, MS 72, Box 2, 717N.

45. Jean-Jacques Dessalines to the Citizens of the City of Le Cap, 19 November 1803, NLJ, MS 72, Box 2, 852N.

46. On 30 November 1803, Captain John Bligh, esq, of His Britannic Majesty's Ship The Theseus, signed a treaty at Cap François with Jacques Boyer, brigadier-general of the French army, and Captain Henry Barré, commander of the naval forces at Saint Domingue. This treaty established that the captured French ships would become the possession of the British and that the passengers, then prisoners of war, would be sent to Europe. The British would send the sick and wounded directly to Europe while the rest would pass through Jamaica. The treaty also respected personal property. "Copie de l'accord pour l'évacuation du Cap," John Bligh and Jacques Boyer, BNAM, 6807-183-4, 326.

47. John Thomas Duckworth to Evan Nepean, 12 November 1803, TNA, ADM 1/-253.

48. He claimed to rule the entire island of Hispaniola (what had formerly been French Saint Domingue and Spanish Santo Domingo). For more on the origins of this name, see "The Naming of Haiti," in Geggus, Haitian Revolutionary Studies.

49. Nugent included the Declaration in a package of documents relating to Saint Domingue/Haiti that he sent to Lord Robert Hobart in London on 10 March 1804. The Declaration of Independence is cataloged with the Jamaican colonial records at TNA. John Thomas Duckworth also obtained a printed copy of the Haitian Declaration of Independence and sent it to the Lords of the Admiralty in London. These two copies of the Declaration of Independence are the only two remaining extant government-issued copies of the document. "Liberty or Death," TNA, CO 137/111, 113. See http://www.nationalarchives.gov.uk/documentsonline/haiti.asp; and "Liberty or Death," TNA, MFQ 1/184.

50. For more on Haitian territory and freedom, see Ferrer, "Haiti, Free Soil, and Antislavery," 40–66.

51. Here I quote a translation provided by an unnamed British official that appears in the Admiralty Records from the Jamaica Station: "The General in Chief to the People of Hayti," TNA, ADM 1/254.

52. "Paix a nos voisins, mais anathème au nom français." "Liberté ou la Mort," TNA, CO 137/111, 113.

53. For more on color and race in independent Haiti, see Nicholls, From Dessalines to Duvalier, 1–2; Trouillot, Haiti, State against Nation, 113; and Dubois, Haiti: The Aftershocks of History, 80–82.

54. Both the British government representatives and Dessalines framed the decisions on the part of the Haitian government as being of Dessalines's own initiative. However, Edward Corbet reported that many of Dessalines's generals were involved in the meetings. According to Corbet, revolutionary leader Henry Christophe was one of Dessalines's primary advisers. Corbet describes color tension within the Haitian leadership and suggests that internal politicking may also have influenced Dessalines's decisions regarding international trade. "No 2 Report," Edward Corbet to George Nugent, 25 January 1804, NLJ, MS 72, Box 3, 349N. For more on the question of internal conflict and political divisions, see Moïse, Constitutions et Luttes de Pouvoir en Haïti; and Saint-Louis, Aux Origines du drame d'Haïti, 224–26.

55. "Copy of a letter from Edward Corbet to General Dessalines respecting the British Government in possession of the Mole," Edward Corbet to Jean-Jacques Dessalines, 15 January 1804, NLJ, MS 72, Box 3, 911N.

56. Dessalines destroyed nearly all of the coastal forts and began erecting new forts further inland. "By this system they will leave they say, the invading army without cover of defense but such as they may create themselves." "No 2 Report," Edward Corbet to George Nugent, 25 January 1804, NLJ, MS 72, Box 3, 349N.

57. "La demande du gouvernement Britannique ne m'inspire aucune méfiance sur sa loyauté et sa bonne foi!" "Upon the subject of what was proposed respecting Môle Saint Nicholas, received 17th." Jean-Jacques Dessalines to Edward Corbet, 16 January 1804, NLJ, MS 72, Box 3, 812N.

58. "No 2 Report," Edward Corbet to George Nugent, 25 January 1804, NLJ, MS 72, Box 3, 349N.

59. "Il est de mon devoir d'accorder une protection signale à tous ceux (les Français rigoureusement et de droit exceptés) à tous ceux qui voudront entretenir des relations amicales et des rapports commerciaux avec le peuple indigène. . . . Toute mesure diplomatique ou commerciale de la part de cette nation qui ne tendra ni au détriment de l'indépendance consacrée en ces lieux, ni aux droits d'un privilège absolument exclusif, sera prise par moi en considération." "Upon the subject of the commercial proposition, received 17th." Jean-Jacques Dessalines to Edward Corbet, 16 January 1804, NLJ, MS 72, Box 3, 902N.

60. Jean-Jacques Dessalines declared himself emperor only in October 1804.

61. Nugent, *Lady Nugent's Journal of Her Residence in Jamaica from 1801 to 1805*, 250.

62. "No 2 Report," Edward Corbet to George Nugent, 25 January 1804, NLJ, MS 72, Box 3, 349N.

63. "French copy of treaty," NLJ, MS 72, Box 3, 741. Dessalines took similar steps to repatriate Haitians who were in the United States and published proclamations in various newspapers inviting these individuals to return and promising to cover the cost of travel. "From St. Domingo," *Federal Spy*, Springfield, Mass., 3 April 1804, 3. He also offered to pay for the passage of "blacks and men of color" in Martinique and Guadeloupe. Elisabeth, "Les relations entre les Petites Antilles françaises et Haïti," 179.

64. Edward Corbet to George Nugent, 16 February 1804, NLJ, MS 72, Box 3, 502N. According to Laurent Dubois's research, the population of the colony in 1789 was 465,000 slaves, 31,000 whites, and 28,000 free-coloreds. Dubois, *Avengers of the New World*, 30. Mats Lundahl's research reveals significantly different numbers from Dubois's and Corbet's contemporary evaluation: "The population had decreased from 520,000 in 1789, to 38,000 according to the census [taken by Dessalines in 1805]." See Lundahl, "Defense and Distribution," 85.

65. Girard, "Napoleon Bonaparte and the Emancipation Issue in Saint-Domingue," 591.

66. "Le gouverneur-général, considérant qu'un grand nombre de noirs et d'hommes de couleur supportent, aux Etats-Unis, toutes sortes de privations, parce qu'ils n'ont pas les moyens de retourner en Haïti, décrète qu'il sera compte aux capitaines de navires américains la somme de quarante piastres pour chaque individu qu'ils pourront ramener dans le pays. Ce décret sera imprimé, publie, aussitôt

expédié, et une copie en sera immédiatement envoyée au Congres des Etats-Unis." Jean-Jacques Dessalines, 14 January 1804, quoted in Madiou, Histoire d'Haïti, 154.

67. George Nugent to Jean-Jacques Dessalines, 8 March 1804, NLJ, MS 72, Box 3, 315N.

68. "Dont la majeure partie de Noirs et gens de couleur pour la rentrée desquelles Dessalines a promis jusqu'à 40 dollars par tête." Elisabeth, "Les relations entre les Petites Antilles françaises et Haïti," 179.

69. Jean-Jacques Dessalines, "Empire d'Hayti, Ordonnance, 22 Octobre 1804," Gazette Politique et Commerciale d'Haïti, 13 December 1804, 4.

70. In an 1816 revision of his 1806 constitution, Alexandre Pétion expanded this recruitment of new citizens to the free country to include "all Africans, Indians, and their descendant and blood relatives, born in the colonies or foreign lands." The constitution declared that these individuals could "come to live in the Republic, [and] will be recognized as Haitian; but will only enjoy the rights of citizenship after a year's residence." This article, paired with the first article of the constitution—"Slavery cannot exist in the territory of the Republic; it is abolished forever"—essentially created Haiti as a haven for slaves in the Caribbean and elsewhere, if they could make it to the island. The national boundaries of Haiti, then, continued to limit and demarcate the confines of universal freedom. By setting foot on the soil, any nonwhite would become Haitian and would be declared free. Sheridan, "Jamaican Slavery to Haitian Freedom," 399; Ferrer, "Haiti, Free Soil, and Antislavery in the Revolutionary Atlantic," 40–66; Revision of the Constitution (1816), 6 February 1816, http://www.modern-constitutions.de/nbu.php?page_id=8294 b7496ae06609fa222b156332446b#Haiti, courtesy of Houghton Library, Harvard University, Cambridge.

71. "St. Domingo," 18 June 1804, Times (London), 3.

72. Edward Corbet to Jean-Jacques Dessalines, 10 February 1804, NLJ, MS 72, Box 3, 501N.

73. Ibid.

74. Ibid.

75. House of Commons Hansard, 1803/4, Commons Sitting of Tuesday, 13 June 1804, http://gateway.proquest.com/openurl?url_ver=Z39.88-2004&res_dat=xri: hcpp-us&rft_dat=xri:hcpp:rec:CDS1V0002P0-0046.

76. See also, for example, House of Commons Hansard, 1803/4, Commons Sitting of Thursday, 7 June 1804, http://gateway.proquest.com/openurl?url_ver=Z39.88-2004&res_dat=xri:hcpp-us&rft_dat=xri:hcpp:rec:CDS1V0002P0-0043.

77. House of Commons Hansard, 1803/4, Commons Sitting of Tuesday, 13 June 1804, http://gateway.proquest.com/openurl?url_ver=Z39.88-2004&res_dat=xri: hcpp-us&rft_dat=xri:hcpp:rec:CDS1V0002P0-0046.

78. House of Commons Hansard, 1803/4, Commons Sitting of Friday, 8 June 1804, http://gateway.proquest.com/openurl?url_ver=Z39.88-2004&res_dat=xri: hcpp-us&rft_dat=xri:hcpp:rec:CDS1V0002P0-0044.

79. John Jeffreys Pratt, 2nd Earl of Camden, responded to Dessalines's request for black laborers on 31 August 1804: "You [Nugent] will therefore inform him that it is impossible for His Majesty's Government to countenance, by agreeing to this

proposition, the importation of slaves into any country not in His Majesty's Possession." John Jeffreys Pratt to George Nugent, 31 August 1804, NLJ, MS 72, Box 3, 468N.

80. "Préserver la Jamaïque de la contagion que le vent de St-Domingue souffle sur elle." "De Londres, le 8 Juin 1804," *Gazette Politique et Commerciale d'Haïti*, 30 January 1806, 3.

81. "Flattons son orgueil; ayons l'air d'embrasser la même chimère que lui; annonçons à ses sujets que nous sommes la seule puissance du monde qui puisse vivre de bonne intelligence avec eux, qui veuille ratifier leur indépendance, et les reconnaître pour de bons et dignes alliés." Ibid., 4.

82. Edward Corbet to Jean-Jacques Dessalines, 27 February 1804, NLJ, MS 72, Box 3, 601N.

83. Edward Corbet to George Nugent, 29 February 1804, NLJ, MS 72, Box 3, 665N.

84. George Nugent to Jean-Jacques Dessalines, 8 March 1804, NLJ, MS 72, Box 3, 315N.

85. George Nugent to Robert Hobart, 19 March 1804, NLJ, MS 72, Box 3, 616N.

86. Ibid.

87. "D'abord, votre Excellence me permettra de lui représenter que le général Toussaint traitait avec le gouvernement britannique comme sujet ou préposé du gouvernement français, que dans les circonstances actuelles, je ne puis ni ne dois traiter que comme chef du peuple que je commande . . . moi chef unique de mon pays, je traite pour mes concitoyens, ce que je ne doit compte a aucune puissance de mes actions ni m'attends l'attache d'aucun gouvernement pour souscrire a des accommodement ou traites." Jean-Jacques Dessalines to George Nugent, 13 May 1804, NLJ, MS 72, Box 2, 628N.

88. "L'intention de mon gouvernement est uniquement de se tenir en garde contre le gouvernement français et ses alliés, de s'armer contre son oppression et de ne rien attenter contre les puissances qui sont assez généreuses pour regarder ce gouvernement comme perfide, régicide et tyran." Ibid.

89. "Le 22 du même mois [February 1804], [Dessalines] rendit un décret qui ordonnait aux généraux commandants des divisions, de faire arrêter toutes les personnes (les blancs) qui seraient convaincues ou soupçonnées d'avoir pris part aux massacres et aux assassinats ordonnés par Leclerc et Rochambeau, afin de les livrer 'au glaive de la justice.'" Ardouin, *Etudes sur l'Histoire d'Haïti*, 14.

90. "Extract from the Secret Deliberations of the Government of the Island of Hayti," quoted in Rainsford, *An Historical Account of the Black Empire of Hayti*, 213.

91. Here I quote a translation provided by an unnamed British official that appears in the Admiralty Records from the Jamaica Station: "The General in Chief to the People of Hayti," TNA, ADM 1/254.

92. Girard, "Caribbean Genocide," 142.

93. "Proclamation of Dessalines," 26 September 1804, *Times* (London), 3.

94. Edward Corbet to George Nugent, 23 March 1804, TNA, CO 137/111, 228.

95. John Perkins to John Thomas Duckworth, 17 March 1804, TNA, ADM 1/254.

96. John Perkins to John Thomas Duckworth, 8 April 1804, TNA, ADM 1/254.

97. Girard, "Caribbean Genocide," 147.

98. "Tous les *Baux-a-ferme* des Habitations, sont et demeurent résiliés." Gouvernement D'Hayti, Jean-Jacques Dessalines, "Arrêté," 2 January 1804, TNA, MFQ 1/184.

99. "Tout individu, ci-devant attaché a la Culture, devra pour exercer sa profession de Marchand, obtenir des Commandans de Place et d'Arrondissement, un certificat qui atteste qu'il a des moyens suffisants; faute de quoi, il sera renvoyé, sous les vingt-quatre heures, sur l'habitation ou il était attaché." "Les femmes attachées aux officiers et soldats comprises dans les dispositions du présent Arrêté, seront assujetties à la même décision." Gouvernement D'Hayti, Jean-Jacques Dessalines, "Ordonnance," 20 January 1804, TNA, MFQ 1/184.

100. "No 2 Report," Edward Corbet to George Nugent, 25 January 1804, NLJ, MS 72, Box, 349N. Mats Lundahl argues that a series of decrees issued between 1804 and 1806 "completed the transformation of all land into government property." See Lundahl, "Defense and Distribution," 91.

101. "Toute propriété qui aura ci-devant appartenue à un blanc français, est, incontestablement et de droit, confisquée au profit de l'État." "Constitution d'Haïti," 20 May 1805, http://www.modern-constitutions.de/nbu.php?page_id=8294 b7496ae06609fa222b156332446b#Haiti, courtesy of American Philosophical Society, Philadelphia.

102. W. L. Whitfield, 9 March 1804, Centre for Kentish Studies, London, U840, 0211/4.

103. George Nugent to Robert Hobart, 10 June 1804, NLJ, MS 72, Box 3, 613. Nugent's letter may not have been entirely truthful, because, according to a letter written by Dacres to Duckworth on 15 May 1804, Dessalines had been given a letter from Nugent on 12 May. The contents of the letter are not listed, but the conversation between Dacres and Dessalines emphasizes that the negotiations between Dessalines and Nugent had come to a close. Dessalines refused to discuss matters further until a decision had been made by the British government in London regarding the proposals that Dessalines had asked to be referred for its consideration. James Richard Dacres to John Thomas Duckworth, 15 May 1804, TNA, ADM 1/254. John Jeffreys Pratt, 2nd Earl of Camden, responded to Dessalines's request for black laborers on 31 August 1804: "You [Nugent] will therefore inform him that it is impossible for His Majesty's Government to countenance, by agreeing to this proposition, the importation of slaves into any country not in His Majesty's Possession." John Jeffreys Pratt to George Nugent, 31 August 1804, NLJ, MS 72, Box 3, 468N.

104. See, for example, "Draft of a Convention between the Governor of Jamaica and General Dessalines," Lord Robert Hobart, attached to a letter dated 7 April 1804, TNA, CO 137/111, 18.

105. Robert Sutherland to William Fawkner, 1 October 1806, TNA, WO 1/75.

106. John Jeffreys Pratt to George Nugent, 31 August 1804, NLJ, MS 72, Box 3, 468N.

107. John Jeffreys Pratt to George Nugent, 6 September 1804, NLJ, MS 72, Box 3, 545N. The Times (London) published an initial report on the massacres on 23 July 1804 and followed up with another report a month and a half later. "Affairs of St. Domingo," 23 July 1804, Times (London), 3; Times (London), 1 September 1804, 3.

108. Gould, Among the Powers of the Earth, 29.

109. Gould argues that a hierarchy of treaties was common throughout the British Empire and emphasizes that treaties signed between British and Indians were not seen as being on the same level as European treaties. "What the British and their European rivals refused to concede was that agreement[s] with indigenous people in North America were comparable to the treaties that they made with each other in Europe." Ibid., 30.

110. Ibid., 50.

111. Extracts of a letter from Mr. Whitfield, dated Kingston, Jamaica, 9 March 1804, Centre for Kentish Studies, London, U840 0211/4.

112. John Jeffreys Pratt, "Thoughts on a Treaty with Dessalines," undated [mid-1804], TNA, CO 137/111, 170.

113. John Jeffreys Pratt to George Nugent, 31 August 1804, NLJ, MS 72, Box 3, 468N. This hope was perhaps misguided, because, as David Geggus has shown, slaves in Jamaica were well aware of events in Saint Domingue beginning with the first uprisings in 1791. Geggus, "The Enigma of Jamaica," 276.

114. John Jeffreys Pratt to George Nugent, 31 August 1804, NLJ, MS 72, Box 3, 468N.

115. John Jeffreys Pratt to George Nugent, 6 September 1804, Centre for Kentish Studies, London, U840, 027/5.

116. "[Illegible] for a Treaty with the government of Hayti," undated, TNA, CO 137/111, 182. As in earlier proposed treaties, Pratt also called for British regulation of Haitian maritime movement.

117. George Nugent to John Jeffreys Pratt, 12 October 1804, NLJ, MS 72, Box 3, 560N.

118. George Nugent to John Jeffreys Pratt, 31 August 1804, NLJ, MS 72, Box 3, 609N.

119. Sheller, "Sword-Bearing Citizens," 233.

120. For a larger discussion of Dessalines's nomination as emperor, see Jenson, *Beyond the Slave Narrative*, 142.

121. Article 12, "Constitution d'Haïti," 20 May 1805, http://www.modern-constitutions.de/nbu.php?page_id=8294b7496ae06609fa222b156332446b#Haiti, courtesy of American Philosophical Society, Philadelphia.

122. The inclusion of Germans and Poles as citizens in independent Haiti was a result of their participation in the war of independence. This topic is discussed in detail in Pachonski and Wilson, *Poland's Caribbean Tragedy*. It was thought at the time that Poles were sympathetic to the blacks' goals for freedom, and so they were often accorded better treatment than the French. This assumption is controversial, but Dessalines seems to have been sympathetic to the Polish military forces in Haiti.

123. "Toutes les constitutions jusqu'a celle de 1918, adopté sous l'occupation Américaine, a l'exception de celles de Christophe (1807 et 1811), reconduisent ces interdictions avec plus ou moins de nuances. A partir de 1867, la formulation strictement raciale sera abandonnée au profit de terme générique d'étranger." Moïse, *Constitutions et Lutte de Pouvoir en Haiti*, 32.

124. Constitution of 1805, Article 7.

125. Rainsford, *An Historical Account of the Black Empire of Hayti*, 217.

126. Ibid., 217–18.
127. Matthew Brown, "Introduction," 9.
128. Gallagher and Robinson, "The Imperialism of Free Trade," 8.

CHAPTER 3

1. I would like to thank Lauren Benton, Mitch Fraas, Nathan Perl-Rosenthal, Edward J. Balleisen, the Triangle Legal History Seminar, and the Warwick University Law School Conversations Reading Group for reading an earlier version of this chapter and for their thoughtful comments and suggestions.
2. Benton, "Strange Sovereignty"; Benton, "Oceans of Law."
3. The cases in Chapter 1, however, suggest that not all ships brought prizes into the courts of their own islands.
4. Benton, "Abolition and Imperial Law," 357.
5. Ibid., 358.
6. Benton, "Strange Sovereignty."
7. The decisions handed down in the cases of the *Manilla* and the *Pelican* were then subsequently referenced in the civil cases of the *Ben Lomond* and the *Elizabeth and Mary*. The cases in this final pairing expanded the diplomatic implications of the law and indeed completely erased the earlier rulings that Haiti was to be considered part of enemy territory.
8. In exchange for which they would receive coffee, cotton, and sugars. In the end, logwood was substituted for sugar. Jean-Jacques Dessalines was nominated Emperor of Haiti in October 1804.
9. Exhibit No. 1, "General Clearance," LS David Lyon, Customs House, New York, 15 October 1804, TNA, HCA 42/426.
10. Court of Vice-Admiralty, Nova Scotia, Examination of Thomas Walmsby Story, master of the *Happy Couple*, 19 March 1805, TNA, HCA 42/426.
11. "Ship News," *Royal Gazette and Bahama Advertiser* 1, no. 63 (12 February 1805).
12. Ibid.
13. "Nassau," *Royal Gazette and Bahama Advertiser* 1, no. 71 (12 March 1805): 3.
14. Jenson, "States of Ghetto, Ghettos of States," 167.
15. Stewart, *Cases Determined and Argued in the Court of Vice-Admiralty*, 67.
16. Ibid., 68.
17. Croke moved to the Vice-Admiralty Court of Nova Scotia in 1801. "His rigid enforcement of the Navigation Acts did not endear him to the merchant community." *Oxford Dictionary of National Biography*, http://www.oxforddnb.com/view/article/6729?docPos=1.
18. As will be discussed in Chapter 4, some American congressmen and the French representatives in the United States and Santo Domingo would have argued otherwise. Stewart, *Cases Determined and Argued in the Court of Vice-Admiralty*, 69.
19. For more on French privateering from the city of Santo Domingo, see Jenson, "States of Ghetto, Ghettos of States," 156–71.
20. Stewart, *Cases Determined and Argued in the Court of Vice-Admiralty*, 71.
21. Ibid., 72.

22. "No. 39," extract of a letter signed Jack, to his wife, Mrs. Eliza Hacker, in New York, dated Port au Prince, 17 February 1805; "No. 40," extract of a letter from J. Faber to Henry Messoniere, merchant Baltimore, Gonaives, 20 February 1805; Court of Vice-Admiralty, Nova Scotia, Examination of Thomas Walmsby Story, master of the *Happy Couple*, 19 March 1805, TNA, HCA 42/426.

23. Court of Vice-Admiralty, Nova Scotia, Examination of Thomas Walmsby Story, master of the *Happy Couple*, 19 March 1805, TNA, HCA 42/426.

24. Ibid.; Exhibit No. 25, Thomas W. Storey to Elias Kane & Co and John B. Murray, undated [shortly after 22 February 1805], TNA, HCA 42/426.

25. Stewart, *Cases Determined and Argued in the Court of Vice-Admiralty*, 72.

26. Ibid.

27. Archibald Kane later signed another contract with the government of Haiti, and this second agreement is discussed in Chapter 4.

28. Court of Vice-Admiralty, Nova Scotia, Testimony of Thomas Walmsby Story, master of the *Happy Couple*, 23 March 1805, TNA, HCA 42/426.

29. According to Emer de Vattel, "contraband" is defined as "Commodities particularly useful in war. . . . Such are arms, ammunition, timber for ship-building, every kind of naval stores, horses,—and even provisions, in certain junctures, when we have hopes of reducing the enemy by famine." Vattel, *The Law of Nations*, 337.

30. Stewart, *Cases Determined and Argued in the Court of Vice-Admiralty*, 72.

31. Ibid., 73.

32. Nessler, "A Failed Emancipation?" chap. 4.

33. For more on this, see Dubois, *Avengers of the New World*, 254.

34. Stewart, *Cases Determined and Argued in the Court of Vice-Admiralty*, 73.

35. Ibid., 74.

36. Ibid.

37. "Nassau," *Royal Gazette and Bahama Advertiser* 1, no. 71 (12 March 1805): 3. For more on these treaties, see Chapter 2.

38. Stewart, *Cases Determined and Argued in the Court of Vice-Admiralty*, 74.

39. Court of Vice-Admiralty, Nova Scotia, Examination of Thomas Walmsby Story, master of the *Happy Couple*, 19 March 1805, TNA, HCA 42/426.

40. Exhibit No. 16, Archibald Kane to Elias Kane, 11 February 1805, NAUK, HCA 42-426.

41. See, for example, "No. 37," extract of a letter from Archibald McElroy jun. to his wife in Pennsylvania, dated St. Marc, 22 February 1805; "No. 43," extract of a letter from A. J. Lewis to Mrs. Huldah Nandyke, St. Marc, 21 February 1805; extract of a letter from M. D. Lewis to Mr. Sam'l McCall, Philadelphia, dated St. Marc, 19 February 1805; "Exhibit No. 17," Archibald Kane to Elias Kane, 20 February 1805; "No. 41," extract of a letter from Nath'l Dillhorn to Mr. C. Collins, St. Marc, 22 February 1805; "No. 46," extract of a letter from Wm. Ely to Mr. J. Catling, St. Marc, 20 February 1805; all in TNA, HCA 42/426.

42. "No. 44," extract of a letter from Nath'l Dillhorn to Capt. Silas Swain, St. Marc, 22 February 1805, TNA, HCA 42/426.

43. Court of Vice-Admiralty, Nova Scotia, Examination of Thomas Walmsby Story, master of the *Happy Couple*, 19 March 1805, TNA, HCA 42/426.

44. "No. 45," extract of a letter from William Ely to W. E. White, St. Marc, 20 February 1805, TNA, HCA 42/426.

45. Court of Vice-Admiralty, Nova Scotia, Testimony of Thomas Walmsby Story, master of the *Happy Couple*, 23 March 1805, TNA, HCA 42/426.

46. Ibid.

47. Stewart, *Cases Determined and Argued in the Court of Vice-Admiralty*, 75.

48. Ibid.

49. Ibid.

50. Ibid., 76.

51. "List of Prizes Adjudged in the Vice-Admiralty Court of the Bahama Islands, from the 26th of June, to the 26th of December, 1805," 4 April 1806, Supplement to the *Royal Gazette*.

52. "Happy Couple," TNA, HCA 42/396.

53. "Capture of the Dart, Nichols, of Baltimore, Bound to Hayti with Military Stores," *Aurora General Advertiser*, 9 March 1805, Philadelphia, 2.

54. "Les anglais mènent a la Jamaique et a Tortole les navires qui vont ou viennent d'hayti, ils en condamnent partie, et ransonnent l'autre partie; le découragement est général pour ce sorte de commerce." Lartigue to Ferrand, 4 October 1806, AN, CC9a41.

55. James Stephen to [Charles Middleton, 1st Baron Barham], 14 June 1805, TNA, CO 245/1, 187.

56. "St Domingo, Letter to His Majesty's Adv. Genl. to prepare the draft of an order for allowing British Subjects to trade to a part of that Island." Stephen Cottrell to His Majesty's Advisor General, 8 July 1806, TNA, PC 2/170.

57. *Oracle and Daily Advertiser* (London), 2 July 1799, issue 22, 025.

58. "Order allowing British ships to go to certain ports and Places in the Island of St Domingo," 21 July 1806, TNA, PC 2/170.

59. "Licence, Messrs MacKenzie and Glennie to Export a Cargo of British Goods and to Import the Return Cargo," 13 August 1806, TNA, PC 2/171.

60. Ibid.

61. Ibid.

62. For example, "Messrs McKenzie and Glennie, Geddes & Co., Robert Sutherland, Doval & Co., Reid Irving & Co., Richard and William E. Lee, Mr. Hamlet, Nathaniel Dowick, and three ships from Halifax to bring fish to Haiti," TNA, PC 2/171.

63. Order in Council, 19 November 1806, and Order in Council, 15 July 1807, TNA, PC 2/171.

64. John Phillips for ship *Echo*, April 1807, National Archives of the Netherlands, the Hague, ALG Rijks Archief, O.A.C. INV NO 451, Film 63.

65. "Licence, Messrs MacKenzie and Glennie," 13 August 1806, TNA, PC 2/171.

66. John Downie to William Fawkener, 3 January 1807, TNA, WO 1/75.

67. The judge's reference was to the initial order of July 1806 and the two others that gave the governors of the Bahama Islands, the Leeward Islands, and Halifax the

authority to issue licenses. 19 April 1805, TNA, HCA 42/426; Stewart, *Cases Determined and Argued in the Court of Vice-Admiralty*, 76.

68. "J'ai eu l'honneur de vous prévenir que les anglais qui croisent sur les cotes de St Thomas, prenaient tous les batimens venant d'Hayti, soit Danois, soit américains." Arnaud André Roberjot Lartigue to Louis Ferrand, 29 October 1806, AN, CC9a41.

69. "Dessalines sera surpris de cela, surtout le roi d'angleterre ayant permis au commerce d'entretenir des relations commerciales avec Dessalines." Arnaud André Roberjot Lartigue to Louis Ferrand, 29 October 1806, AN, CC9a41.

70. Benton, "Abolition and Imperial Law," 357. Benton gives some examples of how sailors "gamed the system": "They seized ships not authorised under their commissions, avoided prize proceedings, sought sympathetic forums with questionable jurisdiction, disposed of goods and ships before cases were complete, sailed with falsified or purchased commissions, flew flags without authorisation, conducted sham sales of ships in order to change their nationality, transshipped goods in neutral ports to 'color' enemy goods, and adopted many other tactics designed to evade regulation and reduce or avoid penalties."

71. "Les danoise et les américains n'iront plus a Hayti." Arnaud André Roberjot Lartigue to Louis Ferrand, 29 October 1806, AN, CC9a41.

72. "Les anglais continuent d'arrêter les bâtiments qui viennent de chez les révoltés de St Domingue, ils ne les relâchent qu'après une forte contribution." Arnaud André Roberjot Lartigue to Louis Ferrand, 17 September 1806, AN, CC9a41.

73. Arnaud André Roberjot Lartigue to Louis Ferrand, 25 August 1806, AN, CC9a41.

74. Louis Ferrand issued a proclamation stating: "Tous les individus, quels qu'ils soient, qui seront trouvés sur des bâtiments alliés ou neutres, expédiés pour les ports de Saint-Domingue, occupés par les révoltés, seront punis de mort." "Arrêté," Louis Ferrand, 5 February 1805/16 Pluviose an XIII, Danish National Archives, Generalguvernementet, Breve fra fremmede autoriteter, 1774–1807, A–C, #2.18.1.

75. Edwards, *Reports of Cases Argued and Determined in the High Court of Admiralty*, 1011.

76. Ibid., 1012.

77. Privy Council to William Scott, 1 December 1806, TNA, PC 2/171.

78. "At the outset of his career on the Admiralty bench he [William Scott] affirmed that a prize court should apply international law, and that even during a war in which Britain was fundamentally engaged, the court must 'administer with indifference that justice which the law of nations holds out to independent states, some happening to be neutral and some belligerent.' . . . Americans, however, whose ships carried the lion's share of neutral trade during the Napoleonic period, felt that Scott did not always afford sufficient protection to the rights of neutrals, and this view has some merit." *Oxford Dictionary of National Biography*, http://www.oxforddnb.com/view/article/24935?docPos=28. The case of the *Manilla* refers to the Order in Council issued on 19 November 1806 that authorized the governor of the Bahama Islands and the governor of the Leeward Islands to grant licenses for trade to Haiti. The content of this appears to be the same as that issued 21 July 1806. Edwards, *Reports of Cases Argued and Determined in the High Court of Admiralty*, 1159.

79. This was a temporary measure, since British captains who had intended to land at Buenos Aires could no longer do so in 1807 because the British had lost control of the city. The Order in Council was translated into French and published in the *Gazette Officielle de l'Etat d'Hayti* 3 (21 May 1807): 3.

80. Ibid.

81. Edwards, *Reports of Cases Argued and Determined in the High Court of Admiralty*, 1160.

82. Ibid., 1013.

83. "Il est arrive a la fin d'octobre au Cap un convoy anglais de 17 voiles, venant de Londres et convoyé par deux frégates." Arnaud André Roberjot Lartigue to Louis Ferrand, 16 November 1806, AN, CC9a41.

84. "Les conséquences en sont désastreuse pour toutes leur colonies." Ibid.

85. "Je vous ai expose l'incohérence et les contradictions que cette incertitude sur l'état d'Hayti, occasionne dans les jugements de vos cours d'amirauté. Je vous supplie encore de faire naitre a la fin un ordre de choses fixe; d'établir un system de politique et de jurisprudence qui soit uniforme; et de prévenir ainsi tout sujet d'irritation future." Jean-Gabriel Peltier to Edward Cooke, 18 June 1808, TNA, WO 1/79.

86. For more on this prohibition, see Chapter 4.

87. "Before the Most Noble and Right Honorable the Lords Commissioners of Appeals in Prize Causes, Pelican, Walter Burke, Master" (unknown: Woodall, printer).

88. Arnaud André Roberjot Lartigue to Louis Ferrand, 1 August 1806, AN, CC9a41.

89. *The English Reports, Ecclesiastical, Admiralty, and Probate and Divorce*, Full Reprint (London: W. Green & Son, Ltd.; Edinburgh Stevens & Sons, Ltd., 1923), Appendix D, HeinOnline, 165 Eng. Rep. 1160 (1752–1865).

90. "Order in Council," 14 December 1808, TNA, PC 2/179.

91. "La déclaration de sa Majesté en conseil qui annonce que les ports d'Haity ne sont point en hostilité avec la grande Bretagne, et que le commerce y est libre comme avec tout autre pays neutre, a causé la plus vive sensation, et le plus grand enthousiasme parmie [sic] les habitants d'Haity. Ils sont pénétrés de reconnaissance pour cet acte envers sa majesté et ses ministres." Jean-Gabriel Peltier to Robert Stewart, Viscount Castlereagh, 5 May 1809, TNA, WO 1/79.

92. The lawyers for the claimants are listed as F. Laurence and JAS. Stephen.

93. *The English Reports, Ecclesiastical, Admiralty, and Probate and Divorce*, Appendix D.

94. Ibid.

95. "Humble memorial of the British merchants residing in Port au Prince Hayti [Robert Sutherland and twenty others] to the Honorable Members of the Board of Trade," 18 September 1810, TNA, WO 1/76.

96. Dickinson discussed these four cases briefly in the early twentieth century, in "The Unrecognized Government," 29–45.

97. Johnson v. Greaves, 1810, *The English Reports, Volume CXXVII, Common Pleas*, (Edinburgh: William Green & Sons; London, 1912), 1111.

98. Blackburne v. Thompson, 4 February 1812, *The English Reports, King's Bench Division*, Max. A. Robertson and Geoffrey Ellis, eds. (Edinburgh: William Green & Sons, 1910), 775–781. HeinOnline, 104 Eng. Rep 775 (1378–1865), 775–781.

99. "Free Trade with Hayti," *Morning Chronicle* (London), 17 December 1808, issue 12354, 2. For more on Jean-Gabriel Peltier, see Chapter 5.

100. *The English Reports, King's Bench*, 781.

101. "Licence, Messrs MacKenzie and Glennie to Export a Cargo of British Goods and to Import the Return Cargo," 13 August 1806, TNA, PC 2/171.

102. T. W. Brown, John Ritchie, John Hornby, Duncan Taylor, Walter Roe, W. D. Robertson, and B. Smith to James Richard Dacres, August 1807, Clements Library, University of Michigan, 6912/14, 167.

103. Mr. Hallam to Edward Cooke, 4 February 1808, TNA, WO 1/75.

CHAPTER 4

1. Jacob Lewis to James Madison, Port-au-Prince, 1 October 1804, NARA, State Department Consular Despatches, Cape Haitian Series, vol. 4, 5 January 1802–10 December 1813.

2. Historian Rayford Logan, in his 1941 study of the relationships between the United States and Haiti, used diplomatic correspondence to describe the attitudes and conflicts between American and French representatives over the issue of economic support and Haitian independence in the first years after 1804. Historians Tim Matthewson and Gordon S. Wood have also undertaken an extensive study of Haiti's relationship with the United States during the revolution and in the first years after independence. See Logan, *The Diplomatic Relations of the United States with Haiti*; Matthewson, *A Proslavery Foreign Policy*; Gordon S. Brown, *Toussaint's Clause*; and Montague, *Haiti and the United States*.

3. Quoted in Matthewson, *A Proslavery Foreign Policy*, 129.

4. Jacob Lewis to James Madison, Port-au-Prince, 1 October 1804, NARA, State Department Consular Despatches, Cape Haitian Series, vol. 4, 5 January 1802–10 December 1813.

5. Gordon S. Brown, *Toussaint's Clause*: 233–44.

6. Ibid., 126–43.

7. Ibid., 143.

8. "Les Américains, particulièrement soucieux de développer leur commerce, devinrent, au cours des deux premières années d'indépendance, les plus importantes partenaires d'Haïti." Nicholls, "Race, Couleur et Indépendance en Haïti," 181.

9. Arnaud André Roberjot Lartigue to Louis Ferrand, 1 August 1806, AN, CC9a41.

10. "At Port-au-Prince (St. Domingo) Mr. Archibald Kane, Merchant, Late of the House of James and Archibald Kane, of This City, Died," *Albany Gazette*, 15 November 1817, 2.

11. "Happy Couple," TNA, HCA 42/426.

12. Archibald Kane to Elias Kane, 9 February 1805, from St. Marc, Haiti, TNA, HCA 42/426.

13. *National Intelligencer and Washington Advertiser*, 12 May 1804, 3. This article was also published in the *Philadelphia Evening Post* on 7 March 1804.

14. Archibald Kane to Elias Kane, 13 February 1805, St. Marc, TNA, HCA 42/426.

15. Extract of a letter from William Ely to Mr. J. Catling, 20 February 1805, St. Marc, TNA, HCA 42/426.

16. "Quelle confiance pourriez-vous avoir en ce banqueroutier frauduleux, en cet aventurier nommé Lewis, qui s'est déshonoré, autant par sa faillite à New-York, que

par le tort qu'il a fait au gouvernement haïtien, en partant furtivement de la rade du Port-au-Prince, sans avoir satisfait aux frais d'exportations?" Henry Christophe, "Etat d'Hayti, Proclamation, 23 Juin 1807," *Gazette Officielle de l'État d'Hayti* 15 (13 August 1807): 4.

17. Ibid.
18. Archibald Kane to James [Kane], St. Marc, 11 February 1805, TNA, HCA 42/426.
19. Archibald Kane to André Vernett, 24 January 1805, TNA, HCA 42/426.
20. André Vernett and Archibald Kane, "No. 12, Aux Gonaïves," 4 February 1805, TNA, HCA 42/426.
21. Archibald Kane to André Vernett, 24 January 1805, TNA, HCA 42/426.
22. George Nugent to John Jeffreys Pratt, 2nd Earl of Camden, 15 December 1804, NLJ, MS 72, Box 3, 511N.
23. 24 January 1805, at St. Marc, Haiti, TNA, HCA 42/426.
24. Archibald Kane to James [Kane], from St. Marc, Haiti, 11 February 1805, TNA, HCA 42/426.
25. Matthewson, *A Proslavery Foreign Policy*, 120.
26. Logan, *The Diplomatic Relations of the United States with Haiti*, 161.
27. Matthewson, *A Proslavery Foreign Policy*, 125.
28. Logan, *The Diplomatic Relations of the United States with Haiti*, 157.
29. Ibid., 160.
30. Ibid., 161.
31. Ibid., 163.
32. André Pichon, 6 June 1804, quoted in ibid., 166.
33. Ibid., 169.
34. Gordon S. Brown, *Toussaint's Clause*, 248.
35. Matthewson, *A Proslavery Foreign Policy*, 125.
36. Ibid., 121.
37. Logan, *The Diplomatic Relations of the United States with Haiti*, 165.
38. Rep. John W. Eppes, 13 December 1804, *Proceedings and Debates of the House of Representatives of the United States, at the Second Session of the Eighth Congress Begun at the City of Washington, Monday, November 5, 1804*, http://memory.loc.gov/cgi-bin/ampage?collId=llac&fileName=014/llac014.db&recNum=336.
39. Thomas Lowndes, 13 December 1804, ibid.
40. William Eustis, 13 December 1804, ibid.
41. Joseph Clay, 13 December 1804, ibid.
42. Ibid.
43. Quoted in Gordon S. Brown, *Toussaint's Clause*, 256.
44. George Logan, Wednesday, 27 February 1805, *Proceedings and Debates of the Senate of the United States, at the Second Session of the Eighth Congress*.
45. Gordon S. Brown, *Toussaint's Clause*, 262.
46. "Ont continuellement harassés notre commerce, et même capturés nos navires, quoiqu'ils fussent employés dans un commerce ordinaire et légal." "Etats-Unis d'Amérique," *Gazette Politique et Commerciale d'Haïti* 14 (14 March 1805): 1.
47. "Les algériens de notre hémisphère." "Etats-Unis d'Amérique," *Gazette Politique et Commerciale d'Haïti* 14 (14 March 1805): 1.

48. Logan, *The Diplomatic Relations of the United States with Haiti*, 171.

49. "New York, June 13," *Albany Register*, 25 June 1805, 3.

50. "Boston, June 17," *City Gazette and Daily Advertiser*, 4 July 1805, 2.

51. *Aurora General Advertiser* (Philadelphia), 17 June 1805, Issue 4512, 2; also cited in Matthewson, *A Proslavery Foreign Policy*, 127; and Jenson, *Beyond the Slave Narrative*, 178. Tim Matthewson argues that "King's toast was deliberate provocation, aimed at embarrassing the president, and it expressed Federalist contempt for slaveholders who preached the equality of man while holding slaves in bondage." See Matthewson, *A Proslavery Foreign Policy*, 127.

52. "Etats-Unis d'Amérique, Chambre des Représentans au Congres," *Gazette Politique et Commerciale d'Haïti*, 6 February 1806, 4. The newspaper noted that it would reprint the relevant debates in forthcoming issues. I have not been able to find any reference in the issues that are still available—the extant issues, however, are not a complete run of the newspaper.

53. Gordon S. Brown, *Toussaint's Clause*, 269.

54. John Quincy Adams, 19 December 1805, *Proceedings and Debates of the Senate of the United States, at the First Session of the Ninth Congress, begun at the City of Washington, Monday, December 2, 1805*, http://memory.loc.gov/cgi-bin/ampage?collId=llac&fileName=015/llac015.db&recNum=2.

55. Gordon S. Brown, *Toussaint's Clause*, 263.

56. Samuel L. Mitchill, 20 December 1805, *Proceedings and Debates of the Senate of the United States, at the First Session of the Ninth Congress*.

57. Matthewson, *A Proslavery Foreign Policy*, 127.

58. For more on Dominguan migration to the United States, see White, *Encountering Revolution*.

59. Samuel White, "Mr. White's Speech in the Senate of the United States, on the bill interdicting all intercourse between the United States and the island of St. Domingo; February 20, 1806" (no publication information, 1806), http://www.archive.org/details/mrwhitesspeechinoowhit.

60. Ferris, "Samuel White and His Father," 3.

61. Ibid., 13.

62. Ibid., 8.

63. White, "Mr. White's Speech in the Senate," 10–11.

64. Ibid., 11.

65. Ibid. White cites from Vattel's chapter on civil war, in *The Law of Nations*, 424. Benton highlights that, thirteen years later, President James Monroe defined the "status of Spain's former colonies as belligerents in a civil war." Benton, "Strange Sovereignty."

66. White, "Mr. White's Speech in the Senate," 11–12.

67. Ibid., 11.

68. Ibid.

69. Ibid., 12.

70. Ibid., 17.

71. Ibid., 8.

72. Ibid., 19.

73. Logan, *The Diplomatic Relations of the United States with Haiti*, 179.
74. White, "Mr. White's Speech in the Senate," 21.
75. Ibid.
76. Ibid.
77. Ibid., 27.
78. Ibid.
79. Logan, *The Diplomatic Relations of the United States with Haiti*, 177.
80. Ibid., 179.
81. James Madison to Armstrong, 15 March 1806, quoted in ibid., 177.
82. Matthewson, *A Proslavery Foreign Policy*, 129.
83. Logan, *The Diplomatic Relations of the United States with Haiti*, 181.
84. This is not the same ship as the one in Chapter 3.
85. Lowrie and Clarke, *American State Papers*, 717.
86. Logan, *The Diplomatic Relations of the United States with Haiti*, 182.
87. Ibid.
88. "Yeaton and others., claimants of the schooner *General Pinkney*, and *Cargo v. the United States*," Cranch, *Reports of Cases Argued and Adjudged in the Supreme Court of the United States*, 281.
89. The *General Pinkney* provided precedent for other similar cases. For example, a similar appeal regarding the *Rachel* in 1810 referenced the case of the *General Pinkney* and also concluded that the trade was legal. "The Schooner *Rachel v. the United States*," Cranch, *Reports of Cases Argued and Adjudged in the Supreme Court of the United States*, 329.
90. "The United States v. Ship Helen," Cranch, *Reports of Cases Argued and Adjudged in the Supreme Court of the United States*, 203.
91. Quoted in Dickinson, "The Unrecognized Government," 35.
92. Washington, *Reports of Cases Determined in the Circuit Court of the United States*, 101.
93. Editorial Staff of the National Reporter System, *Federal Cases*, 932.
94. Ibid.
95. Here the judge referenced another case, *Rose v. Himely*, from 1804, but argued that it did not apply as precedent. "Rose v. Himely," Cranch, *Reports of Cases Argued and Adjudged in the Supreme Court of the United States*, 313.
96. Peters, *By Authority of Congress*, 350.
97. Washington, *Reports of Cases Determined in the Circuit Court of the United States*, 106.
98. "Ne fut guère suivie d'effet, car les marchands américains ne voulaient pas céder la place aux anglais." Brière, *Haïti et la France*, 54.
99. Trouillot, *Haiti, State against Nation*, 53.
100. Matthewson, *A Proslavery Foreign Policy*, 37.

CHAPTER 5

1. Madiou, *Histoire d'Haïti*, 406.
2. Dubois, *Haiti: The Aftershocks of History*, 55.
3. "Aussitôt qu'il a été sûr du pouvoir, il s'est empressé a se faire le héros de la révolution de St. Domingue; se tirant a son naturel féroce et orgueilleux, il n'a plus vu l'état que dans lui, sans déguise . . . il a cru que l'art de gouverner ne consistait qu'a

faire sa volonté tyrannique et a se livrer a la plus crapuleuse débauche." Laurent Férou to Eyre Coote, 20 October 1806, TNA, CO 137/117.

4. Ibid.
5. Eyre Coote to William Windham, 2 November 1806, TNA, CO 137/117.
6. Ibid.
7. Sheller, "Sword-Bearing Citizens," 247.
8. Robert Sutherland to William Fawkener, 1 October 1806, TNA, WO 1/75.
9. Robert Sutherland to George Shee, 12 October 1806, TNA, WO 1/75; Edward Corbet, "No 2 Report," 25 January 1804, NLJ, MS 72, 349N.
10. Peltier, The Trial of John Peltier.
11. "Une ennemi de Buonaparte aussi intrépide que vous l'êtres, est nécessairement un de nos amis. Votre Journal est la lecture favorite des Haïtiens elle est devenue un besoin pour eux." Bruno Blanchet to Jean-Gabriel Peltier, 31 July 1807, TNA, WO 1/79.
12. "Par lequel le gouvernement d'Haïti annonce aux puissances qui ont des colonies dans son voisinage, sa résolution inébranlable de ne point trouble le régime par lequel elles sont gouvernées." Gazette Officielle de l'Etat d'Hayti (20 August 1807): 4.
13. Robert Sutherland to George Shee, 12 October 1806, TNA, WO 1/75.
14. Ibid.
15. Jean-Jacques Dessalines to John Downie, 15 August 1806, TNA, WO 1/75.
16. John Downie to William Fawkener, 3 January 1807, TNA, WO 1/75.
17. G[eorge] S[hee] to Robert Sutherland, [undated, end of 1806], TNA, WO 1/75.
18. James Richard Dacres to William Marsden, 16 November 1806, TNA, ADM 1/256.
19. "De prendre les rênes du gouvernement, et de nous faire jouir de la plénitude de nos droits, de la liberté, pour laquelle nous avons si longtemps combattu, et d'être dépositaire de nos lois auxquelles nous jurons d'obéir; puisqu'elles seront justes." Alexandre Pétion to Henry Christophe, 18 October 1806, quoted in Madiou, Histoire d'Haïti, 416.
20. "Constitution," 27 December 1806, by the Constitution Committee of the Constituent Assembly, in Documents Constitutionnels d'Haïti, 1790–1860; text also available online at http://www.modern-constitutions.de.
21. "Constitution de l'Etat d'Hayti," 17 February 1807, in Documents Constitutionnels d'Haïti, 1790–1860; text also available online at http://www.modern-constitutions.de; TNA, WO 1/79.
22. "Heureusement que (le General Christophe seul excepte) la cause des Haitiens est la même et que malgré la séparation de la famille, tous savent l'apprécier. Il existe malgré la différence des Gouvernemens, une ligue soumise et tacite contre tous les ennemis de notre Liberté et de notre Indépendance" "sous les point de vue de la cause de la défense du territoire, je ne sais aucune différence de pays, et que mon cœur ne voit sans aucune abstraction qu'Haity." Alexandre Pétion to William Wilberforce and James Stephen, NLJ, MS 692.
23. Henry Christophe to Thomas Clarkson, 18 November 1816, in Henry Christophe and Thomas Clarkson, A Correspondence, 100.
24. "Constitution de l'Etat d'Hayti, 1807," Articles 1 and 2; "Constitution, 1806," Article 1; select paragraphs relating to Haiti's early constitutions are revisions of excerpts from Gaffield, "Complexities of Imagining Haiti," 81–103.

25. "37. Le Peuple d'Haïti ne fait point de conquêtes hors de son Isle, et se borne a conserver son territoire." The other article in this section is: "36. The Government of Haiti declares to the Powers that have colonies in its vicinity its unshakeable decision to not disturb the regime by which they are governed." "36. Le Gouvernement d'Haïti manifeste au puissances qui ont des colonies dans son voisinage, sa résolution inébranlable de ne point troubler le régime par lequel elles sont gouvernées." TNA, WO 1/79. Pétion's constitution contains a similar article: "Art. 2. La République d'Haïti ne formera jamais aucune entreprise dans les vues de faire des conquêtes, ni de troubler la paix et le régime intérieur des iles étrangères." Pradine, *Recueil General des Lois et Actes du Gouvernement d'Haïti*, 169.

26. Nicholls, *From Dessalines to Duvalier*, 59.

27. Gaffield, "Complexities of Imagining Haiti," 93.

28. "L'assemble étant constituée, du vingt au trente novembre, douze personnes de son département qu'elle croit les plus propres à remplir les fonctions de Sénateur. Ces personnes ne peuvent être pris que parmi les citoyens qui exercent ou qui ont exercé une fonction civile ou militaire avec probité et honneur." Constitution of 1806, Article 48.

29. "Tout autre Président que celui nomme par la présente Assemblée constituante, ne pourra être pris que parmi les citoyens qui auront été ou seront membres du Sénat ou Secrétaire d'Etat." Constitution of 1806, Article 111.

30. "Que l'union, le travail, le commerce et l'industrie de tous les Citoyens, en fournissant au Gouvernement les moyens de se soutenir avec dignité et de remplir avec honneur ses engagemen[t]s, lui donnent aussi le pouvoir de faire votre bonheur et de vous préserver de tous les pièges de nos Ennemis." Henry Christophe, "Adresse. Le Chef du Gouvernement D'Hayti, aux Habitans et Cultivateurs," 22 January 1807, TNA, WO 1/79.

31. "Que ceux qui voudront lier des relations politiques ou jouir des avantages de notre Commerce, trouvent une réciprocité équitable; n'offrons que la mort et les combats aux autres." Henry Christophe, "Adresse: Henry Christophe, Président et Généralissime des Forces de Terre et de Mer de L'Etat d'Haïti, A L'Armée et au Peuple," 17 February 1807, TNA, WO 1/79.

32. Constitution of 1807, Article 49.

33. Constitution of 1807, Article 41.

34. "Le Président a vu avec plaisir les offres de service que vous faites au Gouvernement d'Hayti [sic], et vos intentions favorables à son égard. Personne ne peut mieux que vous remplir son but, et travailler efficacement à amener le Gouvernement Anglais a entrer en traite avec l'Etat d'Hayti. Vous connaissez toute l'étendu des avantages que peut retirer le commerce de la Grande Bretagne en liant des relations commerciales avec nous." Rouanez, jeune, to Jean-Gabriel Peltier, 5 April 1807, TNA, WO 1/79.

35. "Les immenses relations commerciales qui existent déjà entre l'Angleterre et l'Etat de Haïti, et les encouragements que le ministre Britannique a donnés jusqu'à ce jour un examen approfondi et une surveillance rigoureuse des principes, des moyens et de l'objet des deux partis; et a cet égard, je suis assure de pouvoir démontrer a votre seigneurie que S.E. le Président Christophe est parfaitement digne de la bienveillance, de l'estime et des faveurs politiques du gouvernement de S.M." Jean-Gabriel Peltier to Robert Stewart, Viscount Castlereagh, 8 June 1807, TNA, WO 1/79.

36. "La reconnaissance de l'indépendance de cet Etat par le Gouvernement Anglais, engagerait peut-être les autres nations a imiter son exemple: mais l'avantage d'un pareil acte serait tout en faveur de l'Angleterre. Son commerce, sa marine trouveraient toujours dans nos ports un Gouvernement dispose à leur offrir tous les genres d'hospitalité de préférence aux sujets des autres nations." Rouanez, *jeune*, to Jean-Gabriel Peltier, 5 April 1807, TNA, WO 1/79.

37. "L'intention du peuple d'Hayti est tellement éloignée de donner des inquiétudes aux nations qui ont des possessions dans son voisinage qu'il en a fait un des principaux articles de sa constitutions nouvelle et il serait a désirer que les Anglais fréquentassent assez nos Ports pour pouvoir juger par eux mêmes des égards qu'ils y trouveront." Ibid.

38. "Après la mort de Dessalines, a la quelle Christophe avait coopéré non pas en l'armant contre lui, il le craignait trop, mais par des propositions adroitement communiquées aux Généraux Pétion et Gerin de se défaire du tyran, Christophe fut proclame provisoirement chef du gouvernement." Bruno Blanchet to Jean-Gabriel Peltier, 31 July 1807, TNA, WO 1/79.

39. "Il s'est empare de toutes les denrées des habitants et des cultivateurs en leur remettant un bon payable a une certaine époque, c'est-a-dire, du papier en échange; la plupart des députés du Nord a l'assemblée constituante qui ont eu l'imprudence de retrouver dans leurs communes n'existent plus; tous les hommes de couleur qu'il a pu attendre n'existent plus; des femmes, des enfants ont été les victimes de sa férocité." Ibid.

40. "Cependant la fin tragique de Dessalines aurait du lui prouver que Les Haïtiens savent repousser la tyrannie sous quelque forme et quelque couleur qu'elle se présente." Ibid.

41. "Tantôt le poursuivre avec l'arme du ridicule que vous maniez si adroitement. Dans les moments de répit que vous auorderez [aborderez] a l'Empereur Napoléon, je vous recommande de vous occuper un peu de l'empereur Christophe, qui se qualifie de successeur naturel et légitime de Dessalines." Ibid.

42. "Marchait a pas de géant a la domination universelle." Ibid.

43. "Pusillanimité a l'égard de la France, et peut-être d'une haine invétérée a l'égard de la Grande Bretagne." Ibid.

44. "Votre Seigneurie m'ayant fait savoir par M. Cooke, que soit en raison des troubles civils qui s'étaient élevés dans ce pays, soit par d'autres motifs, le Gouvernement de Sa Majesté ne jugerait pas convenable de prendre encore ces ouvertures en considération sérieuse." Jean-Gabriel Peltier to Robert Stewart, Viscount Castlereagh, 5 October 1807, TNA, WO 1/79.

45. "Un Etat qui vous tend les bras, qui ouvre a votre marine les plus beaux ports, les plus belles positions, qui vous offre son sang, ses sucurs et ses trésors de préférence a toute autre nations, un pays fier d'être la plus belle isle du monde après l'Angleterre, et qui demande a sa sœur ainée de la prendre sous sa protection; un pays qui, seul avec vous, a vaincu Buonaparte, et qui seul veut encore aujourd'hui le combattre avec vous; un pays aussi naturellement votre allie, peut-il continuer d'entre encore traite a l'insta_ d'une colonie ennemi?" Ibid.

46. "De proposer aux ministres de sa Majesté de reconnaître l'isle d'Haity comme état libre et indépendant, et son gouvernement comme gouvernement souverain sous

la protection de l'Angleterre." Henry Christophe, "Instructions pour M. Richardson, envoyé auprès du Cabinet Britannique," 13 July 1807, TNA, WO 1/79.

47. Ibid.

48. "Il est aisé de sentir que les commerçants et les colons Britanniques, tant a Londres qu'a la Jamaïque doivent mieux aimer apercevoir a Haity 60 Mille cultivateurs, la houe a la main, que 60 mille soldats la bayonette au bout du fusil; qu'aux yeux des philosophes l'esprit d'industrie est beaucoup plus a désirer pour le progrès de la civilisation que l'esprit militaire." Jean-Gabriel Peltier and Thomas Richardson to Robert Stewart, Viscount Castlereagh, [undated, 1807], TNA, WO 1/79.

49. "Ce commerce peut vous rapporter un jour autant que celui de toutes vos colonies ensemble, et il ne vous en coutera ni frais de gouvernement, ni frais d'administration, ni d'armée, pour vous en assurer les avantages, un traite, un ministre résident et trois consuls suffiront pour cela." Ibid.

50. Matthew Brown, "Introduction," 9.

51. Thomas Richardson and Jean-Gabriel Peltier to Robert Stewart, Viscount Castlereagh, "Note," 28 October 1807, TNA, WO 1/79.

52. "Narrative of the proceedings," James Walker and Hugh Cathcart, 27 August 1803, NLJ, MS 72, Box 2, 493N.

53. Ferrer, *Freedom's Mirror*, 204.

54. See, for example, B. S. Rowley to W. W. Pole, 17 March 1809, TNA, ADM 259; and W. Charlton to B. S. Rowley, 6 December 1809, TNA, ADM 260.

55. "Si par la suite, il s'introduit d'autres religions, nul ne pourra être empêché, en se conformant aux lois, d'exercer le culte religieux qu'il aura choisi." Constitution of 1806, Article 37.

56. Constitution of 1807, Article 30.

57. Jean-Gabriel Peltier to Robert Stewart, Viscount Castlereagh, "Hayti Trois Mémoires," October 1807, TNA, WO 1/79.

58. "Cette reconnaissance d'un Etat nouvellement forme, et dont le territoire non seulement dépanadait en dernier lieu d'une grand puissance Européenne, mais même dont les habitants étaient, en majeure partie, esclaves des sujets de cette puissance, étonnée au premier aspect, et la nouveauté de la circonstance fait naitre d'abord une foule d'objections que nous croyons aisé de dissiper." Ibid.

59. "L'indépendance d'Haity est une chose de fait; qui a déjà existe, qui existe, et qui existera." Ibid.

60. "Reconnus par tous les souverains de l'Europe et formant aujourd'hui des Gouvernements réguliers dans la société des Etats." Ibid.

61. "Ce serait perdre sont temps que de répondre a l'objection qu'on pourrait faire sur le danger de la reconnaissance de la souveraineté d'une peuplade d'hommes nouveaux, dont les trois quarts ont été rassembles au hasard de toutes les parties d'Afrique lorsque tous les gouvernements Européens ont des traites avec plusieurs potentats Africains et Mahométans." Ibid.

62. "Aujourd'hui, il aspire à être compte pour quelque chose. Il s'élevé par ses formes a la hauteur des gouvernements européens. Il a des tribunaux, des temples, des prêtres, des ministres qui ne seraient déplacées dans aucun cabinet européen, un hôtel des monnaies, des salles de spectacles, des forts, des citadelles, des écoles

publiques, une armée de 70 mille hommes organisée a l'Européenne; et cependant l'incertitude de sa position lui fait désirer qu'une main ferme et puissante dirige sa marche et fixe son existence ; il veut entrer en contact avec un gouvernement européen; il se fixe sans hésiter sur le Gouvernement Britannique; il veut coopérer avec lui a la destruction de l'ennemi commun, s'honorer autant que s'affermir par la protection de sa majesté, et offrir au commerce anglais des avantages qu'il refuse aux autres nations; quel plus beau spectacle! Qu'elle plus heureuse circonstance quel hommage plus brillant en l'Angleterre peut-elle recevoir! et quelle réponse y fera-t-elle?" Ibid.

63. Luster, *The Amelioration of the Slaves in the British Empire*, 10; Fergus, *Revolutionary Emancipation*, 40.

64. "Par la raison qu'on montre aux noirs qu'ils ne sont pas destines à être éternellement esclaves." Jean-Gabriel Peltier to Robert Stewart, Viscount Castlereagh, "Hayti Trois Mémoires," October 1807, TNA, WO 1/79.

65. "C'est remettre sous l'influence européenne une population qui avait jure de s'y soustraire." Ibid.

66. "Alors il ne faut plus rechercher quelle peut être l'influence morale de la reconnaissance de l'indépendance de Haity sur vos colonies, il faut songer a prendre de bonne heures des précautions physiques contre les dangers de l'état de choses plus hostile qu'amical, que vous créez ou au moins que vous tolérez ainsi." Ibid.

67. "Toussaint et Dessalines ont péri, sans que la mort de l'un ni de l'autre ait du exciter aucun regret en Angleterre, aucun des deux ne fut dispose favorablement pour elle. Toussaint ne témoigna jamais une envie franche de se lier avec l'Angleterre qui l'avait combattu sans Fruit. Dessalines envoya a son tour un agent pour proposer aux Etats-Unis un traite d'alliance et de commerce exclusif entre l'Amérique et Haity." Ibid.

68. Ibid.

69. Nicholls, *From Dessalines to Duvalier*, 40, 266n22; DuBois, *Haiti: The Aftershocks of History*, 55.

70. Griggs and Prator, *Henry Christophe and Thomas Clarkson*; Daut, "'Alpha and Omega' of Haitian Literature," 49–72; Garraway, "Empire of Freedom, Kingdom of Civilization," 1–21.

71. "J'ai donne au Gouvernement des notes et des preuves sans nombre que Christophe était un homme d'honneur, un homme bien intentionné, bien pensant, en un mot un grand homme dans un temps ou il y en a tant de petits a la tête des affaires de ce pauvre monde. J'ai prouvé de même par leurs propres lettres que Pétion et ses adhérents étaient des meurtriers, des lâches, des parricides, des républicains, des Buonapartistes, enfin." Jean-Gabriel Peltier, "Note Verbale," 10 November 1807, TNA, WO 1/79.

72. "Je sais que vous me répéterez à cet égard qu'un gouvernement neutre n'a point le droit de s'interférer dans les querelles intérieures d'un autre pays. Cet axiome peut être juste, quand on ne va pas dans un pays ; mais quand on y va commencer comme vous allez maintenant le faire a St. Domingue, la neutralité entre un chef légitime, et des révoltes, est impraticable. Vos intérêts et les devoirs de l'humanité vous préservèrent d'interposer votre influence dans cette querelle entre Henry Christophe, chef légitime, et Pétion soldat révolte contre son chef." Ibid.

73. Rouanez, *jeune*, "Mémoire Présenté par l'ordre de Monseigneur le Président et Généralissime des forces de terre et de mer de l'Etat d'Haïti a Right Honorable Lord Castlereagh," undated [late 1807 or early 1808], TNA, WO 1/79.

74. I have not found the law that Peltier was referring to.

75. Jean-Gabriel Peltier to Robert Stewart, Viscount Castlereagh, 5 March 1808, TNA, WO 1/79; Jean-Gabriel Peltier, "Note, Orders in Council, Their Operation with Respect to the Future Trade with Haity," 5 March 1808, TNA, WO 1/79.

76. "Ces cargaisons ont consistés principalement en draps fins et communs, en toiles de toute espèce, serges, casimirs, basins, nankins, soieries, étoffes de coton de toute espèce, bas, mousselines, batistes, armes, sellerie, ouvrages en fer de Birmingham, gallon, Chapeaux, poudre a canon, bijouterie, mouchoirs, papeterie, librairie, voitures, harnais, meubles, verrerie, poisson sale, morue, harengs, pilchards, vin de prise, porter, marchandises des Indes, &c." Ibid.

77. "Haity est, si non nominalement, au moins par le fait, par ses besoins, par ses relations déjà établies avec la Grande Bretagne, une véritable colonie Anglaise." Ibid.

78. "Combien chaque jour et chaque évènement qui se succèdent, rendent manifeste la propriété de fixer enfin l'existence de l'Etat d'Haity, en reconnaissant son indépendance, en y entretenant des agents reconnus." Ibid.

79. "M. Canning a dit avant-hier dans la chambre des communes; que 'tout pays qui se révolterait contre l'oppresseur-général du monde, et l'ennemi de la Grande Bretagne, devenait par cela seul, dans quelques circonstances qu'il se trouvât, l'allie de l'Angleterre!' J'invoque ce sentiment pour mes commettants les Haytiens. Plus heureux que les Espagnols, leur révolte contre l'oppresseur des nations, est terminée. Vous faites un grand commerce avec eux ; et loin de les traiter en amis et en allies, vous les traitez *en ennemis!*" Jean-Gabriel Peltier to Edward Cooke, 18 June 1808, TNA, WO 1/79.

80. "My Lord Castlereagh m'avait demande, au mois de janvier dernier, si j'aurais des objections à ce que le gouvernement de sa majesté reconnut l'indépendance des deux gouvernements actuels d'Hayti?" Ibid.

81. "Il me charge de vous annoncer qu'il n'est pas au pouvoir d'aucune puissance ni d'aucun gouvernement de morceler celui d'Haïti. Si Pétion s'est mis en état de révolte contre son autorité, le Président possède les moyens de le réduire par la force." Extract of "Nouvelles D'Haity," Rouanez, *jeune*, to Jean-Gabriel Peltier, 17 March 1809, TNA, WO 1/79.

82. John Goff to the Robert Jenkins, 2nd Earl of Liverpool, 4 May 1811, TNA, WO 1/79.

83. John Goff to the Robert Jenkins, 2nd Earl of Liverpool, 16 May 1811, TNA, WO 1/79.

84. Ibid.

85. Jean-Gabriel Peltier to Edward Cooke, 10 November 1807, TNA, WO 1/79; Jean-Gabriel Peltier to Robert Stewart, Viscount Castlereagh, 10 November 1807, TNA, WO 1/79; Jean-Gabriel Peltier to Edward Cooke, 18 June 1808, TNA, WO 1/79.

86. Thomas Richardson to Robert Stewart, Viscount Castlereagh, 29 November 1807, NAUK, WO 1/79; Thomas Richardson to Edward Cook, 14 January 1808, TNA, WO 1/79; Thomas Richardson to Robert Stewart, Viscount Castlereagh, 14 January

1808, TNA, WO 1/79; Richardson to Robert Stewart, Viscount Castlereagh, 22 January 1808, TNA, WO 1/79.

87. "Il faudrait au moins que vous expliquassiez au chef d'Haity sous quel titre vous reconnaissez cet état et son Gouvernement, ou si vous le regardez comme une abstraction, un *non-descript*." Jean-Gabriel Peltier to Robert Stewart, Viscount Castlereagh, "Hayti Trois Mémoires," October 1807, TNA, WO 1/79.

88. Jean-Gabriel Peltier to unknown, 27 June 1810, TNA, WO 1/79.

89. "Il est rare, monsieur, que des relations commerciales entre deux peuples n'ameneur a leur suite quelques relations politique." Bruno Blanchet to William Windham, 23 April 1807, TNA, WO 1/75.

90. Ferrer, *Freedom's Mirror*, 256.

91. Quoted in ibid., 258; Junta to Someruelos, Real Orden, 18 February 1809, AGI, leg. 12, exp. 57, Estado, Ministerio de Guerra.

92. Ferrer, *Freedom's Mirror*, 258.

93. For more, see Dessens, *From Saint-Domingue to New Orleans*.

94. Dubois, *Haiti: The Aftershocks of History*, 57.

CONCLUSION

1. I would like to thank David Lambert for his thoughts on the significance of diplomatic recognition and the importance of customary and traditional practices between governments.

2. Plummer, *Haiti and the United States*, 33.

3. Jean-Jacques Dessalines, Henry Christophe, Augustin Clervaux, "St. Domingo, 29 November 1803," *Times* (London), 6 February 1804, issue 5938, 3.

4. "Que l'union, le travail, le commerce et l'industrie de tous les Citoyens, en fournissant au Gouvernement les moyens de se soutenir avec dignité et de remplir avec honneur ses engagemen[t]s, lui donnent aussi le pouvoir de faire votre bonheur et de vous préserver de tous les pièges de nos Ennemis." Henry Christophe, "Adresse: Le Chef du Gouvernement D'Hayti, aux Habitans et Cultivateurs," 22 January 1807, TNA, WO 1/79.

5. "No 2 Report," Edward Corbet to George Nugent, 25 January 1804, NLJ, MS 72, Box 3, 349N.

6. Sexton, "An American System"; Sanders, "Congressional Reaction in the United States"; Reinhold, "New Research on the First Pan-American Congress."

7. For more on metaphorical slavery in the American Revolutions, see Christopher Leslie Brown, *Moral Capital*, chap. 2.

8. For more on territory and freedom, see Ferrer, "Haiti, Free Soil, and Antislavery."

9. Gould, *Among the Powers of the Earth*, 2.

10. The British sent a consul, Charles Mackenzie, to Haiti in 1826, after the French recognized Haitian independence. See Zavitz, "From Amity and Commerce to Slave Trade Suppression."

11. See ibid., quoting Charles Mackenzie to George Canning, 30 November 1826, TNA, PRO F.O. 35/6; and Nicholls, *From Dessalines to Duvalier*, 51. According to Zavitz's research, "Mackenzie claims the British duty was lowered by Alexandre Pétion to 7%,

while Madiou states for 1819 'manufactures anglaises qui ne payaient jamais que cinq pour cent.' In either case, the British had an advantageous commercial position." Mackenzie, Notes on Haiti.

12. Jacob Lewis to John Q. Adams, Port-au-Prince, 5 June 1818, NARA, General Claims, compiled ca. 1799–ca. 1844, ARC identifier 1174286/MLR number PI 177 238.

13. James Richard Dacres to William Marsden, 2 May 1805, TNA, ADM 1/255.

14. "Copy of the Secret Additional Articles to the Treaty between Great Britain and France, Signed at Paris 30th of May 1814," 22 September 1815, Boston Public Library, Haitian Collection, MS Haiti 66–246 (2); Dubois, Haiti: The Aftershocks of History, 76.

15. Marques de Campo Sagrado, Secretario del Despacho de la Guerra, to D. Jose Garcia de Leon y Pizarro, Secretario del Despacho del Estado, 24 February 1817, AGI, leg. 17, n. 46, Estado, Ministerio de Guerra.

16. I am extremely grateful for the generosity of Charlton Yingling, PhD candidate at the University of South Carolina, who shared these documents with me. His dissertation is tentatively titled "Colonialism Unraveling: Radicalism and Religion, Race and Nation in Santo Domingo during the Age of Revolutions, 1784–1822." Ibid; see also Yingling, "The Maroons of Santo Domingo."

17. Julien Prévost to Thomas Clarkson, 20 November 1819, in Griggs and Prator, Henry Christophe and Thomas Clarkson, 173.

18. Popkin, A Concise History of the Haitian Revolution, 152.

19. Charles Mackenzie described this scene in 1830 in a published account of his time in Haiti, Notes on Haiti, 88–89.

20. Zavitz, "From Amity and Commerce to Slave Trade Suppression."

21. Ibid.; Brière, Haïti et la France, 244–45; Geggus, "Haiti and the Abolitionists," 137.

22. Zavitz, "From Amity and Commerce to Slave Trade Suppression."

23. Ibid.

24. John Henry Temple, Viscount Palmerston, to George William Conway Courtenay, "Slave Trade," 29 June 1839, TNA, FO 84.293 I would like to thank Erin Zavitz for generously sharing the sources on the slave trade and the commercial treaties.

25. TNA, FO 84330.

26. TNA, FO 35/28.

27. Matthew Brown, "Introduction," 3.

28. Blaufarb, "The Western Question," 755.

29. Foreign Office [author unknown] to Edward James Dawkins, "Draft, Mr. Dawkins, No 5, [Foreign Office,] March 18th, [18]26, Communicating the Opinions of HM Gov't Respecting Peace between Sp[anish] America and Spain; and Respecting Cuba," TNA, FO 35/1.

30. Blaufarb, "The Western Question," 755.

31. Gordon S. Brown, Toussaint's Clause, 286.

32. Ibid., 292.

33. Gaffield, "Outrages on the Laws of Nations."

34. "Toutes les révolutions ont un bus et une fin. La notre fondée sur la loy [sic] la plus sacrée de la nature, est juste & ne peut rencontrer d'ennemis que dans ceux de l'humanité et de la raison. C'est aux gouvernements éclairés par le genie de la

philosophie et de la philanthropie de le mettre audessus des préjugés d'Epidermes et de nuances qui sont le prétexte injuste dont veulent se servir nos ennémis, et a ne voir dans les hommes que le mérite et le vertus qui seul pensent et doivent les distingué." Alexandre Pétion to William Taylor, Port-au-Prince, 9 April 1815, NARA, State Department Consular Despatches, Cape Haitian Series, vol. 4, January 5, 1802–December 10, 1813.

35. "Le Gouvernement des Etats-Unis, Monsieur le Secrétaire d'Etat, est le premier de tout les gouvernement auquel celui d'Hayti adresse officiellement la communication de sa situation politique, en demandant qu'un acte régulier de la législature de sa sœur ainée reconnaisse son indépendance qui compte déjà sa dixneuvieme année." "Le Peuple haytien ne pense pas que le Peuple américain, qui dans d'autres temps s'est trouvé dans la même position que lui est qui a éprouvé le même besoin, puisse lui refuser la justice qui lui est due." B. Inginac to John Quincy Adams, Port-au-Prince, 6 July 1823, NARA, State Department Consular Despatches, Cape Haitian Series, 1797–1906, Roll T-5, vol. 5.

36. Fanning, *Caribbean Crossings*, 166.
37. Ibid., 122.
38. Gordon S. Brown, *Toussaint's Clause*, 294.
39. Plummer, *Haiti and the United States*, 51.
40. Logan, *The Diplomatic Relations of the United States with Haiti*, 304.
41. Robertson, "The Recognition of the Spanish Colonies," 91.
42. Blaufarb, "The Western Question."

Bibliography

MANUSCRIPT COLLECTIONS

Boston, MA
    Boston Public Library
        Haitian Collection
Copenhagen, Denmark
    Danish National Archives (Statens Arkiver)
        Department of Foreign Affairs, West Indies
        Foreign Correspondence
The Hague, Netherlands
    National Archives of the Netherlands (Nationaal Archief)
        ALG Rijks Archief
Kingston, Jamaica
    National Library of Jamaica
        George Nugent Papers
London, England
    Center for Kentish Studies
        George Charles Pratt Correspondence and Papers
    National Army Museum
        Miscellaneous Correspondence Relating to the West Indies
    The National Archives of the United Kingdom
        Colonial Office
        Foreign Office
        High Court of Appeals for Prizes
        Letters from Senior Admiralty Officers
        Privy Council Registers
        Sir John Nicholl Papers
        War and Colonial Department
        War Office
Paris, France
    Archives Nationales
        Colonial Archives, Saint-Domingue
        Moreau de Saint-Méry Papers
        Secrétariat d'État à la Marine, Guadeloupe
Seville, Spain
    Archivo General de Indias
        Estado, Ministerio de Guerra
Spanish Town, Jamaica
    Jamaican National Archives

  Minutes of the Council, Jamaica
Washington, DC
  National Archives and Records Administration
    General Claims, 1799–1844
    State Department Consular Despatches, Cape Haitian Series

SECONDARY SOURCES

Ardouin, Beaubrun, Etudes sur l'Histoire d'Haïti Suivies de la Vie du Général J.-M. Borgella. Port-au-Prince: F. Dalencour, 1958.

Armitage, David. "The Contagion of Sovereignty: Declarations of Independence since 1776." South African Historical Journal 52 (2005): 1–18.

———. The Declaration of Independence: A Global History. Cambridge: Harvard University Press, 2007.

Armitage, David, and Julia Gaffield. "Introduction: 'We Must Live Independent or Die': The Haitian Declaration of Independence in an Atlantic Context." In The Haitian Declaration of Independence, edited by Julia Gaffield. Charlottesville: University of Virginia Press, forthcoming, fall 2015.

Bellegarde, Dantès. "Alexandre Pétion: The Founder of Rural Democracy in Haiti." Caribbean Quarterly 3, no. 3 (1953): 167–73.

Bellegarde-Smith, Patrick. "Haitian Social Thought in the 19th Century: Class Formation and Westernization." Caribbean Studies 20, no. 1 (1980): 5–33.

Benton, Lauren. "Abolition and Imperial Law, 1790–1820." Journal of Imperial and Commonwealth History 39, no. 3 (2011): 355–74.

———. "Oceans of Law: The Legal Geography of the Seventeenth-Century Seas." Conference Proceedings, Seascapes, Littoral Cultures, and Trans-Oceanic Exchanges, Library of Congress, Washington, DC, 12–15 February 2003.

———. A Search for Sovereignty: Law and Geography in European Empires, 1400–1900. Cambridge: Cambridge University Press, 2010.

———. "Strange Sovereignty: The Provincia Oriental in the Atlantic World." Mexico 20/10, La Modernidad en el Atlantico Iberoamericano, 1750–1850 (2012) 1, http://www.20-10historia.com.

Blackburn, Robin. "The Force of Example." In The Impact of the Haitian Revolution in the Atlantic World, edited by David P. Geggus. Columbia: University of South Carolina Press, 2001.

Blancpain, François. Un Siècle de Relations Financières entre Haïti et la France: 1825–1922. Paris: L'Harmattan, 2001.

Blaufarb, Rafe. "The Western Question: The Geopolitics of Latin American Independence." American Historical Review 112, no. 3 (2007): 742–63.

Bose, Sugata. A Hundred Horizons: The Indian Ocean in the Age of Global Empire. Cambridge: Harvard University Press, 2006.

Brière, Jean-François. Haïti et la France, 1804–1848: La Rêve Brisé. Paris: Kathala, 2008.

Brown, Christopher Leslie. Moral Capital: Foundations of British Abolitionism. Chapel Hill: Published for the Omohundro Institute of Early American History and Culture by University of North Carolina Press, 2006.

Brown, Gordon S. *Toussaint's Clause: The Founding Fathers and the Haitian Revolution.* Jackson: University Press of Mississippi, 2005.

Brown, Matthew. "Introduction." In *Informal Empire in Latin America: Culture, Commerce, and Capital,* edited by Matthew Brown. Malden, MA: Blackwell Publishing, 2008.

Bryan, Patrick. "Emigrés: Conflict and Reconciliation, the French Emigrés in Nineteenth Century Jamaica." In *The Haiti-Jamaica Connection.* Fifth in Seminar Series on Intra-Regional Migration. Latin-American Caribbean Centre, University of the West Indies, Mona, 2004.

Bulmer-Thomas, Victor. *The Economic History of the Caribbean since the Napoleonic Wars.* Cambridge: Cambridge University Press, 2012.

Burnham, Thorald. "Immigration and Marriage in the Making of Post-Independence Haiti." PhD diss., York University, Canada, 2006.

Cooper, Frederick. "Alternatives to Empire: France and Africa after World War II." In *The State of Sovereignty: Territories, Laws, Populations,* edited by Douglas Howland and Louise White. Bloomington: Indiana University Press, 2009.

Cranch, William. *Reports of Cases Argued and Adjudged in the Supreme Court of the United States in February Term, 1809.* New York: Isaac Riley, 1812. HeinOnline, 9 U.S. 281 (1809).

Curry-Machado, Jonathan. *Cuban Sugar Industry: Transnational Networks and Engineering Migrants in Mid-Nineteenth Century Cuba.* New York: Palgrave Macmillan, 2011.

Daut, Marlene. "The 'Alpha and Omega' of Haitian Literature: Baron de Vastey and the U.S. Audience of Haitian Political Writing." *Comparative Literature* 64, no. 1 (2012): 49–72.

Dessens, Nathalie. *From Saint-Domingue to New Orleans: Migration and Influence.* Gainesville: University Press of Florida, 2007.

Dickinson, Edwin D. "The Unrecognized Government or State in English and American Law." *Michigan Law Review Association* 22, no. 1 (1923): 29–45.

Dubois, Laurent. *Avengers of the New World: The Story of the Haitian Revolution.* Cambridge: Belknap Press of Harvard University Press, 2004.

———. *Haiti: The Aftershocks of History.* New York: Henry Holt, 2012.

Dubois, Laurent, Julia Gaffield, and Michel Acacia. *Documents Constitutionnels d'Haïti 1790–1860.* New York: De Gruyter, 2013.

Duffy, Michael. *Soldiers, Sugar, and Seapower: The British Expeditions to the West Indies and the War against Revolutionary France.* Oxford: Clarendon Press, 1987.

Editorial Staff of the National Reporter System, eds. *The Federal Cases: Comprising Cases Argued and Determined in the Circuit and District Courts of the United States, Book 5.* St. Paul, MN: West Publishing Company, 1894.

Edwards, Thomas. *Reports of Cases Argued and Determined in the High Court of Admiralty, Commencing with the Judgements of the Right Hon. Sir William Scott, Easter Term 1808.* London: A. Strahan, 1812. HeinOnline 165 Eng. Rep. 1011 (1752–1865).

Elisabeth, Léo. "Les relations entre les Petites Antilles françaises et Haïti: De la Politique du Refoulement a la Resignation, 1804–1825." *Outre-Mer* 90, nos. 340–41 (2003): 177–206.

Enthoven, Victor. "An Assessment of Dutch Transatlantic Commerce, 1585–1817." In *Riches from Atlantic Commerce: Dutch Transatlantic Trade and Shipping, 1585–1817*, edited by Johannes Postma and Victor Enthoven. Boston: Brill, 2003.

Fanning, Sara. *Caribbean Crossing: African Americans and the Haitian Emigration Movement*. New York: New York University Press, 2015.

Fergus, Claudius K. *Revolutionary Emancipation: Slavery and Abolitionism in the British West Indies*. Baton Rouge: Louisiana State University Press, 2013.

Ferrer, Ada. *Freedom's Mirror: Cuban Slave Society and the Haitian Revolution*. Cambridge: Cambridge University Press, 2014.

———. "Haiti, Free Soil, and Antislavery in the Revolutionary Atlantic." *American Historical Review* 117, no. 1 (2012): 40–66.

———. "Speaking of Haiti: Slavery, Revolution, and Freedom in Cuban Slave Testimony." In *The World of the Haitian Revolution*, edited by David Patrick Geggus and Norman Fiering. Bloomington: Indiana University Press, 2009.

Ferris, Benjamin. "Samuel White and His Father." *Papers of the Historical Society of Delaware* 37. Wilmington: Historical Society of Delaware, 1903.

Fick, Carolyn. "Emancipation in Haiti: From Plantation Labour to Peasant Proprietorship." *Slavery and Abolition* 21, no. 2 (2000): 11–40.

Fouchard, Jean. "Quand Haïti exportait la liberté aux Antilles." *Revue de la Société Haïtienne d'Histoire et de Géographie* 143 (1984): 41–47.

Gaffield, Julia. "Complexities of Imagining Haiti: A Study of National Constitutions, 1801–1807." *Journal of Social History* 41, no. 1 (2007): 81–103.

———. "Haiti and Jamaica in the Remaking of the Early Nineteenth-Century Atlantic World." *William and Mary Quarterly* 69, no. 3 (2012): 583–614.

———. "'Outrages on the Laws of Nations': American Merchants and Diplomacy after the Haitian Declaration of Independence." In *The Haitian Declaration of Independence*, edited by Julia Gaffield. Charlottesville: University of Virginia Press, forthcoming, fall 2015.

———, ed. *The Haitian Declaration of Independence*. Charlottesville: University of Virginia Press, forthcoming, fall 2015.

Gallagher, John, and Ronald Robinson. "The Imperialism of Free Trade." *Economic History Review* 6, no. 1 (1953): 1–15.

Garraway, Doris. "Empire of Freedom, Kingdom of Civilization: Henry Christophe, the Baron de Vastey, and the Paradoxes of Universalism in Postrevolutionary Haiti." *Small Axe* 16, no. 3 (2012): 1–21.

Garrigus, John. *Before Haiti: Race and Citizenship in French Saint-Domingue*. New York: Palgrave Macmillan, 2006.

Gaspar, David Barry. *Bondmen and Rebels: A Study of Master-Slave Relations in Antigua with Implications for Colonial North America*. Baltimore: Johns Hopkins University Press, 1985.

Geggus, David Patrick. "The Enigma of Jamaica in the 1790s: New Light on the Causes of Slave Rebellions." *William and Mary Quarterly* 44, no. 2 (1987): 274–99.

———. "Haiti and the Abolitionists: Opinion, Propaganda, and International Politics in Britain and France, 1804–1838." In *Abolition and Its Aftermath, 1790–1916*, edited by David Richardson. London: Frank Cass, 1985.

———. *Haitian Revolutionary Studies*. Bloomington: Indiana University Press, 2002.
———. *Slavery, War, and Revolution: The British Occupation of Saint Domingue, 1793–1798*. Oxford: Clarendon Press, 1982.
———. "The Slaves and Free Coloreds of Martinique during the Age of the French and Haitian Revolutions: Three Moments of Resistance." In *The Lesser Antilles in the Age of European Expansion*, edited by Robert L. Paquette and Stanley L. Engerman. Gainesville: University Press of Florida, 1996.
Girard, Philippe R. "Black Talleyrand: Toussaint Louverture's Diplomacy, 1798–1802." *William and Mary Quarterly* 66, no. 1 (2009): 87–124.
———. "Caribbean Genocide: Racial War in Haiti, 1802–1804." *Patterns of Prejudice* 39, no. 2 (2005): 138–61.
———. "Napoleon Bonaparte and the Emancipation Issue in Saint Domingue, 1799–1803." *French Historical Studies* 32, no. 4 (2009): 587–618.
———. *The Slaves Who Defeated Napoléon: Toussaint Louverture and the Haitian War of Independence, 1801–1804*. Tuscaloosa: University of Alabama Press, 2011.
Gonzalez, Johnhenry. "The War on Sugar: Forced Labor, Commodity Production, and the Origins of the Haitian Peasantry, 1791–1843." PhD diss., University of Chicago, 2012.
Gould, Eliga. *Among the Powers of the Earth: The American Revolution and the Making of a New World Empire*. Cambridge: Harvard University Press, 2012.
Griggs, Earl Leslie, and Clifford H. Prator, eds. *Henry Christophe and Thomas Clarkson: A Correspondence*. Berkeley: University of California Press, 1952.
Hall, Neville. *Slave Society in the Danish West Indies: St. Thomas, St. John, and St. Croix*. Baltimore: Johns Hopkins University Press, 1992.
Jean-Baptiste, St. Victor. *Le Fondateur Devant l'Histoire*. Ca. 1954. Port-au-Prince: Presses Nationales d'Haïti, 2006.
Jenson, Deborah. "Before Malcolm X, Dessalines: A French Tradition of Black Atlantic Radicalism." *International Journal of Francophone Studies* 10, no. 3 (2007): 329–44.
———. *Beyond the Slave Narrative: Politics, Sex, and Manuscripts in the Haitian Revolution*. Liverpool: Liverpool University Press, 2011.
———. "Dessalines's American Proclamations of the Haitian Independence." *Journal of Haitian Studies* 15, no. 1/2 (2009): 72–102.
———. "From the Kidnapping(s) of the Louvertures to the Alleged Kidnapping of Aristide: Legacies of Slavery in the Post/Colonial World." *Yale French Studies: The Haiti Issue: 1804 and Nineteenth-Century French Studies* 108 (2005): 162–86.
———. "States of Ghetto, Ghettos of States, Haiti and the 'Era de Francia' in the Dominican Republic, 1804–1808." *Global South: States of Freedom: Freedom of States* 6, no. 1 (2012): 156–71.
Johnson, Michael P. "Denmark Vesey and His Co-Conspirators." *William and Mary Quarterly* 58, no. 4 (2001): 915–76.
Jordaan, Han. "Patriots, Privateers, and International Politics: The Myth of the Conspiracy of Jean Baptiste Tierce Cadet." In *Curaçao in the Age of Revolutions, 1795–1800*, edited by Wim Klooster and Gert Oostindie. Leiden: KITLV Press, 2011.
Jordan, Winthrop D. *Tumult and Silence at Second Creek: An Inquiry into a Civil War Slave Conspiracy*. Baton Rouge: Louisiana State University Press, 1993.

Knight, Franklin W. *Slave Society in Cuba during the Nineteenth Century*. Madison: University of Wisconsin Press, 1970.

Knox, John P. *A Historical Account of St. Thomas, W.I., with Its Rise and Progress in Commerce, Missions and Churches, Climate and Its Adaption to Invalids*. New York: Negro Universities Press, 1854.

Kraska, James. "Prize Law." *Max Planck Encyclopedia of Public International Law*. Oxford: Oxford University Press, 2011.

Logan, Rayford Whittingham. *The Diplomatic Relations of the United States with Haiti, 1776–1891*. 1941. Chapel Hill: University of North Carolina Press, 2011.

Lowrie, Walter, and Matthew St. Clair Clarke, eds. *American State Papers: Documents, Legislative and Executive, of the Congress of the United States, from the First Session of the First to the Third Session of the Thirteenth Congress, Inclusive, Commencing March 3, 1789, and Ending March 3, 1815*. Washington, DC: Gales and Seaton, 1832.

Lubin, Maurice. "Les Premiers Rapports de la Nation Haïtienne Avec L'étranger." *Journal of Inter-American Studies* 10, no. 2 (1969): 277–305.

Lundahl, Mats. "Defense and Distribution: Agricultural Policy in Haiti during the Reign of Jean-Jacques Dessalines, 1804–1806." *Scandinavian Economic History Review* 32, no. 2 (1984): 77–103.

———. *Peasants and Poverty: A Study of Haiti*. London: Croom Helm, 1979.

———. "Toussaint L'ouverture and the War Economy of Saint-Domingue, 1796–1802." *Slavery and Abolition* 6, no. 2 (1985): 122–38.

Luster, Robert E. *The Amelioration of the Slaves in the British Empire, 1790–1833*. New York: Peter Lang, 1995.

Mackenzie, Charles. *Notes on Haiti, Made during a Residence in That Republic, Vol. II*. London: A. J. Valpy, 1830.

Madiou, Thomas. *Histoire d'Haïti, Tome III, 1803–1807*. 1847. Port-au-Prince: Editions Henri Deschamps, 1989.

Matthewson, Tim. *A Proslavery Foreign Policy: Haitian-American Relations during the Early Republic*. Westport, CT: Praeger, 2003.

Miller, Christopher L. "Forget Haiti: Baron Roger and the New Africa." *Yale French Studies: The Haiti Issue: 1804 and the Nineteenth-Century French Studies* 107 (2005): 39–69.

Mintz, Sidney. "Labor and Sugar in Puerto Rico and in Jamaica, 1800–1850." *Comparative Studies in Society and History* 1, no. 3 (1959): 273–81.

Moïse, Claude. *Constitutions et Luttes de Pouvoir en Haïti, Tome 1, 1804–1915*. Montreal: CIDIHCA, 1988.

Montague, Ludwell Lee. *Haiti and the United States, 1714–1938*. Durham: Duke University Press, 1940.

Nash, R. C. "The Organization of Trade and Finance in the British Atlantic Economy, 1600–1830." In *The Atlantic Economy during the Seventeenth and Eighteenth Centuries: Organization, Operation, Practice, and Personnel*, edited by Peter A. Coclanis. Columbia: University of South Carolina Press, 2005.

Nesbitt, Nick. *Universal Emancipation: The Haitian Revolution and the Radical Enlightenment*. Charlottesville: University of Virginia Press, 2008.

Nessler, Graham Townsend. "A Failed Emancipation? The Struggle for Freedom in Hispaniola during the Haitian Revolution." PhD diss., University of Michigan, 2011.

Nicholls, David. *From Dessalines to Duvalier: Race, Colour, and National Independence in Haiti*. Cambridge: Cambridge University Press, 1979.

———. "Race, Couleur, et Indépendance en Haïti, 1804–1825." *Revue d'Histoire Moderne et Contemporaine* 25 (1978): 177–212.

Nugent, Maria. *Lady Nugent's Journal of Her Residence in Jamaica from 1801 to 1805*. Mona, Jamaica: University of the West Indies, 2002.

Pachonski, Jan, and Reuel K. Wilson. *Poland's Caribbean Tragedy: A Study of Polish Legions in the Haitian War of Independence, 1802–1803*. Boulder: East European Monographs, 1986.

Paquette, Robert. *Sugar Is Made with Blood: The Conspiracy of La Escalera and the Conflict between Empires over Slavery in Cuba*. Middletown, CT: Wesleyan University Press, 1988.

Peabody, Sue. "Free upon Higher Ground: Saint-Domingue Slaves' Suits for Freedom in U.S. Courts, 1792–1830." In *The World of the Haitian Revolution*, edited by David Patrick Geggus and Norman Fiering. Bloomington: Indiana University Press, 2009.

Peltier, Jean-Gabriel. *The Trial of John Peltier, Esq., for a Libel against Napoleon Buonaparté, First Consul of the French Republic: At the Court of the King's Bench, Middlesex, on Monday the 21st of February 1803*. London: M. Peltier, 1803.

Peters, Richard, ed. *By Authority of Congress, the Public Statutes at Large of the United States of America, Vol. II, Ninth Congress, Sess. 1, CH 6, 7, 8, 1806*. Boston: Charles C. Little and James Brown, 1848.

Picó, Fernando. *One Frenchman, Four Revolutions: General Ferrand and the Peoples of the Caribbean*. Princeton: Markus Wiener Publishers, 2011.

Plummer, Brenda Gayle. *Haiti and the United States: The Psychological Moment*. Athens: University of Georgia Press, 1992.

Popkin, Jeremy D. *A Concise History of the Haitian Revolution*. Malden, MA: Blackwell Publishing, 2012.

Pradine, Linstant de. *Recueil General des Lois et Actes du Gouvernement d'Haïti depuis la Proclamation de son Indépendance jusqu'à nos jours, Tome 1ère*. Paris: Pedone-Lauriel, 1886.

Rainsford, Marcus. *An Historical Account of the Black Empire of Hayti*. 1805. Edited by Paul Youngquist and Grégory Pierrot. Durham: Duke University Press, 2013.

Reinhold, Fraces L. "New Research on the First Pan-American Congress Held at Panama in 1826." *Hispanic American Historical Review* 18, no. 3 (1938): 342–63.

Robertson, William Spence. "The Recognition of the Spanish Colonies by the Motherland." *Hispanic American Historical Review* 1, no. 1 (1918): 70–91.

Rupert, Linda Marguerite. *Roots of Our Future: A Commercial History of Curaçao*. Netherlands Antilles: Curaçao Chamber of Commerce and Industry, 1999.

Saint-Louis, Vertus. *Aux Origines du drame d'Haïti: Droit et Commerce Maritime, 1794–1806*. Port-au-Prince: Bibliothèque Nationale d'Haïti, 2006.

Sanders, Ralph. "Congressional Reaction in the United States to the Panama Congress of 1826." *Americas* 11, no. 2 (1954): 141–54.

Scott, Julius. "The Common Wind: Currents of Afro-American Communication in the Era of the Haitian Revolution." PhD diss., Duke University, 1986.

Scott, Rebecca J. "'She . . . Refuses to Deliver Up Herself as the Slave of Your Petitioner': Émigrés, Enslavement, and the 1808 Louisiana Digest of the Civil Laws." *Tulane European and Civil Law Forum* 24 (2009): 115–36.

Sexton, Jay. "An American System: The North American Union and Latin America in the 1820s." In *Connections after Colonialism: Europe and Latin America in the 1820s*, edited by Matthew Brown and Gabriel Paquette. Tuscaloosa: University of Alabama Press, 2013.

Sheller, Mimi. *Democracy after Slavery: Black Publics and Peasant Radicalism in Haiti and Jamaica*. Gainesville: University Press of Florida, 2000.

———. "Sword-Bearing Citizens: Militarism and Manhood in Nineteenth-Century Haiti." *Plantation Societies in the Americas* 4, no. 2/3 (1997): 233–78.

Sheridan, Richard B. "Jamaican Slavery to Haitian Freedom: The Case of the Black Crew of the Pilot Boat, Deep Nine." *Journal of Negro History* 67, no. 4 (1982): 328–39.

Stark, Francis. *The Abolition of Privateering and the Declaration of Paris*. New York: Columbia University Press, 1897.

Stein, Robert. "The Abolition of Slavery in the North, West, and South of Saint Domingue." *Americas* 41, no. 3 (1985): 47–55.

———. "From Saint Domingue to Haiti: French Policy toward Newly Independent Haiti, 1804–1825." *Journal of Caribbean History* 19, no. 2 (1984): 189–226.

Stewart, James. *Reports of Cases Argued and Determined in the Court of Vice-Admiralty at Halifax, Nova Scotia: From the Commencement of the War in 1803 to the End of the Year 1813, in the Time of Alexander Croke, Judge of That Court*. London: Printed for J. Butterworth and Son, 1814.

Stinchcombe, Arthur. "Class Conflict and Diplomacy: Haitian Isolation in the 19th-Century World System." *Sociological Perspectives* 37, no. 1 (1994): 1–23.

Taylor, Charles Edwin. *Leaflets from the Danish West Indies: Descriptive of the Social, Political, and Commercial Condition of These Islands*. London: Printed by Wm. Dawson and Sons, 1888.

Trouillot, Michel-Rolph. *Haiti, State against Nation: The Origins and Legacy of Duvalierism*. New York: Monthly Review Press, 1990.

———. *Silencing the Past: Power and the Production of History*. Boston: Beacon, 1995.

Vattel, Emmerich de. *The Law of Nations, Or, Principles of the Law of Natures, Applied to the Conduct and Affairs of Nations and Sovereigns*, edited by Joseph Chitty. Cambridge: Cambridge University Press, 1834.

Washington, Bushrod. *Reports of Cases Determined in the Circuit Court of the United States, for the Third Circuit, Comprising the Districts of Pennsylvania and New Jersey, Commencing at April Term, 1803*. Vol. 2. Philadelphia: Philip E. Nicklin, Law Bookseller, 1827. HeinOnline 165 Eng. Rep. 1011 (1752–1865).

White, Ashli. *Encountering Revolution: Haiti and the Making of the Early Republic*. Baltimore: Johns Hopkins University Press, 2010.

Yingling, Charton, "The Maroons of Santo Domingo in the Age of Revolutions: Adaptation and Evasion, 1783–1800," *History Workshop Journal* 79, no. 1 (Spring 2015): 25–51.

Zavitz, Erin. "From Amity and Commerce to Slave Trade Suppression: British Conventions and Haitian Recognition, 1825–1840." Presented at the Haitian Studies Association's Annual Conference, November 2010, Brown University.

Index

Abolition: British bill on, 80–81; in British Caribbean, 173–75; French, 142, 173; in Haitian Declaration of Independence, 187; laws and, 87; repatriation of ex-slaves, 77–78, 214 (n. 63), 215 (n. 70); in Saint Domingue/Haiti, 9, 73–74, 161, 211 (n. 30), 215 (n. 70)
Abul Hasan, Mirza, 179
Acte de l'Indépendance, 1, 12. *See also* Haitian Declaration of Independence
Act to Regulate the Clearance of Armed Merchant Vessels (1805): deliberations, 134–37; signing of, 138
Adams, John Quincy, 125, 139, 193
Agents. *See* British agents; French agents
Agricultural production, 61, 64, 77, 191; exports, 22, 63, 156; promotion of, 163, 169. *See also* Plantations
Albany Register, 138
American Civil War, 194
American Declaration of Independence, 7–9, 90
American merchants, 15, 106, 188; commercial agents and, 193; at Curaçao, 50; experiences in Haiti, 127–29; French privateers and, 132–33; imports, 152; promotion of trade, 126–27; trade prohibition and, 146–48, 166. *See also* American ships
American Revolution, 6, 8–9, 137, 195
American ships: arming of, 130–31, 133–38; capturing of, 18, 94; *Dart*, 95, 97, 100–102, 105, 118; *General Pinkney*, 147–48, 227 (n. 89); *Happy Couple*, 95, 98–106, 111, 118; *Helen*, 148; *Indostan*, 138; *Manilla* (sailing from Nantucket) 146–47; *Manilla* (sailing from New York), 95, 112–16, 119–20, 219 (n. 7); ports, 116; *Rachel*, 227 (n. 89); safety of, 126; *Sea Nymph and Emma*, 149; slaves aboard, 78; trade prohibition and, 49, 147–48
Armitage, David, 8–9
Arrests, 54
Aurora General Advertiser (Philadelphia), 105, 138
Autonomy, 7, 82, 88, 168

Bahama Islands, 97, 106–7, 109, 113; Vice-Admiralty Court, 98, 105, 112
Barré, Henry, 213 (n. 46)
Batavian Republic (Netherlands), 13, 32; Dutch merchants, 25, 27, 42, 136; French-Dutch relations, 24–25, 29–30, 33, 38–39; government, 37–38, 45, 48; jurisdictional authority, 40; neutrality of, 4, 210 (n. 14)
Bayley, Judge, 121
Bay of Baracoa, 41
Bellegarde, Dantès, 7
Bellegarde-Smith, Patrick, 3
Benton, Lauren, 226 (n. 65); on layered sovereignty, 12–13, 184; on maritime law, 93, 111–12, 222 (n. 70); on neutral shipping, 94
Blanchet, Bruno, 155, 179; letter to Peltier, 165–66
Blaufarb, Rafe, 192, 195
Bligh, John, 213 (n. 46)
Blockades, 59, 71, 79; at Cap Français, 68, 72–73; at city of Santo Domingo, 103, 168; siege at Curaçao, 32–33, 38
Bonaparte, Napoléon, 101, 180; Haitian-British alliance and, 157, 164, 167; military strategy, 17, 66; United States and, 166

Boyer, Jacques, 213 (n. 46)
Boyer, Jean-Pierre, 181, 191, 193–94
Brazil independence, 195
Breda, Mr. (Saint Domingue inhabitant), 52
British Admiralty Courts, 109, 110, 149, 196; deliberations on Haitian independence, 14, 93, 96–97, 121, 123; neutral nations and, 46, 121; power, 95; rule on prize cases, 94, 95–96, 112–15
British agents, 22, 68–69, 138; merchants acting as, 122–23; in Saint Domingue/Haiti, 68–69, 73, 77, 158; in Virgin Islands, 48
British Empire: aid, 8, 66, 79, 103, 156; amelioration policy, 173–74; economic policy, 95, 97, 118, 119, 121, 190; Haitian Revolution and, 157; Latin American states and, 169, 192; military agreement with France, 189; occupation of Curaçao, 28, 31, 59–60, 188; occupation of Saint Domingue, 65–66, 72, 212 (n. 30); occupation of St. Thomas, 59–60, 188; U.S. relations, 7, 77, 132, 173. See also British-Haitian relations; Franco-British war
British-Haitian relations: administrative gap in, 122–23; agents and British ministers, 155, 172–77, 178–79; economic, 14, 109, 115, 121, 123; evidence of alliance, 101–5; first commercial treaty, 191–92; impact of Haitian massacre on, 63, 85–86; imports/exports and, 64, 74, 108, 170, 176; Jamaican treaty negotiations and, 72–78, 79–81, 87–90, 92, 192; military alliance, 167–69, 189; military bases and, 70–72, 74–76, 170; naval protection, 74, 103–4; official diplomatic recognition, 190–92; trade treaty proposals, 156–57, 163–64, 166–72, 176–77
British merchants, 86, 88, 90, 169; arrival in Haiti, 157; Danish trade prohibition and, 48; Dessalines and, 158; duty on trade, 170, 176, 188, 234 (n. 11); legal permission to trade, 92, 95, 113; licenses for, 108–10, 114, 119–20, 121, 188; poor treatment of, 118–19; preferential treatment of, 168, 188–89; as unofficial agents, 122–23, 155, 157
British Navigation Acts, 60
British ships: Ben Lomond, 119–20, 219 (n. 7); Cambria, 97, 99; captains, 96; capturing of foreign ships, 97, 109, 116, 213 (n. 46); cargo, 61, 109–10, 120; Elizabeth and Mary, 120–21, 219 (n. 7); flag of truce, 74, 79; Halifax, 112; Lark, 116; manipulation of legal system, 111–12, 222 (n. 70); naval protection, 103–4; permission to trade, 192; provisions from Haiti, 104; repatriation of Haitians aboard, 77; Sarah Ann, 97; siege at Curaçao, 28; Superior, 104; trade regulations, 114–15, 119–21; of war, 122
Brown, Gordon, 127, 139, 193–94
Brown, Matthew, 92, 169, 192
Burke, Walter, 115–16
Burnham, Thorald, 2, 198 (n. 5)

Cap Français, 17, 27; British blockades at, 68, 72, 213 (n. 46).
Cap Haïtien. See Cap Français
Cathcart, Hugh: mission in Saint Domingue, 68–69; negotiations with Dessalines, 70–72
Cazeau de franquevill, 57
Chamber of Commerce (Philadelphia), 137–38
Changuion, Pierre-Jean: correspondence with Ferrand, 32–36; ship processing conflict, 37–44; trade prohibition proclamation, 34–36
Christophe, Henry, 1, 11, 15, 22, 181, 213 (n. 54); American merchants and, 128–29; appeal to Spanish colonies, 180; Blanchet's critique of, 165–66;

claim to leadership, 154–55, 159; constitution (1807), 157, 159, 161–63, 170–71, 186; control of ports, 119–20; Dessalines's assassination and, 153; Peltier's support for, 166–69, 174–75, 179; recognition as ruler, 168; trade treaty proposals, 167–72
Circuit Court of Pennsylvania, 149, 152
Citizenship, 91, 156, 218 (n. 122)
City Gazette and Daily Advertiser (Charleston), 138
Civil war, 46, 104, 226 (n. 65); British-Haitian trade treaty and, 156, 167, 173; de Vattel on, 143, 149; Haitian, 128, 150, 156, 159–60, 176, 181; Haiti-France, 142–44
Claiborne, W. C. C., 212 (n. 30)
Clarkson, Thomas, 160, 190
Clark v. The United States, 148–51
Clay, Joseph, 136
Clervaux, Augustin, 11, 185
Club Haitien, 53
Coffee: duty on, 176; production in Haiti, 22, 156; ship transport, 41
Colonial Council: at Curaçao, 25, 28, 31, 42, 44; at Trinidad, 55
Colonialism, 4, 9, 63, 187; benefits of, 169; end of French rule, 7, 17; Haiti's challenges to, 2, 185
Colquhoun, Patrick, 48
Columbian Centinel (Boston), 137
Congress of Panama (1826), 194
Congress of Vienna (1814–1815), 189
Conspiracies, 52, 54–58, 209 (n. 182)
Constitutions: Christophe's (1807), 157, 159, 161–63, 165, 186; Dessalines's (1805), 90–91; Louverture's (1801), 91, 100–101, 150, 168; Pétion's (1806, 1816), 159, 161–63, 165, 215 (n. 70); religious practice and, 171; white landownership and, 170, 212 (n. 39)
Contraband of war: aboard American ships, 131–32; de Vattel's definition, 220 (n. 29); neutral nations and, 96, 98, 100; supplied by British navy, 103–4; trading of, 46, 50, 95, 97, 136, 139–40
Cooke, Edward, 166, 177
Coote, Eyre, 122, 153–54, 160
Corbet, Edward, 68, 73, 156; report on Haitian massacre, 84–85, 89; treaty negotiations with Dessalines, 74–77, 79–83, 186, 213 (n. 54)
Corsairs. *See* Privateers
"Corsairs of Guadeloupe, The," 23
Cotton, 22, 64, 139, 156
Courtenay, William Conway, 191
Court of Common Pleas, 119
Court of the King's Bench, 119–20
Courts. *See* British Admiralty Courts; Court of Common Pleas; Court of the King's Bench; Prize Cases
Croke, Alexander, 99–101, 150, 219 (n. 17)
Cuba, 19, 206 (n. 127); ports, 34; privateers, 137; sugar production, 62; trade with Haiti, 180
Cultivateurs. See Laborers
Curaçao: British occupation, 59–60, 188; French-Dutch relations in, 24–25, 29–30, 33, 38–39; government, 14, 29–32; jurisdictional power in, 37–44, 58; merchants, 109–10; population, 24; recognition of French agents in, 37–39; trade center, 20, 23–25, 199 (n. 19); trade prohibition, 21, 33–36, 50, 58–59, 92, 188
Curiel, Jan Valentin, 42–43

Dacres, James Richard, 68, 122, 188, 217 (n. 103)
Danish Empire, 4, 112, 199 (n. 19); merchants, 21, 22, 46–48, 59, 116; trade prohibition, 48–50
Dawkins, Edward James, 192
Denmark. *See* Danish Empire
Deportation, 54, 57
Dessalines, Jean-Jacques, 11, 49, 187; advisers to, 74, 213 (n. 54); *Arrêté* on plantations, 85; assassination, 153–54, 165; assistance to slaves, 53;

Dessalines, Jean-Jacques (continued)
declaration as emperor of Haiti, 56, 90; emissaries sent by, 51–55, 57; Haitian Declaration of Independence, 1, 7, 9, 12, 73; invitation to Nugent, 61, 63–65, 69; letter to Jefferson, 126; massacre of French white citizens, 84–87; military strategy, 19; national constitutions, 90–91; trade negotiations with Jamaica, 69–72, 73–77, 85–90, 92; wife, 128

Deverell, Robert, 80

Diplomatic recognition/non-recognition: by British Empire, 70, 87–89, 91–92, 101–5, 172–74, 179–80; Christophe and Pétion's efforts at, 163, 177–78; economic recognition and, 10, 13, 125, 183; by foreign governments, 13–15, 132, 183–85, 194; by France, 190–91; Haitian dignity and, 185–86; Haitian internal divisions and, 153–54; isolation of Haiti and, 2, 4, 13; of Latin American colonies, 192, 195; by Spain, 189–90; by United States, 125, 144, 152, 193–94

Dominican Republic. *See* Santo Domingo

Dominion vs. control, 113–14

Downie, John, 110, 158

Dubois, Laurent, 214 (n. 64)

Duckworth, John Thomas, 62, 68, 103–4, 213 (n. 49); letter to Nepean, 69, 72–73

Dutch merchants, 21, 59, 136; in Curaçao, 25, 27–28, 42

Economic policy: British, 60, 95, 97, 116–18, 119, 121, 190; in Haitian constitutions, 162–63; law of nations and, 141, 185; U.S. court system and, 152

Economic recognition: diplomatic non-recognition and, 10, 13, 125, 183–84, 186–87; Haitian massacres and, 87–88

Ely, William, 103–4, 128, 145

Embargo Act (1807), 148

Emissaries: British, 19; of Haitian government, 115, 117; in Saint Domingue/Haiti, 68, 99; in St. Thomas, 51–55, 57

Eppes, John W., 135

Ernouf, Jean Augustin, 47, 53

Eustis, William, 135

Export crops, 22, 62–64, 156

Fanning, Sara Connors, 194

Férou, Laurent, 153–54

Ferrand, Jean-Louis: correspondence with French agents, 30–32; correspondence with Lartigue, 51–57; efforts to assert French control, 18–19; exchanges with Changuion, 38, 40–41, 43–44; French and Batavian governments and, 32–33; prohibition of trade, 21, 23, 34–36, 46–48, 144–45; in Santo Domingo, 30, 33, 168, 170

Ferrer, Ada, 19, 171, 180, 206 (n. 127)

Fitzsimons, Thomas, 137

Flags of truce, 74, 79

Flemish independence, 197 (n. 1)

Floridas, acquisition of the, 133, 152

Foreign policy: British, 92; United States, 139

France: archives in, 4; Batavian Republic and, 24–25, 29; claims to Haiti, 7–8, 10, 64, 100–101, 113–15, 150; Haitian isolation goal, 14, 17, 20–21, 58, 182; military agreement with Britain, 189; ports, 148; recognition of Haitian independence, 190–91; rejection of Haitian independence, 5, 17–20; U.S. relations, 132–33, 134–36. *See also* Franco-British war; French agents; French army

Franco-British war, 3, 7–8, 68–69; British exports and, 64; British military bases, 70, 75, 170; Haitian independence and, 96, 104, 187–88, 192; peace treaty, 65, 66, 211 (n. 22)

248   Index

Freedom: individual, 9, 187; sovereignty and, 183; universal, 73, 79, 174, 184, 215 (n. 70). *See also* Abolition

French agents, 5, 138; in Curaçao, 21, 29–32; in Guadeloupe, 27–28; recognition and authority of, 37–39, 44, 58; in St. Thomas, 21, 44–45, 105–6

French army: attack on American ships, 131; defeat at Santo Domingo, 19, 103–4; evacuation from Haiti, 17, 72, 79, 127, 176, 185; occupation of the Netherlands, 24; reinforcements, 8, 27, 61–62, 68; in Saint Domingue, 17, 27–28, 67, 72

Fuller, Mr. (British Parliamentarian), 80–81

Gallagher, John, 92
Gazette Officielle de l'Etat d'Hayti, 113, 129, 157, 166
Gazette Politique et Commerciale d'Haïti, 81, 137–38, 139, 226 (n. 52)
Geggus, David, 51, 218 (n. 113)
George III (king), 86, 95, 116
Gérin, Étienne, 159, 165
Girard, Philippe, 211 (nn. 20, 22)
Goff, John, 178
Gonzalez, Johnhenry, 63
Gouges, Jean-Pierre: as French agent in Curaçao, 21, 31–32; ship sentencing, 37–44; trade prohibition efforts, 33–36, 50, 59
Gould, Eliga, 6, 87, 90, 218 (n. 109)
Grant, William, 118
Guadeloupe: French agents in, 27–28; privateers from, 32; rumor of slave revolt in, 51–53; trade prohibition, 23

Haiti: arms and ammunition, 77, 80, 89, 97, 100; consuls in, 60, 190–91; courts, 170; European-style government, 173; imports/exports, 62–64, 74, 108, 130, 152, 156; internal divisions, 74, 89, 153–54, 159, 177–78, 213 (n. 54); militarization of, 90, 154, 187; naming of, 73, 213 (n. 48); official diplomatic recognition of, 13–15, 88, 190–94; Polish and German citizens, 90, 218 (n. 122); population, 77–78, 173, 198 (n. 5), 214 (n. 64); rights of, 145; ships, 19, 171. *See also* British-Haitian relations; Diplomatic recognition/non-recognition; Isolation, Haitian; Saint Domingue; Sovereignty, Haitian

Haitian Declaration of Independence: copies of, 213 (n. 49); Dessalines's proclamation of, 1, 7, 9, 12, 73; diplomatic recognition and, 2, 7, 13–15, 182; individual freedom and, 187; liberty and, 9; as public statement, 184; renaming of Saint Domingue in, 73, 213 (n. 48); traitors and enemies and, 83–84; U.S. independence and, 9–10

Haitian Indigenous Army (Armée Indigène), 1, 7–8, 89, 90; war matériel, 100, 103–4

Haitian Revolution: American merchants and, 126–27; Caribbean-wide fear of, 3, 47, 50–58, 86, 182–83; constitutional laws on, 161, 165; containment of, 11, 66, 73, 78, 83, 92; French planters and, 67; success of, 1–2; trade implications of, 20, 45

Halifax Vice-Admiralty Court, 97, 98, 100, 111, 150, 219 (n. 17)
Hall, Neville, 54
Hallam, Mr. (British agent), 122–23
Hierarchy: in British-Haitian relations, 176, 186; in imperial relations, 69; international, 101; plantation, 67, 71; racial, 1, 133, 183; of treaties, 6, 218 (n. 109)
Hillhouse, James, 139
Hispaniola, 151, 180, 212 (n. 30), 213 (n. 48); French colonialism, 7, 18; French privateers at, 99, 137; merchant communities, 29; Spanish colonialism, 19

Index 249

Hobart, Robert, 62, 68, 82, 85, 213 (n. 49), 217 (n. 103)
Humanity, community of, 11–12

Identity: American, 90, 141–42; Haitian, 2, 160–61
Imports, 22, 26, 60, 64, 84, 152
Informal empire, 169, 172, 177, 192
Inginac, Joseph Balthazar, 193–94
Isolation, Haitian: antislavery and, 73; diplomatic non-recognition and, 2, 4, 13; diversity and, 11, 198 (n. 5); foreign governments and, 10; France's goal of, 14, 17, 20–21, 58, 182; United States' role in, 124–25, 131–32

Jackson, James, 140
Jamaica: blockades, 68, 168; British merchants and, 188–89; Dutch merchants, 25; economic opportunities with Haiti, 14–15, 61, 65; French refugees, 67, 70, 86; imports, 22; slavery, 77, 81, 218 (n. 113); sugar economy, 62; trade negotiations with Saint Domingue/Haiti, 66–70, 73–77, 85–90, 154, 192; Vice-Admiralty Court, 116
Jefferson, Thomas, 133, 140; armed merchant vessels bill, 134, 138; letter from Dessalines, 126; trade prohibition bill, 116, 166
Jenkins, Robert, 178
Jenson, Deborah, 18, 51, 98
Jérémie, 79, 84, 122
Jurisdictional authority, 58, 187; in territorial waters, 37, 39–41

Kane, Archibald, 97, 103, 220 (n. 27); New York West India Company, 129–31; time in Haiti, 127–28
Kane, Elias, 97, 129
King, Rufus, 138
Knox, John P., 26–27

Laborers (*cultivateurs*), 62, 77–78, 162, 169; military service and, 156

L'Ambigu (London), 157, 166
Landownership, 71–72, 85, 90–91, 170
Lartigue, Arnaud André Roberjot, 21, 115; fear of Caribbean-wide revolution, 50–58; as French agent in St. Thomas, 44–45, 111–12; trade prohibition efforts, 45–50, 59
Latin American independence movements, 169, 192, 195
Law of nations: contraband of war and, 98, 132; customary practices of, 3–4, 10, 94; economic policy and, 141, 185; Haiti and, 8, 187; neutral nations and, 96; prize courts and, 94, 222 (n. 78); trade prohibition and, 146, 152; United States and, 133, 141–42, 146, 152
Le Blanc, Judge, 121
Leclerc, Victor Emmanuel, 20, 83
Lewis, Jacob, 124–25, 126, 188; condemned by Christophe, 128–29
Lidman, Aaron, 115
Lincoln, Abraham, 194
Livermore, Edward, 147
Logan, George, 137, 138, 140
Logan, Rayford, 138, 144, 146–47, 224 (n. 2)
Louverture, Toussaint, 22, 71, 87, 127; British secret convention, 66, 107, 211 (nn. 20, 22); constitution (1801), 91, 100–101, 150, 168
Lowndes, Thomas, 135
Lucas, John, 136
Lundahl, Mats, 59, 214 (n. 64), 217 (n. 100)

Mackenzie, Charles, 190–91, 234 (nn. 10, 11)
Madiou, Thomas, 153, 235 (n. 11)
Madison, James: British agents and, 138; law of nations and, 146; letter from Jacob Lewis, 124, 126; trade agreements, 131–32
Maitland, Thomas, 66, 102, 107
Malter, M., 190

Mansfield, James, 119
Manufactured goods, 22, 64, 74, 176, 211 (n. 17)
Marchand(e)s (hucksters), 156
Maritime law, 94, 111–12
Marshall, John, 147
Martinique, 51; privateers, 32; rumor of slave revolt in, 51–53
Massacre of French citizens, 63, 90, 217 (n. 107); British-Haitian relations and, 63, 85–86; recount of, 83–85, 128; U.S. policy and, 133
Matthewson, Tim, 133, 146–47, 224 (n. 2), 226 (n. 51)
Merchants: acceptance of Haitian independence, 105; in Curaçao, 25, 27–28, 33–36; Danish, 21, 22, 46–48, 59, 116; Dutch, 25, 27, 42, 136; laws for, 93, 98; punishment, 36, 112; religious practice, 172; slaves and, 78, 81; trade opportunities with Haiti, 10, 15, 20, 184; as unofficial agents, 186. *See also* American merchants; British merchants
Merry, Anthony, 131–32, 140
Migration, 78, 194, 198 (n. 5)
Military strategy, 11, 96; Bonaparte's, 17, 66; British, 8, 62, 68, 187, 189; Dessalines's, 19
Mitchill, Samuel L., 139–40
Moïse, Claude, 90
Môle Saint Nicolas, 70, 75, 170
Monroe, James, 226 (n. 65)
Moreau, General, 52–53
Morning Chronicle: London, 120; New York, 55
Mühlenfels, Balthazar Frederik, 45, 54; ban on trade, 48–49

National Intelligencer and Washington Advertiser, 128
Nation building, 93, 154–55, 160
Naturalization, 90–91, 218 (n. 122)
Nepean, Evan, 69, 72
Nessler, Graham, 18

Netherlands. *See* Batavian Republic
Neutral nations, 4, 96, 137, 149, 210 (n. 14); civil war and, 143–44; ports and, 120–21; trade rules and, 30, 46, 50, 64, 116, 131, 151, 188; United States as, 132, 145, 222 (n. 78)
Neutral ships: Atlantic warfare and, 94–95; capturing of (Lille), 38–44, 58; contraband trading and, 98, 100; Privy Council Order on, 113; punishment and, 23, 36; trade licenses for, 119–20
Nicholl, John, 118
Nicholls, David, 90, 161
Non-Intercourse Act (1809), 148
Nugent, George: letter from Rochambeau, 61–62; letter from/to Dessalines, 61, 63–65, 217 (n. 103); reports to Hobart, 62, 68, 82, 85, 213 (n. 49), 217 (n. 103); trade negotiations with Dessalines, 66–69, 73–78, 79–83, 85–90, 92, 186, 192
Nugent, Maria, 76–77

Panama Congress (1826), 186, 192
Peasant farming, 62–63
Peltier, Jean-Gabriel: Blanchet's appeal to, 165–66; British-Haitian treaty proposal, 155–56, 164, 166–70, 176–77; diplomatic recognition of Haiti and, 115, 120, 163, 166, 177; letters/memoires to Stewart, 172–75, 178–79; popularity among Haitians, 157; reaction to trade restrictions, 117
Perkins, John, 84
Pétion, Alexandre, 1, 15, 128, 170, 177–78; appeal to U.S. agent, 193; Blanchet's defense of, 165–66; claim to leadership, 159; constitutions (1806, 1816), 159, 161–63, 171, 215 (n. 70); Dessalines's assassination and, 159, 165; efforts to connect with British ministers, 155, 178; nation building, 154, 160; Peltier's criticism of, 175
Pichon, Louis-André, 78, 132–33, 140

Piracy, 27, 39, 77, 131. See also Privateers
Plantations: compensation for French planters, 190; Dessalines's Arrêté on, 85; exports, 63; female laborers, 156; slave labor, 62, 173–74; white owners, 31, 70–71, 84, 212 (n. 39)
Plummer, Brenda Gayle, 185
Politics of the skin, 74
Port-au-Prince, 84, 116, 159; assassination of Dessalines at, 153–54; harbor, 129, 146; U.S. agents at, 193
Portugal, 195
Possession and ownership, 114–15
Power: British naval, 64, 94; Dessalines's, 153; European, 24, 28, 99, 131, 172, 174, 183; foreign, 103, 105, 123, 140, 177, 183, 190; Haitian government, 98, 159, 161–62; international jockeying over, 25; military, 167; slaveholding, 1, 2; sovereign, 95, 101, 150
Pratt, John Jeffreys, 68, 215 (n. 79); trade agreement with Haiti, 86–89, 218 (n. 116)
Prévost, Julien, 190
Prisoners, 79, 213 (n. 46)
Privateers: British, 97, 111; Cuban, 75; at Curaçao, 28, 30–31, 58; French, 8, 18–19, 99, 130, 132, 137–38; prizes captured by, 31–32, 37–44, 202 (n. 86); Spanish, 18–19, 64, 130, 138
Privy Council for Trade and Foreign Plantations: Haitian sovereignty and, 110, 113–15; Order in Council (1799), 107–8; Order in Council (1806), 107–9; Order in Council (1808), 116–18, 119–20, 188; Order on neutral ships, 112–13; trade licenses, 108–10, 116, 119–20, 179
Prize cases, 31–32; Haitian independence and, 98; *Happy Couple* and *Dart*, 95, 97–106; *Lille*, 38–44, 58; *Manilla* and *Pelican*, 95, 112–17, 119–21, 219 (n. 7)
Public Sale, 119

Puerto Rico, 56–57
Punishment, 91, 106; for illegal trade, 36, 37, 112, 145

Race: Haitian independence and, 3, 9, 173, 183; humanity and, 7, 12
Racism, 2, 4, 146, 183, 195
Rainsford, Marcus, 7, 65–66, 83, 91
Refugees: in Cuba, 180; in Jamaica, 67, 70, 86
Religion, 171–72
Repatriation, 77–78, 79, 214 (n. 63)
Richardson, Thomas, 155, 167–70, 172, 176, 178–79
Rights: citizen, 78, 153, 186, 215 (n. 70); human, 99, 196; to independence, 7, 8, 144; individual, 186–87; of neutral nations, 145, 222 (n. 78); of new states, 6–8; trading, 131, 164, 169
Robinson, Christopher, 112
Robinson, Ronald, 92
Rochambeau, Donatien, 83; appeal for military aid, 27–28; French army evacuation treaty, 72, 87; invitation to Nugent, 61–62
Roman Catholicism, 171–72
Rouanez, *jeune* (secretary of state), 155, 163–64, 176–77
Roullit, Captain, 39–40, 42–43
Royal Gazette and Bahama Advertiser, 97–98, 100, 102
Rupert, Linda, 24–25, 28, 59–60

Saint Domingue (colonial Haiti), 1, 7; British occupation, 65–66, 72, 212 (n. 30); British request for military bases, 70–72, 74–76, 214 (n. 56); constitution (1801), 91, 100–101, 150, 168; economy, 20, 22, 62–63, 65; French army in, 17, 27–28, 67, 72; French evacuation, 30, 68–69; plantation owners, 70–71, 212 (n. 39); renaming of, 73, 213 (n. 48); trade negotiations with Jamaica, 66–70, 73–77, 85–90

St. John, 59, 199 (n. 19)

Saint-Méry, Médéric Louis Élie Moreau de, 57

St. Thomas: British occupation, 59–60, 188; Danish rule, 25; French agents in, 21, 44–45, 105–6, 115; government, 14; merchants, 46–50, 59; rebel conspiracy in, 51–52, 54–58; as trade center, 20, 23, 25–27; trade prohibition, 45, 46–50, 59–60, 92, 188

Samaná, 170

Santa Marta, 41

Santo Domingo, 28, 180; Dessalines's attack on, 19, 103–4; diplomatic recognition of Haiti, 189–90; Ferrand at, 30, 33, 168, 170, 176; independence, 189; trade, 48

Scott, Julius, 11

Scott, William, 113–15, 118, 119–21, 222 (n. 78)

Shee, George, 157–58, 167

Ships. *See* American ships; British ships; Neutral ships

Slave revolution. *See* Haitian Revolution

Slavery: in British Caribbean, 173–75; in Curaçao, 24; foreign slave systems, 73, 79, 91; humanity and, 11–12; importation of slaves, 81, 215 (n. 79); international coalition against, 191; in Jamaica, 67, 69, 77, 218 (n. 113); laws and, 87; liberty and, 9; merchants and, 46–47; on plantations, 62, 173–74; in Saint Domingue, 67, 211 (n. 30); in St. Thomas, 26. *See also* Abolition

Smilie, John, 145–46

Sovereignty, Haitian: British ambiguity on, 101–2, 104, 114–15, 118, 123, 196; Dessalines's political title and, 82; dominion and control and, 113–14; establishing/constructing, 1, 8, 22, 93, 98; foreign acceptance of, 2, 7, 103; in Haitian Declaration of Independence, 9, 183; interpretations of, 96; layered, 13, 94; official recognition of, 60, 125, 191; power, 101, 161; temporary recognition of, 13, 114, 121, 144, 184

Spain: alliance with France, 8, 18–19; colonies, 195, 226 (n. 65); Haiti and, 180, 189; trade, 33; war with Britain, 3

Stephen, James, 106–7, 160

Stewart, Robert, 155; failure to respond to Peltier, 175–77, 178–79; Peltier's letters/memoires to, 164, 167–68, 172–75

Story, Thomas, 98–99, 103–4

Sugar production, 22, 62–63, 180, 199 (n. 23)

Sullivan, John, 62

Supreme Court, 147–48, 152

Sutherland, Robert, 86, 118; on Haitian agricultural production, 22, 156; Haitian Revolution and, 157–58

Tacky's Rebellion (1760), 173–74

Taylor, William, 193

Temple, John Henry, 191

Thilorier, J., 33, 37; as French agent in Curaçao, 21, 27–32

Tiburon, 70, 72, 170

Times (London), 12, 84, 87, 217 (n. 107)

Tortola, 48–49, 105

Trade: Britain-Haiti agreement (1844), 191–92; Caribbean islands–Haitian relations, 11, 34; of contraband of war, 96, 97, 139–40; in Curaçao, 20, 23–25, 30, 199 (n. 19); neutral nations and, 30, 46, 64; regulation of, 14–15, 79, 114–17, 123, 179, 193; in St. Thomas, 20, 23, 25–27, 45–50, 58; Spanish, 33; U.S.-Haitian relations, 18–19, 129–31, 146–47, 188, 193–94. *See also* Trade prohibitions

Trade prohibitions: American ships and, 49, 147–48; city of Santo Domingo, 144–45; Curaçao, 21, 33–36, 50, 58–60, 92, 188; foreign influence on, 146; French control and, 149–52; Guadeloupe, 23; St. Thomas, 45,

Index 253

Trade prohibitions (*continued*)
  46–50, 59–60, 92, 188; United States and foreign nations, 148; United States and Haiti, 14–15, 116, 125–27, 138–41, 144–45, 152, 193
Treaty of Alliance (1778), 6, 195
Treaty of Amiens (1802), 66, 67–68
Treaty of Basel (1795), 100
Treaty of Paris (1783), 7
Treaty of Paris (1815), 60
Treaty of Ryswick (1627), 100
Treaty-worthiness, 6–7, 89, 187
Trinidad, 51–52, 54–58
Trinidad Gazette, 55
Trouillot, Michel-Rolph, 90, 211 (n. 18)

United States: alliance with Haiti, 174–75; commercial agents, 152, 193; court system, 125; foreign policy, 139; foreign pressure on, 126, 132, 138, 142, 150, 188; French representatives in, 131, 132, 136, 224 (n. 2); government, 102, 131–34, 149–52; migration of free people, 194; non-recognition/recognition of Haiti, 125, 144, 152, 193–94; occupation of Haiti, 170, 212 (n. 39); relations with Britain, 77, 173; relations with France, 46–47, 195; role in Haitian isolation, 124–25, 131–32; slavery, 78, 133, 139–40, 214 (n. 63); trade treaty with Haiti, 194. *See also* American merchants; American ships; U.S. Congress
U.S. Congress, 124, 131; arming of merchant vessels bill, 134–38; trade prohibition bill, 14, 49, 125–27, 138–41, 145–47; White's speech in, 141–45, 150, 152

Vattel, Emer de, 8–9, 94, 210 (n. 183), 220 (n. 29); on civil war, 143, 149
Vermont independence, 197 (n. 1)
Vernet, André, 71, 130
Viallet, Noel, 191
Villaret, General, 47, 53

Walker, James: mission in Saint Domingue, 68–69; negotiations with Dessalines, 70–72
War matériel. *See* Contraband of war
West India Company: Danish, 25; Dutch, 25; New York, 129–31
White, Samuel: Adams and, 125; speech in Congress, 141–45, 150, 152
Whitfield, W. L., 85, 87
Wilberforce, William, 80–81, 160
Wood, Gordon S., 224 (n. 2)
Wynne, William, 118

Yong, Mr. (informant), 52–53

Zavitz, Erin, 188, 190, 234 (n. 11)

www.ingramcontent.com/pod-product-compliance
Lightning Source LLC
Chambersburg PA
CBHW051214300426
44116CB00006B/577